SAGE was founded in 1965 by Sara Miller McCune to support the dissemination of usable knowledge by publishing innovative and high-quality research and teaching content. Today, we publish over 900 journals, including those of more than 400 learned societies, more than 800 new books per year, and a growing range of library products including archives, data, case studies, reports, and video. SAGE remains majority-owned by our founder, and after Sara's lifetime will become owned by a charitable trust that secures our continued independence.

Los Angeles | London | New Delhi | Singapore | Washington DC | Melbourne

POVERTY AND DEPRIVATION

Thank you for choosing a SAGE product!
If you have any comment, observation or feedback,
I would like to personally hear from you.

Please write to me at **contactceo@sagepub.in**

Vivek Mehra, Managing Director and CEO, SAGE India.

Bulk Sales

SAGE India offers special discounts
for purchase of books in bulk.
We also make available special imprints
and excerpts from our books on demand.

For orders and enquiries, write to us at

Marketing Department
SAGE Publications India Pvt Ltd
B1/I-1, Mohan Cooperative Industrial Area
Mathura Road, Post Bag 7
New Delhi 110044, India

E-mail us at **marketing@sagepub.in**

Subscribe to our mailing list
Write to marketing@sagepub.in

This book is also available as an e-book.

POVERTY AND DEPRIVATION

Changing Contours

Social Change in Contemporary India

Series Editor: Manoranjan Mohanty

Volume V

Edited by

K. B. SAXENA

Los Angeles | London | New Delhi
Singapore | Washington DC | Melbourne

First published in 2021 by

SAGE Publications India Pvt Ltd
B1/I-1 Mohan Cooperative Industrial Area
Mathura Road, New Delhi 110 044, India
www.sagepub.in

SAGE Publications Inc
2455 Teller Road
Thousand Oaks, California 91320, USA

SAGE Publications Ltd
1 Oliver's Yard, 55 City Road
London EC1Y 1SP, United Kingdom

SAGE Publications Asia-Pacific Pte Ltd
18 Cross Street #10-10/11/12
China Square Central
Singapore 048423

Published by Vivek Mehra for SAGE Publications India Pvt. Ltd. Typeset in 10.5/13pt Bembo by Fidus Design Pvt. Ltd, Chandigarh.

Library of Congress Control Number: 2021943079

ISBN: 978-93-91370-76-3 (HB)

SAGE Team: Amrita Dutta, Syed Husain Naqvi, Aishna Bhatt

Contents

List of Abbreviations   vii
About the Series   ix
Foreword by Manoranjan Mohanty   xiii
Introduction by K. B. Saxena   xix

Section I: Poverty: Rural and Urban

Sectional Introduction

Chapter 1   Dimensions of Rural Poverty   5
    E. Narayanan Nair
Chapter 2   The Structure of Poverty: Case of Bihar   19
    Ramashray Roy and V. B. Singh
Chapter 3   Urban Development and the Poor   41
    S. R. Hashim

Section II: Dimensions of Poverty

Sectional Introduction

Chapter 4   Sociology of Poverty: Conceptual Issues   63
    Arun Kumar Ghosh
Chapter 5   Women and Poverty: Rural–Urban Dimensions   70
    Preet Rustagi
Chapter 6   Poverty and Disability in India   113
    Ambati Nageswara Rao
Chapter 7   Children Toiling at a Tender Age   131
    Helen R. Sekar and Manju Khurana
Chapter 8   Industrial Pollution and Health Hazards in Jharkhand   141
    Bijay Sarkar
Chapter 9   Some Cognitive and Motivational Concomitants of Poverty   155
    Durganand Sinha

Section III: Disparities
Sectional Introduction

Chapter 10   Rural Households' Access to Basic Amenities
in India: Deprivation and Socio-economic
Exclusions   169
Arjun Kumar

Chapter 11   Disparity and Development in Uttar Pradesh 209
Prashant Kumar Trivedi

Chapter 12   Development and Poverty in an Indian State:
A Study of KBK Districts of Orissa   227
Satya Prakash Dash

Section IV: Programmes for Poverty Alleviation
Sectional Introduction

Chapter 13   Planning for Alleviation of Rural Poverty
in India: Experience and Lessons   257
Kamta Prasad

Chapter 14   Supplementary Nutrition to Women and
Children: A Situational Analysis of
Anganwadis in Tribal Areas of Gujarat   272
Ratnawali

Chapter 15   Socio-economic Impact of Implementation of
Mahatma Gandhi National Rural Employment
Guarantee Act in India   305
T. Haque

About the Editors and the Contributors   336
Index   341

List of Abbreviations

ALs	Agricultural labourers
AP	Andhra Pradesh
APL	Above the poverty line
AWC	Anganwadi centres
AWW	Anganwadi worker
BPL	Below the poverty line
CDPO	Child Development Project Officer
CDPs	City development plans
CSD	Council for Social Development
CSR	Child sex ratio
DPAP	Drought Prone Area Programme
DPRs	Detailed project reports
EGS	Employment Guarantee Scheme
FHHs	Female-headed households
HCR	Head count ratio
IAY	Indira Awas Yojana
ICDS	Integrated Child and Development Services
ILO	International Labour Organization
IMR	Infant mortality rate
IRDP	Integrated Rural Development Programme
JnNURM	Jawaharlal Nehru National Urban Renewal Mission
KBK	Kalahandi, Balangir and Koraput
LR	Land reforms
MDGs	Millennium Development Goals
MGNREGA	Mahatma Gandhi National Rural Employment Guarantee Act
MGNREGS	Mahatma Gandhi National Rural Employment Guarantee Scheme
MHUs	Mobile health units
MMR	Maternal mortality rate
MPCE	Monthly per capita consumption expenditure

MPI	Multidimensional Poverty Index
NABARD	National Bank for Agriculture and Rural Development
NEC	Not elsewhere classified
NFHS	National Family Health Survey
NGOs	Non-governmental organizations
NREP	National Rural Employment Programme
NSDP	Net state domestic product
NSS	National Sample Survey
NSSO	National Sample Survey Office
OBC	Other Backward Class
OLs	Other labourers
ORMs	Other religious minorities
PAHs	Polycyclic aromatic hydrocarbons
PDS	Public distribution system
PHCs	Primary health centres
PMJAY	Pradhan Mantri Jan Arogya Yojana
PRIs	Panchayati Raj Institutions
PURA	Provision of Urban Amenities to Rural Areas
RIDF	Rural Infrastructure Development Fund
RLEGS	Rural Landless Employment Guarantee Programme
RLTAP	Revised Long-term Action Plan
SCs	Scheduled Castes
SECC	Socio-Economic and Caste Census
SFDA	Small Farmers Development Agency
SMEs	Small and medium-sized enterprises
STs	Scheduled Tribes
THPS	Tetrakis hydroxymethyl-phosphonium sulphate
TRYSEM	Training of Rural Youth for Self-employment
UC	Utilization certificate
UNDP	United Nations Development Programme
UNESCO	United Nations Educational, Scientific and Cultural Organization
UP	Uttar Pradesh
UPSS	Usual principal and subsidiary status
USMR	Under-5 mortality rate
WHO	World Health Organization
WPR	Work participation rate

About the Series

Social Change in Contemporary India is a series of thematic volumes carrying selected articles from the journal *Social Change* which is celebrating its golden jubilee. They are offered as important contributions capturing the momentous experience of the people of India and their institutions since Independence.

Social change in Independent India has gone through three distinct phases. The first two decades saw the impact of the freedom struggle in most arenas where policymakers and common people shared some perspectives to initiate concrete steps to reduce poverty, hunger and scarcity with the objective of making progress towards the goals enshrined in the Constitution of India. Planned development with a focus on industrialization, the Green Revolution in agriculture, building educational institutions of high quality and, above all, promoting democratic institutions and procedures to meet the aspirations of all sections of society characterized most of this era. The pluralistic character of Indian society, culture and polity was acknowledged, and some important policy initiatives emerged.

But by the late 1960s, the crisis of this model had already surfaced. The food riots in 1966, the Naxalbari uprising in 1967 and the beginning of non-Congress governments in many states were symptoms of the emerging environment. That heralded the second phase, 1970–1990, which witnessed the unfolding of most major contradictions in the Indian Republic. Assertion of rights by ethnic groups in different parts of the country was responded to by a certain centralization of power by the union government, which, in turn, was challenged by the emergence of strong regional parties and movements. Poverty eradication was prominent on the agenda, but progress was tardy. Education and health facilities have expanded but not to the extent needed. An Indian middle class did emerge but was increasingly alienated from the masses. Challenges accumulated, leading to mass movements and the Republic saw the declaration of the Emergency followed by the rule of alternative forces and the return of the Congress to power. In the process, civil society organizations pursuing citizens' rights emerged and the struggle for democratic rights continued to expand. Internal disturbances, communal riots and atrocities on dalits, minorities and women occurred from time to time. But the democratic structure continued to get consolidated and people's consciousness to defend constitutional values continued to grow.

In 1991, the neoliberal economic reforms were launched in the wake of a serious economic crisis. At that time, India was also experiencing a social upsurge over the rights of dalits, backward classes, religious minorities and women. By this time, environmental issues had also acquired much attention and thus began the third phase. The Indian elite, cutting across the dominant political parties, accepted the agenda of globalization, liberalization and privatization. Mobilization on caste and religious issues took a new turn with Hindu nationalist forces becoming stronger by the day. Initially, the Congress, through its alliance of parties, was able to stem this trend. They handled contradictions for a decade with a strategy that promoted rapid economic growth, tried to provide rural employment and food security to the poor and addressed the grievances of minorities. But corruption and inefficiency made them unpopular and the BJP-led government came to power. This third phase of neoliberal growth, steered by Hindu nationalism, is in full swing though alternative forces continue to occupy a significant space.

This story of independent India is captured by scholars and commentators as it unfolded during the past 50 years as contributions to the Council for Social Development's (CSD) social science quarterly, *Social Change*. They narrate the multidimensional dynamics of social change experienced by various sections of people at local, regional and national levels and also in the global context. We decided to share these contributions on specific themes in several volumes with a wider readership for good reasons.

First, *Social Change* is a unique, interdisciplinary journal that covers not only research papers in social sciences but also policy analysis and reports from the field in areas of social development. Right from the start, Durgabai Deshmukh, the founder of the Council of Social Development, wanted theory, policy and ground-level experience to be integrated, each benefitting from the other. So each volume in this series has papers by authors defining concepts, explaining theoretical frameworks, analysing policies and presenting survey results and other evidence from rural, urban and tribal areas.

Second, the journal carried contributions from not only senior scholars such as Nirmal Kumar Bose, B. N. Ganguly, T. N. Madan and B. K. Roy Burman, policymakers like C. D. Deshmukh and social activists like Devaki Jain but also from a large number of young academics from all over the country who used the forum to present their findings from their most important research projects. Some of them later became eminent academics and important policymakers. The contributions by these writers over a 50-year period can help us identify key points in the history of policymaking as well as discourses during the three major phases of contemporary India. Some contributions clearly impacted public discourse and the policy process. Thus, we are able to capture shifts in policy in the early 1970s when the state took many active initiatives and also the big change in 1991 when a new role of the state was visible in the economy, giving a substantial role to the private sector. That trend continued in the first two decades of the 21st century. We may note the changing perspectives and the linkage with the global processes not only on theoretical issues of social development but also on policy debates concerning questions of the privatization of health, education, rural development, forest and environment. Their implications for people's welfare and human rights have also been dealt with by many authors in recent years.

Third, an equally important consideration underlying these volumes is the fact that the CSD has a mission to serve the interests of marginalized groups through its research, publications and advocacy, and this journal reflects that commitment. Therefore, the volumes carry articles on selected themes such as health, education, poverty and agriculture with special focus on the marginalized groups, including the adivasis, dalits, minorities, women and urban and rural poor. Each of these volumes reflects what has been done in respect of the specific marginalized groups and analyses the nature of the development experience from the vantage point of the marginalized.

Each volume is edited by an expert who has done considerable work on the subject. A major and substantive introduction by the editor of the volume not only puts the papers in perspective but also identifies the strengths as well as the gaps in the treatment of the subject. The editor's introduction also addresses current concerns in theory and policy, discourse and practice and presents suggestions for further thinking and action. These volumes are designed as studies on a theme for ready reference and use by students, researchers and general readers.

Manoranjan Mohanty
Series Editor

Foreword

In normal times, the value of this volume would be immense both for researchers on poverty and policymakers, but in the COVID-19 context, it is a critical reference tool for anyone thinking and researching about poverty and deprivation in India. It is now clearly established that during the pandemic-struck year of 2020/2021, more people—estimates vary from 80 to 140 million—slid back into the abyss of poverty than ever before in independent India, with at least 150 million being added to the number of the global poor. What this collection of articles points to is that already more and more people were slipping below the poverty line even before the pandemic because of the neoliberal policies that focused on achieving high economic growth.

The story of poverty eradication efforts in independent India is presented in this volume by a set of contributions selected from the pages of *Social Change* published over five decades, all reflecting public policy and field experience. Many historical moments of shifts and turns in policy are identified, and their effects on the ground are analysed in concrete terms. The positive thrust on poverty alleviation in the 1980s through integrated rural development is analysed in some depth. As economic reforms came into force, the gradual shift in policy in the 1990s led to a slowdown in the process of poverty eradication. But the need for legitimation in a democracy demanded pro–poor initiatives. So we saw, along with an impetus towards neoliberal policies during 2004–2014, a set of 'right-based' measures to guarantee rural employment, food security and elementary education among others. These were very significant steps and proved to be subsistence support for the masses of the rural poor, but whether they introduced long-term processes of creating productive assets for the poor was debatable. The high degree of insecurity of millions of rural and urban poor was exposed abundantly during the pandemic.

This historical account of India's much debated record of poverty eradication is introduced by one of India's most distinguished experts on the subject, Professor K. B. Saxena. With his field experience in the state and association with policymaking at the centre, he is eminently qualified to present this work. Like his late colleagues, legendary civil servants B. D. Sharma, S. R. Sankaran and P. S. Krishnan, Saxena's record as a young officer in Bihar as well as in senior positions was known for his absolute commitment to the cause of the poor and oppressed sections of the population. As the Union Health Secretary and Rural Development Secretary, Government of India, Saxena directly initiated many important policies. After he retired, the inherent academic in him made him intensify his research and field investigation into issues of the poor and the downtrodden. His report on the status of the Scheduled Castes in India for the National Human Rights Commission remains a momentous document. As a distinguished professor at the CSD, his many research projects and publications, especially on Mahatma Gandhi National Rural Employment Guarantee Scheme (MGNREGS) and public health, testify to his expertise and commitment.

Saxena's Introduction is a comprehensive essay on the subject of poverty and deprivation and their various dimensions, reflecting his full grasp of the theoretical, policy level and ground reality in India over the decades. He presents an assessment of the major perspectives on the definition of poverty from various viewpoints. Saxena explains and critiques most of them—from the calorie-based food intake access to the capability approach, from the income poverty approach to consumption expenditure and basic needs. He sees positive elements in each of them while identifying inadequacies in each of them. That poverty is multi-dimensional is now acknowledged by the United Nations Development Programme (UNDP), which has moved beyond the notion of 'income poverty' even though 'income poverty' still dominates the statistical systems worldwide. For Saxena, the social dimensions of poverty are extremely important. Women, dalits, adivasis, the landless agricultural labour, unorganized workers, the disabled and religious minorities are structurally deprived due to long-standing social, economic and cultural conditions. Therefore, while nutrition, health, education, housing and employment are relevant aspects of poverty eradication programmes, the social structure that creates these conditions of deprivation must also be targeted. In fact, this outlook had informed the concept of 'social development', which drove Durgabai Deshmukh to establish the CSD and its journal, *Social Change*, nearly five decades ago. The biennial

India Social Development Report that the CSD produces also carries this perspective as an advance over the UNDP's *Human Development Report*. The UNDP has also moved in the direction of defining poverty in multidimensional terms.

'Poverty is a situation where an individual or household is unable to meet the basic necessities of life and to attain a minimum level of well-being.' This simple sentence from the Introduction by Saxena carries in it the multiple aspects of poverty eradication of which has been designated by the United Nations Educational, Scientific and Cultural Organization (UNESCO) as a human right.

Hence, the essays selected for this volume reflect this multi-dimensionality of poverty and deprivation. It squarely relates poverty with social deprivation. That the experience has varied from one region to another is evident from the case studies that have been included. While the magnitude of rural poverty remains high, the growing phenomenon of urban poverty is also a cause of anxiety. The mining projects in the adivasi-inhabited forest areas causing displacement of people and destroying the natural environment are a major source of impoverishment, pushing many into poverty. Feminization of poverty—women losing their source of earning due to the changing agrarian economy and corporatization of many arenas of production are yet other trends. Environmental degradation and climate change have emerged as new causes of loss of livelihood and well-being. Have the 'right-based' programmes, like MGNREGS, helped in reducing poverty? Perhaps yes, to some extent, but only temporarily. That this programme played a key role in providing some support during COVID-19 showed its merit. Yet the neoliberal growth process causes so many pressures on the working population that this kind of programme looks grossly inadequate.

An important proposition advanced in this work is the relationship between poverty and inequality. Contrary to the neoliberal viewpoint that the two are unrelated, and a rapidly growing economy can address poverty successfully, it is argued that historically gross inequalities of class, caste, race and gender have been a principal cause of many people remaining poor or becoming poor. While the former approach led to giving subsistence income support through precarious jobs with some promises of minimum wages and dependence on a government's willingness to fund such programmes, it did not create structural conditions to build permanent capacities through access to productive assets, education and health. That did not lead to substantive employment and entitlement to decent wages and ensuring 'basic necessities' for 'well-being' or a meaningful life. It is argued here that only when the social roots of poverty lying in unequal structures are addressed, can the problem of poverty be truly addressed. In fact, this phenomenon was starkly demonstrated during the pandemic when the rural and urban poor, in general, and migrant workers, in particular, belonging to the lower caste, tribal groups, minorities and women as well as people from backward regions, were pushed into conditions of poverty and insecurity in large numbers.

The human rights perspective on poverty eradication necessarily involves moving the policy discourse clearly from a 'welfare' perspective where the state performs a 'duty' to deliver welfare services to the population below the poverty line to the extent it can, according to the wish of the prevailing regime, to the 'rights' perspective where the state is obliged to implement a constitutional right of the citizen, namely the 'right to life'. Under this right guaranteed under Article 21 of the Indian Constitution, several basic needs such as food security, education, health and dignity have been declared by the Supreme Court as part of the right to life. This should be the rationale for people, including the poor, exercising power through political institutions from the village panchayats upwards to ensure concrete progress on poverty eradication. Instead, panchayats have been functioning as mechanisms of top-down 'welfare' services rather than institutions of people's empowerment. Therefore, poverty eradication—not only alleviation—should be the central issue of democratic politics. This volume chronicles how such voices were raised from time to time though 'welfare' orientation with some varying slogans patronizing the poor—*antyodaya* to *gareeb kalyan*—remained in mainstream policy even when the 'rights' perspective was declared as a public commitment.

The United Nations' (UN) Sustainable Development Goals aim at eradicating 'absolute poverty' by 2030. But if we take the multidimensional perspective, especially the structural dimensions of poverty, and assess the existing policies, then the scenario looks uncertain.

Even though the extent of people below the poverty line—defined as minimal purchasing power capacity—had continued to fall from some 40 per cent in the 1980s to about 21 per cent in 2018, the magnitude of poverty and deprivation remained high. On the global index of multidimensional poverty, India ranks at a low 67. At a time when the world is talking about the 'rise of India', such a scale of poverty and deprivation is unacceptable, to say the least. Now, the poor and the deprived have woken up, and therefore, they are no longer satisfied as passive recipients of government doles. Demand for living wages, work and dignity along with healthcare and education as a matter of right is steadily growing. Therefore, the poor are not going to wait for growth to trickle down to them in due course. The reality is that the prevailing pattern of neoliberal growth is generating more and more inequality across the board. Therefore, eradication of poverty and empowerment of common people are very urgent. For policymakers, researchers and social workers, this volume is an important pointer.

Manoranjan Mohanty
Council for Social Development
New Delhi

Introduction

K. B. Saxena

Poverty is a situation where an individual or household is unable to meet the basic necessities of life and to attain a minimum level of well-being. It is one of the most fundamental social and economic problems the country has faced since before Independence. In extreme cases, poverty can force people to end their own lives, as reported frequently in the media, but even when it does not kill, it cripples the very possibility of human development. Eradication of poverty, therefore, is accepted now as a basic human right and a moral commitment, both at the national and the global level.

APPROACHES TO DEFINE POVERTY

There are four approaches to define and measure poverty—monetary, capability, social exclusion and participatory (Hughes et al., 2009). The monetary approach defines poverty as a lack of adequate income and suggests increasing it by growth or redistribution. The capability approach tends to lay stress on the provision of public goods—education, health and nutrition—and therefore emphasizes the need to increase public expenditure to make them available. The social exclusion approach points to social barriers that block attempts to improve living conditions, limit choices and constrain freedom of action, and therefore, they need to be dismantled by the redistribution of resources to disadvantaged groups and combating discriminatory practices. The participatory approach draws attention to a lack of voice and power in decision-making and requires eliminating inequalities in income, wealth and opportunities and deepening democracy. But there is considerable interconnectedness in the four approaches and targeting one type of poverty necessitates the other type. In India, poverty is defined in terms of lack of income and reliance is placed on economic growth to increase it. This is supplemented by poverty alleviation programmes for the same purpose. But other approaches to poverty alleviation have been addressed by general development programmes for the entire population as elaborated in the paper later.

MEASUREMENT OF POVERTY

The concern with poverty is intimately associated with our freedom struggle, and the earliest expression of it was articulated by Dadabhai Naoroji in 1877 with his paper on 'Poverty in India' and subsequently published in his book, *Poverty and Un-British Rule in India*, in 1899 (Himanshu, 2020; ICPR, 2011). Several Indian leaders before and after Independence voiced their commitment to ending poverty. The Directive Principles in the Indian Constitution contain several guiding principles for the state to achieve this goal. There have been several attempts at estimating poverty and identifying the poverty line, ranging from Naoraji's subsistence level income of ₹16–33 per capita, per year at 1867–1868 prices and K. T. Shah's ₹15–20 per capita, per month (1939) prior to Independence to the Planning Commission's (1962) per capita expenditure of ₹20 per month at 1960–1961 prices and V. M. Dandekar and N. Rath's (1971) money equivalent to provide 2,250 kcal per capita, per day in both rural and urban areas. The normative basis of the poverty line that was accepted by the Planning Commission was worked out by the Task Force (1977) headed by Professor Yoginder Alagh as 2,400 kcal per capita, per day in rural areas and 2,100 kcal per capita, per day in urban areas which required consumer expenditure of ₹49.63 per month for rural areas and ₹56.76 per month for urban areas to obtain with the base year of 1973–1974. As per this norm, the poverty ratio was 56.4 per cent in rural areas and 49 per cent in urban areas. This norm was lowered in actual application to 2,200 kcal for the first official estimate itself (Nayyar & Nayyar, 2016). This norm has been criticized on methodological grounds and was reviewed by an expert group (headed by Dr D. T. Lakdawala) in 1993, which continued with the calorie-based norm and updated it using the consumer price index for industrial workers in urban areas and agricultural labourers in rural areas. It disaggregated the national-level poverty line into state-specific poverty lines using state-specific prices. The continued use of a consumption basket for defining poverty faced criticism on grounds, among others, of inadequacy of expenditure for providing a minimum level of standard of living, changes in the consumption pattern of the poor and failing to take into account an increase in private expenditure on education and health. Therefore, another expert group headed by Professor Tendulkar was tasked to review it which abandoned the caloric base for determining actual food expenditure, used the same consumption norm for rural as well as urban poor and made explicit provisions for private expenditure on education and health. On this basis, the poverty line for 2004–2005 was raised to ₹356.30 per capita per month in rural areas and ₹538.68 for urban areas and the proportion of persons below the poverty line (BPL) combined for rural and urban areas increased from 27.5 per cent, based on the old method, to 37.2 per cent. This poverty line at 2005–2006 prices approximated to $1 per day, which was lower than the $1.25 per day of the international poverty line (World Bank, 2011), though Ahluwalia considers it roughly equal to it (Ahluwalia, 2020). But the controversy about norms as well as estimate of poverty did not subside. It was again reviewed by the Rangarajan Expert Group which recommended raising the poverty line in 2011 from the Tendulkar-based estimate of 22 per cent to 29 per cent, which has not been officially accepted yet and which the NITI Aayog Vice Chairperson, Rajiv Kumar, was asked to look into (Nayyar & Nayyar, 2016). There is no official estimate of poverty and inequality after 2011–2012. The report of the latest consumption survey on the basis of which the poverty line is calculated carried out in 2017–2018 was not officially released as it is reported to show a decline in the consumption expenditure in rural areas and a marginal increase in urban areas, implying an increase in overall poverty. Other indicators such as unemployment, wages and income corroborate this conclusion (Himanshu, 2020).

ALTERNATIVE ESTIMATES

There have been alternative estimates of poverty and its normative basis, the most important being one made by the National Commission for Enterprises in the Unorganized Sector (NCEUS, 2007), which found that 76.70 per cent of people lived on an average income of ₹16.24 per capita daily in 2004–2005, and 36 per cent of them were in the vulnerable category (ICPR, 2011). A different approach to identifying the poor was attempted by carrying out a census of the poor so as to target them for providing assistance under poverty alleviation programmes in 2002. This census adopted an indicator-based scoring approach for classifying households as poor and non-poor. Three such censuses in 2002, 2007 and 2009 were carried out, and the methodology adopted in each successive census was progressively refined to address shortcomings. This method of identification was also critiqued on several grounds. As a result, the Socio Economic and Caste Census was carried out in 2011 to accurately identify the poor deserving benefits of poverty alleviation programmes. This was done by identifying those to be automatically excluded, those to be automatically included and the rest to be identified through a scoring criterion using various deprivation indicators. On this basis, 39.3 per cent of rural households were automatically excluded, 0.92 per cent were automatically included, and 106.9 million were considered for deprivation. Currently, the results of this census are being used to ensure that programme benefits reach the deserving poor. The next such census will be carried out in 2021 by revamping the parameters of the 2011 census (*Economic Times*, 2020). Since 2010, a UN-sponsored global initiative of multidimensional poverty index has been developed, which computes poverty by scoring each surveyed household on 10 parameters. In this, India ranks 62 among 107 countries. One scholar has also attempted to measure poverty based on three types of deprivation and found that the proportion of poor is 83.3 per cent based on one of the three deprivations (Radhakrishna, 2015). This periodical reconsideration of poverty estimates and their methodological basis arises from the basic fact that the official poverty estimates are set very low and have no correspondence with ground reality. It is actually labelled as the destitute line (World Bank, 2011), but they have no credibility in the public eye and the lived-in experience. This is the sharp divergence from people's own perception of poverty, which is called the 'community poverty line' (Narayan, 2008) and is 10–20 per cent higher than the official line (World Bank, 2011).

GRADATIONS IN POVERTY

Poverty is not a uniform condition characterized by a lack of income and consumption. It has variations and grades. An 'absolute poverty line' is determined in terms of a standard indicator as in the case of India. This poverty line is used for comparing the level of poverty and its reduction over time. Relative poverty indicates the position of different segments of the population in the income hierarchy, which is of little use in our country with its high incidence of poverty. But there is a category called 'severe poverty'/'chronic poverty' where the poverty is entrenched and is of a long and continued duration. Economic growth, poverty alleviation programmes or cash transfers do not improve the poverty situation of households in this category as they suffer from multiple deprivations and experience different forms of discrimination, which are 'mutually reinforcing' (Hughes et al., 2009). The poor in this category transmit the condition to future generations. Chronic poverty is disproportionably high among Scheduled Castes (SCs), Scheduled Tribes (STs), elderly, women and the disabled due to structural factors. The chronically poor are roughly half of those below the official poverty line (ICPR, 2011). They require group specific policies and substantial and continued assistance for longer duration to enable them to reduce their poverty. 'Transient poverty' is where people are sometimes poor, not always, but an economic shock can push them to chronic poverty (Hughes et al., 2009).

PROFILE OF THE POOR

Who are the poor? There is a geography, sociology, occupational specificity and rural–urban typology of the poor. The geographical picture of rural poverty indicates its concentration in 'backward' states, such as Bihar, Madhya Pradesh, Uttar Pradesh, Odisha and Assam. Jharkhand, Uttarakhand and Chhattisgarh also fall in this category, whereas the urban poor are concentrated in Uttar Pradesh, Maharashtra, West Bengal, Madhya Pradesh, old Andhra Pradesh and Odisha (ICPR, 2011; Radhakrishna & Ray, 2005). The chronically poor are also larger in number in these regions. This is indicative of unequal regional economic development, particularly post-reforms.

These poorest states are predominantly rural and agrarian and contain a large number of the poorest districts identified by the Planning Commission in 1997 (ICPR, 2011). The sociology of poverty conveys the social category-wise concentration of poverty. SCs/STs and most backward castes are among the poorest historically. Poverty among them is deeply entrenched, and SCs/STs constitute the largest number of hard core, long-duration, chronically poor in rural areas, more than their share of the rural population. The SC rural poor are concentrated in Uttar Pradesh, Madhya Pradesh, Bihar and West Bengal and the urban poor in Uttar Pradesh and Madhya Pradesh. Poverty among STs is the highest among social groups, and the reduction of poverty among them is the slowest. They are mostly concentrated in Jharkhand, Odisha, Chhattisgarh, Gujarat, Madhya Pradesh and Maharashtra. STs are at the bottom of every human development indicator and belong to the lowest per capita consumption group. They live in far-flung areas, are deficient in physical and social infrastructure and suffer from multiple deprivations. They have experienced large-scale displacement and alienation of their land. Occupational poverty is defined by the nature of work and its conditions. Poverty is the most commonly found in casual labour households, both in rural and urban areas, and their growing dependence on the casual labour market is indicative of uncertainty of work, job insecurity, low wages, lack of any social security which, in the case of the urban poor, is compounded by sub-human living conditions with a lack of access to basic amenities.

The rural–urban specificity in the nature of poverty is defined by their work status and environment. Rural poverty is characterized by a lack of assets for income generation or marginal access to land and dependence on wage labour for subsistence. Rural poor households consist of landless wage earners or farmers operating very small landholdings. This may also include a small percentage of those who engage in other occupations, including self-employment such as artisanal households and service providers. SC and ST households are overwhelmingly poor as they depend upon daily wage earnings from agricultural and non-agricultural work. Even among them, those who depend upon casual labour as a main or a major occupation are chronically poor, and coming out of poverty for them is more difficult as compared to other poor people. Women are concentrated in this category and they only get occasional casual work. The number of casual hired labourers is on the increase.

URBAN POVERTY

Urban poverty is related to the nature of the work, living conditions and social environment. The urban poor are heavily dependent on the labour market because they have no assets other than their labour power. Their vulnerability is related to the type of work which is irregular, with low wages and no social protection. Increasing casualization and segmentation characterize the labour market. Those who engage in self-employment lack access to credit and skill development opportunities. Most urban poor are migrants from rural areas and live in overcrowded and unclean settlements, temporary shelters and on encroached land and feel insecure due to the ever-present threat of eviction and violence. They are poorly serviced by public infrastructure and basic amenities. They also lack social capital, face hostility of the host population and are socially excluded. Market-oriented reforms have aggravated inequity in the provision of civic amenities where they reside (Loughhead & Mittal, 2000).

POLITICS OF POVERTY

There is also the politics of poverty as the increasing number of disadvantaged people from deprived and discriminated regions are turning to Left-wing extremism to get relief and justice against corporate industrialization and indifference of the government to their suffering, indicating a deficit of trust, democracy and legitimacy (ICPR, 2011; Kumar, 2011).

DIMENSIONS OF POVERTY

Poverty has been variously defined to refer to multiple deprivations which make it difficult for a household to attain a minimum level of well-being. Measuring poverty, however, is not a simple task because well-being includes not only economic but also non-economic dimensions, particularly the latter, which are also difficult to capture and quantify. Generally, only income and consumption-based norms, that is, an 'economic' approach, are used to estimate poverty, as has been done in India too. But this approach ignores other critical dimensions and interventions to tackle low income, and inadequate consumption may fail to get people out of a poverty trap. It is, therefore, necessary to encompass, in any strategy of poverty eradication, multiple deprivations which cause poverty. The mapping of this multidimensionality of deprivation should be based not only on findings of research and investigation but on people's own perception of what it means to be poor (Radhakrishna & Ray, 2005). An attempt to capture different dimensions of poverty brings out the following.

Poverty as Material Deprivation

Poverty in India is largely equated with an inadequate level of income or consumption below a certain standard, which in this country is the normative basis to obtain the required food basket. The insufficiency of income is due to the lack of or irregular employment/underemployment and low wages. The standard approach, including that of the World Bank, is to address it through faster economic growth, which will also benefit the poor through a trickle-down effect. This would increase employment opportunities and growth in rural wages. It suggests that a one percentage point growth in a country's main income is likely to reduce the incidence of poverty by 2.4 percentage points (World Bank, 2006, cited by Mosley, 2012). The assumption is that, on average, growth is distribution-neutral and poor groups gain as much as rich groups. This is not true for many reasons but the most significant one is an inequality in the distribution of income, assets and power, which blocks an equal chance of participating in the market and access to jobs. International institutions have pushed the view that job creation through growth would achieve equity rather than through independent policies (Mosley, 2012). India does rely primarily on economic growth as a route to poverty reduction but recognizes that a trickle-down mechanism may not happen, and growth may bypass the poor, particularly the severely poor. It has, therefore, combined economic growth with programmes directly benefitting the poor to reduce inequities in growth and achieve synergy between the two.

Poverty as Deprivation of Resources, Access and Social Capital

The poor generally lack assets or have low quality assets which do not generate much income. They only depend on their labour to survive. In rural areas, dominant landowners control their livelihood by providing them with land in tenancy or work on their farms and thus continue to exercise social, economic and political control over them[1]. Land reforms have failed to provide the landless poor with some land. Distribution of other income generating assets under poverty alleviation programmes did not significantly change the assetlessness of the poor. The poor are also deficient in human assets——education, skills and good health. In addition to the poverty of private resources, their access to public assets such as community infrastructure, basic social services and development programmes is also limited. This is compounded by a poverty of social relationships and political voice, that is, social and political capital (Kozel & Parker, 2005). Labour being their only private asset, they need secure jobs with better wages outside agriculture to improve their earning and status. But there is an increasing casualization of jobs in the non-farm sector, which has failed to provide secure and decent jobs.

Enhanced human capital is also an important asset for the poor for accessing better paying jobs for which access to basic social services is essential. Though these public services are available free of cost, the poor have difficulties in accessing them due to social constraints. The settlements of the poor are equally neglected in the provision of infrastructure such as roads, electricity and transport.

The poor are disadvantaged not only in natural and human capital but also in social capital, that is, social relationships, networks and institutions, that can support the poor in need. This is because the poor lack resources to contribute to any network which can provide them with any economic assistance. The poor have not shown any inclination to build their own network except when facilitated by non-governmental organizations (NGOs) under a government supported programme. Their only social capital is the landowners with whom they work with in a patron–client relationship (Kozel & Parker, 2005). In the political sphere also, they have little contact, which can mitigate their situation or give them access to government programmes, unlike the rich who use their political capital to corner a higher share of public resources.

The poverty alleviation programme, besides providing wage employment, had also a programme for the creation and distribution of assets, though discontinued now. Self-employment is promoted with state-supported credit and skill development and capacity building. They also provide food security and nutrition supplements as well as social security. Social capital is sought to be built by promoting group activity among the poor. A minimum needs programme is intended to improve access to social services.

Poverty as Deprivation of Capability

Poverty may not be reduced by economic growth through the creation of employment opportunities because the poor may not be able to participate in the growth process so as to take advantage of opportunities offered by it. That is where Amartya Sen is relevant. He has shifted the focus on poverty from just material deprivation to inadequacies of 'capabilities' which tend to restrict choices for the poor and constrain their freedom to action to lead a life they can and wish to live. This concept has been extensively used by the UNDP to promote human development through the provision of basic social services—education, health, drinking water, sanitation and nutrition—to enable the poor to 'function' effectively, while equalizing capabilities will enable the poor to lead a long and healthy life with freedom, dignity and self-respect (Hughes et al., 2009). An improvement in the quality of life is also essential for increased productivity of labour. Education enables access to decent jobs in the labour market and upward mobility and creates greater self-confidence. Good health is necessary for sustained hard work, achieving increased productivity and career advancement. However, even when these services are available to all citizens, the poor may fail to access them as they face social barriers. They also reside in segregated colonies in urban areas, which are poorly serviced by municipal agencies. Low-educational achievements condemn the poor to low-paid insecure jobs in the informal sector. Similarly, due to the lack of good health, the poor face a higher burden of disease and have a lower life expectancy and higher fertility. Therefore, efforts to tackle income poverty alone will fail to eradicate poverty in the absence of focused measures to improve their access to social services as also the removal of social constraints to equalize capabilities and expand freedom of action. With these capabilities, even economic growth becomes effective. For this to happen, economic and social sector policies should be integrated, and the former should be compatible with the latter (Mehrotra & Delamonica, 2007). An increase in the public expenditure of the social sector with a pre-eminent role for the state's provisioning of these services is the route to realize this objective. India has pursued the policy of providing minimum needs to all its citizens as an important goal of development ever since the Fifth Five-Year Plan, not as a poverty alleviation measure but as a perquisite for the balanced human development for all its citizens.

Poverty as a Deprivation of a Barrier Free Social Environment

India's social structure is characterized by deep and continuing inequalities where discrimination against certain groups is widely practised based on caste, ethnicity, gender and, lately, religion. The social exclusion of SCs/STs is entrenched and has been found to be the least amenable to social change. This structural condition is deeply linked to the poverty of households of these groups. Persons from these groups usually work in low-paid and low-status jobs, like agricultural labourers who live in thatched and mud houses, have low educational attainments and suffer frequent illnesses. They face widespread discrimination in access to jobs in the labour market, as sellers of goods in the product market, as seekers of credit from state financial institutions and state provided public services. Development programmes, even when specifically targeted for them, fail to reach them. They are more likely to suffer material deprivation than people from the higher castes as they are disproportionally engaged in low-skilled work and insecure jobs with lower incomes, whether in farm or non-farm sectors, than individuals from the upper castes. SCs lack productive assets and are largely landless. STs have owned land, though of poor quality, but have been deprived of it due to illegal alienation and development-induced acquisition and are, therefore, increasingly becoming landless. SCs and STs are at the bottom of all human development indicators and have continued to be in this position. The bulk of people suffering from chronic poverty belong to these groups, and some of them are forced to work as the bonded labourers of rich landowners.

The discrimination against Muslims has been elaborately documented in the Sachar Committee Report (Sachar Committee Report, 2006). Disability is also a major cause of poverty as well as a consequence of it. Persons with disabilities are excluded from the labour market, and if they are employed at all, they work for fewer hours with low wages. Social security schemes do not provide them with a living wage. Their needs remain peripheral to development planning. Their segregation contributes to their marginalization, increased vulnerability and exclusion (see Chapter 6). Therefore, interventions to tackle income poverty would fail to lift them above the poverty threshold unless this discrimination is effectively eliminated.

This would require anti-discriminatory policies which should cover both regulatory and developmental aspects. Regulatory aspects would include enactment of laws, making regulatory provisions, issuance of directions. The developmental aspects would cover affirmative action, effective implementation of existing programme and taking of new programmes and giving these groups a voice in decision-making, along with deepening of democracy through grassroots level support. Gender-based discrimination has to eliminate biases in inter- and intra-household allocation of resources, empowering women with access to productive assets and credit support, and special attention to the provision of educational and health services. Redistribution of resources towards those groups would link the 'capability' approach to social exclusion and participation (Hughes et al., 2009). State interventions have been made to neutralize these barriers through a number of policies and programmes—regulatory, developmental and financial—to eliminate discrimination against all socially excluded groups.

Poverty Based on Gender Identity

Gender-based deprivations have multiple dimensions which add to poverty-related vulnerability. Poverty is most acute in the case of women-headed households. Female workers are engaged in the lowest-paid activities and are usually concentrated on low-paid work in agriculture such as casual labourers. They generally get lower wages than men for the same or similar work. They are also under-represented in the workforce as compared to men. Their work participation has gone down even further in the post-reforms period. Their work within the household fails to get any recognition. Socially governed norms prevent women from taking to many occupations and using other opportunities to participate equally with men in political and economic life. They are regarded as a burden. They are discriminated against by their families in accessing education, food distribution and seeking healthcare. They suffer from a triple burden—reproductive, social and economic. The poverty level is also marginally higher among women than among men in both rural and urban areas, particularly in female-headed households. The situation of elderly women in households is even worse. Widows and girls within poor households also suffer from chronic energy deficiency, indicating a nutritional deficiency. Therefore, targeting poor households for income generation without addressing biases against women within and outside the household will not alleviate their poverty (see ICPR, 2011; Radhakrishna & Ray, 2005; Chapter 5). India has been implementing several measures, legal and developmental, aimed at providing physical security against violence, promoting education and addressing their health problems.

Poverty as Deprivation of Nutrition and Incidence of Child Labour

Poverty among children is linked to the economic status of a household, both in rural and urban areas, and is associated with their malnutrition. The share of children in poor households is quite high. This results in a higher degree of malnutrition among them. The problem is more severe among children below the age of five years. According to the National Family Health Survey (NFHS) 2015–2016, 35.8 per cent of children are underweight and 38.4 per cent are stunted in the country. Globally, India has 28 per cent of undernourished people (Gulati & Jose, 2020). Nutritional deficiency is the result of inadequate food and a lack of access to health services and environmental sanitation. It is also linked to a mother's education and access to antenatal care. Poverty is a major cause of food scarcity. Malnutrition causes poverty because it debilitates the physical condition, affects one's capacity to undertake hard and sustained work and lowers resistance to disease. But undernutrition is not confined to children. According to the NFHS 2015–2016, 37.4 per cent of adult males and 39.4 per cent of adult females suffer from chronic energy deficiency. Intervention to tackle nutritional deficiency requires not only an enhancement of incomes but also access to education, health services and food security. This dimension of poverty has been addressed through the provision of food security, additional food supplements and measures to eliminate infant mortality rate (IMR), maternal mortality rate (MMR) and mortality under the age of 5.

Incidence of Child Labour

Another manifestation of household poverty is child labour. It is also a cause of poverty as such children grow up illiterate without any skills for upward mobility. Poverty forces parents to send their children to work. Child workers experience not only severe exploitation—physical, social, psychological and sexual—but also violence from their employers and risk to their life and health for being engaged in hazardous occupations. Improving the economic condition of families who send their children to work is the most enduring solution to the menace of child labour. The incidence of child labour is sought to be eliminated through the enforcement of law and special programmes to wean such children and enrol them into schools.

Environmental Dimension of Poverty

The environment is linked to poverty in multiple ways. The most important of them is related to people inhabiting large areas of the country, described as rainfed agro-ecological zones, parts of which are semi-arid and are characterized by the poor quality of land, lack of infrastructure and frequent crop failure due to the failure of the monsoon. People residing in hill areas suffer from a paucity of cultivable land, lack of infrastructure and employment opportunities and poor access to basic services (ICPR, 2011). Not only the challenging natural environment but also the man-made environmental degradation as a result of economic growth exacerbates poverty. Mineral extraction, industrial pollution and chemical inputs in agriculture not only degrade productive resources like land, water and forest but also contribute to the poor quality of life due to pollution of air and water sources. Some of the worst hotspots of environmental degradation are to be found in tribal concentration areas which aggravates their existing higher level of poverty. Environment degradation contributes to poverty primarily in two ways: first, as a determinant of health, fertility and mortality and, second, as affecting access to environmental goods and services such as food, timber and fossil fuels (Hughes et al., 2009). The poor also live in ecologically fragile areas, which makes them vulnerable to natural disasters. Lately, climate change has added to their vulnerability. But the environmental factor is rarely discussed in poverty analysis and its eradication, though area development programmes are implemented for backward regions. Industrial pollution is sought to be checked by regulatory measures and mitigation strategies have been outlined for coping with climate change.

Conflict Dimension of Poverty

Areas affected by violent conflict experience higher levels of poverty. Conflict destroys human and economic capital, reduces employment opportunities and makes the provision of basic social services difficult. Poverty, inequality and injustice make it easier to mobilize affected people against the government leading to violent conflicts (Hughes et al., 2009). In India, three areas are currently affected by violent conflict—Jammu & Kashmir, the Northeast and central India (the Maoist belt). In the first two, poverty is not a proximate driver of conflict. But central India is home to tribals, the poorest of the poor, who also face discrimination, neglect and apathy from the government for their multiple deprivations. Government policies have adversely impacted them by dispossessing them of their land for development projects, which impoverishes them further (see, Fernandes, 2006). They are also denied access to forest resources by not implementing the rights granted to them under the law. Development programmes introduced for their benefit fail to reach them. They are powerless in influencing decisions of the government which affect them notwithstanding the political reservation they enjoy in legislative bodies and in Panchayati Raj Institutions (PRIs). When they are mobilized to violently resist injustice and apathy, it is treated as a 'law-and-order' problem (see Chapter 12), and they are exposed to military action which results in serious human rights violations. Due to these security operations, they suffer food insecurity, loss of livelihood, absence of essential social services, restrictions on their physical movement and total control over the flow of information to and from the area. People affected have now been trapped in chronic poverty. Here, poverty and injustice have caused conflict, and conflict management has aggravated poverty and injustice. Conventional poverty alleviation measures would be of no avail in this complex situation. A political solution is required to end military operations, address their grievances and to engage them politically to restore peace.

Vulnerability and Powerlessness

The poor are vulnerable to the possibility of sliding into chronic poverty and destitution from which it is difficult to come out as they neither possess assets nor have any social support (Kozel & Parker, 2005). They are always haunted by a serious risk of suffering and a sudden mishap like serious illness requiring costly treatment, death or disability of the main earner of the household, asset loss due to fire or theft or death of a livestock. These shocks may compel them to borrow and fall into a debt trap. In the case of women, widowhood or desertion by the spouse with no social support often leads to destitution. Economic shocks include crop failure, floods, erosion or wasted investment in a failed dug well or compulsory acquisition of their land and so on. They continue, therefore, with low-paying economic activities and are reluctant to take any risk with economic activities which may bring higher economic returns and thus perpetuate their poverty (Kozel & Parker, 2005). This intervention would require state-provided comprehensive social security, safety nets and insurance policies. The state has made modest interventions in this direction.

Powerlessness and Poverty

Poverty is not merely an economic and social phenomenon, but it is political as well which reflected in the unequal distribution of power. Power is the capacity to get the desired outcomes. The poor lack this power in the system which is dominated by the rich and middle class. It is the most serious of all structural inequities and 'self-reinforcing' (Royce, 2015). This powerlessness leads to helplessness, despair and resignation and generates loss of morale which inhibits action to change existing conditions (see, Roy & Singh in this volume). The powerlessness of the poor comes from marginalization processes rooted in the social structure and gets replicated and reinforced in other spheres. These processes need to be 'arrested and reversed' through structural change for which the initiative should come from the state along with measures to empower the poor. As a first step, many deprivations the poor suffer from have to be addressed by the implementation of existing and new programmes and the 'poor to be assisted to gain entry into mainstream institutions and networks that exercise power for participation on equal terms with others' (Radhakrishna & Ray, 2005 p. 164) and to form organizations for collective assertion of their rights and shed their dependency. The government took some measures to improve the participation of the poor in development programmes through social mobilization by external agencies but that process ceased long ago.

Cognitive Dimension of Poverty

Poverty is such a deeply debilitating phenomenon that its impact goes beyond social, political and economic effects and influences the development of cognitive abilities and motivation. This translates into psychological inadequacy to cope with problems of life and makes the poor fatalistic and inferior, developing notions of self-pity (see, Sinha in this volume). As a result, they have a strong tendency to ascribe success to external factors rather than their own efforts, while failure is often ascribed to them. These psychological traits accentuate the condition of poverty due to a lack of self-confidence to make the effort to move up. The measures suggested above to eradicate poverty are expected to neutralize the psychological dimension of poverty.

It is evident from the above that, though relying primarily on economic growth, India has not confined its approach to a single strategy but a combination of interventions to tackle the complexity of poverty, irrespective of whether they are taken as poverty alleviation measures or general development programmes. The poverty eradication strategy has also evolved over a period of time: from being focused on income poverty to an emphasis on basic needs and further to participation, through decentralized governance and social mobilization, and then to right-based entitlements in the post-reforms period. The strategy for tackling income poverty has also shifted from being individual centric to group centric and from asset transfer to capacity building for participation in the growth process (Radhakrishna & Ray, 2005). But the contours of poverty have been changing, and existing strategies do not address them and require interventions focused on each one of them.

Changing Contours of Poverty and Deprivation

Demographic Transition Is Changing

The profile of poverty is changing demographically. Living longer leads to a larger proportion of elderly people in poor families. Due to the low-earning capacity, the poor generally are in no position to make provisions for old age. The position of elderly women is worse as they usually live longer. The case of persons with disabilities, whether young or old, is even more precarious. As younger people in poor households migrate to seek work, elderly people are left behind to survive on begging and foraging. Economic growth will not address this vulnerability. Only comprehensive state-funded social security will help (Radhakrishna & Ray, 2005).

Priority to Human Capital Development over Growth

Evidence has emerged that even with faster growth and poverty alleviation programmes, poverty persists among those who lack physical and human capital and/or suffer from social exclusion. Focused interventions to enhance their human capital and eliminate discrimination will help them participate in the growth process. This should receive priority over economic growth (Dev, 2016a; Gaiha & Kulkarni, 1998; Radhakrishna, 2015).

Eliminate Child Poverty

There is a large incidence of child poverty, both in rural and urban India, with an increase in the proportion of children among the poor. The inability of households to feed their children due to disability or chronic illness or the death of the main breadwinner forces them to push their children into the labour market not only for their own survival but also to support the family, more so in a post-COVID-19 situation. This results in a high incidence of malnutrition and loss of education among them, not to speak of the multifaceted exploitation and even violence that they face. Child labour is substantially higher among ST households than in other social groups. The government's attempt to enrol such children in school will not succeed in curbing it and requires a specific strategy of reducing the poverty levels of families which pushes their children to work.

Feminization of Poverty

Female work participation rates as compared to males and the rate of growth of employment of women have gone down after the introduction of economic reforms (Radhakrishna & Ray, 2005). This is evident, especially after mid-2016, in both rural and urban areas (Vyas, 2020), with the decline more evident in the former than the latter. More women work in the informal sector and engage in work of a casual nature, earning lower wages than men. They are additionally burdened with domestic duties which limit their employability. Women also face discrimination within the family and outside. There is thus an emerging feminization of poverty which poverty alleviation programmes targeting households do not neutralize. This requires targeting women in poor households and employing multipronged action to empower them specifically in rural areas.

Agrarian Distress Retards Poverty Reduction

The farm sector in the post-reforms period has witnessed acute distress, leading to farmers' suicides. This distress has resulted from the unviability of agriculture due to the high cost of inputs and low returns from the market, withdrawal of state support, trade liberalization, reduction in public investment and shrinking credit support. Farmers are caught in a perpetual debt trap because of the wide gap between their average monthly expenditure and their income from cultivation and other sources. The recently introduced cash transfer to them does not bridge this gap. This, along with increasing landlessness from 28 per cent in 1951 to 55 per cent in 2011, indicates the level of impoverishment (Misra & Iqbal, 2020). The farm sector requires comprehensive state support and intervention on multiple fronts in respect of small and marginal farmers to alleviate their poverty.

Growth-induced Impoverishment

Besides those poor who are left out of the growth process, there are some who are its victims (Roy cited in Gopalan, 2020). The latter are those who are affected by the acquisition of their land for development projects. This results in the large-scale displacement of people from their land, habitat, livelihood, access to social services and network of social relationships with meagre compensation and absence of rehabilitation. The 2013 law on land acquisition, though an improvement over the 1894 law, does not arrest their slide into chronic poverty overnight. STs suffer from both dimensions of poverty. They not only have the highest incidence of poverty and its lowest reduction by economic growth but also have a disproportionally high share (more than 40%) of this displacement compared to their share of the population (8%; Fernandes, in this volume). The loss of land and the denial of access to forest resources are at the root of it. Without a determined effort to prevent alienation of their land and implement their rights to forest resources, the existing intergenerational transmission of poverty among them will continue.

Unprecedented Unemployment

The slowing down of the economy resulting from demonetization and the ill-prepared Goods and Services Tax (GST) has led to the retrenchment of workers in many establishments and the closure of many small and medium-sized enterprises (SMSEs), leading to a huge loss of jobs (11 million in 2018 and 27 million in April 2020) with no social security to fall back upon. The country's rural areas account for 84 per cent of jobless people who are concentrated in women, wage labourers, agriculture labourers and small traders (Vyas, 2019). The unemployment rate shot up to 7.4 per cent in December 2018, and now, COVID-19 has only worsened it. This has pushed the existing poor into chronic poverty because job losers have to compete for fewer jobs with new entrants joining the labour force. Not only the revival of the economy but the composition of growth has to change to provide for secure jobs, along with expanded Mahatma Gandhi Employment Guarantee Act (MGNREGA) and its urban extension and state-funded social protection.

Regressive Labour Reforms

The precarity of employment is emerging as a major cause of poverty. With already 82.4 per cent of workers employed in the informal sector and increasing informalization in the formal sector (Srivastava, 2020), radical changes in labour laws pushed by the government recently to give employers freedom to hire and fire workers, settle terms of employment and drastic curtailment in trade union activity will lead to many secure workers in the formal sector turning into informal workers with a fall in wages and loss of social security. This will result in the non-poor falling into poverty and some into chronic poverty. This regressive measure needs to be withdrawn along with a firm adherence to labour standards.

Let us now see how far India has succeeded in eliminating poverty through various interventions.

GROWTH AND POVERTY

Growth being valued as the primary driver of poverty reduction, its impact on achieving it is assessed on the basis of consumption surveys that are carried out periodically. As per this assessment, poverty has been reduced by 1.3 per cent per annum between 1974 and 1987, 0.4 per cent per annum between 1987 and 1994 and 0.74 per cent per annum between 1993–1994 and 2004–2005 (ICPR, 2011). Officially, it is claimed that poverty reduction post-reforms in the 1990s was higher than the pre-reform period of the 1980s, which is however strongly contested (Deaton & Dreze 2002, Saxena & Farrington, 2003). It is also mired in controversy about the recall period in the consumption survey schedule (Deaton & Kozel, 2005). The 1980s had more equitable consumption and growth, ensured faster reduction in poverty and a decrease in inequality (Dhamija & Bhide, 2010). But between 2004 and 2005 and 2011, its decline was faster, that is by 2.2 per cent, which was officially attributed primarily to the higher rate of economic growth, leading to an increase in per capita income, though agricultural growth and MGNREGA also contributed to it (Ahluwalia, 2020). Non-official assessments ascribed this reduction to the right-based entitlements during this period, shifting the discourse on poverty from poverty alleviation to capability issues (Himanshu, 2020). Patnaik, however, considers this decline as spurious as also incredible due to the virtual collapse of employment growth, rapid global food price inflation, and the drought of 2009–2010 during this period. But, more importantly, it was because of the divergence between the nutrition and invariant poverty line and the official poverty line. This decline in poverty is on account of the standard calorie intake measurement of poverty being lowered over time. The percentage of poor would be 75 per cent as per this measurement in 2009–2010 (Patnaik, 2013). In any case, notwithstanding higher poverty reduction, the poverty levels of SCs/STs are higher than other groups and, for STs, two times that of the national average (Dev, 2016a). Besides, the growth process has led to a widening of regional inequalities with poorer states benefitting less than developed states. This has increased rural–urban disparity and intensified intra-urban inequalities (Radhakrishna, 2015).

GROWTH AND INEQUALITY

Faster growth post-reforms has been accompanied by rising consumption inequality between the rich and the poor, indicating that growth in this period was pro-rich (Radhakrishna, 2015). Inequality, in fact, is far greater in income and wealth. Income inequality is corroborated by the National Council for Applied Economic Research (NCAER) Human Development Survey between 2004–2005 and 2011–2012 (Dev, 2016b). It is to the extent of ₹500:1 or even ₹1,000:1 if the salaries of the private sector top officials are taken into account, which has disturbed even the government (ICPR, 2011). Wealth inequality is the most glaring. According to Credit Suisse's report, the richest 1 per cent in India owned 53 per cent of the country's wealth, while the share of the top 10 per cent was 76.3 per cent (Dev, 2016a). Inequalities between the rich and the poor are much higher if access to education and health, particularly education, is taken into account (World Bank, 2011). Inequalities in income and wealth have led to an unequal distribution of power. Wealthy people occupy strategic command posts in the economy and politics to get the desired outcomes (Royce, 2015). Inequalities have not only an economic dimension but also have a social dimension. The gap is more pronounced when caste, ethnicity, gender and religion are factored in. This gap is not bridged by economic growth even with redistribution and requires social change to achieve it. An increase in inequalities poses a serious challenge to poverty reduction and affects its pace. Even growth may be adversely affected (Dev, 2016a; Kapoor, 2013). The government should, therefore, focus on giving primacy to distribution with a view to making income more equal before stressing on high growth (Kapoor, 2013).

POVERTY ALLEVIATION PROGRAMMES

The benefits of growth not trickling down to the poor were recognized by policymakers, and therefore, it was supplemented by a direct attack on poverty through various programmes targeting the poor. A poverty alleviation strategy was conceptualized in the initial phase in terms of, first, a change in the agrarian structure through land reforms and, second, improving agriculture production and productivity through the Green Revolution. The first sought to break the concentration of land through the abolition of intermediaries and giving secure rights to the tiller of land through tenancy reforms so as to end their exploitation by owners and to redistribute surplus land obtained from the imposition of ceiling on agricultural land holdings to the landless poor. But land reforms only benefitted the upper layer of tenantry, bypassing the oral tenants. The real cultivators, who were not recorded in land records, were evicted. The ceiling programme could not realize its objective because of the meagre land declared surplus and distributed. The programme failed, except in Kerala and West Bengal, due to a lack of political commitment and the absence of the poor being organized effectively. The Green Revolution only helped large landowners who had access to water and credit and sufficient resources of their own to invest in.

DIRECT ATTACK ON POVERTY

The 1970s led to a change in strategy to a direct attack on poverty and introduced two types of programmes, one focused on improving arid and semi-arid drought prone and desert areas and the other on assisting small and marginal farmers to enhance income through cultivation. Both programmes could achieve meagre benefits due to inadequate allocations and design and implementation problems (Radhakrishna & Ray, 2005). The 1980s and 1990s witnessed a major thrust on poverty reduction through a number of centrally sponsored schemes which can be clubbed under three thematic categories: (a) employment programmes which consisted of self-employment through asset building and training and wage employment in public works, (b) public distribution system (PDS) and nutrition and (c) social security. These programmes were added to the other general development programmes for all sections of the population from which benefits were likely to accrue to the poor. The nomenclature and design of these programmes have undergone several changes over a period of time without any change in their objectives. The period 2000 onwards is marked by a further improvement in strategy with some of these programmes (wage employment and food and nutritional security) converted into right-based statutory entitlements.

EMPLOYMENT
Self-employment

In the category of employment programmes, self-employment is aimed at providing productive assets as a stable source of income generation to the targeted household through the supply of credit to purchase them along with working capital and skill development to start economic activities. The major programme in this category was the Integrated Rural Development Programme (IRDP). An evaluation of the programme revealed several shortcomings which include sub-critical investment, non-viable projects, design defects, poor quality of assets, corruption and so on (Radhakrishna & Ray, 2005; Saxena & Farrington, 2003). It was redesigned as Swarnajayanti Gram Swarojgar Yojana (SGSY), shifting from an individual to a group approach to entitlement with mandated social mobilization of the poor, organizing them into self-help groups for taking up economic activities in a cluster. Inadequate credit availability and difficulties in designing viable projects failed to produce better results. There has been a further change in the programme, now called the National Urban Livelihood Mission (renamed most recently as Deen Dayal Antyodaya Yojana) consisting of several sub-programmes aimed at capacity building, organizing the poor into groups and providing the self-employed and entrepreneurial-oriented poor with skills, financial linkage for establishing micro-enterprises and creating linkages with livelihood opportunities. In short, the poor now have no programme for asset building, the lack of which is the main cause of persistent poverty.

Wage Employment

Wage employment is designed to provide gainful work to unskilled rural poor seeking work in a manner that enables them to get some income and also creates productive assets/economic infrastructure for sustainable employment. The programme has undergone several changes, both in nomenclature and in content and design. Starting with Food for Work, it was changed to Jawahar Rozgar Yojana, then to Jawahar Gram Samridhi Yojana, later to the Employment Assurance Scheme and finally culminating in the MGNREGA. The Act guarantees 100 days of work to a household as a right at wages fixed by the government. It is not targeted but work is offered on a self-selection basis. The previous wage employment programmes suffered from many shortcomings, ranging from the low-level of employment created to thinly spread resources, flawed selection of projects and corrupt practices (Radhakrishna & Ray, 2005; Saxena & Farrington, 2003). MGNREGA fares better in comparison, both in terms of financial allocations and the average number of days of employment provided. It has also destabilized traditional power relations (Vijayabaskar & Balagopal, 2019). However, the employment provided is still lower than the mandated 100 days. The recent changes in the Act and policy guidelines have privileged infrastructure creation over provision of work, centralization of direction over panchayat-level decision-making and technocratizing monitoring. Notwithstanding these and other negative features, the programme has great potential for reduction in income poverty. If mandated provision of employment is increased from 100 to 200, notified minimum wages in the states are paid, the guarantee is made applicable to the individual rather than the household, adequate allocations are provided to bridge the unmet demand, and wage payment delays are addressed.

Recently, a cash transfer scheme called Kisan Samman Nidhi has been introduced for small and marginal farmers to alleviate their economic distress under which ₹6,000 is credited to their account per year which does not address their distress.

Urban Poor

For the urban poor, three categories of programmes have been introduced: habitat-based programmes for improving basic services and provision of shelter; generation of employment through the creation of assets with skill development and credit support, and the integrated development of small and medium towns. PDS and nutritional schemes are also extended to these areas. These programmes have had no significant impact on reducing urban poverty considering inadequate resource allocation and coverage, poor targeting, and design problems and difficulties in obtaining credit. The strategy lacks a differentiated approach to different strata of urban poor, an effective mechanism for beneficiary participation and building community support and ignores in situ upgradation of shelter among others. The need for an urban National Rural Employment Guarantee Act has also been ignored.

Public Distribution System

The programme has evolved from being as an instrument of price stabilization and restricted to urban areas in the 1970s to its restructuring as a measure for poverty alleviation since the Sixth Five-Year Plan and its extension to rural areas in the 1980s and thereafter to targeted PDS in 1997 by entitling BPL families to get 25 kg of food grains per month at subsidized prices. It also covered people above the poverty line (APL) but at a higher issue price. A component of the programme, Antyodaya Anna Yojana, provided 25 kg of food grains to the poorest households at highly subsidized prices. The PDS performance has faced severe criticism for inefficient implementation, weak targeting, leakages to open market, low quality of food grains supplied and so on (Radhakrishna & Ray, 2005). The programme was revamped in 2013 with the enactment of the National Food Security Act and covers 75 per cent of households in rural areas and 50 per cent in urban areas. The distinction between BPL and APL categories has been abolished. It has also incorporated food grain requirements for nutritional programmes such as Integrated Child Development Services (ICDS), Midday Meals Scheme and cash transfer for Maternity Benefit Scheme with food security. Some states have expanded the coverage of entitled households, reduced issue prices, added pluses and edible oil to commodities supplied through the PDS and deprivatized ration shops along with doorstep delivery (Vijayabaskar & Balagopal, 2019). While this arrangement needs to be universalized, the overall food security measures, however, have not had the desired impact in eliminating hunger considering that India ranks 94 out of 107 countries in the Global Hunger Index 2020 behind Nepal, Pakistan and Bangladesh. (Express Web Desk, 2020) There is pressure from the neoliberal lobby to replace PDS with cash transfer. This needs to be resisted and food security should ensure nutritional security (Vijayabaskar & Balagopal, 2019).

Nutrition

The incidence of acute malnutrition among children and women was sought to be tackled by three programmes. One was a food supplementation programme called the Integrated Child Development Services (ICDS), mentioned earlier. Started in 1975, it provides children in the 0–6 years of age group and pregnant and lactating women with food supplements and, in addition, has been mandated to impart nutrition education to mothers and pre-school education to children.

This programme has been universalized. The second programme provides food supplements to adolescent girls to address nutritional deficiency and anaemia. The third programme is the Midday Meals, which provides nutritional cooked food to school-going children with the additional objective to incentivize their attendance in school. The National Maternity Benefit Scheme, which provides cash transfer of ₹5,000 to pregnant women, is also being implemented, though with restricted eligibility. The ICDS programme suffers from inadequate financial allocation to fully universalize it, a lack of infrastructure in anganwadis (childcare centres), disruption in food supplies, low unit cost of food supplements (it has been revised recently), neglect of childcare education and so on. The lack of sufficient resources affects the implementation of other programmes also. The progress in reducing malnutrition is slower relative to the pace of economic growth (Dev, 2016a)[1], considering that according to the NFHS 2015–2016, the nutritional status of children, though improved as compared to 2005–2006, is still very high, with 38 per cent of children stunted and 36 per cent of underweight children (IIPS, 2017).

Social Security

A social security system was started for the first time in 1995 targeting three groups: elderly persons in poor households in the age group of 60 years and above through a National Old Age Pension Scheme; households affected by the death of a primary bread earner through the National Family Benefit Scheme and lastly pregnant women, through the National Maternity Benefit Scheme. All three involved a cash transfer to beneficiaries. The pension scheme has also been provided for widows and persons with disability. The pension schemes suffer from inadequate coverage due to inadequate financial allocations with huge unmet demands, with a very low amount of pension which has not been increased for the past many years (some states have supplemented it with their contribution) and irregular payments. The second scheme suffers from a lack of awareness, with no formal system of information dissemination. The third scheme is now incorporated into the National Food Security Act and is being implemented with restricted eligibility. The coverage of the second and third schemes is suboptimal because of cumbersome procedures, which require several certificates and proofs. Under the present (NDA) government, a number of new pension schemes have been introduced for different categories of unorganized workers such as farmers, street vendors, rickshaw pullers and ragpickers, self-employed and small traders and unorganized workers (Ray, 2020). There are also two life insurance schemes. These schemes involve beneficiary contribution rather than cash transfer and are voluntary in nature. It is unrealistic for unorganized workers, with no regularity of employment, to deposit their contributions over 20–30 years (Katiyar, 2019). To address the vulnerability of the poor due to a sudden large health expenditure, a publicly funded health insurance scheme called the Ayushman Bharat Pradhan Mantri Jan Arogya Yojana (PMJAY) has been introduced to replace the Rashtriya Swasthya Bima Yojana which provides cashless hospitalization in case of certain specified catastrophic diseases. None of the above measures have provided effective social protection to the poor who require employment security, pension on retirement, comprehensive health insurance and protection against risk. The Unorganized Workers Social Security Act, 2008, has not registered much progress.

Human Development

This dimension of poverty has been addressed through the provision of basic essential services to all citizens to improve their standard of living. These services include publicly financed education, health services, drinking water and sanitation. Education is provided up to the secondary level, free in government-administered and government-aided institutions. Entitlement to free and compulsory education for children in the age group of 6–14 years has been made a statutory right, in fact, a fundamental right. There is no right-based entitlement in respect of healthcare. But health services are provided in rural areas through three-tier primary healthcare institutions at the block level and referral services at a government-funded hospital at the district level and above. Tertiary healthcare is made available in government funded medical college hospitals. In addition, vertically administered programmes for infectious and non-infectious diseases have also been implemented. But the availability of services does not ensure their smooth access to the poor. The poor, particularly marginalized sections, face numerous constraints in availing them.

Health Services

Although improvements have been made in key health indicators, such as infant and under-five mortality, institutional deliveries, antenatal care, immunization and nutritional status as reflected in NFHS-4, the progress is slow, and their status is substantially worse among the poor than among the rich and among the SCs/STs than the higher castes. The disparity in health status exists not merely across classes and social groups but also across states. Self-reported morbidity in India is high, which adversely impacts productive capabilities. This is due to the neglect of the public health system in financial allocations and the promotion of private sector healthcare, which the poor cannot afford. As a result, the poor depend upon unqualified medical practitioners at great risk to their lives and the severely poor do not access healthcare at all. Public sector health units in rural areas suffer from non-availability of doctors, dilapidated infrastructure, non-supply of medicines in rural areas and overcrowding and under-resourced hospitals in urban areas.

Education

Education does not fare much better. Although school attendance has increased substantially, the disparity in the attendance of girls in schools has reduced though literacy has risen (World Bank, 2011), but learning levels are low relative to the curriculum and grades. Inequities in learning outcomes are very high, not only across states but within states as well. The most important reasons are non-functional public schools with an inadequate number of teachers, deficiency in infrastructure, untrained teachers, teacher absenteeism, among others, due to which even the poor are shifting to low budget private schools even though they cannot afford them. The closure of many existing government schools on grounds of efficiency is a regressive step which impacts negatively on access to education, particularly of children from poor and disadvantaged groups. Evidently, right-based entitlement in education has made little difference to the overall improvement in educational attainments.

Drinking Water and Sanitation

As for drinking water, while it is available for free in rural areas, access to it by lower caste groups is impacted by exclusionary practices. Besides, the availability of water is a huge problem in summer in arid and semi-arid areas. The new scheme, Jal Jeewan Mission, promises tap water to all households. In urban areas, access to water is priced, which excludes the poor due to their inability to pay. The colonies of the poor are not serviced by municipalities due to their unrecognized status, and the poor have to depend upon public taps for water. Basic sanitation has registered an improvement in rural areas due to the priority assigned to it in the last few years. But the poor in urban areas who live in slums have to depend on community toilets, the maintenance of which is a serious problem, exposing them to health hazards. It is clear that rapid economic growth has not improved human development outcomes. Notwithstanding the improvement registered by India in its Human Development Index value from 0.437 to 0.640 between 1990 and 2017, it ranks 129 among 189 countries in the UN Human Development Index 2019, below that of Nepal, Sri Lanka and Bangladesh.

Social Exclusion

Widespread discrimination practised against the SCs on the basis of caste and untouchability practices and STs on the basis of ethnicity has been recognized ever since the colonial period, and measures to combat it have been incorporated in the Constitution. As a result, these two communities have been given the benefit of reservation in government jobs, entry into higher educational institutions and representation in legislative bodies and PRIs. Laws have been enacted to criminalize the practice of untouchability, caste-based violations of civil rights and atrocities inflicted on the two communities. Manual scavenging has been prohibited under law with the state's commitment to liberate manual scavengers and rehabilitate them. SCs and STs have also earmarked the share of public funds pooled from different development schemes for their exclusive welfare besides a specified share in beneficiary-oriented schemes. Two national commissions, one each for SCs\STs and a third statutory commission, exclusively for manual scavengers, have been set up as watchdog bodies for overseeing measures introduced for the welfare of the concerned groups. STs have also been protected in law against alienation of their land by non-STs and have also been given legal recognition of their traditional rights in forests. Despite this impressive policy and institutional architecture, there is no significant improvement in the condition of these groups and the disabilities they suffer from. They continue to face discrimination in society, the market space and in the public sphere, including government institutions. There is no let-up in atrocities committed on them. Jobs in government have shrunk after the onset of economic reforms while access to private sector jobs is constrained by their lack of skills and discrimination. Political participation in democratic institutions has not translated into power and a voice in decision-making. They continue to be bypassed by economic growth as they cannot participate in it due to these formidable constraints. Most of these measures for eliminating social exclusion and violence suffer from a lack of adequate political commitment, ineffective implementation and societal resistance, and have no significant impact on reducing their poverty.

Gender Discrimination

Gender discrimination has been addressed by various measures which include giving them a specified share in beneficiary-oriented development schemes, providing training, skill development and access to credit to promote self-employment, making stringent provisions in law to deal with violence, particularly sexual violence against them, enacting laws to deal with domestic violence, sexual harassment at the workplace and prohibition against giving and taking of dowry in marriage. The Hindu Succession Act has given women a share in parental property. Schemes relating to tackling nutritional deficiency, prevention of violence against women, promotion of education and healthcare, facilitation of income-generating activities and social mobilization and support have the objective of combating discrimination against them.

A separate commission has also been set up to oversee their interests and gender budgeting has been introduced to ensure that women get an adequate share of development resources. But India ranks 135 among 147 nations in terms of women empowerment according to the UN Human Development Index (*Economic Times*, 2020), 112 among 153 countries in the Global Gender Gap Index 2020 and 150 in the health and survival component, below its small neighbouring countries (Ghosh & Sen, 2020). This indicates that policy and institutional initiatives have had no significant impact on neutralizing their disabilities and a reduction in their poverty. The task is no doubt complex as discrimination against them is also practised within the family against the girl child at birth, in social norms, in the allocation of resources, opportunities and decision-making.

Participation and Social Mobilization

The dimension of powerlessness and voicelessness of the poor is addressed through three measures to empower them. The most important of them is the institutional mechanism for participation of the poor in planning, implementation and monitoring of development programmes in PRIs. The reservation of seats for SCs/STs/women ensures the prevention of the elite capture of these institutions. But social hurdles on the grounds of caste still operate for the lower caste heads of Panchayats to exercise powers vested in them. Even otherwise, this measure has failed to realize its objectives due to the reluctance of state governments, except in Kerala, to devolve finances, functions and functionaries to these institutions and loosen control over them.

The second mechanism of empowerment of the poor is collective action in economic activities through the formation of self-help groups (particularly of women), encouraged by the government with funds and subsidies and NGOs providing capacity building, activating participation of members and helping them with project formulation and execution. Self-help groups are largely engaged in thrift and credit activities. Where they engage in economic activities, they require continuing support in dealing with market and business practices. The experience so far does not hold out much hope of economically empowering the poor and reducing their poverty through this measure. The third mechanism is empowering the poor through social mobilization by an external agency, which involves organizing them for collective action to break their dependence on the non-poor and emboldening them to demand a change in the basic norms and institutions of society loaded against them (Radhakrishna & Ray, 2005). But such a measure requires an enabling environment, suitable external agents and political commitment to pursue it. This strategy was modestly tried in the Five-Year Plan, which ceased long ago and is unlikely to be pursued to be relevant in the current political dispensation. Even rudimentary social mobilization by NGOs runs into conflict with local power structures and government agencies since it threatens to disturb the status quo. The prospects of such social mobilization are bleak. Overall, the strategy of political and economic empowerment has contributed little to the reduction of poverty or even to giving the poor a voice in decision-making.

Environmental Degradation

Watershed programmes have been implemented in arid and semi-arid areas. Laws have been enacted to check environmental degradation and its restoration, and there is a National Green Tribunal to oversee their enforcement. An action plan for mitigating climate change is also in place. But the implementation is more in breach than in adherence, as it seems that the government privileges growth over the environment and contributes to its degradation and climate warming.

Social Sector Expenditure

It is recognized that poverty reduction and sustainable development require, besides equitable economic growth, the enhancement of human capital. The commitment to achieve this objective is judged by the allocation of sufficient resources for the provision of basic social services such as education, health, nutrition and social security in central and state budgets. India's social sector expenditure growth, by both the centre and states, has been very small with only 7.7 per cent of GDP and a mere 1.1 per cent point increase between 2015 and 2019 as per the *Economic Survey 2019–2020* (Nanda, 2020). The growth in allocation was far higher in the year 2008–2009 and even in 2014–2015 (Reserve Bank of India, 2019). Of this expenditure, the share of education was 3.1 per cent, far lower than the 6 per cent recommended by experts and that of health at 1.6 per cent, far lower than the 2.5 percent of GDP advocated by the National Health Policy and the rest going to other social sub-sectors. This expenditure was also lower in international comparison (Nanda, 2020). Worse, central expenditure on education and health has been either stagnant or declining, both as a percentage of the GDP as well as that of total expenditure (Centre for Budget and Governance Accountability, 2019, 2020). The bulk of the social sector expenditure is incurred by states as many subjects fall in the state's list of the Constitution. State-level expenditure is marked by interstate disparities between financially strong and better resourced states in the south and west and the resource-poor states in the north and east (Dev, 2016a). Evidently, faster growth has not been translated into higher social sector expenditure and matched by enhanced human development attainments.

Composition of Expenditure

Besides inadequate social sector expenditure, the composition of the expenditure also impacts negatively on poverty reduction. In education and health, most of the expenditure goes towards the payment of salaries with very inadequate resources for non-salary components which adversely impacts the quality of services provided (Radhkrishna & Ray, 2005). Public services are criticized for their inefficiency which is caused by insufficient resources, and therefore, they require, not only an increase in the overall allocation of resources, but the intra-sector allocation of resources between basic and non-basic services is equally important because health and education spending discriminates against the poor. Targeting an increase in primary healthcare and school education has better distribution effects and produces more effective social outcomes in the context of poverty reduction (Mehrotra & Delamonica, 2007). Besides, social sector expenditure has to be accompanied by comprehensive social protection consisting of social insurance, pension schemes, legal support to labour standards and housing (Loughhead & Mittal, 2000).

Macroeconomic Policies for Poverty Reduction

Even with higher resource allocation for human capital development, poverty reduction is unlikely to be realized unless macroeconomic policies are compatible with social policies and are harmoniously integrated so as to benefit the poor. In the neoliberal political economy, macroeconomic policies are directed towards limiting the supply of money, lowering government expenditure and budget deficits, reducing the size and role of government in the production sector as well in provisioning of services and liberalizing trade, which reinforce existing inequities and further marginalize the poor. An alternative paradigm of political economy is needed which benefits the poor proportionately more than the non-poor in income distribution, public expenditure and improving working conditions and the social environment where the very poor reside (Mehrotra & Delamonica, 2007). This requires a revision of existing fiscal, monetary and trade policies and halting the increasing privatization and dilution of labour laws. It should reduce inequalities in income and assets, inequities in social and physical infrastructure and uneven spatial growth. The former will require effective redistributive measures while the latter will necessitate helping backward states with greater resource transfers, infrastructure creation and measures to assist the poor to participate in the local economy (Radhakrishna, 2015). The composition of growth will need to shift to economic activities which focus on, first, a provision of full employment to 25–30 of per cent BPL households from the 150 poorest districts as suggested by Bhaduri (2003) through a range of measures, including an expanded MGNREGA and an urban version of it. This should be accompanied by credit and skill development support for self-employed and the production of low-skill intensity goods. Second, protection for small agricultural landowners with state support, cost reducing technology, formation of collectives for access to formal credit and non-formal employment (Radhakrishna, 2015). Third, policies and programmes for upgrading informal sector activities to micro, small and medium enterprises with an adherence to labour standards, along with the social protection of the labour force to cover at least health, old age pension and death benefit to be wholly financed by the government through pro-poor taxation (Mehrotra & Delamonica, 2007). The growth process should have a stronger domestic orientation and avoid foreign investment. Pro-poor institutions that can deliver poverty-reducing inputs and access to work and capital are also needed (Mosley, 2012).

Strategic Shifts in Policy Orientation

Besides moving to pro-poor growth, non-economic policy changes are required to tackle hardcore and persistent poverty. Context-specific changes have been indicated in the paper. Overall, four areas of strategic shifts are highlighted here. These consist of social policies, participation of the poor, combatting social exclusion and governance reforms. Social policies should concentrate on improving human capital and all the dimensions of deprivation with a considerably higher level of social sector expenditure, which should include social security and safety nets for all categories of the poor. Participation of the poor should be accomplished not only by devolution of functions, functionaries and finances to PRIs and an extension of a rights-based approach to drinking water, sanitation, health and housing, along with the implementation of existing rights but also social mobilization of the poor for collective action that unites poor people to influence policy and implementation and strengthening institutions of the poor to protect them from market and non-market risks (Radhakrishna & Ray, 2005). Social exclusion should be combated through land reforms to loosen the existing oppressive agrarian and social structure for improve the bargaining power of the poor. This should be followed by asset building to landless and effective protection against land acquisition and displacement, besides sincerely implementing existing regulatory and developmental interventions in favour of marginalized groups. Structural change is the key for which political parties should take a lead and involve NGOs, community-based organizations, social activists and social movements in this task. In conflict-affected tribal areas, closure should be sought through dialogue with the movement and accommodation of genuine demands to address the trust deficit and bringing underground organizations on board to raise issues concerning them. Governance reforms should include differentiated policies/programmes for the poor, designed in consultation with them, taking into account their heterogeneity and specificity of their poverty and their effective implementation, monitoring and social auditing. Better targeting and effectiveness of the delivery system should be achieved by exerting pressure from the top as well as from below to make implementing agencies accountable, responsive and responsible (Mehrotra & Delamonica, 2007).

CONCLUSION

The slowing down of growth has already increased overall poverty levels with a decline in consumption expenditure in rural areas and an increase in unemployment. The large-scale economic disruption caused by the COVID pandemic will have pushed many non-poor to poverty and the existing poor to chronic poverty. We have a very bleak situation at hand, and the task of poverty eradication is more challenging than ever before.

NOTE

1.   Kozel & Parker, 2005.

REFERENCES

Ahluwalia, Montek Singh (2020). *Backstage: The story behind India's high growth years*. Rupa

Bhaduri, Amit. (2005). *Development with dignity: A case for full employment*. National Book Trust.

Centre for Budget and Governance Accountability. (2019). *Promises and priorities: Analysing the Union Budget, 2019–20*. New Delhi. https://www.cbgaindia. org/wp-content/uploads/2019/07/Promises-and-Priorities-An-Analysis-of-Union-Budget-2019-20-1.pdf

———. (2020). *Decoding priorities: An analysis of the Budget 2020–21*. https://www. cbgaindia.org/wp-content/uploads/2020/02/Decoding-the-Priorities-An-Analysis-of-Union-Budget-2020-21-2.pdf

Deaton, Angus, & Kozel, Valerie (Ed.). (2005). *The great Indian poverty debate*. Macmillan India.

Deaton, Angus, & Dreze, Jean. (2002). Poverty and inequality in India: A re-examination. *Economic & Political Weekly, 37*(36). https://www.epw.in/journal/2002/36/special-articles/poverty-and-inequality-india.html

Dev, S. Mahendra (2016a). *Economic Reforms, Poverty and Inequality*. Indira Gandhi Institute of Development Mumbai, March, 2016.

———. (2016b). Poverty and inequality after reforms. *Mint,* July 26. https://www.livemint.com/Opinion/Mr2DS2Qv4ika8zEuScxN1L/Poverty-and-inequality-after-reforms.html

Dhamija, Nidhi, & Bhide, Sashank. (2010). Dynamics of poverty in India. *Economic & Political Weekly,* 45(13). https://www.epw.in/journal/2010/13/special-articles/dynamics-poverty-india-panel-data-analysis.html

The Economic Times. (2020). Socio Economic Caste Census-2021 to define eligibility of rural household for benefits under government schemes. October 26, 2020. https://economictimes.indiatimes.com/news/politics-and-nation/rejig-of-socio-economic-caste-census-criteria/articleshow/74663021.cms

Fernandes, Walter (2006). Liberalisation and Development Induced Displacement' *Social Change,* 36(1).

Gaiha, Raghav, & Kulkarni, Vani. (1998). Is growth central to poverty alleviation in India? *Journal of International Affairs, 52*(1), 145–180.

Express Web Desk. (2020). Global Hunger Index 2020: India ranks 94 out of 107 countries, under 'serious' category. *The Indian Express,* October 19.

Gopalan, Aparna. (2020). Rights politics and politics of rights in neo-liberal India. *Social Change, 50*(2). https://doi.org/10.1177/0049085720920238

Gulati Ashok, & Jose, Shyana. (2020). Challenge to nurture India has become bigger with outbreak of COVID-19. *The Indian Express,* September 14. https://indianexpress.com/article/opinion/columns/poshan-maah-india-malnutrition-index-global-hunger-index-6594794/

Himanshu. (2020). Freedom struggle was about combating poverty: There has been a setback. *The Indian Express,* April 15. https://indianexpress.com/article/opinion/columns/british-colonialism-independence-economic-growth-poverty-in-india-6555157/

Hughes, Barry B., Irfan, M. T., Khan, Haider, Kumar, Krishna B., Rothman, Dale S., & Solorzano, Jose R. (2009). Reducing global poverty: Patterns of potential human progress (vol. 1). Oxford University Press.

India Chronic Poverty Report (ICPR). (2011). *Towards solutions and new compacts in a dynamic context*. Indian Institute of Public Administration, New Delhi. http://www.chronicpoverty.org/uploads/publication_files/India%20Chronic%20Poverty%20Report.pdf

Ghosh, S., & Sen, S. (2020). Where does India stand in the Global Gender Gap Index. *The Hindu,* January 6. https://www.thehindu.com/data/data-where-does-india-stand-in-the-global-gender-gap-index/article30494545.ece

Kapoor, Radhicka. (2013). Inequality matters. *Economic & Political Weekly, 48*(2). https://www.epw.in/journal/2013/02/special-articles/inequality-matters.html

Katiyar, Sudhir. (2019). Pension Scheme for unorganised workers is yet another illusion. Centre for Labour Research and Action, February 2. https://thewire.in/labour/budget_2019_schemeunorganised_workers_mirage

Kozel, Valerie, & Parker, B. (2005). A profile and diagnostic of poverty in Uttar Pradesh. In Angus Deaton, & Valerie Kozel (Eds.), *The great Indian poverty debate*. Macmillan India.

Kumar, T. M. Vinod, & Gayatri. (2000). Urban poverty: Issues, policies and actions. *Social Change, 30*(1/2).

Kumar, Anand. (2011). Poverty, peoples and paradigm shift: New trajectories of policies and governance in LPG era. In *India Chronic Poverty Report*. Indian Institute of Public Administration.

Kundu, Amitabh. (2000). Urban poverty in India: Issues and perspective in development. *Social Change, 30* (1/2). https://doi.org/10.1177/004908570003000202

Loughhead, Susan, & Mittal, Omkar. (2000). Urban poverty and vulnerability in India: A social policy perspective. *Social Change, 30* (1/2). https://doi.org/10.1177/004908570003000203

Mehrotra, Santosh, & Delamonica, Enrique. (2007). *Eliminating human poverty: Macroeconomic and social policies for equitable growth*. Orient Longman.

Ministry of Rural Development Government of India. (2018). Deendayal Antodaya Yojana—National Rural Livelihood Mission: Alleviating rural poverty and fostering diversified livelihoods through sustainable community institutions of the poor. Press Information Bureau Delhi, April 3. https://rural.nic.in/press-release/deendayal-antodaya-yojana-%E2%80%93-national-rural-livelihoods-mission-alleviating-rural

Misra, Udit, & Nushaiba Iqbal. (2020). Explained: How remunerative is farming in India? Here is what data shows. *The Indian Express*, September 27. https://indianexpress.com/article/explained/simply-put-the-farmer-a-field-report-6606785/

Mosley, Paul. (2012). *The politics of poverty reduction*. Oxford University Press.

Nanda, Prashant K. (2020). Social sector expenditure as portion of GDP grows at a snail pace: Eco survey. *Mint*, January 3. https://www.livemint.com/budget/economic-survey/social-sector-expenditure-as-portion-of-gdp-grows-at-a-snail-pace-eco-survey-11580489661656.html

Narayan, Deepa (ed.). (2008). *Moving out of poverty, Vol. 3, The promise of empowerment and democracy in India*. Palgrave Macmillan and the World Bank.

International Institute for Population Sciences (IIPS). (2017). *National Family Health Survey (NFHS-4), 2015–16: India*. http://rchiips.org/nfhs/nfhs-4Reports/India.pdf

Nayyar, Gaurav, & Nayyar, Rohini. (2016). India's 'poverty numbers': Revisiting measurement of poverty. *Economic & Political Weekly, 51*(35). https://www.epw.in/journal/2016/35/special-articles/indias-poverty-numbers.html

Press Information Bureau. (2020). Press note on Global Multidimensional Poverty Index and India. September 07. https://pib.gov.in/PressReleasePage.aspx?PRID=1651981

Patnaik, Utsa. (2013) Poverty trends in India 2004–05 to 2009–10. *Economic & Political Weekly, 48*(40). https://www.epw.in/journal/2013/40/special-articles/poverty-trends-india-2004-05-2009-10.html

Radhakrishna, R., & Ray, Shovan (Ed.). (2005). *Oxford handbook of poverty in India: Perspectives, policies, and programmes*. Oxford University Press.

Radhakrishna, R. (2015). Well-being, inequality, poverty and pathways out of poverty in India. *Economic & Political Weekly, 50*(41). https://www.epw. in/journal/2015/41/special-articles/well-being-inequality-poverty-and-pathways-out-poverty-india.html

Ray, Surya Sarathi (2020). PM pension schemes for very poor, small traders gets off to a slow start. *Financial Express,* May 16. https://www.financialexpress.com/ money/pm-pension-schemes-for-very-poor-small-traders-get-off-to-a-slow-start/1960583/

Reserve Bank of India. (2019). *Handbook of statistics on the Indian economy, 2018–2019.* https://rbidocs.rbi.org.in/rdocs/Publications/PDFs/0HB2018-19A91 A298806164470A2BCEF300A4FE334.PDF

Royce, Edward. (2015). *Poverty and inequality: The problem of structural inequality* Rawat.

Sachar Committee Report. (2006). Social, economic and educational status of the Muslim community of India: A report. Prime Minister's High Level Committees Cabinet Secretariat, Government of India. http://www.minorityaffairs.gov.in/ sites/default/files/sachar_comm.pdf

Saxena, N. C., & Farrington, John. (2003). Trends and prospects for poverty in rural India: Context and options (Working Paper No. 198). United Nations Research Institute for Social Development, Geneva. https://www.files.ethz. ch/isn/100556/wp198.pdf

Sen, Abhijit. (2011). Foreword. *India Chronic Poverty Report,* Indian Institute of Public Administration, New Delhi.

Srivastava, Ravi. (2020). There is much in the labour codes that needs to be discussed and debated. *The Indian Express,* October 5. https://indianexpress. com/article/opinion/columns/economic-crisis-migrant-labour-bills-covid-19-change-6671565/

The World Bank. (2011). Perspectives on poverty in India: Stylized facts from survey data. World Bank, Washington. https://openknowledge.worldbank. org/handle/10986/2299

UNDP. (2019). Gender Inequality Index 2018. *Human development report 2019: Beyond income, beyond averages, beyond today: Inequalities in human development in the 21st century.* http://hdr.undp.org/sites/default/files/hdr2019.pdf

Vijayabaskar, M., & Balagopal, Gayatri. (2019). The politics of poverty alleviation: Strategies in India (Working Paper 2019-7). United Nation Research Institute for Social Development, Geneva. https://www.unrisd.org/80256B3C 005BCCF9/(httpAuxPages)/423E4B35EE9F8450802584C800546863/$file/ WP2019-7--Vijayabaskar_Balagopal.pdf

Vyas, Mahesh. (2019). 11 million jobs lost in 2018, rural areas worst hit: CMIE. *Business Today,* January 9. https://www.businesstoday.in/current/economy-politics/india-lost-11-million-jobs-in-2018-rural-areas-worst-hit-cmie/ story/306804.html

Vyas, Mahesh. (2018). The bitter truth of female labour participation. *Business Standard,* October 9, 2020. https://www.business-standard.com/article/opinion/ the-bitter-truth-of-female-labour-participation-118100800412_1.html

Section I

Poverty: Rural and Urban

Sectional Introduction

K. B. Saxena

Poverty is the inability to meet subsistence needs and maintain minimum well-being. It is spread over both rural and urban areas. However, as three quarters of India's poor live in rural areas, the number, as well as the percentage of poor, is much higher in the rural areas than in urban areas. The characteristics of poverty are also different in the two areas, with some common features shared by them.

In rural areas, the ownership of land determines the divide between the poor and non-poor. In urban areas, the nature of wage employment and level of wages defines the incidence of poverty. Rural poverty is increasingly concentrated in landless households engaged in agricultural labour and marginal farmers whose landholding is not sufficient to meet subsistence needs or those who have poor quality of assets with low returns and have to depend on wage labour to supplement income from farming. It is acute in far-flung areas with a scattered population. Urban poverty is linked to households engaged in wage labour in manufacturing and services or self-employment. Urban poverty is to be found in households employed as casual labour with low wages, uncertainty of work, no assets except their labour power and no social security or social capital. In rural areas, the share of agricultural labourer households has been increasing over the years, and in contrast, the share of self-employment (farmers) among the poor has been falling. Similarly, the number of casual labour households among urban poor households is increasing due to their dependence on the casual labour market, which subjects them to uncertainty of work availability and aggravates their poverty (Radhakrishna & Ray, 2005).

Voicelessness and powerlessness are common to both the rural and urban poor. Both face constraints in access to basic services, the urban poor more than the rural poor. In the rural areas, it is due to the caste factor and segregated settlements, while in the urban areas, it is due to a lack/inadequate provisioning in slums and unauthorized colonies. Both experience a lack of access to formal credit and skills under development programmes.

But there are marked differences as well. While fuel, wood and water are freely available in rural areas, the urban poor require cash expenditure to access them. They also have to meet the transportation costs to the worksite or market. The urban poor also have to pay higher prices for goods and services, all of which make them dependent on cash income. They are, therefore, more vulnerable to a rise in the prices of essential communities of daily use (Kumar & Gayatri, 2000). A large section of the urban poor are migrants from rural areas who live in poor quality, congested and temporary shelters, often in environmentally degraded areas, poorly serviced by the provision of public infrastructure and basic essential services. The most vulnerable poor live on pavements and survive on begging, foraging, charity feeding and occasional casual work. Poverty in rural areas is associated with a lack of access to land to generate income, absence of employment opportunities for wage labour, except in agriculture for a short period of sowing and harvesting, and a non-payment of minimum wage. As their expenditure exceeds their total income from all sources, they are forced to borrow to meet subsistence and other social needs. They, therefore, remain perpetually indebted with some agricultural households slipping into debt bondage of their employers.

Urban poverty is generally associated with the size of the city with its concentration (80%) in small and medium towns, particularly of backward states, which are neglected in the development of infrastructure and basic social services, while larger cities are able to generate employment to the new entrants in the labour market. But Amitabh Kundu argues that even industrialized states have a high share of poverty, not due to a lack of development itself but to the nature of development which is associated with casualization and marginalization of the workforce. Urban poverty is also underestimated due to the rural bias of policy orientation (Kundu, 2000).

The papers included in this section bring out some of these aspects. Narayanan Nair's paper locates rural poverty in the stratification created by the method of sharing surplus with the ruling hierarchy, resulting in the concentration of land in a few hands and the emergence of a class of small farmers with uneconomic holdings and an increase in agricultural labourers with low wages, high indebtedness and bondage. This process is supported by a pernicious caste system. The culture of fatalism of the weaker sections makes the articulation of alternative social relations extremely difficult. Based on the study of a backward village in Gujarat, the author finds class and caste stratification highly correlated. Maldistribution of land is a huge impediment to the physical development of the village and, along with indebtedness, acts as a bar to the generation of human and economic capital, resulting in an alarming level of inequality in consumption expenditure and level of living. It also prevents the rational employment of land, labour and capital. Clan and caste relations perpetuate this arrangement.

The paper by Ramashray Roy and V. B. Singh, based on two Bihar villages, dwells on the structure of poverty which is embedded with an unequal distribution of productive resources, rooted in the way societal resources are controlled and distributed among social groups. It determines not only the capacity to maintain a lifestyle and chances of improving it, but it also reflects on income distribution and the pattern of expenditure on basic necessities. Landless and marginal farmers who are forced to borrow to survive are bonded to the landowners. This signifies not only an inequality in living conditions, but also in life chances. Far more damaging is the unequal distribution of power between the poor and rich. The lack of power instils in the poor a culture of poverty which breeds helplessness and despair and is self-perpetuating.

S. R. Hashim's paper relates urban poverty to the size of the city. Large cities have a lower incidence of poverty due to the capacity to generate work for the poor as compared to small and medium towns. Urban poverty is also underestimated and this estimation does not reflect changing conditions. It is largely concentrated in migrants from rural areas and is characterized by three vulnerabilities—residential, occupational and social. Residential poverty is reflected in houselessness/insecurity/temporary shelters and a lack of access to basic social services and a poor quality of living environment. Occupational poverty is characterized by uncertain employment/casual work, irregular wage payments and a total absence of any social security. Social vulnerability is observed in poorly serviced infrastructure, hostile host population and social exclusion.

REFERENCES

Kumar, T. M. Vinod, & Gayatri. (2000). Urban poverty: Issues, policies and actions. *Social Change, 30*(1/2).

Kundu, Amitabh. (2000). Urban poverty in India: Issues and perspective in development. *Social Change, 30*(1/2). https://doi.org/10.1177/00490857 0003000202

Radhakrishna, R., & Ray, Shovan (Ed.). (2005). *Oxford handbook of poverty in India: Perspectives, policies, and programmes.* Oxford University Press.

Chapter 1
Dimensions of Rural Poverty[*]

E. Narayanan Nair

INTRODUCTION

After considerable planning, at national, state and local levels, income disparities remain sizeable in rural India. In aggregate terms, the rate of economic growth can be considered as remarkable, but the benefits of progress failed to trickle to the majority at the bottom of the socioeconomic hierarchy.[1] The failure to maintain an equitable distribution of the economic gains of our plan has seen the largest and most spectacular in relation to the growing inequality in the place of development activities in different sectors, unequal distribution of activities over space, and inequality of distribution of income and wealth, etc. This was the result of the so-called orientation in both agriculture and industry, resulting in concentrating attention on those categories of existing producers which are already in the most favourite position to produce. Most agricultural production programmes have proved lopsided not only between crops but also between categories of producers. The benefits mostly are cashed by large and middle-class farmers in the intensive irrigated areas. Inevitably, the distance between the insecure dry areas and the irrigated and between the small and large areas has been greatly widened in the process.[2] As a result of this orientation of our plan proposals throughout rural India, nearly 230 million people lived below subsistence level in 1968–1969 (using ₹20/- as minimum per capita consumption per month at 1960–1961 prices).[3]

---

[*] *Social Change* Vol 8, no. 4 (December 1978): 3–7.

The legacy of poverty which we have inherited should be looked at through the historical perspective of the development process. In the literature of economic history, the pre-colonial traditional Indian village was usually depicted as a politically autonomous, economically self-sufficient and more or less static community. Peasant castes, on the one hand, and artisan and serving castes, on the other, collaborated on a footing of equivalence and reciprocity.[4] The significant point is that, to a substantial degree, this system did provide for acquisition and maintenance of infrastructure, resources and employment. The village itself consumed a major portion of its produce. This was reinforced by the comparative isolation in which the villages were held by a virtual absence of a network of communications. This spatial and economic isolation has developed an in-built mechanism to reinvest in the villages whatever net surplus acquired from agriculture, and it percolated to some extent to the weaker sections of society. The image of the idyllic village community, characterized by reciprocity instead of competition, by solidarity instead of exploitation, compared favourably with the structure of the rural community as it was said to have come into being under British rule.[5]

Rural British India existed under a strong survival of feudal structure. Tillers of the soil comprised the most oppressed class in the British tenurial system. There existed a long stratification of landowners, tenants and sub-tenants with the actual tillers being mostly at the bottom. The penetration of British power in the Indian economy not only weakened the rural economy through the destruction of handicraft industries, but it also hastened the growth of the commodity economy. By controlling trade and administration, the colonialists designed institutions for extracting the agricultural net surplus. The impact of the British industrial revolution was initially to weaken the natural and potentially hopeful relationship of rural villages to neighbouring towns by linking rural India with urban British,[6] and this rural–urban continuum resulted in the drain of rural produce in the form of rent, which sustained the urban structure of life.[7] There is a considerable agreement between economic historians on the formation of economic classes in the traditional society of British India. The method of sharing the agricultural surplus of the peasants with the ruling hierarchy and the existence of a 'caste system' that supported this class stratification created a situation in which the majority of rural holds emerged as 'deficit households'. With the passage of time, these households found themselves in the cultches of rural rich, resulting in landlessness and bonded labourers.[8] The process was responsible for increasing concentration of wealth in the hands of a few, the emergence of a class of small farmers with uneconomic holding and an increase in the production of agricultural labour class. This phenomenon of concentrating large land in few hands results in low utilization of land and labour compared to small farms,[9] the kind of investment that is undertaken, the purposes of scale on which the saving is done, as well as the need and ability to borrow and lend.[10]

Miserable low wages, high indebtedness and bondage of labour resulted in wide spread poverty.

The agricultural development programme initiated in the 1960's have been fully cashed by the privileged few, and the so-called agrarian reforms have only reshuffled the power structure, leaving the underprivileged weaker section in the same condition of poverty. Two decades of favourable terms of trade for agriculturists[11] have not benefited those living below the poverty line. Since the outlets were not adequate to invest this vast accumulated surplus within the traditional frame of agriculture by the top strata of rural society, they were diverted to money-lending activities and purchase of land and assets.[12] A good portion of this net surplus is flown back to the urban areas as a consequence of their economic and social interaction with the urban system. Even though this increase in net surplus may have a percolation effect on small farmers in certain region, this effect is only marginal[13]; on the contrary, this leads to an increase in the price level of food grains and, consequent to it, an increase in the price level of industrial commodities as well.[14] The poorer sections of the rural community are, thus, caught in pincers.

The influence of these various factors of the historical development process on the traditional rural system has made it an inadequate organization for the ideals of contemporary India.[15] Even though villages vary in physio-climatic conditions, population sizes, linkages and the urban orientation of the local elites, the old system prevails to varying degrees, keeping the socio-economic structure intact.[16] In this transforming rural system, the privileges of the patron classes have been retained more easily than their responsibilities. Together with this, Myrdal[17] has pointed out that the condition of 'softness' of the government sections makes it difficult for an alternative, better articulated system to replace the traditional social organization. Today, local hierarchies exist in a mutually supportive relationship with scarcity and maldistribution of resources, employment and infrastructure. The result is that the elite top of these local hierarchies increasingly have access to the amenities which their villages lack. In accordance with the theory which underlies the concept of 'softness', what is lacking is an alternative set of social relations which would permit more effective utilization of resources and even distribution of the economic benefits. The cultural and psychological fatalism of the weaker section of the rural system who finds 'security within insecurity'[18] in the present social relations, does make effective, alternative articulated social organization and planning that actually involves the non-elite extremely difficult.

Case Study: Village Gandiali

The need to study a micro-level and locality-oriented approach for the above framework arises out of the dissatisfaction with aggregate data at national or regional level which underplays the complexity of relationships among a multitude of social, economic and political factors.[19] The main objective of this case study at the village level is to analyse the components of the traditional system and understand the mechanisms which are in force to degenerate the rural economy and perpetuate as well as accentuate the skewed income and wealth distribution even at a lower level of economic development. This analysis of the rural economy will give us some guidelines for designing a better articulated alternative village organization.

Methodology

After a brief study of the various backward districts of Gujarat state, Banaskantha district was taken as the region from which a micro-level backward village was chosen for study. Taluka Tharad figured as a backward taluka with the help of well-known indicators of development (mostly data which can be assembled from the 1971 census).[20] Various typologists of backward villages were found. We have decided to take the village of Gandiali as our sample village due to its low level of agricultural development, lack of social services and physical infrastructure, spatial isolation and small population. A 100 per cent household survey was conducted in 1976, and information tabulated and analysed according to the frame work earlier discussed.

Gandiali Village

Gandiali village, which lies on the northern boundary of Tharad taluka, has dry land. The soil is sandy, porous and dry and easy to till but has a poor capacity for retention of moisture. The total geographical area of the village is 1,395 acres, with 1,222 acres of agricultural land. The population of the village is 462, with 235 males and 227 females, comprising 86 families. The annual population growth between 1961 and 1971 was about 1.05 per cent as against the district growth rate of 2.7 per cent. The land pressure of the village is about 2.41 acres per capita. In village Gandiali, only about 0.8 per cent of the agricultural land is irrigated as against the district which has 12.5 per cent of land under irrigation.[21] The main economic activity is agriculture. About 95 per cent of the workforce of 68 per cent of the population depends directly or indirectly on agriculture.

The occupational pattern of the workforce in the village is shown in Table 1.1.

The comparison of the occupational pattern of the village and the district shows that the percentage of cultivators is less in the village, and the percentage of agricultural workers is higher.

There is not much occupational and geographical mobility in the village. About 7 per cent of the workforce go out to the nearest village for work on a daily basis during peak seasons.

The caste structure of the village is as follows: Brahmins (11.70%), Barot (16.7%), Patel (13.3%), Kanbi (37.2%), Suthar (7.06%), Harijans (15.1%). Brahmins play a dominant role in social life, whereas Barots and Patels control the economic side of village life. Under the compulsory education scheme, the total number of children enrolled in the village is about 70.6 per cent of the number of children at that age. But the school-going children are only 34 per cent, with 86.5 per cent

Table 1.1 *The Occupational Pattern of the Workforce in Gandiali*

Sr. Occupation No.	Percentage of Workforce Employed in Gandiali	Banaskantha District
1. Cultivators	40.25	63.68
2. Agriculture labourers	25.97	16.20
3. Animal husbandry and allied activities	11.28	2.57
4. Household industry	1.29	3.16
5. Transportation and construction trade and commerce	2.58	7.43
6. No work	15.59	—[a]
7. Mining and quarrying, non-household industry and other activities	—	6.96

Source: The Table is based on (a) village questionnaire and (b) *Census, 1971, Banaskantha District Handbook*, 68, 69.
Notes: The total workers in Banaskantha District is about 31 02 per cent of its population.
[a] The census does not have any information on workers who are unemployed.

boys and 13.5 per cent girls. Besides this, 16.6 per cent of the school-going children go to the primary school at Bhorol, which is 5 km away, and one boy studies in college at Palanpur. This boy is the son of the Barot who owns maximum amount of land. There is no health institution in the village. The village is not properly connected with nearby villages. Drinking water is a severe problem in the village. The existing six wells dry up during the summer, and they get water from a polluted tank and, inevitably, have a high incidence of guinea worms, malaria and small pox diseases.

Having this background of the village's physical environment, we will go to the social structure of the village system. The main aspects of rural social structure which interact to maintain the traditional system in Gujarat, as elsewhere, are (a) land distribution, (b) indebtedness and (c) caste loyalty.

Rural Indians attribute great economic, social and political importance to land. The distribution, ownership and labour relationship patterns have traditionally penetrated every form of social organization. Relationships of mutual support between landholding patterns and caste or ethnic stratification systems have evolved for centuries. This is explicit in the land distribution pattern of village Gandiali. It was found that 14.3 per cent of the families have no land and this comes to about 18.9 per cent of the population. About 24.0 per cent of the families or 22 per cent of the population share land below 5 acres. By classifying the whole family into three classes: A (having no land and below 5 acres), B (between 5 and 25 acres) and C (above 25 acres). We found that Class A had 38.3 per cent of families or 40.6 per cent of the population, Class B had 57 per cent of families or 55.7 per cent of the population, and Class C had 4.7 per cent of families or 3.7 per cent of the population. This also shows the inverse relationship between income and family size. The distribution of total agricultural land by the three classes is as follows: Class A, having 40.6 per cent of the population, possesses 55 per cent of the total land; Class B, having 55.7 per cent of population, possesses 59.9 per cent of the land, and Class C, that is, 3.7 per cent of the population possesses

34.6 per cent of the land. These figures amply show the skewed distribution of land. The low productivity of land due to the lack of irrigation facilities inevitably requires a high acreage per capita. Using the criteria of subsistence level of income ₹45/- per capita/month,[22] the viable land needed per capita is calculated as 3.6 acres (taking the average productivity of one acre of land, 5 maunds of Bajri and a single crop with a village price of ₹30/- per maund of Bajra).[23] Accordingly, it is found that about 75 per cent of the total agricultural families own land below the viable minimum landholding (excluding the 14.3% of the families who do not possess any land). It can be concluded that the present land pressure of 2.41 acres per capita is high compared to the viable minimum per capita land of 3.6 acres and the future population growth will result in added pressure on land.

The present pattern of land possession has a positive correlation with the possession of fixed assets, cattle, agricultural implements, net agricultural surplus (Table 1.2).

Table 1.2 Correlation of Ownership of Land with Ownership of Fixed Assets

		Share of Assets and Net Saving/Year			
Class	Percentage of Population	Value (%) of Land[a]	Value (%) of Agri. Implements[b]	Value (%) of Cattle[c]	Net Saving (%)[d]
A	40.6	5.60	18.26	21.07	Nil
B	55.7	60.54	62.50	55.26	45.94
C	3.7	33–86	19.24	23.68	54.06

Notes: [a] Value of land occupied, computed on the basis of three types of land available having a value of ₹500, ₹300 and ₹200 per acre. It was found that Barots and Patels own a lot of good quality land.
[b] Values of bullocks, tilling implements, etc., are taken
[c] Different values for buffalos, cows, bulls, goats and sheep are taken into account.
[d] Net saving is the saving which people had after all expenses, and we got this figure from the household questionnaire.

The class stratification and the caste stratification is found to be highly correlated even though this is a widely known and accepted phenomenon. The social stratification maintains the traditional system even though the nature of patronage is different in the transformed traditional system.

Barot families control about 53.07 per cent of the total agricultural land and Patels and Kanbi come next in possession. Even though both these castes get the same share, the per capita land share of Patel is much higher than Kanbi, which had a large number of families (Table 1.3).

The maldistribution of rural land is a positive impediment to the physical development of villages and other settlements. It has, for example, maintained long standing reciprocities with indebtedness and, thereby, has acted indirectly as a bar to the generation of economic and human capital. The preliminary findings on indebtedness in Gandiali are similar to those of various other studies on indebtedness and inequalities. There is a considerable degree of indebtedness among the non-elite to the elite. Table 1.4 shows the income distribution of the families in Gandiali village.

It is clear from Table 1.4 that the bottom 20 per cent of people share about 12.6 per cent of the income and the top 20 per cent share 32.5 per cent of income. At the first instant, this distribution

Table 1.3 Caste versus Landholding

Caste	Percentage of Landholding
Harijans	3.25
Bhel	1.14
Suthar	1.14
Suthar	5.02
Kanbi	13.96
Barot	53.07
Patel	14.52
Brahmins	8.93
Total	100.00

Table 1.4 *Income Distribution (Lorez Ratio)*

Percentage of People	Actual of Income	Percentage Distribution
0		0
20		12.6
40		26.8
60		46.1
80		68.5
100		100.0

is not much disturbing, but when one relates this to the distribution of per capita expenditure, the level of inequality and people below poverty line is quite alarming.

Categorizing the percentage of people into different strata of per capita expenditure per month into (a) below subsistence level (₹45 per capita per month), (b) one time above subsistence level, (c) two times above subsistence level, and captioning it as A, B and C, respectively, we get the following distribution.

The percentage of people below the poverty line is about 66.60. We found that the levels of living have a significant relation with the operational landholding pattern of the village. In fact, 66.60 per cent of people below subsistence level control only 11.74 per cent of land, whereas the top 4.60 per cent of the people (according to the concentration criteria of ₹90 and above per capita/month) control about 57.54 per cent of the agricultural land. From the analysis on the land distribution, we found that Class C, which owns land more than 25 acres/family and forms about 3.7 per cent of the population, possesses 34.6 per cent of the land. This brings out the relationship between land possession and the level of living (Table 1.5).

This relationship between landholding and per capita expenditure was clearer from analysis done on the consumption pattern. The average family of the bottom Class A spends about 91.6 per cent of its expenditure on food and clothing (6.6%), health (3.3%) and fuel (1.3%), whereas an average family from the top

Table 1.5 *Income Distribution per Capita*

Class	Percentage of People
A (₹45 per capita/month)	66.60
B (₹45–90)	23.80
C (₹90 and above)	4.60

Class C spends about 39.28 per cent on food, 12.85 per cent on milk products, 27.85 per cent on education, 8.57 per cent on clothing and 4.28 per cent on recreation. The diversification of consumption items and the expenditure elasticities are found to have a positive relationship with income.

The employment pattern of the village is interesting as compared to the above class stratification. About 95 per cent of the workforce is engaged in agriculture, either partially or fully, as agriculture workers (25.97%), farmers (40.25%) and depending upon animal husbandry (14.28%). About 15.59 per cent of the work force is without any work. Table 1.6 shows clearly the relation between employment pattern and consumption stratified groups.

The analysis shows that about 91 per cent of the labourers and 58 per cent of the small and marginal farmers are in the category of the consumption range of ₹45 per capita per month.

Present ownership patterns, the cropping and work habits associated and the appropriation of the agricultural surplus do not enable effective and rational employment of land, labour and capital. The well-to-do section acquires the agricultural surplus, and they make use of this accumulated surplus to buy land, money lending and a certain portion of it goes to the nearest urban area as part of education, recreation and industrial consumption goods. The inevitable result is the deteriorating condition of the 66 per cent of the people who are below the poverty line, and their indebtedness perpetuates and even accentuates as time passes.

Besides the vivid economic reasons for the indebtedness and poverty of the large section of rural society, clan-caste relations represent a potential economic liability. Even though caste

Table 1.6 *Employment Pattern in the Village*

Class	Percentage of Employment in Each Activity					
	Agriculture Labour	Farmer	Animal Husbandry	Carpentry	Transport	No Work
A (below ₹45/capita/month)	90.41 9.59	58.06	54.5	100	100	46.15
B (₹45–₹90)	100.00	38.70	27.2			30.76
C (₹90 & above)		3.24	18.3			23.09
Total		100.00	100.00	100 00	100.00	100.00

relations can be a potential asset, in a saturated rural economy like ours, especially for these poor sections, it has been on the liability side and ultimately drawing them into the hands of the money lender.

Money lending has tended to be the monopoly of one or few castes in the rural economy. The often permanent state of being a creditor for one or more families, which members of these castes have enjoyed, has been a powerful support for land distribution pattern and, consequently, caste inequality itself. During the times when these factors, in mutual support, also served the functions of settlement management, even money lending had some rational justifications. Today, it merely misdirects resources and has the effect of self perpetuation. It has been supported by caste loyalties and can never be completely rooted out without a redirection of these loyalties to alternate forms of social relations.

The combined influence of land distribution, debt and caste have acted and continues to act, as support to the traditional patronage system. The encroachment of modernity, the cities and via central, state and local organizations, 'all have eroded' the capacity of this system to develop rural India effectively. Its capacity to maintain itself despite its loss of function can be understood if we note the lessons of history. Despite the Moghul invasions and conquest, British colonial administration and the post-Independence rural development policies, a fully articulated and effective alternative to the traditional system has never been adopted. When we, today, seek functional alternatives to counter this existing traditional pattern, it is for these reasons that one must question seriously and try to understand why the traditional pattern continues to persist before becoming very optimistic about new ideas on patterns and process of rural development.

NOTES

1. P. C. Mahalanobis, 'The Asian Drama, an Indian Review,' *Sankhyā: The Indian Journal of Statistics* Series B 31, no. 3/4 (1969).

2. D. R. Gadgil, 'Planning without a Policy Frame,' *Economic & Political Weekly* 2, no. 3/4 (1967).

3. B. N. Minhas, *Planning and the Poor* (New Delhi: S. Chand & Co., 1974).

4. J. Breman, *Patronage and Exploitation* (Berkeley, CA: University of California Press, 1974), 3.

5. Ibid., 5.

6. Robinson, Ronald and Johnson, Peter, ed., *The Rural Base for National Development* (Cambridge: Cambridge University Press, 1968), 8.

7. Daniel Thorner and Alice Thorner, *Land and Labour in India* (New Delhi: Asia Publishing House, 1962), 52.

8. Pradhan H. Prasad, 'Employment and Income for Rural India,' *Economic & Political Weekly* 7, no. 18 (June 1972).

9. C. H. Hanumantha Rao, 'Alternative Explanation of the Inverse Relationship between Farm Size And Output Per Acre in India,' *Indian Economic Review* 1, no. 2 (October 1966).

10. K. N. Raj, 'Ownership and Distribution of Land,' *Indian Economic Review* 5 (1970).

11. B. N. Minnas, 'Rural Poverty and the Minimum Level of Living: A Reply,' *Indian Economic Review* 6, no. 1 (April 1971), and Reserve Bank of India, *Report on Currency and Finance 1974–75* (Vol. 2), Statement 17.

13. A. V. Jose, 'Trends in Real Wage Rates of Agricultural Labourers,' *Economic & Political Weekly* 9, no. 13 (March 1974).

14. Ashok Mitra, 'Industrial Growth and Income Distribution,' *Social Scientist* 5, no. 54–55 (Jan–Feb 1977): 9–23.

15. Daniel Lerner, *The Passing of Traditional Society* (New York, NY: Free Press, 1963); see for the model study of de-traditionalization.

16. Breman, *Patronage and* Exploitation, Chapter 11.

17. Gunnar Myrdal, *The Challenge of World Poverty* (London: Penguin Books, 1971).

18. Szyman Chodak, *Societal Development* (Oxford: Oxford University Press, 1974).

19. In the case of India, there is no dearth of such micro-level studies. British administrators such as Harold Hann and G. Slater carried out village studies, and in recent times, D. R. Gadgil, R. K. Mukherjee, C. N. Vakil and G. S. Ghurye studied aspects of rural life. The problem in the Indian context is not so much of scarcity of micro-level data but of lack of research interest in generating the experience of villages in different parts of the country.

20. Main indicators are agricultural land–man ratio, employment pattern, literacy ratio, irrigated agriculture area, accessibility and level of amenities.

21. *Census* 1971, Banaskantha District.

22. Taking the minimum subsistence level of ₹20 per capita/month (source: Minnas, 'Rural Poverty and the Minimum Level of Living') and converted it into the current price of 1976 taking the general consumer price index as 276 (Source: Labour Bureau, Government of India, Shimla).

23. Village survey.

Chapter 2

The Structure of Poverty*
Case of Bihar

Ramashray Roy and V. B. Singh

I

The phenomenon of poverty has, in recent years, attracted a lot of attention in both intellectual and policy-framing circles. The one aspect that has stimulated extensive discussion pertains to the relationship observed between the persistence of inequality in the distribution of income and the process of development within and among nations. This relationship underlines the failure of economic development in mitigating, if not radically ceasing, economic disabilities, measured in terms of income of people inhabiting the lower echelons of the economic hierarchy.

The tendency of the poor to get poorer in the process of economic development, understood as a movement towards industrialization, is frequently underplayed. One factor responsible for this is, no doubt, the belief that, as development proceeds, the tendency of inequality in income to widen in the early stages of development is not only halted but certainly reversed in the later stages. This belief has been remarkably sustained by Simon Kuznets' statistical demonstration of its empirical foundations by analysing time-series aggregate economic

---

* *Social Change* Vol 14, no. 2 (June 1984): 25–33.

The paper presented in the seminar on 'Poverty and Development' with a special reference to eastern region, held at A. N. S. Institute of Social Studies, Patna, on 16–18 April.

data with respect to several countries and advancing a hypothesis of the U-shaped pattern of economic development.[1]

Kuznets' hypothesis may reassure the rulers in the developing countries that their promise to remove inequalities and reduce poverty, if not completely eliminate it, will bear fruit in the long run. The catching at the straw of 'the long run' may assuage the rulers' guilt feelings and may sustain them in the stupendous task of transforming the economic face of their society. However, what for most of the poor in India is of special significance is not the distant future, even though painted in the most hopeful of colours, but the distressing present. As will be clear later on, for most of the poor in this country, the future is already mortgaged to the unplacatable present any way. If the present is the clue to the shape of the poor's future, Kuznets' U-shaped pattern of development only helps to make the poor the sacrificial goat at the altar of somebody else's hope. Their own hope does not even survive the first cold blast of their stark existential reality[2].

Whatever may be the consequences of the doomed hopes of the poor of this country, we are concerned in this paper not with retailing the factors that frustrate the hopes of the poor yet prevent them from demanding and getting equitable access to and share in societal resources. What we are concerned with is simply the nature of poverty that exists in the Indian countryside. We are also interested in identifying some of the correlates of the structure of poverty that, in our view, are responsible not only for keeping them poor but also for making it very difficult for them to breakout the vicious circle that the phenomenon of poverty invariably creates. We base our analysis on empirical data drawn from total household surveys conducted during 1980 in two blocks of Bihar—Mahnar (Vaishali district) and Hariharganj (Palamu district).

II

Discussions about poverty usually revolve around two of its aspects: What constitutes poverty, and who precisely are the poor? Invariably, the counting of the heads of the poor begins by identifying the components that supposedly constitute the phenomenon of poverty. The easiest and, by far, the most deceptive but popular strategy to define poverty is to settle on a single factor, for example, per capita income, and to treat all those who fall below a particular level of income as poor. Considered as an indicator, this single factor signifies a particular level of income denoting the capacity or lack of it to satisfy certain needs whose fulfilment assures subsistence. Once the line of poverty is thus well demarcated, its validity can then be established by means of identifying a multiple of correlates, such as housing, education, employment, health, fertility and mortality, whose main manifestation in a particular way are supposed to be the characteristics of poverty.

Whether the inclusion of these multiple correlates of poverty as a part of its definition or its indicator confuses between the determinants and the consequences of poverty is a question that we do not intend to discuss here. However, when a unidimensional definition or indicator of poverty, like the level of income, is chosen, it generally stands as a proxy for something else. This is either the bare minimum level of living or consumption pattern or some such thing. Whether it is an empirical or a theoretical consumption pattern that provides the basis of demarcating the line of poverty, an estimate of a fixed minimum monthly or annual sum of money is made which, it is supposed, is desirable to enable families to secure the necessities of life based on standards rather stringently drawn.

Since 1960, a lot of intellectual exercises have, following Rowntree's example at the turn of this century, taken place to define and re-define the poverty line[3]. In 1962, for example, a study group appointed by the Government of India settled upon a per capita consumption of ₹20 per month at 1960–1961 prices (excluding expenditure on health and education) as the bare minimum level of living in India. Following this, a spate of studies have, taking this as a base figure, criticized, amended and reformulated the poverty line. It is not possible here to discuss the various lines of argument advanced in favour of or opposition to a particular cut-off point for determining the poverty line. But what is remarkable about these studies is the poverty of human concerns.

A variety of methodology is applied to almost the same body of data to arrive at different estimates for not only the bare minimum level of consumption pattern but also the number of persons below or on the poverty line and various categories of the poor.[4]

It is true, as Dantwala points out,[5] that these studies 'leave no doubt about the pervasive stark poverty' that exists in India. However, such an approach creates a number of difficulties. First, emphasizing as it does the necessity of raising the level of income of the poor as a means of alleviating, if not eradicating completely, the consequences of poverty, it tends to encourage simplistic solutions to the problem ignoring the complex nature of economic backwardness and its determinants. One obvious example of this is the 'additive rather than transformative conception of rural development in this country'.[6] Second, the attempt to identify poverty on the basis of some barest minimum level of livelihood 'implies that there is some easily discovered, absolute and apparently universal, line below which there is poverty and above which there is not....'[7] However, the components that constitute the bare minimum level of livelihood are an artifact of the analyst's own minds; they may not have any meaningful empirical referent in the poor's cognition or experience. As Townsend observes:

> It may be that people do not know what goods arc 'necessary' and where they can be obtained cheaply. Or it may be that spending habits are determined by the conventions of the lowest stratum of society, and by economic and social measures ... currently adopted by the community as a whole. All this is quite apart from individual habits and inclination.[8]

Even more important than this, what Townsend most vehemently objects to is the fact that the inflexible, but easily understood, formulation of a fixed poverty line narrowly defines what is necessary for a healthy existence. 'If clothing, money for travel to work and newspapers are considered to be "necessaries", why not tea, handkerchiefs, laundry, contraceptives, cosmetics, hairdressing and shaving, and life insurance payments.'[9]

One can object to this as being true of only the rich, industrialized countries with a particular style of living. However, it is not very difficult to translate these into the terms of our own style of living and come to the conclusion that the barest necessities that are supposed to compose the bare minimum level of living have only a limited empirical relevance. But more important than this is the fact that the determination of the line of poverty does not so much depend on what the analyst of poverty deems it to be but, more significantly, on what social conventions make it to be. As such, the conception of poverty appears to be not so much as an absolute universal standard but a relative phenomenon, a matter of conventions that are socially formed. But once we recognize this, we open up Pandora's box and encounter insurmountable difficulties in defining poverty.[10]

And, lastly, poverty is not simply an economic phenomenon. Much more than the loss of economic well-being and the inability to satisfy certain strongly felt needs, poverty denotes also the important loss of power. In the words of Coates and Silburn, 'poverty is not so much a simple lack of wealth as more basic lack of power.... Loss of power is the most serious of all the losses entailed in poverty, because it is the most permanent and self-reinforcing.'[11] This is so for the simple reason that the realization of the inability to change things in order to open the way for greater access to and control over societal resources, instils among the poor what Oscar Lewis characterizes as 'the culture of poverty'.

The culture of poverty is not merely a matter of deprivation or disorganization; it is something positive with its own consequences. As Lewis puts it:

> The culture of poverty is both an adaptation and a reaction of the poor to their marginal position in a class-stratified, highly individualized, capitalist society. It represents an effort to cope with feelings of hopelessness and despair which develop from the realization of the improbability of achieving success in terms of the values and goals of larger society.[12]

The culture of poverty denotes an adaptive style on the part of the poor which signifies the helplessness of the poor in silently enduring a situation of deprivation which is not of their own making, making do with whatever resources they can harness to sustain their existence and abjectly surrendering to hostile forces when they cannot be coped with. But the culture of poverty tends to be transmitted, as is poverty, from one generation to the next. Thus, the culture of poverty is self-perpetuating and those who live by it are pictured by Lewis as removed and alienated, ignorant and uninterested and uninvolved and apathetic.

All this points to a situation where the poor have reconciled themselves to their fate and feel powerless to change their condition. The poor, because they have no means to alter the condition society has callously imposed on them, are driven to the walls. To quote Coates and Silburn again,

> To the burden of individual deprivation, they too have to add the additional imposts of social neglect, and of consequent exclusion from even such normal opportunities for self-defence as might exist for people only slightly more favoured than they themselves. *Material lack becomes loss of morale*: and this in turn may Well serve to inhibit collective action in any form, and still further atomize and intimidate the poor community.[13]

In view of these considerations, the attempt to reduce the multifaceted phenomenon of poverty to simply the lack of economic resources and to measure poverty in a unidimensional frame of reference, like income or a stringent subsistence level, is, to say the least, strange. It is true that the solution of a problem involves an understanding of its structure which, in turn, requires rigour in analysing the problem. But to sacrifice the complexity of a particular phenomenon in the name of convenience of analysts is equivalent not only to mortgaging one's understanding but also to disowning moral responsibility. 'Placed in this context, the stringently calculated subsistence level of poverty line is seen to be an aberration on the part of those whose yearning for precision and parsimony exceeds not only their common humanity, but also their desire for sociological sophistication.'[14]

The inadequacy of a single factor in defining poverty and illumining its various dysfunctionalities is beyond doubt. Moreover, the meaning of poverty changes depending upon cultural values and the level of economic growth. Also, the phenomenon of poverty cannot be fully explicated with the help of the culture of poverty or the cycle of poverty theory, even though they shed significant light on its structure. It is true that the accident of birth in poor families precludes the poor from taking advantage of the numerous opportunities society makes available for economic advance. It may also be true that economic deprivation is instrumental in instilling in the poor an outlook of despair and resignation, breeding in them feelings of incompetence and marginality, making them incapable of participating in the affairs of the larger society and inclining them to violence.

As such, it is conceivable that living in poverty has its own destructive effects on human capacities, and these impairments become part of the whole process of perpetuating poverty. However, the origin of poverty is embedded more in the unequal distribution of societal resources. This inequality is not an individual phenomenon; it is associated with social structural factors. Poverty is related, as Valentine argues, with

> The total amounts of consumable resources available in relation to the population, the distribution of control over resources within the social structure, the cultural standards of value and adequacy, the proportion of society's membership whose level of disposable resources stands below such standards and the degree of contrast in welfare between higher and lower socio-economiestrata.[15]

III

Given the fact that poverty has a structural dimension and has certain consequences individually for the poor, it is necessary to see it in both these respects. In its structural dimension, poverty must be viewed in terms of the pattern of inequality exhibited in a particular community. Such a pattern gets manifested in the available stock of resources, their distribution and the way they are owned or controlled by various groups in that community. The extent of control over and access to these resources by various groups determines their capacity not only for maintaining a particular lifestyle but also for improving their life chances and helping their offspring to have a better start in life. Unequal distribution of resources determines not only unequal life chances but also an unequal distribution of power. In the words of Meade:

> A man with much property has great bargaining strength and a great sense of security, independence and freedom; and he enjoys those things not only vis-a-vis his property less fellow citizens but also vis-a-vis the public authorities. An unequal distribution of property means an unequal distribution of power, even if it is prevented from causing too unequal a distribution of income.[16]

It is true that in a democratic system like India, everybody has, theoretically speaking, an equal opportunity to compete with everybody else for access to and control over societal resources. However, the face of acquiring goods and services gets loaded against the poor since they start from a position of weakness. The initial locational advantage in the race usually determines its outcome. The structural factors associated with inequality in the distribution of resources affect, in significant ways, not only the extent of resources the poor people have but also the use of these resources mainly for life-sustaining rather than life-chance enhancing purposes. As a result, disabilities that accompany the poor become self-perpetuating, creating a vicious circle that becomes so obdurate that self-effort on the part of the poor does not help in breaking out of the culture of poverty. Our data drawn from two blocks in Bihar fully substantiate these observations.

Mahnar and Hariharganj blocks are, topographically and resource wise, two dissimilar units. While Mahnar, north to the River Ganges, is a flat land and has rich Gangetic alluvial soil, Hariharganj, the northern most tip of the Chota Nagpur Plateau, is interspersed with hills and has alluvial soil but very poor in quality. Both the blocks are primarily agricultural, but the total geographical area of Mahnar is only 24,800 acres as compared to 55,403 acres in Hariharganj. However, the advantage of Hariharganj in terms of size is totally lost if we compare the pattern of land use in both the blocks (Table 2.1).

It is interesting to note that while Hariharganj block has more than double the total land area of Mahnar block, the net area sown is only 23 per cent as compared to 74.30 per cent in Mahnar. Note also that the area under double cropping in Hariharganj is only 8.90 per cent as against 47.50 per cent in Mahnar. In terms of irrigation, only 10.70 per cent of total land in Hariharganj as against 20.10 per cent in Mahnar is under irrigation. One interesting fact that stands out clearly is that farmers in Hariharganj have to invest a larger effort to get adequate return from farming. Note, for example, that the total irrigated area as the proportion of the net area sown in Hariharganj comes to 46.70 per cent as against 27.10 per cent in Mahnar, indicating a larger input for getting adequate yield from land. These facts point to the differential conditions prevailing in the two blocks. In so far as the land resources are concerned, Hariharganj block, while very richly endowed, can use only a very small part of it for agricultural purposes and that also at greater effort. It is interesting to note that if we take net area sown as a base, Mahnar has to support only 3.5 persons per acre of land as against 4 persons in Hariharganj.

If the two blocks symbolize two very different types of economic units—the one more favoured than the other—they do not differ greatly in so far as the distribution of resources within each of the blocks is concerned. Both the blocks demonstrate quite clearly the intermeshing of social and economic factors and its impact on how resources are distributed among various social sectors. The convergence of social status and the access to and control over land resources in these blocks is one of the most significant aspects of rural society. It is this convergence that keeps a large part of rural India marooned in the desolate sea of inequality, domination and stagnation. The convergence of social status and wealth means a great inequality in life opportunities. Table 2.2 presents the distribution of land caste-wise to emphasize this fact.

As Table 2.2 indicates, the pattern of land distribution both in Mahnar and Hariharganj is almost the same and reflects extreme inequality in the access to and control over one resource, land, which is vitally important for the economic well-being of the people in these blocks. Note, for example, that the upper castes (Brahmins, Bhumihars, Rajputs) own almost half of the land in both the blocks, while they constitute even less than one-fourth (22% in Mahnar and only 14%

Table 2.1 *Land Utilization: Mahnar and Hariharganj*

Land Use	Mahnar		Hariharganj	
	Area in Acres	(%)	Area in Acres	(%)
Total geographical area	24,800.00	100.00	55,403.74	100.00
Net area sown	18,416.11	74.30	12,738.19	23.00
Area sown more than once	11,781.68	47.50	4,936.16	8.90
Total cropped area	30,107.79	121.80	17,674.35	31.90
Area irrigated	4,986.97	20.10	5,946.44.	10.70
Area irrigated more than once	2,885.24	11.60	1,084.09	2.00
Current fallow	477.90	1.90	11,812.80	21.30
Land not available for agriculture	8,770.69	35.40	31,454.78	56.80

Source: This and all other tables in this chapter are based on the household surveys conducted by the Centre for the Study of Developing Societies during 1980.

Table 2.2 *Caste and Land Ownership in Mahnar and Hariharganj (in %)*

Caste	Mahnar		Hariharganj	
	Population	Land Ownership	Population	Land Ownership
Brahmins & upper castes	22.0	51.7	14.1	45.6
Business castes	8.1	6.7	10.9	6.0
Upwardly mobile castes (peasants)	25.2	33.1	22.4	25.5
Service and low castes	16.7	4.3	11.5	6.1
Schedule Castes and Tribes	23.5	2.8	35.3	15.3
Muslims	3.5	1.1	5.8	1.3
Total	99.0[a]	99.7[a]	100.0	100.0

Note: [a] Total less than 100 per cent because of cases not ascertained.

in Hariharganj) of the population. In contrast, the three lowest castes (service castes, low castes and Scheduled Castes and Scheduled Tribes[17]), which constitute 40.2 per cent of the population in Mahnar and 46.8 per cent in Hariharganj, own only 7.1 per cent and 21.6 per cent of land, respectively. There is no doubt that the three lowest castes taken together own more land in Hariharganj than what is the case in Mahnar. It is also true that the average size of landholding for service and low castes in Mahnar is 13.2 katha[18] as against 46.1 katha in Hariharganj and 5.6 katha for Scheduled Castes in Mahnar as compared to 30.5 Kathas in Hariharganj. However, this advantage is lost since cultivation in Hariharganj demands more labour input, especially irrigation, in comparison to Mahnar.

Apart from the unequal distribution of land, there is also the fact that, both in Mahnar and Hariharganj, as one moves up the caste hierarchy, the viability of household farming units also increases. Out of a total of 10,200 households in Mahnar, 39.9 per cent are landless, 27.8 per cent marginal farmers, 9.9 per cent small farmers and 22.4 per cent viable farmers. The picture in Hariharganj is not very dissimilar. Out of 7,870 households, 31.6 per cent are landless, 26.3 per cent marginal farmers, 16.5 percent small farmers and 25.6 per cent viable farmers. As Table 2.3 further indicates, talking of landless alone, the largest proportion, about two-thirds, is constituted by the three lower castes in Manhar as against 68.3 per cent in Hariharganj. Of the marginal farmers, about 46 per cent in Mahnar and about 65 per cent in Hariharganj are made up of, again, the three lower castes. As we move on to the categories of small and viable farmers, the proportions of the three lower castes in both the blocks dwindle precipitately. For instance, in Mahnar, the proportion of small farming households in the three lower castes comes to 11.1 per cent and of viable farmers only 5 per cent. In Hariharganj, while the lower castes make up a sizeable proportion of small farmers (44.6%), their proportion in respect of viable farming households comes down to 19 per cent.

If the pattern of landownership indicates unequal distribution, not less so in income distribution. Generally speaking, about 55 per cent of households in Mahnar and 53 per cent in Hariharganj have a monthly income varying between less than ₹100 and 25. It should be noted here that the Gadgil Working Group had recommenced in 1962 a national

Table 2.3 *Households, Landholding and Caste (in %)*

| | Mahnar | | | | | Hariharganj | | | | |
	Landless	Marginal Farmers	Small Farmers	Viable Farmers	No.	Landless	Marginal Farmers	Small Farmers	Viable Farmers	No. of
Brahmins & upper castes	4.2	15.6	20.0	60.1	1,914	3.1	7.2	13.3	76.5	979
Business castes	45.6	27.8	9.6	17.0	801	44.2	20.9	16.7	18.1	807
Upwardly mobile castes (peasants)	13.8	34.4	17.1	34.7	2,426	5.3	23.2	26.6	44.9	1,599
Service & low castes	54.5	36.9	4.5	4.1	1,764	28.3	37.2	18.3	16.2	826
Scheduled Castes and Tribes	74.3	23.1	1.2	1.4	2,766	45.5	33.7	13.3	7.4	3.220
Muslims	56.2	36.5	2.3	5.0	387	73.4	14.0	6.5	6.1	428
Total	39.9	27.8	9.9	22.4	10,200	31.6	26.3	16.5	25.6	7,870

minimum consumption standard of ₹100 per month for a household of five persons in rural areas and ₹125 in urban areas at 1960–1961 constant prices. If we accept this as the definition of the poverty line and take into account the large erosion in the purchasing power of the rupee since then, it is beyond doubt that close to two-thirds of the households in both the blocks suffer from serious economic disabilities. Even if we estimate on the basis of only a threefold increase in the price index since 1962, the proportion of the households below the poverty line in both the blocks is, according to our data, very high. Note, for example, that the proportion of households with a monthly income of ₹300 is 66 per cent in Mahnar and 60 per cent in Hariharganj.

Apart from the phenomenon of pervasive poverty as reflected in the pattern of income distribution, there is also the fact that severe economic disability strikes the marginal farmers much more than any other population segments in both the blocks. In Mahnar, for example, 23.5 per cent of marginal farmers' households as compared to only 126 per cent of the landless households have a monthly income of up to ₹100. Similar is the case in Hariharganj where 25 per cent of the marginal farmers households as against only 17 per cent of the landless have the lowest per month income. It is true that the category 'landless' includes those who have no land but have independent means of living, such as businessmen, traders, service men, etc. But it should be emphasized here that the proportions of such people, that is, traders, shopkeepers, professional and white-collar job holders, etc., comes to only 4.1 per cent and 3.1 per cent of the population in Mahnar and Hariharganj, respectively. Moreover, if anything, such people earn more income per month and fall into higher income brackets. Anyway, what is incontrovertible is the fact that the marginal farmers are even less than those who have nothing else but their labour power to sell.

IV

The discussion in the preceding section highlights some of the factors that constitute the structure of poverty in two blocks. These factors point to the gross inequality that exists in the distribution of resources in these blocks. But apart from this, they also imply certain consequences for the poor in these blocks, not simply in terms of the quality of living conditions but also in terms of their capacity to improve their own life situations and secure better life chances for their progeny.

The fact that almost two-thirds of the households in these blocks suffer from acute economic disability has its impact also on the overall style of their living. Economic status seems to have a very close relationship with the size of family. As one moves up the economic hierarchy, the average size of family increases. In both the blocks, the average size of the household for the landless is five; it is six for the marginal farmers and seven for the small farmers. In the case of viable farmers, the average size is eight in Mahnar and nine in Hariharganj. This is no doubt related to the type of family. For example, 79.5 and 74.5 per cent of the landless in Mahnar and Hariharganj, respectively, have nuclear families as compared to about 41 per cent of viable farmers in the two blocks. It is true that an economically better-off household can support a large family. However, in terms of dependency ratio, there is not any marked difference in the landless and viable farmer's household in respect of the economic burden each has to bear. Note, for example, that the dependency ratio for the landless in Mahnar is 0.71 as against 0.74 for the viable farmers.

Similarly, in Hariharganj, the dependency ratio for the landless is 0.88 as compared to 0.90 for the viable farmer.

This points to the fact that, given the same scale of responsibilities, the poor as against the comparatively rich in these blocks have less resources to discharge their responsibilities. Much more significant, however, is the sociological aspect of poverty. This refers to the fact that poor households, even when it may be to their advantage to sustain a joint family for better deployment of resources, are forced to splinter under the strain and stress of scarcity, which makes harmonious living a difficult proposition. In contrast, the rich families, even while, the joint-family system breeds acrimony and tolerates inefficiency, are forced to maintain a joint family in order to insure a particular level of economic well-being and social prestige. It is interesting, therefore, to note that the problem of maintaining or raising a particular level of economic well-being evokes two very different types of responses in so far as familial relations are involved.

One of the significant reflections of the paucity of resources is the pattern of expenditure on basic necessities. As Table 2.5 shows, there is a clear pattern indicating the decreasing proportion of income spent on food as economic status rises. Note, for example, that in Mahnar, while the landless spend 67.1 per cent of their income on food, the marginal farmers spend only 58.7 per cent, the small farmers 44.9 per cent and the viable farmers only 33.7 per cent. Similar is the pattern in Hariharganj, another noteworthy feature pertains to the higher proportion of income spent on education by comparatively richer households. Also, in so far as other expenses are concerned, the proportion of expenditure goes up as we move up in the economic hierarchy (Table 2.4).

This will, no doubt, seem to be natural inasmuch as these patterns are in keeping with the general observation that the higher the economic status, the greater the proportion of expenditure on education and other non-food items. However, these patterns conceal one fact of great significance. This relates to the phenomenon of homogeneity of lifestyle across economic hierarchy, which is effectively camouflaged, when one focusses exclusively on differential proportions of income spent on food items by different economic groups. This is confirmed by the fact that, keeping per capita expenditure on food in mind, if the landless spend, on the average, ₹24 per person per month, the viable farmers spend even less, only ₹22 per person per month. It is true that the farming community can supplement its expenditure on food with the produce of the land it tills. However, this does not make for a radical difference in lifestyle. In matters both of food and clothing, there is a large degree of homogeneity in living style. Given this homogeneity, however, great differences in the pattern of the satisfaction of basic needs exist.

While this is also true of Hariharganj, the pattern is slightly different and in favour of the landless. It is interesting to note that, keeping per capita per month expenditure on food in mind, the pattern gets reversed. While the landless spend on average ₹30 per person, the marginal farmers spend ₹20, the small farmers ₹14.5 and the viable farmers only ₹12.3. One reason for this is the fact that the larger the farm size, the less the need to buy food grains for household consumption. Whatever may be the case, the conclusion seems to be unavoidable that despite so much talk of the rise of capitalist farming and the differential impact of the Green Revolution, there is not much differentiation in the lifestyle of the rich and the poor in the rural areas, at least in Bihar.

The persistence of this homogeneity should not, however, blind us to the fact of inequality not only in life conditions but also in life chances. This is indicated by two facts. First, so far as the question of education of children is concerned, the richer households spend a larger proportion of their income as compared to the poor and not so rich households. Note, for example, that if the landless in Mahnar spend only 1 per cent of their income on education, the viable farmers spend 10 times of that. Similarly, in Hariharganj, the landless spend 2.1 per cent of their income on education as compared to 7.2 per cent by viable farmers. Second, it is true that a large part of what we call 'other expenditures' is constituted by what F. G. Bailey calls 'contingent expenditure' relating to religious rituals and social prestige, not an insignificant part of this is spent on inputs into farming operations. These two factors taken together help in generating capacities for the richer elements in rural society to make better use of their resources. In other words, the most significant difference between the rich and the poor, at least in Bihar if not anywhere else, pertains not so much to life conditions as to life chances. There are, no doubt, great inequalities in life conditions as well. However, what is important is that while the rich have available to them greater advantage in improving life chances, the poor are denied these advantages. As a result, the depressed condition of the poor remains depressed and they endure this helplessly. We do not need to adduce more than a couple of pieces of evidence in this regard. First, if education opens up new channels of opportunity for status mobility, most of the poor in the two blocks are prevented from taking advantage of the new avenues because of their economic disability. The much vaunted free primary education remains out of their reach because the present economic necessity of using their children's labour to supplement their meagre income forecloses future opportunities. It should be pointed out that so far as literacy goes, it is very low in both the blocks; 60.7 per cent of males and 82.9 per cent of females in Mahnar (70.4% of persons) and 689 of males and 91.1 per cent of females in Hariharganj (79.1% of persons) are illiterate. Given this general picture, however, the proportion of illiterate persons increases as one goes down the economic hierarchy. Note, for example, that 86.8 per cent of landless males as against 32.6 per cent of males from viable farmers' households in Mahnar and 72.9 per cent of landless males as against 55.5 percent of male viable farmers in Hariharganj are illiterate.

These proportions are, however, somewhat misleading. If we calculate the proportions of illiterates in different economic categories, the picture changes radically in Hariharganj. If, in Mahnar, higher economic status retains its advantage in respect of literacy, the picture gets altered in Hariharganj. Note, for example, that, in Hariharganj, out of 19,014 illiterate males, 27.7 per cent come from landless families, 26.6 per cent from marginal farmers, 18.7 from small farmers and 27 per cent from viable farmers' families. In other words, it is only the small farmers that show a marked inclination towards removing illiteracy. But when it comes to higher education, we again revert back to the phenomenon of higher economic status proving to be the stepping stone to higher education. This is true in both the blocks. For example, in Mahnar, out of 830 males who have completed 11 or more years of education, 5.3 per cent come from the landless, 17.3 per cent from marginal farmers, 15.2 per cent from small farmers and 62.1 per cent from viable farmers. In Hariharganj, 20 per cent come from the landless, 12.7 per cent from marginal farmers, 11.2 per cent from small farmers and 56.2 per cent from viable farmers.

Second, the foreclosure of future opportunities for the poor is indicated also by their inability to meet current expenditures as well as to meet the expenses of farming operations. As our data reveal, most landless and marginal farmers live beyond their means. This is possible only when they are able to convert either their goodwill or physical resources or both into ready cash. The landless farmers have no other resource than to contract loans from village money lenders. In the case of the others, either loan can be contracted, or land can be sold to procure cash to sustain themselves. But once the loans are contracted, there is no release, especially for the landless, from them since repayment becomes difficult. If marginal and small farmers either sell or mortgage their land to repay the loan or to meet current expenses, it only further weakens their economic condition.

That the situation of the poor, especially the marginal and the small farmers, is really depressing can be gleaned from the data on land transactions. To take Mahnar first, it is interesting to note that both the marginal and the small farmers lease in more land than they lease out. Note, for example, that, during 1980, the marginal farmers leased 538.3 acres of land but leased out 146 acres; the small farmers leased

146 acres as against 225 acres that they leased out, and the viable farmers leased 160 acres when they leased out 1,154 acres, When a marginal or a small farmer leases their land out as compared to a viable farmer, two distinct modes of economic behaviour are suggested. In the case of the non-viable farmer, the leasing out of land suggests distress; that is to say, it denotes either a mortgage or their inability to invest the necessary inputs for farming. In contrast to this, the viable farmer leases out their land not because they cannot meet the expenses of farming but because they have to lease their land out in order to retain the services of farm labourers to preserve the domain of their influence or to get additional return to land they cannot themselves profitably cultivate.

The picture is slightly different in Hariharganj. Except for the viable farmers, both the marginal and small fanners lease in more land than they lease out. 511.4 against 387 acres in the case of marginal farmers, and 426 against 241 acres in the case of small farmers. The viable farmers lease 378 acres as against 1,687.5 acres of leased out land. What is significant is the data on the sale and purchase of land in this regard. During 1976–1980, in Mahnar, for example, the marginal farmers sold 50 acres of land and bought almost an equal amount of land, the small farmers sold 38 acres and bought 61.3 acres, and the viable farmers sold 125 acres against the 216 acres they bought. Similarly, in Hariharganj, the marginal farmers sold 53.4 acres and bought 73 acres; the small farmers sold 80 acres and bought 91 acres, and the viable farmers sold 241 acres and bought 440 acres. Here again, two distinct types of economic behaviour become discernible. This can be explained with the help of the average buying and selling prices that different categories of farmers receive and pay. For example, in Mahnar, the marginal farmers received a selling price of ₹429.8 per Katha but had to pay ₹622.4 per katha, and the small farmers sold their land at the rate of ₹510 per katha but had to pay a buying price of ₹582 per katha. In contrast to the marginal and the small fanners, the viable farmers received ₹456.6 per katha but paid only ₹387.1 per katha. Similar is the case in Hariharganj as well. When marginal farmers sell their land, they receive a selling price of ₹177.7 per katha; it's against the buying price of ₹246 per katha. The corresponding figures for a small farmer are ₹156.3 and ₹248.3, respectively. However, in the case of the viable farmer, the situation is reversed. He receives the selling price of ₹202.4

Table 2.4 Landowning Status of Households and Monthly Income (in %)

	Landowning Status									
	Landless	Marginal Farmers	Small Farmers	Viable Farmers	Total	Landless	Marginal Farmers	Small Farmers	Viable Farmers	Total
Up to ₹100	12.6	23.5	17.2	6.7	1,504 (14.8)	17.0	25.0	24.4	11.6	1,492 (19.0)
₹101–250	58.5	38.0	28.4	16.3	4,115 (40.3)	47.8	47.0	29.0	8.7	2,713 (34.5)
₹251–500	25.6	29.3	32.3	37.7	2,063 (30.0)	23.4	19.7	22.6	14.1	1,567 (20.0)
Above ₹500	3.3	9.2	22.1	39.3	1,518 (14.9)	11.8	8.3	24.0	65.6	2,098 (26.7)
Total	4,072	2,835	1,011	2,282	10,200	2,490	2,068	1,299	2,013	7,870

Table 2.5 *Type of Farmer Household and Their Monthly Income (in %)*

Household Type	Mahnar				Hariharganj			
	Landless	Marginal Farmers	Small Farmers	Viable Farmers	Landless	Marginal Farmers	Small Farmers	Viable Farmers
Food	67.1	58.6	44.7	37.2	75.2	71.9	61.6	40.5
Clothing	11.1	10.3	10.5	9.0	9.1	9.1	10.2	10.1
Education	1.0	2.9	6.6	10.3	2.2	1.6	2.7	7.2
Health	4.9	4.8	5.1	4.5	3.3	3.2	3.3	3.4
Festival, birth, death, etc.	13.8	14.7	15.6	17.3	9.0	10.3	13.0	17.3
Agricultural wage, etc.	0.2	4.5	11.0	14.6	0.0	1.6	5.4	15.3
Others	1.9	4.3	6.6	7.1	1.3	2.3	3.7	6.1
Total (per month)	₹179.2	₹259.9	₹355.7	₹472.3	₹199.6	₹163.1	₹164.6	₹274.0

per katha as against the buying price of ₹162.1 per katha. It is evident, then, that when marginal and small farmers sell their land, it is more or less distress selling. But when viable farmers sell their land, it is for profit. It does not rule out the possibility of distress selling in the case of viable farmers. However, in many cases, it is profitable for viable farmers to engage in the selling and buying of land.

V

The analysis presented in this paper sharply brings out several factors. First, if one goes by the general economic situation in both the blocks, it is quite depressing. The prevalence of extreme inequality in the distribution of resources makes it still more depressing. Second, given the overall depressed economic condition in the two blocks, what is of the greatest significance is the inability of most of the poor in these blocks to improve their life chances, In so far as the question of a generalized lifestyle is concerned, our data show little difference across the echelons of the economic hierarchy. However, when it comes to the utilization of whatever resources various economic groups have available to them to improve their life chances, the significance of inequality in the distribution of resources at once gets magnified. Generally speaking, the higher the economic status, the largest resources are deployed for improving life chances.

It should be emphasized here that, given the general economic condition, the lot of marginal farmers seem to be much more deplorable than the landless. However, the fact remains that in the present general economic depression, both the landless and the marginal farmers constitute perhaps the one large group suffering acute economic disabilities. And lastly, given the data, it is vital to look at the phenomenon of poverty from a new, more realistic perspective informed more by human sympathy than by intellectual objectivity and rigour.

NOTES

1. Simon Kuznets, 'Economic Growth and Income Inequality,' *American Economic Review* 45, no.1 (March 1955): 1–28, and 'Quantitative Aspects of the Economic Growth of Nations: VIII. Distribution of Income by Size,' *Economic Development and Cultural Change* 11, no. 2 (January 1963): 1–80.

2. For a discussion on this theme, see Ken Coates and Richard Silburn, *Poverty: The Forgotten Englishman* (Harmondsworth: Penguin Books, 1970), 22–23.

3. A few of such studies are B. H. Minhas, 'Rural Poverty, Land Redistribution and Development Strategy: Facts and Policy,' *Indian Economic Review* 5, no. 1 (April 1970): 97–128, P. K. Bardhan, 'On the Minimum Level of Living and the Rural Poor,' *Indian Economic Review* 5, no. 1 (1970): 129–136., Reprinted in T. N. Srinivasan and P. K. Bardhan, eds., *Poverty and Income Distribution in India* (Calcutta: Statistical Publishing Society, 1974), V. M. Dandekar and Nilakanta Rath, *Poverty in India* (Poona: Indian School of Political Economy, 1971). For a discussion on the substantive aspects of these studies, see, among others, M. L. Dantwala, *Poverty in India: Then and Now, 1870–1970* (New Delhi: Macmillan, 1973), and C. K. Johri and S. M. Pandey, 'Dimensions of Poverty and Income Policy,' *Indian Journal of Industrial Relations* 14, no. 1 (July 1978).

4. Ibid, p. 3; Johri and Pandey, for example, talk of three categories of people below the poverty line, 'severely destitute', 'destitute' and 'poor'.

5. Dantwala, *Poverty in India*, 21.

6. For a brief discussion on this theme, see Ramashray Roy, *Against the Current* (Patna: Institute for Rural Development, 1981), 7–87.

7. Coates and Silburn, *Poverty*, 22.

8. Peter Townsend, 'Measuring Poverty,' *British Journal of Sociology* (1954): 131, quoted in Coates and Silburn, *Poverty*, 24.

9. Ibid.

10. For a discussion on the point, See Ramashray Roy, 'The Meaning and Measurement of Poverty,' in *Depreciation: Its Social Roots and Psychological Consequences*, eds. D. Sinha, R. C. Tripathi and G. Mishra (New Delhi: Concept Publishing, 1982), 5–16.

11. Coates and Silburn, *Poverty*, 25–26.

12. Oscar Lesis, La Vida : *Puerto Rican Family in the Culture of Poverty* (New York: Random House, 1966), p. 34.

13. Coates and Silburn, *Poverty*, p. 26.

14. Coates and Silburn, *Poverty*, p. 28.

15. Charles A. Valentine, *Culture and Poverty. Critique and Counter-proposals* (Chicago, IL: University of Chicago Press, 1970), 13.

16. J. E. Meade, *Efficiency, Equality and Ownership of Property* (London: George Allen and Unwin, 1964), Quoted in Coates and Silburn, *Poverty*, 27.

17. There are no Scheduled Tribes in Mahnar: Only 0.2 per cent of the population in Hariharganj is Scheduled Tribes.

18. About 23 Kathas constitute one acre.

Chapter 3

Urban Development and the Poor*

S. R. Hashim

INTRODUCTION

The process of urbanization in India has been exceptionally slow and India is one of the least urbanized countries in the world. There could be many reasons for the slow rate of growth of urbanization, but the question is whether the same slow pace of urbanization in India can be projected into the future also? A reasonable bearing on this question is crucial for dealing with urban growth and urban poverty in a way that urbanization becomes a supporting stimulant rather than a stumbling block to the level and quality of development that the nation aspires to. Even with a low level of urbanization, India has not been able to manage, so far, healthy living conditions for the urban poor and satisfactory provision of essential urban amenities and services to most urban residents. Urban governance has been poor. The question is whether even this slow pace of urbanization has been too much for the country to manage, and if so, what happens when urbanization grows at a faster pace? We would like to emphasize that urbanization in India is not a single, uniform, monolithic experience. There are states which have experienced high levels of urbanization, and there are states with urbanization levels which the country as a whole experienced in the early 20th century. Also, it is generally seen that states with higher levels

* *Social Change* Vol 44, no. 4 (December 2014): 505–18.

of urbanization have been able to manage their urban units much better than states with primitive levels of urbanization.

SLOW PACE OF URBANIZATION

All human activities are spurred by close interaction and mutual support within a large community of people living in a habitat. Commerce and industry grow in clusters and agglomerations. Cities have been the centres of advancement of education and knowledge, language and arts, invention and innovations and broadly of culture and civilization. With economic growth and increasing diversification of economic activities away from agriculture and animal husbandry, urbanization has been constantly expanding all over the world. As per Census 2011, the urban population in India was 31.16 per cent, and the growth rate of the urban population over the two decades, 1991–2011, has been just around 2.7 per cent per annum, which is a little lower than the average rate of urban growth obtained during 1951–91 (Table 3.1). The level of global urbanization was around 15 per cent

Table 3.1 *Urbanization and Urban Growth in India*

Census Years	Percentage of Urban Population	Annual (Exponential) Growth Rates of Urban Population
1901	10.84	–
1911	10.29	0.03
1921	11.18	0.79
1931	11.99	1.75
1941	13.86	2.77
1951	17.29	3.47
1961	17.97	2.34
1971	19.91	3.21
1981	23.34	3.83
1991	25.72	3.09
2001	27.78	2.73
2011	31.16	2.70

Sources: INDIA Urban Poverty Report 2009 and Census, 2011.

at the beginning of the 20th century when India was 11 per cent urbanized. The world today is about 60 per cent urbanized, while urbanization in India remains at around 31 per cent. In 1980, when India had an urban population of 23 per cent, China only had 20 per cent. Today, China is reported to be 54 per cent urban. During the last three and half decades, since China has experienced an unprecedentedly high rate of economic growth and since restrictions on rural–urban migration were somewhat relaxed, urbanization in China has grown at a very fast pace. In developed countries, urbanization ranges between 75 and 90 per cent, and the rural population has shrunk in keeping with the dependence of the workforce on agriculture, which in turn becomes more or less proportional to the contribution of agriculture to GDP. The contribution of agriculture to GDP in India has come down to about 14 per cent (2012–2013), while agriculture is still burdened by nearly 50 per cent of the workforce. This accounts for extreme inequality between rural–urban incomes, and the underdevelopment of the rural sector in all respects.

A typical worker in India, by tradition and by habit, is a reluctant migrant. They just do not flock to the city looking for jobs. They only move when they clearly find a job opportunity, that too, through established connections. Most of the time, they move alone leaving the family behind and keep their connection with the community back home alive. They move to the city when the city needs work from they. An educated person is more likely to migrate from rural to urban areas but only after being reasonably sure about finding work. Poverty is not a key factor in migration (Kundu & Sarangi, 2005). Hence, all the noise about rural poor flocking to the city and adding to poverty in urban areas is unfounded. Urban poverty is not a result of the push factor (Hashim, 2009). In fact, it is this reluctance about insecure and purposeless migration which even today has contained more than two-thirds of the Indian population in rural areas, though most of them do not have full time productive work in hand.

India's economic growth in the first three decades after Independence was very slow in spite of emphasis on industrialization from the Second Five-year Plan onwards. Later, when the growth picked up after liberalization and even accelerated to higher levels, the structure of growth was such that it did not create jobs for the masses. Higher growth achievement of the last two decades or so has been based on the growth of the services sector, particularly of the type which creates fewer jobs, that too for well-educated and skilled population. India jumped from primary sector to tertiary sector by passing the growth of manufacturing against the historical experience of developed countries and of China in more recent times. The service sector accounts for 60 per cent of the GDP. The share of manufacturing which was 16.2 per cent in 2010–2011 is projected to fall to about 15 per cent in 2012–2013. This is despite the pronounced aim of the government to take it to 25 per cent. India's share in world manufacturing is negligible. In the year 2009, the USA with a share of 18.7 per cent and China with a share of 18.1 per cent dominated world manufacturing. Japan had a share of 10.1 per cent, while India had a meagre share of 2.1 per cent in world manufacturing. The consequence is that GDP growth has not contributed to growth in job opportunities. More than 93 per cent of the work force remains employed in informal sectors with low incomes and no security. Lack of industrial/manufacturing job creation has contributed to the slow growth of urbanization. The high-level of fast growing industrialization and industrial exports was the main basis of Chinese growth. The pattern of growth that we in India have experienced in the last two decades is unsustainable. Our growth pattern has to change with emphasis on industrialization.

Industrialization demands a high level of infrastructure, energy, transport, ports and airports. Industrialization creates clusters and agglomerations. It creates jobs to draw people away from agriculture and rural areas. This is precisely the process of urbanization. Industrialization, job creation and urbanization are thus one and the same process. In the interest of sustaining economic growth, we have to induce and encourage this process. A high level of urbanization is not only unavoidable but necessary for growth and development. And therefore, it is important to realize at this stage that the rate of urbanization in India has to break from the past trend and grow at an unprecedented higher pace. With certain reasonable assumptions about the rate of economic growth and job creation, it would be reasonable to assume an urban population of nearly 50 per cent by 2031. This perspective has to be kept in policymaking if we want to avoid absolutely chaotic urbanization.

THE PATTERN OF URBAN GROWTH

The pattern of urban spread that has emerged in the country, even though unplanned, is not too skewed. The distribution of cities of size 1 lakh and above in states and union territories is shown in Table 3.2. A number of meaningful observations can be made from this table. It is not that the experience of a high level of urbanization does not exist in the country. There are a number of states, quite a few of them very large, where urbanization is already in the neighbourhood of 50 per cent or even more, even if we exclude from consideration the city territories, like NCT of Delhi and Chandigarh. Puducherry, Goa and Mizoram have an urbanization level of more than 60 per cent. Big states such as Tamil Nadu (48.45%), Kerala (47.74%) and Maharashtra (45.23%) have urbanization in the neighbourhood of 50 per cent. In general, South India is more urbanized, and North and East India are much less urbanized. The level of development (indicated in Table 3.2 by per capita net state domestic product [NSDP]) is highly correlated with the level of urbanization. The distribution of cities by size classes appears to be quite balanced on the whole. All the mega cities (eight in total) are located in the more urbanized states. What is even more interesting is to note that Goa, Sikkim and Arunachal Pradesh do not have a single city of size 1 lakh and above, though Goa is the most urbanized state. Kerala, a relatively larger state which has urbanization level of 47.74 per cent does not have a single city of size 10 lakh and above. The relatively more urbanized states with population share of 46.8 per cent have 252 towns in the size group 1–10 lakh, while the relatively less urbanized states with population share of 53.2 per cent have only 198 towns in this size group. To say that a very high level of urbanization will encourage only mega cities and will be at the cost of smaller cities is not borne out by data.

In fact, Goa and Kerala, the two most urbanized states, present the best example of urbanization where rural and urban areas are a continuum, and there is little difference between the two in terms of infrastructure and facilities. The more urbanized states of the South are also known for better governance structure for the cities and better management of the problems than the less urbanized states in the north.

Table 3.2 *Distribution of Cities (Size 1 Lakh and above) in States/Territories 2011*

	States/Union Territories	Percentage of Urbanization 2011	Per Capita NSDP at FC 2011-2012	Number of Cities by Population Size (in Lakh)				State Population Millions
				1-10	10-20	20-40	40 & Above	
1	NCT of Delhi	97.50	112,626	14			1	16.8
2	Chandigarh	97.25	89,351	1				1.1
3	Puducherry	68.31	80,558	2				1.2
4	Goa	62.17	112,602					1.5
5	Mizoram	51.51	39,546	1				1.1
6	Tamil Nadu	48.45	57,546	29	2		1	72.1
7	Kerala	47.74	53,877	7				33.4
8	Maharashtra	45.23	62,457	34	8	2	1	112.4
9	Gujarat	42.58	57,508	25	2		2	60.4
10	Karnataka	38.57	41,959	25			1	61.1
11	Punjab	37.49	46,364	15	2			27.7
12	Andaman Nicobar	35.67	68,356	1				0.4
13	Andhra Pradesh	33.49	42,119	39	2		1	84.5
14	West Bengal	31.89	33,117	59	1		1	91.2
15	Uttarakhand	30.55	50,303	6				10.1
16	Nagaland	28.97	43,267	1				2.0
17	Madhya Pradesh	27.63	24,395	28	4			72.6

18	Jammu & Kashmir	27.21	28,999	2	1			12.5
19	Tripura	26.18	39,542	1	1			3.7
20	Rajasthan	24.89	28,851	26	2	1		68.5
21	Haryana	24.25	62,078	19	1			25.3
22	Jharkhand	24.05	25,634	8	2			33.0
23	Chhattisgarh	23.24	26,979	8	1			25.5
24	Uttar Pradesh	22.28	18,217	57	4	2		199.8
25	Manipur	20.21	23,957	1	1			2.6
26	Meghalaya	20.08	36,937	1	1			3.0
27	Orissa	16.68	24,134	10				42.0
28	Assam	14.08	22,910	4	1			31.1
29	Bihar	11.30	13,226	25	1			104.1
30	Himachal Pradesh	10.04	48,923	1				6.9
	INDIA	31.16		450	33	5	8	1210.0

Source: Constructed from Census of India Tables (Provisional), 2011.

Notes: 1. Cities enumerated in this table are cities defined by the statutory limits, that is, municipal corporations. As such, the extension of a city outside the corporation limits is counted as a separate city. Thus, Kolkata and Howrah are separate cities. In National Capital Territory of Delhi, only the city defined by MCD is the one metro city, and there are 14 other cities including New Delhi. In their economic functioning the cluster of these cities together along with the closely located other cities constitute one big agglomeration. Thus, Mumbai, Delhi, Kolkata and Chennai make big agglomerations.

2. The eight cities enumerated in this table in the category 40 lakh above are: Greater Mumbai (MC), Delhi (MCD), Kolkata (MC), Chennai (MC), Bangalore (MC), Greater Hyderabad (MC), Ahmedabad (MC) and Surat (MC). Among the 5 cities in the next category (size 20 to 40 lakh) are: Pune (MC), Nagpur (MC), Jaipur (MC), Lucknow (MC) and Kanpur (MC).

TOWN SIZE, BASIC AMENITIES AND POVERTY

Analysing access to basic amenities and urban security in cities, Kundu (2009) finds that Class I towns, particularly the metropolises, enjoy a distinctly higher level of basic amenities (access to drinking water, electricity and toilet facilities).

A study of six small and medium towns across the country brings out some stark facts about the basic amenities in those towns (IHD, 2012). The six towns studied are given in Table 3.3.

Sources of drinking water in these six towns together were public hand pump (27.9%), public stand post (16.3%), private hand pump (17.4%), well (7.1%), piped water supply (9.6%), purchase of water (10.1%) and others (21.6%). Parbhani had 19.1 per cent of piped water supply and Bidar had 9.9 per cent. All other towns had less.

Open defecation was widely prevalent (among 57.2% of households). This was true of bigger towns even more: Parbhani 81.3 per cent, Bidar 53.8 per cent, Madhubani 60.6 per cent, Pakur 71 per cent.

Drainage in these towns was mostly informal (*Kuchcha*), mostly uncovered and did not have proper outfall.

Sewerage connections served only centrally located settlements and have not been extended to peripheral areas. Even in central areas, many poor settlements have been left out.

Table 3.3 *Selected Small and Medium Towns and their Population*

Town	State	Population (2011) (in '000)
Parbhani	Maharashtra	259
Bidar	Karnataka	173
Mansa	Punjab	73
Madhubani	Bihar	66
Jangaon	Andhra Pradesh	44
Pakur	Jharkhand	36

Source: Institute for Human Development (2012).

Table 3.4 *Percentage of Poor in Different Size Classes of Cities/Towns*

City/Town Size	1973–1974	1999–2000
Large towns/cities	18.4	14.2
Medium towns/cities	27.6	20.4
Small towns	33.2	24.2
All urban areas	27.4	19.9
Rural areas	35.7	23.9

Source: Institute for Human Development (2012).

As regards housing, thatch, grass, tarpaulin and asbestos as roofing material dominated the houses of three lower quintiles of households.

It has also been observed that large cities exhibit distinctly higher, demographic growth, better infrastructural facilities, higher levels of education and lower poverty ratios. The quality of employment, productivity and returns to education are likely to be better in larger cities than in smaller towns (Hashim, 2009). On the point of incidence of poverty by size class of towns, Table 3.4 reproduced from Kundu and Sarangi (2005) will be of much interest.

Small towns were almost at par with rural areas in respect of incidence of poverty.

The situation in less developed states in this respect is even worse. 'About a fifth of the population in these towns lives in totally dehumanized conditions, as they have to do without safe drinking water, electricity and toilet facilities' (Kundu, 2009). Local bodies, particularly those of smaller towns, face more severe resource crunch in less developed states. At the same time small and medium towns in these states have experienced a rapid growth in population. It, thus, appears that the quality of urban development depends more on the quality and nature of governance (the basic cause for disparities in development) rather than on the level of urbanization.

PLANNING FOR URBANIZATION

Urbanization in India has not followed any pre-planned frame of development or a pre-planned pattern of urbanization. Planning for urbanization, in that sense, would have meant outlining a perspective on urban growth as a whole, visualizing a desirable spread of urban units over various states, planning infrastructure accordingly and 'seeding' the growth of urban units and nudging the location of industries (particularly manufacturing industries) according to the visualized pattern. Physical planning of urban units, particularly keeping in mind the needs of workers and the needs of the relatively poorer sections of the population in these urban units, would be an important part of planning of urban units (or urban planning). Yet another relatively more neglected part of urban planning has been the planning and putting in place effective urban governance machinery with adequate provision of resources to be able to take care of expanding needs in the future. In this respect as well, the relatively more urbanized and more developed states have performed better.

The attitude towards urbanization was somewhat ambivalent in the earlier stages of planning. The First Five-year Plan almost entirely focused on agriculture and rural community development (FFYP, 1951). The Second Plan took note of the urban problems only in the context of 'housing'. It said:

> Large towns have attracted to themselves new industries and services and the problem of providing housing and other amenities have become increasingly acute. Rise in the land values, speculative buying of lands in the proximity of growing towns, high rentals and the development of slum areas are features common to most large towns …. For the urban development to proceed on desirable lines, competent municipal administration with adequate powers, resources and administrative and technical staff are essential. (SFYP, 1956: 297)

Thus, urbanization appears to be only a problem, and the problems mentioned earlier have, since, become even more acute, though there have been a number of schemes and programmes to address them under subsequent Five-year Plans. The problem of urban governance was sought to be tackled through a landmark legislative measure, that is, the 74th Amendment of the Constitution effective from April, 1993, which provides a common framework for the structure and mandate of urban local bodies for effective democratic decentralization.

It was the Tenth Five-year Plan which, while noting the problems, took a more positive view of urbanization, as can be seen from the following quotation:

6.1.12 Attitudes to urban growth within the country tend to swing between two extremes. Cities are seen either as an unavoidable evil or in a more positive way as "engines of growth". The former view is held by those who focus on the growth of slums and squatter colonies, the congestion on the roads and environmental degradation. The others, in contrast, focus on the bustling formal and informal sectors in urban areas and their contribution to the economy, the diversification of occupations away from traditional land-based ones to newer forms of production and services, and the lower levels of poverty as compared to rural areas. (TFYP, 2002: 613)

There has been no urban planning in the broader sense of the term. Except for Kalyani in West Bengal (in the early fifties), Chandigarh in the north and Gandhinagar in Gujarat, no green field planned city has come up in the country not counting the metropolises—induced satellite towns with infrastructural support from state governments and which have become integral part of the big urban agglomeration. Kalyani, which was supposed to share the load of Kolkata spill over, refused to grow into a full-fledged dynamic city for lack of supporting activities and industries. Chandigarh grew into a large beautiful city, but failed to visualize the future needs of service providing workers and their residential needs. The result is that it is now dotted with and surrounded by sprawling slums. Gandhinagar has done relatively better but is now almost a part of the fast growing mega city, Ahmedabad. The so-called urban planning in India has been only a lagged response to problems arising in unplanned urban units, that is, slums, shortage of drinking water, absence of drainage and sewerage, inadequate or non-existent public transport system, and in more recent years, increasing road congestion and air and water pollution. The Jawaharlal Nehru National Urban Renewal Mission (JnNURM) was one such response. However, the small-and medium-size towns do not get much attention even with reference to these problems.

A number of schemes and programmes for urban poverty alleviation, improvement of the urban environment and slums, improvement of urban basic services, urban housing, etc., were launched under various Five-year Plans (Palitkar, 2009). The JnNURM is the single largest initiative in the urban sector. It was launched by the Government of India in 2005 with a total outlay of 100,000 crores, and was aimed at strengthening infrastructure and the overall quality of life in the 63 cities listed in the Mission document. The Mission has two sub-Missions: Urban Infrastructure and Governance and Basic Services for the Urban Poor. The states were required to submit city development plans (CDPs) and later, detailed project reports (DPRs), justifying their request for funding under JnNURM. Fifteen of the CDPs submitted were analysed by Harini Narayanan and Shipra Bhatia of National Institute of Urban Affairs (2007). This analysis brings out some interesting points which throw light on the way the state governments look at the urban problems, particularly with reference to the urban poor. For example, most of the CDPs identify as an achievement or express the desire for a movement of employment creation opportunities from the primary and secondary sector (particularly manufacturing), to the tertiary sector with particular ambition for IT sector development. CDPs show little concern for the implications of such development for the poor and have hardly any plans for job creation for the poor. Cities look for 'clean' and 'modern sector' development. The growth of informalization of jobs is acknowledged, but there is hardly any plan to remedy the situation. However, cities such as Chennai, Coimbatore, Pune and Ludhiana do appear to value their manufacturing growth and would like to push it with better infrastructural support. The Ahmedabad CDP does try to address the issue of unemployment resulting from the decline of textile industry, and it clearly acknowledges 'the poor contribute to the globalising economy of Ahmedabad as much as the non-poor ... without receiving due economic or other civic facilities or services at par with the non-poor'. It includes plans for credit provision for livelihood and shelter building activities for the poor. 'Many cities discuss the spaces where the poorer sections of the workforce operate only in the context of shifting them out to the periphery of the city', concludes the policy paper (Narayanan & Bhatia, 2007).

URBANIZATION AND POVERTY

Urban development and its relationship with poverty is an important focus of discussion in this article. We have already drawn attention to the relationship between city size and poverty. Larger cities have a generally lower incidence of poverty mainly because of their capacity to generate more work opportunities for the poor. From the available data, one can also discern a clear relationship between the extent of urbanization and the incidence of poverty at the level of states. However, our understanding of the plight of the urban poor will remain totally inadequate unless we also reflect upon the question: Who is the urban poor? In this context, a brief discussion of the official methodology of defining the poor and an alternative way of identifying urban poor will be quite in place. This is what we do in what follows.

The relationship between the level of urbanization and the extent of poverty was examined in a paper (Hashim, 2009) with the help of available data for the years 1993–1994 and 2004–2005, using official poverty estimates released by the Planning Commission. The states were grouped in to four categories according to the extent of poverty: Very Low (VL), Low (L), High (H), Very High (VH). The states were also grouped similarly in to four categories according to their level of urbanization. The information was then tabulated into a matrix as shown in Table 3.5. The matrix shows that a higher degree of urbanization is associated with lower levels of poverty.

Table 3.5 *Urbanization and Poverty*

Urbanization→ Poverty ↓	VL (Very Low)	L (Low)	H (High)	VH (Very High)
VL			Punjab	
L		Kerala	Gujarat	Delhi
			Haryana	Goa
			West Bengal	Tamil Nadu
H	Bihar	Andhra Pradesh	Karnataka	Maharashtra
		Rajasthan		
		Uttar Pradesh		
VH	Orissa	Madhya Pradesh		

Source: Hashim (2009).
Note: Himachal Pradesh, Jammu & Kashmir and Assam are excluded from the analysis for non-availability of comparable estimates.

As per official estimates issued by the Planning Commission (2012), the incidence of urban poverty (the head count ratio) in India was 25.7 per cent in 2004–2005 and 20.9 per cent in 2009–2010. The estimates are based on the methodology recommended by the Tendulkar Committee, according to which the poverty line for the year 2009–2010 was ₹860 per capita per month or an expenditure of ₹28.60 per person per day. Doubts have been widely expressed about the efficacy of such a low poverty line, much lower than $1 ppd, and that too for meeting the cost of living in urban India. It may be noted here that the official estimates of poverty released by the Planning Commission, though have undergone redressing at various intervals, are still rooted in the poverty level consumption basket of 1974–1974 which was the basis of the work of the Task Force chaired by Dr Y. K. Alagh in 1979. Redressing of the Alagh poverty line was done mainly in respect of the question as to which basket to be used—whether all-India basket or state-specific basket, and which price indices to be used for indexing the poverty line (Lakdawala Committee), and more recently, whether urban basket or rural basket is more appropriate (Tendulkar Committee). After all these revisions and adjustments of 'poverty line' at the base of which was a basket of consumption in 1973–1974, one is not sure what basket of consumption it represents today, and whether the basket meets even at the bare minimum level the requirement of a reasonably decent living today. Conditions and patterns of life in urban areas over these last 40 years have changed much more drastically. The revised poverty lines also fall short of the original calorie norms in which they were anchored.

The Copenhagen Declaration (UN Social Summit, 1995) says:

> Absolute poverty is a condition characterised by severe deprivation of basic human needs, including food, safe drinking water, sanitation facilities, health, shelter, education and information. It depends not only on income but also on access to social services.

Historically, the poverty lines were drawn around food requirements alone, and that too reduced to the minimum calories needed. Whatever other things the household consumed along with the minimum calorie consumption, was taken as satisfying its total needs for living (Dandekar & Rath, 1971). An implication of the Engel's law of budget shares is that people rank their necessities for the purposes of allocating expenditure within the constraints of their income. Food expenditure gets the first rank and the highest share in the budget. The point at which just the minimum necessary food requirements (in terms of calories) are met, expenditure on other necessities, such as clothing, housing, health and education, etc., must necessarily be at sub-minimum level. Calorie-centric poverty line is deficient in this respect.

The concept and notion of poverty is relative to economic and social conditions and evolution of society's collective thinking as to what is decent and what is not. Hence, poverty is not comparable over time with a fixed measuring rod.

Another problem with official estimates is that these are only aggregate estimates which tell us the proportion of poor population in a state or in the country. They cannot help to identify the 'poor household'. Given the need for reaching out to the poor household, efforts started first at state levels, to identify the poor households through a census in rural areas. Initially, there were a lot of difficulties with the concepts and methods. Ultimately, a sort of a consensus has evolved to identify poor households on the basis of a number of 'vulnerabilities' which are visible and also easily verifiable in a large-scale census operation.

The Planning Commission constituted an Expert Group (under the chairmanship of the present author) in May 2010 to recommend an appropriate methodology for identification of urban poor.

Taking note of the decision of the Government of India to under-take Socio-Economic and Caste Census (SECC), it was decided to include in SECC questions helpful to the identification of the urban poor. The questionnaire was prepared by the Expert Group in asso-ciation with the Ministry of Housing and Urban Poverty Alleviation. The SECC captures the residential status, the physical conditions of the dwelling, the number of rooms occupied, provision of civic amenities, occupational status, employment conditions, health and education, age and social vulnerabilities.

The urban poor suffer from a large number of vulnerabilities which could broadly be grouped under three categories: residential, occupa-tional and social vulnerabilities. The residential vulnerabilities are the most acute for the urban poor. It includes houselessness or a house with a roof and wall made of plastic or polythene, grass, thatch, bamboo, mud, unburnt bricks, etc., Lack of water connection or water availability, sewer, drain, electricity, etc., add to these vulnerabilities. The quality of surrounding environment in which the house is located is also important. Among occupational vulnerabilities are begging, rag picking, uncertain employment, irregular source of livelihood, casual work, irregular wage payments, etc. Social vulnerabilities include child headed households, households with all or some members with disability or chronic illness, etc.

The group has recommended a three stage identification process: (a) automatic exclusion, (b) automatic inclusion and (c) scoring index. The methodology has been worked out in detail, keeping in view the data which would be available from the SECC. However, the data from the census are not yet available, and hence the exact estimate of poverty based on this methodology could not be made. But whatever little data were available on which the proposed methodology could be tested, based on that, it appears that the magnitude of urban poverty is much larger than what the official estimates indicate.

SUMMING UP

Cities have been the centres of advancement of knowledge, industry, culture and civilization. Urbanization has been constantly expanding all over the world. The world today is 60 per cent urbanized, while urbanization in India remains at 31 per cent only. This is mainly because of slow industrial growth and the slow rate of overall economic development in India. Since the country is looking forward to higher rates of economic growth and job creation, a higher pace of urbanization is unavoidable.

The pattern of urban growth, which has emerged in the country, is fairly balanced. Also a fairly large part of the country (south and west) has experienced high levels of urbanization. Within the country, a higher level of urbanization is strongly associated with higher level of economic development. More urbanized states are also better governed states. Amenities and infrastructure in larger towns are better. Conditions in smaller towns are very dehumanizing in this respect.

There has been no planning for urbanization in India, though city plans exist. The urban poor hardly find a place in city plans. Cities look for 'clean' and 'modern sector' development. The growth of informalization of jobs is acknowledged, but there is hardly any plan to remedy the situation.

There is a relationship between city size and poverty. Smaller towns have a larger incidence of poverty, almost at par with the incidence of poverty in rural areas. The level of urbanization and the extent of poverty are negatively correlated at state level also. In this context, it needs to be noted that the method of estimating poverty (the official method) is quite faulty at present, and there is no method of identifying an urban poor household. A methodology has been proposed which is based on residential, occupational and social vulnerabilities of the urban poor, and which can be applied to data from SECC. SECC data are not yet available. But testing the data on some available data, it is surmised that the extent of urban poverty is much larger than the official estimates.

REFERENCES

Dandekar, V. M., & Rath, N. (1971). *Poverty in India*. Institute of Political Economy.

FFYP. (1951).The First Five Year Plan. Planning Commission, GOI, 1951.

Hashim, S. R. (2009). Economic development and urban poverty. *INDIA Urban Poverty Report, 2009*. Ministry of Housing and Urban Poverty Alleviation, Government of India, Oxford University Press.

IHD (Institute for Human Development). (2012). *Nature of poverty and identification of poor in small and medium towns* (mimeographed). IHD.

Kundu, A. (2009). Access to basic amenities and urban security—An interstate analysis with a focus on the social sustainability of cities. *INDIA Urban Poverty Report*, Ministry of Housing and Urban Poverty Alleviation, Government of India, Oxford University Press.

Kundu, A., & Sarangi, N. (2005). Employment guarantee—The issue of urban exclusion. *Economic and Political Weekly, 40*(30): 3642–3646.

Narayanan, H., & Bhatia, S. (2007). A policy paper, JNURM and the urban poor. Guidance, Hazards Centre Project Assistance, NIUA.

Palitkar, S. (2009). The millennium development goals and the role of cities. *INDIA Urban Poverty Report, 2009*, Govt. of India, Oxford University Press.

Planning Commission. (2012). Press Note on Poverty Estimates, 2009–10, March 2012, Govt of India.

SFYP. (1956).The Second Five Year Plan. Planning Commission, GOI, 1956.

TFYP. (2002).The Tenth Five Year Plan. Planning Commission, GOI, 2002.

UN Social Summit. (1995). *Report of the world summit for social development*. https://undocs.org/A/CONF.166/9

Section II

Dimensions of Poverty

Sectional Introduction

K. B. Saxena

Poverty is generally assumed to arise from a lack of adequate income to meet subsistence needs. However, deep investigations have brought out its more complex and multifaceted character. As a result, poverty is not reduced/eradicated even with faster growth and rise in per capita income and redistribution because many other deprivations intersect with it. These may vary from person to person and need to be tackled along with the income deficit to lift the poor above the poverty line. In our own country, Scheduled Castes (SC)/Scheduled Tribes (STs) present the most glaring example of how entrenched structural barriers block attempts to alleviate their poverty.

These multiple deprivations have been succinctly captured in Amartya Sen's formulation of inadequacies 'of capacities' has in view precisely these multiple deprivations to eradicate poverty. These incapabilities include not only a lack of good health and adequate nourishment for proper 'functioning' of the individual but also the ability to choose and achieve the kind of life the poor can actually lead. This approach implies not only effective state provisioning of basic social services—health, nutrition, education and so on, but also a redistribution of resources towards socially and economically disadvantaged groups and removal of social barriers to expand their freedom, thereby linking a capability approach to those of social exclusion and participation. This requires identification of deprivations/ inabilities of a non-income nature, removing them effectively through specific programmes and focusing on institutions that facilitate an individual's attempt to choose and achieve the kind of life they wish to live (Hughes et al., 2008). The ambit of a 'capability' approach is thus wide enough to encompass any type of constraint that blocks pathways of the poor to lead a life of dignity and self-respect. This approach has been supported by the United Nations, which is reflected in the formulation of a Human Development Index, which aggregates the three dimensions of achievements—standard of living, knowledge acquisition (literacy) and life expectancy. The UNDP has developed a Human Poverty Index which measures deprivation instead of achievements in these three dimensions. In 2010, a Global Multidimensional Poverty Index (MPI) was developed jointly by the Oxford Poverty and Human Development Initiative and the United Nations Development Programme (UNDP), which is computed by measuring progress using 10 parameters. The NITI Aayog is the nodal agency to monitor progress in MPI in India.

This section contains six papers which identify some non-income deprivations in the Indian context, which need to be tackled simultaneously with material deprivation.

Arun Kumar Ghosh in his paper has argued that the shift from material deprivation to social deprivation has broadened the concept of poverty. The poor are not merely deprived of income but also of basic needs such as food, clothing, shelter, water and sanitation. Sen had deviated from an income and consumption approach to the deprivation of capability, which includes not only important social variables, such as education and health, but also social exclusion. The UNDP, drawing upon this approach, views poverty not merely in terms of material impoverishment but a lack of opportunity for the poor to lead valued lives due to social constraints and personal circumstances. These deprivations are linked to a lack of autonomy, self-respect, dignity and power and are embedded in the institutional structure of society based on caste and gender.

Preet Rustagi's paper dwells on women and poverty and brings out its multiple dimensions, particularly gender-based deprivation and discrimination which add to poverty-related vulnerabilities. The combined effects of gender and poverty are examined through women's demographic, educational and employment status as also through access to basic amenities. The difference between men and women in the nature of employment is compared to consumption expenditure quintiles to bring out a gender and poverty interface. She highlights the need for a specific focus on poor women in urban India. Given the decline in female work participation even among the poorer households and increasing recourse to self-employment, intervention should focus on investment in education up to secondary and above levels and measures to assist them in accessing better avenues of work with scope for part-time regular work options.

Disability is also a major cause of poverty and, thus, of its consequences too. People with disabilities are relegated to the margins of society. Ambati Nageswara Rao's paper highlights the multidirectional nature of their poverty, which includes exclusion from the labour market. If they are employed at all, they work for fewer hours with low wages. Social security schemes do not provide a living wage. Their segregation contributes to their marginalization. Disability and poverty reinforce each other and contribute to their vulnerability and exclusion. Their needs remain peripheral to development planning. Nearly 50 per cent of disabilities are preventable. Specific steps are required not only for prevention of disability, but also to enable participation of persons with disability in the development process. The recently enacted law needs to be effectively implemented to achieve it.

Child labour is a symptom of poverty. Helen R. Sekar and Manju Khurana's paper links child labour with the poverty of families, which forces them to send their children to work. Dysfunctional schools are also a factor. It is also a cause of poverty because child workers remain illiterate, devoid of skills, get paid low wages and are subjected to physical, social, sexual and psychological abuse. They are also exposed to health hazards, which are aggravated by malnutrition, as a result of which they suffer from multiple diseases. The risk to health is so grave that some of them become unemployable for life. Child labour has adverse psychological consequences as well. Engaging children in work is a violation of the law and the rights of children. Welfare programmes have not made much dent in the problem. Improving the economic condition of families from where children are drawn into the workforce is the most enduring solution to the problem.

Bijay Sarkar's paper highlights the gravity of health hazards and the risk caused by industrial pollution in Jharkhand. This he does by drawing upon data from published sources in respect of ground water pollution, river water pollution and air pollution. The areas affected most are tribal concentration districts where people suffer from several killer diseases. Government authorities are apathetic; industrialists are non-cooperative, and bureaucrats are servile to the industrial lobby. The problem is rooted in a flawed concept of development, which takes the volume of production as a single yardstick and does not take into account cost in terms of environmental degradation. The absence of any regulatory and reformative initiative is due to the powerlessness of people. The author urges leaders of parties to demand that industrial planning must be weighed against the prospective loss of the environment and people should be educated on the causes and effects of pollution.

Durganand Sinha's paper demonstrates that economic and cultural disadvantages and poverty adversely influence the development of cognitive abilities and motivation. The psychological concomitants of poverty have detrimental consequences on the general functioning of the individual, rendering him/her incapable of overcoming poverty through personal efforts. A vicious circle is created; economic and social factors generate poverty, which, in turn, makes the individual incapable of coping with poverty and further accentuating poverty. Another important consequence of poverty is in the shape of restriction of language and linguistic mode of communication, which is undifferentiated and simplex in contrast to the better-off sections whose linguistic code is elaborated. This renders the poor less capable of performing academic tasks, and they encounter failure and frustration, which renders them less capable of combating their poverty. The poor are also low in motivation and aspiration, apathetic, fatalistic and resigned to their lot. The behaviour is characterized by extreme caution, risk and failure avoidance, over dependence on government and external agencies and lack of self-help. All these elements undermine their competence for coping with poverty.

An unidisciplinary approach is not adequate to combat the phenomenon of poverty. The psychological characteristics of the poor are as important as the socio-economic system which gives rise to poverty.

Chapter 4

Sociology of Poverty*
Conceptual Issues

Arun Kumar Ghosh

Poverty is one of the areas in which social science research has conducted numerous studies. In India, much of the research on poverty
has been the preserve of economists and statisticians because of their
concern with growth and development. Reduction of poverty and
inequality is one of the major objectives of economic planning, and the
Planning Commission has played a leading role in initiating research
studies on poverty. 'The economists were in the forefront of the work
both within and outside the Planning Commission that sought to relate
poverty and inequality to growth and development' (Beteille 2003).

Economists have based their concept of poverty on income/
expenditure, which is easy to measure with some amount of reliability.
Poverty has been defined as the inability to attain a minimum standard
of living as measured by income and expenditure. Absolute poverty
means poverty for which a line is drawn at a need adequacy level. The
poor are those whose consumption level falls below this level. It is
computed on a fixed consumption basket of food which satisfies the
minimum requirement of 2,400 calories in rural areas and 2,100 calories
in urban areas. Most studies on poverty have focused on standardization
in the measurement to determine the number and proportion of the
population below the poverty line. Head count ratio (HCR) is the most
conventional method for measurement of poverty. Data pertaining to

* *Social Change* Vol 35, no. 4 (December 2005): 123–40.

household expenditure reported in various national sample surveys have been used for this purpose.

However, it is not easy to achieve standardization amid such extensive variations and fluctuations in prices across the country, though price adjustments are made with respect to time and space. There are methodological issues involved in the measurement of poverty.

There is no uniformity in the estimation of poverty among economists and statisticians. Debates have been generated in the recent past over the official estimate of poverty. Different scholars have provided alternative estimates for 1999–2000 that are at variance with official poverty figures (Deaton and Dreze 2002; Sen and Himanshu 2004; Sundaram and Tendulkar 2003). Those who used the direct method of calculating poverty based on stipulated calories have come up with an estimate considerably higher than the official estimate (Meenakshi and Viswanathan 2003; Patnaik 2004). The credibility of the estimates based on the direct calorie norm has been questioned (Dev 2005). The poverty estimate based on the HCR approach serves the specific and limited objective of finding out the number and proportion of the poor as defined according to a fixed standard. The concept of absolute poverty is obviously narrow and restrictive if it is defined in terms of the basic requirements as measured by expenditure or income. Closely related to the income/consumption approach is the basic need approach. The poor are deprived of basic needs such as food, clothing, shelter, water and sanitation that are necessary to prevent ill health, undernourishment and the like. The basic needs approach sets an adequacy level for each of these needs, instead of specifying a poverty line based on dietary energy adequacy. Both the income/consumption and basic need approaches focus on the deprivation of basic material needs.

Amartya Sen deviated from the traditional income/consumption approach, viewing poverty as deprivation of capability rather than merely low levels of income. He argued that overemphasis on income poverty had led to the neglect of other important social variables such as ill health, lack of education and social exclusion that are also linked to deprivation of capability.

The United Nations has developed a concept of human poverty drawing heavily on the conceptual framework provided by Sen.

He conceptualized poverty or deprivation in terms of the absence of certain basic capabilities to function. Poverty not only means the lack of the necessities for material well-being, but also denial of opportunities to lead a reasonable level of living: 'In the capability concept the poverty of a life lies not merely in the impoverished state in which the person lives, but also in the lack of opportunity—due to social constraints as well as personal circumstances—to lead valuable and valued lives' (United Nations Development Progamme 1997). UNDP used this conceptual framework to specify some basic capabilities to 'lead a long, healthy, creative life and to enjoy a decent standard of living, freedom, dignity, self-respect and the respect of others' (United Nations Development Progamme 1997). This was a sharp departure from the traditional approach to income poverty.

The concept of human poverty is limited to a few variables that have been operationally defined. It has constructed human poverty indices on the lines of human development indices. This also has the specific and limited objective of finding out the proportion of the population living in poverty and comparing the levels of poverty among different nations. Whether it is income poverty or human poverty, it is the measurement of poverty which has been the central focus of poverty studies.

Sociological studies of poverty came largely from British and American sociologists. In his paper on 'Poverty and Inequality', Andre Beteille (2003) discussed how poverty in Britain emerged as a social problem, which drew the attention of sociologists. In the USA, poverty was linked to the problem of race because poverty in urban America was highly concentrated among Blacks and other racial minorities. Others tried to relate poverty not so much with racial characteristics as with economic, social and demographic characteristics which make the black minority a disadvantaged group (Wilson 1987). Poverty studies in the West were largely confined to urban poverty. The survey method was used to find out the social, economic, demographic and moral characteristics of poverty.

PROBLEM OF DEFINITION

The problem sociologists usually face is formulating a single definition of poverty universally applicable to all varied space and time. Poverty is relative deprivation as defined culturally by the particular society to which the poor belong. Peter Townsend and Abel-Smith (1995) conducted an extensive study of poverty in Britain and made a significant contribution to the sociological understanding of poverty. They discarded the concept of absolute poverty. As Peter Townsend (1979, 38) said,

> In fact, people's needs, even for food, are conditioned by the society in which they live and to which they belong, and just as needs differ in different societies so they differ in different periods of the evolution of single societies. Any conception of poverty as 'absolute' is therefore inappropriate and misleading. (Beteille 2003)

Sociologists in the West in general are critical of the concept of absolute poverty. The concept of relative poverty, too, is subject to criticism for being subjective and impressionistic and not measurable with reliability. However, the concept of relative poverty has dominated the thinking of most sociologists.

The social exclusion approach recently developed by the International Institute for Labour Studies comes close to the 'relative deprivation' concept of poverty propounded by Townsend. Poverty in the social exclusion theory is regarded as a lack of resources to participate in activities and enjoy living standards which are widely accepted in society. There are complex social and economic factors associated with social exclusion which create poverty traps.

In India, poverty has been perceived as an economic problem. It has hardly been considered a social problem, leaving poverty studies to the exclusive domain of economists and statisticians. Sociologists have not studied poverty as a core issue. They have studied slums in urban areas and marginalized groups such as the Scheduled Castes (SCs) and Scheduled Tribes (STs) in rural areas to assess their livelihood status in terms of some socio-economic parameters. They have carried out quantitative analyses of socio-economic data based on the survey method, supplemented by qualitative analyses based on the case study method. There are some excellent social profiles of SCs/STs indicating their livelihood status, their educational status and health and nutritional status. These studies capture some aspects of their poverty in terms of occupations, income, expenditure, moveable assets, level of education and health.

It is true that the bulk of SCs and STs are living below the line of poverty. Hence, there is a need to study poverty among them. Economists have studied the incidence of poverty to arrive at the number of those among them below the poverty line. However, they have not measured poverty among members of individual castes or tribal groups. Sociologists have usually not treated all SCs or STs as a single social group. Rather, they have treated them as broad social categories within which fall a large number of castes and tribal groups that are internally differentiated. They have analysed these groups in a stratification scheme. Groups occupying the bottom of the hierarchy are considered the poorest. However, class differentiation among individual castes and tribes within the broad categories of SCs and STs presents a reality confined to its own universe (Mukherjee and Ghosh 2003). Such analyses will help identify those SCs and STs that need immediate priority for development. Sociologists perceive poverty as a group phenomenon and do not estimate the number of people or households of that group who fall below the poverty line.

POVERTY A CORE SUBJECT

Indian sociologists ought to take up poverty as a core subject. This will add to their knowledge and social theory. The formulation of sound social policies for alleviation of poverty depends upon well-developed social theory. Poverty cannot be studied in isolation. It is a complex social phenomenon. The concept of poverty is holistic, covering a wide range of economic, social, political, cultural and environmental variables, which are casually related. The shift from material deprivation to social deprivation has broadened the concept of poverty. The social deprivation model of poverty includes not only deprivation of basic material needs but also deprivation of capabilities. Elements such as lack of autonomy, powerlessness and a lack of self-respect and dignity are important components of this model. There are structural constraints on enhancement of capabilities resulting from particular social structures. The social system of a particular society may impose certain limits to enhancement of capabilities. It cannot be viewed simply as deprivation of capability without examining the sources of deprivation. These sources are linked to the institutional framework of society. The deprivation of capability arises not merely from income inequality but also from social inequalities such as caste and gender. Deprivation in education and health reflects social and gender inequality. The relationship between inequality and poverty can be examined in a social and historical context. Traditional caste and gender inequalities in India have perpetuated poverty for a long time. Although the traditional forms of inequality have been weakened over the years after Independence, they operate to different degrees across regions in India. It is true that active discrimination against SCs/STs on grounds of caste plays a less important part in reinforcing poverty than in the past. Nonetheless, the social and economic characteristics of some SCs/STs are such that they are unable to move out of the poverty trap. Primitive tribal groups, too, are afflicted with poverty because of their social isolation.

The concept of social exclusion may be further redefined on the basis of research on poverty by examining social and economic characteristics among marginalized SCs/STs, including some marginalized Muslims. Case studies based on qualitative analysis may be conducted in different poverty-stricken areas, such as urban slums or backward villages/blocks or marginalized groups such as SCs/STs. These may help generate some sociological parameters that need to be operationally defined for quantitative analysis based on the survey method. This is a new challenge which sociologists in India must take up.

REFERENCES

Abel-Smith, B., and P. Townsend. 1995. *The Poor and the Poorest*. London: Bell.

Beteille, Andre. 2003. 'Poverty and Inequality.' *Economic and Political Weekly* 38, no. 42: 4455–4462.

Deaton, Angus, and Jean Dreze. 2002. 'Poverty and Inequality in India: A Re-examination.' *Economic and Political Weekly* 37, no. 36: 3129–3148.

Dev, S. Mahendra. 2005. 'Calorie Norms and Poverty.' *Economic and Political Weekly* 40, no. 8: 789–792.

Dreze, Jean, and Amartya Sen. 1995. *India: Economic Development and Social Opportunity*. New Delhi: Oxford University Press.

Meenakshi, J. V., and B. Viswanathan. 2003. 'Calorie Deprivation in Rural India.' *Economic and Political Weekly* 38, no. 4: 369–375.

Mukherji, P. N., and A. K. Ghosh. 2003. 'Scheduled Communities: A Social Development Profile of Scheduled Castes and Scheduled Tribes in Bihar,

Jharkhand and West Bengal: A Report.' Council for Social Development. Sponsored by Planning Commission (Mimeographed).

Patnaik, Utsa. 2004. 'The Republic of Hunger.' *Social Scientist* 32, no. 9/10: 9–35.

Sen, Abhijit, and Himanshu. 2004. 'Poverty and Inequality in India–I.' *Economic and Political Weekly* 39, no. 38: 4247–4263.

Sen, Amartya. 1999. *Development as Freedom.* New Delhi: Oxford University Press.

Sundaram, K., and S. D. Tendulkar. 2003. 'Poverty in India in the 1990s: Revised Results for All India and 15 Major States for 1993-94.' *Economic and Political Weekly* 38, no. 46: 4865–4872.

Townsend, Peter. 1979. *Poverty in the United Kingdom.* Harmondsworth: Penguin Books.

United Nations Development Progamme. 1997. *Human Development Report.* New York, NY: Oxford University Press.

Wilson, William J. 1980. *The Declining Significance of Race.* Chicago, IL: University of Chicago Press.

Wilson, William J. 1987. *The Truly Disadvantaged.* Chicago, IL: University of Chicago Press.

Chapter 5

Women and Poverty*
Rural-urban Dimensions

Preet Rustagi

INTRODUCTION

Rural poverty and its implications for women have received some attention in literature. However, urban poverty is relatively of newer vintage (Mathur, 1994; Rodgers, 1989). Irrespective of the location, there are strong pieces of evidence to suggest that women are the worst sufferers from poverty-related deprivations as they have twin disadvantages of gendered deprivation and inequalities as well as poverty (Masika et al., 1997; Razavi, 2000). Therefore, examination of gender dimensions of poverty are extremely critical both for a better understanding of the interlinkages as well as for effective policy interventions.

Gender dimensions of poverty often gain significance from the notion that women constitute the poorest of the poor, being at the lowest rung of social and economic hierarchies. However, gender and poverty are two distinct forms of disadvantage and therefore should not be collapsed into the notion of 'feminization of poverty' because understanding of women as the poorest of the poor (alone) is not adequate (Jackson & Palmer-Jones, 2000).

* *Social Change* Vol 37, no. 4 (December 2007): 1–36.

The author is grateful to his colleagues Sandip Sarkar and Pinaki Joddar for their help with data analysis and the discussions they held that benefited him in writing this paper. He alone is responsible for any errors that remain.

Also, a frequently made link between gender and poverty is the equation of women-headed households with the poor (Chant, 2003; Gangopadhyay & Wadhwa, 2003; Pearce, 1978). Women-headed households are necessarily poorer and suffer from vulnerabilities when compared with those of men-headed households (Gangopadhyay & Wadhwa, 2003). It is also true that the proportion of women heads who are workers is higher compared to the overall work participation rates of women since, in most cases, the woman head is the active earner of the family. However, it would be incorrect to state that all women-headed households are poor. In fact, many more women-headed households fall into the relatively higher consumption expenditure quintiles. As such, the questions that should be asked are: Who constitutes the women heads? Whether there is a distinction between rural and urban locations? What are the consequences thereof in terms of poverty impact upon women?

Poverty is an income-based concept, defined and measured by the household as a unit. Difficulties in acquiring accurate income data, together with the argument that consumption is a better proxy for household's standard of living, have put the consumption expenditure as a better measure of well-being than income (World Bank, 1990), for current consumption (including consumption from own production) reflects the ability of the household to buffer their standard of living through saving and borrowing, despite income fluctuations. Household consumption expenditure is then used as a benchmark to designate the households below poverty lines. Such measures of poverty are also problematic, particularly in finding out the intra-household inequalities in consumption. However, in the absence of gender-segregated data on women in poor households, their location in the households below poverty lines can be studied to throw up some indicative pointers.

In any case, poverty and women's work is a complex issue. Women tend to be doubly burdened by poverty and are pressurized to seek formal employment because they need to contribute to the household income (Mitra & Pool, 2000), and yet their stereotypical household responsibilities constrain their availability for paid work. In some households where cultural norms and taboos prevent public participation of women as wage earners in the labour market, the burden of reducing costs by deploying their own labour services to avoid market purchases puts women under tremendous stress. Apart from the gender-based division of labour within the domestic spheres, market jobs are also gendered in ways that result in discrimination against women in terms of employment and wage returns.

The chapter addresses these issues in several sections. The first section of the chapter provides an estimation of poverty in absolute numbers across rural and urban areas. The second and third sections deal with the social environment and access to employment avenues which differ from rural to urban locations. As discussed earlier, women-headed households have often been taken as synonymous with poverty. The fourth section touches upon this issue by interrogating the extent to which such a proposition holds in the Indian context along with poor households' rural–urban distribution and changes over time. The fifth section is devoted to the education of women in rural and urban locations and its implications for poorer women. The sixth section is about the dimensions of employment of poorer women vis-à-vis relatively better-off women. It may be compulsion that drives poor women to paid employment, whereas it may be more of an option for the relatively better-off women, which would be reflected in the nature and type of jobs undertaken by the women. Given the variations in landowning households and its bearing upon labour utilization, the rural scenario may be distinct from the urban areas.

POVERTY ESTIMATES

The bulk of the poor remains in rural areas, although the urban areas display an increase in the absolute numbers of the poor over time from 1993–1994 to 2004–2005. Poorer households tend to have a more balanced sex ratio, implying more women have to bear the burden of poverty. This is true in both urban and rural locations. However, manifestations of poverty in the two locations differ in certain respects, especially with regard to access to basic amenities.

The poverty line as defined by the Planning Commission Expert Group for rural areas is ₹356.30, while the figure is ₹538.60 for urban locations per capita per month for 2004–2005. In 1993–1994, the poverty line was ₹205.84 for rural areas and ₹281.35 for urban areas (Table 5.1). As expected, the monthly per capita expenditure is higher

Table 5.1 *All-India Poverty Line and Absolute Number of Poor between 1993–1994 and 2004–2005 (Using Planning Commission Expert Group Method)*

Year	Poverty Line (Rupees per Capita per Month)		Number of Poor (in Lakhs)	
	Urban	Rural	Urban	Rural
1993–1994	281.35	205.84	763.37	2,440.31
2004–2005	538.60	356.30	807.96	2,209.24

Source: GOI (2007).

for urban areas as compared to rural areas. The increase over time in the poverty line is also much more significant in urban areas. In addition, the numbers of those netted under the poverty line would then be expectedly more in urban areas during this period, as is the case.

However, as the proportion of rural population is much higher than the urban counterparts, India's poor are largely in rural areas. As per the poverty estimates in 2004–2002, 28 per cent of the rural population is below the poverty line, while in urban areas, it is 26 per cent (Table 5.2). While rural poverty has declined from 37 per cent in 1993–1994 to 28 per cent in 2004–2005, the urban poverty estimates have declined from 32 per cent to 26 per cent over the same period.

In absolute terms, there are more than 300 million poor people in the country as a whole, with 220.9 million in rural and 80.8 million in urban areas. A simple method of using the actual gender composition as reported among the below poverty line households is adopted to generate the absolute numbers of men and women, rural and

Table 5.2 *Comparison of Poverty Estimates between 1993–1994 and 2004–2005 (Based on Uniform Recall Period)*

Sector	1993–1994	2004–2005
Urban	32.4	25.7
Rural	37.3	28.3
Total	36.0	27.5

Source: GOI (2007).

Table 5.3 *Absolute Number of Poor Women and Men (Estimated) and Growth Rates between 1993–1994 and 2004–2005*

| Sector | Numbers of Poor (in Lakhs) | | | | CAGR (%) between 1993–1994 and 2004–2005 | |
| | 1993–1994 | | 2004–2005 | | | |
	Women	Men	Women	Men	Women	Men
Urban	377.70	385.67	402.53	405.43	0.58	0.46
Rural	1,205.74	1,234.57	1,105.89	1,103.35	−0.78	−1.02

Notes: CAGR: Compound annual growth rate.
National Sample Survey (NSS) unit level data are used to estimate woman–man and urban–rural shares of poverty. These shares are then applied on population adjusted estimates of total poverty available from the Planning Commission to estimate absolute number of poor women and men in urban and rural areas separately. Calculations are done by authors themselves.

urban poor, as provided in Table 5.3. As per 2004–2005 estimates, one half of the poor are women, of which rural women constitute 110.6 million, while urban poor women are 40.3 million (Table 5.3). In urban areas, there has been an increase, while rural areas experience a marginal decline.

Both men and women among the urban poor have increased in absolute numbers. However, the annual compound growth rate for poor women is relatively higher than that for men. The number of urban poor women has increased from 37.8 million in 1993–1994 to 40.3 million in 2004–2005. This is as expected since the sex ratios among the relatively poorer households are more balanced. It is commonly noted that there are relatively more women among the poorer households as compared to their non-poor or prosperous counterparts.

Using the latest NSS consumption data from the 61st round as well as the 50th round to estimate the head count ratio (HCR) across households classified by who heads the household reveals a drop in overall poverty, but the women-headed households (female-headed households [FHHs]) have slightly higher HCR compared to the men-headed households except in 1993–1994 for rural areas where the reverse holds true (Table 5.4).

Table 5.4 HCR (%) of Poverty by Head of the Household between 1993–1994 and 2004–2005

Period	Rural	Urban	Rural + Urban
Woman head			
1993–1994	35.48	36.92	35.88
2004–2005	28.80	28.74	28.78
Man head			
1993–1994	37.34	32.26	36.10
2004–2005	27.99	25.65	27.41
Diff woman ~ man head			
1993–1994	–1.87	4.65	–0.21
2004–2005	0.81	3.09	1.38

Source: Calculated from unit level consumption data of NSS 50th (1993–1994) and 61st (2004–2005) round.
Note: Diff woman ~ man head: Percentage point gap between HCRs of poverty for women- and men-headed households.

DEMOGRAPHIC COMPOSITION

While the overall demographic profile in India reflects a women–deficit in the sex ratio, the share of women is higher among the households with lower monthly per capita consumption expenditure (MPCE) in both rural and urban areas. The variations across MPCE groups in the sex composition show that the households from the bottom quintile is more balanced with systematic declines in the share of women as one moves up to the top quintile (Table 5.5).

In fact, the lowest quintile with a sex ratio of slightly more than 1,000 shows that there are as many women as men among the poorest group of households in both rural and urban areas. The comparisons reveal the urban sex ratios to be generally far worse off. What is noteworthy in both the locations across all the MPCE quintiles is the improvement over time in the sex ratios in that they are becoming relatively more balanced.

The prosperity–poverty connection to lower sex ratios has also been commented upon effectively in the literature (Agnihotri, 2000;

Table 5.5 *Sex Ratios by MPCE Quintiles between 1993–1994 and 2004–2005*

MPCE Quintiles	Rural		Urban	
	1993–1994	2004–2005	1993–1994	2004–2005
Q^1 (bottom 20%)	997	1,019	1,003	1,001
Q^2	958	988	931	948
Q^3	946	953	907	911
Q^4	926	937	883	877
Q_5 (top 20%)	896	917	811	868
All	944	962	905	920

Source: Calculated from unit level employment–unemployment data of NSS 50th (1993–1994) and 61st (2004–2005) round.

Rustagi 2006). Metropolitan cities and some of the newer growing million plus cities also reflect the same situation with slum populations having better sex ratios, compared to the non-slum inhabitants.[1]

The poor households are compelled to depend on their women's labour supplies for their survival. However, employment avenues have to be available. It may be argued that the working status of women is also an outcome of the availability of particular kinds of jobs, especially across income categories. Also, if work has to be ameliorative of poverty, the returns from employment need to be more remunerative, which in turn can be ensured only if investments are made towards educating poor women. Access to public provisioning as well as basic amenities is critical for the overall well-being of poor women. Urban areas are generally better provided for in terms of most of these facilities on average. However, the differences in the context of the poor and non-poor may be starker for urban areas compared to their rural counterparts.

BASIC AMENITIES: URBAN–RURAL COMPARISONS

Basic amenities and lack of access to them forms one significant dimension of poverty. Undoubtedly, urban areas are usually better off in terms of most basic amenities as compared to rural counterparts. The 2001 census reports the location of the source of drinking water within the premises in 65 per cent of households, which is only 29 per cent in villages. In 25 per cent of cases, urban households report the source of drinking water being located near their premises, while in 9 per cent of households the location is a distance away. In urban areas, especially for the poorer households, the issue is not as much of location of source as it is of access and adequacy of supply. Common occurrences of failure in regular or timely water supply, excessive pressure on public stand pipes resulting in frequent conflicts, some of which turn ugly and violent, are frequently reported (Kundu, 1993). Since women are involved in undertaking these chores, they end up being more affected by these problems.

While 70 per cent of urban households have bathing facilities in their homes, there is only 23 per cent in rural areas. Non-availability of latrines is reported in 26 per cent of urban households, whereas it is 78 per cent in rural households. However, it is noteworthy to dwell on the implications of urban deprivation as distinct from rural locations, given the high and increasing density in big towns and cities, leaving little or no space for open defecation. The indignities involved in being so deprived for women are more severe, imposing unimaginable constraints and restrictions on daily routine such as defecation, urination and bathing. The implications for hygiene and health risks thereby affect poorer women, who have limited access to healthcare services given the economic constraints. Even drainage facilities are non-existent in the case of 22 per cent of urban households and a similar proportion of households have no electricity.

The only basic amenity with relatively better rural conditions is the ownership of households. While 29 per cent of urban households inhabit rented accommodation, only 4 per cent of rural households report rented housing tenure. Access to ownership of shelter, whatever the conditions may be, is an option that most villagers can exercise. In urban areas, the poor end up living on pavements, in makeshift shelters and eventually gain entry into slums and squatter settlements. Even with many years of stay, the slum dwellers may lack any documents to prove their citizenship.

Data from the NSS 58th round (July–December 2002) is used to elicit information on the proportion of slum dwellers' citizenship status. Nearly 21 per cent of the slum households have no proof of citizenship, while 30 per cent of them have a ration card. Very few of the slum dwellers have voter identification cards. It must be pointed out that access to several pro-poor services is contingent upon the poor having citizenship. It is in this context that there is an urgent need to ensure universal coverage of voting rights through issuance of voter ID cards to all poor persons. Their registration is especially significant not only as basic citizenship rights, but also for political participation so as to assert them.

UNDERSTANDING POVERTY IN URBAN AND RURAL CONTEXTS

In order to explain and understand the causes of urban poverty, aspects concerning urbanization itself are to be looked into (Mahadevia & Sarkar, 2004, and the references cited therein). Urban growth is an outcome of natural increases in population, rural to urban net migration and reclassification of towns. The latest assimilation of rural hinterland within the city limits or their reclassification into urban areas is beset with a range of problems that manifest urban poverty. The complexities are further magnified for women belonging to erstwhile rural and/or culturally bound households who face constraints over the supply of their labour and also in terms of using the newly available avenues. The poverty faced by these groups of the urban population, especially women, thus assumes an entirely different form, which often defies easy identification and redressal for poverty amelioration.

Rural poverty is an outcome of socio-economic and political ine-qualities as well as the process of marginalization. Landlessness or poor access to land and economic resources, low returns from agriculture, especially for the land, poor who operate with scanty investments, inadequate avenues for remunerative employment, social exclusion and lack of political voice are a few of the prominent factors explain-ing poverty in rural areas. Inadequate employment opportunities due to the low level of non-farm sector development is another major factor which is interlinked with public provisioning of amenities and infrastructure in a substantial manner. With relatively fewer avenues for survival livelihood in rural areas, temporary, periodic or short-term migration is often sought by men, which may increasingly be supported by women joining them as well. Where this migration is for a longer span or results in permanent relocation into urban areas, these rural masses add to the poorer echelons of urban societies. It may be true that they earn better and, in most cases, end up with a higher consumption expenditure as a result, which is indicative of their poverty reduction, since that is how it is calculated and measured. However, in the urban context, they become the net additions to the urban poor (Mitra, 2006). Under such circumstances, migration from rural areas is often seen as fueling urban poverty, albeit not as the major reason, but certainly as one of the causes for the proliferation of slums and unauthorized settlements as well as the increasing pressures on urban amenities. The use of migrant workers, often contractual, for construction and various informal sector activities in urban cities and towns displays the conditions in which these workers live and work. The level of vulnerabilities faced by these workers is extremely high, and they are almost completely at the mercy of the contractors, middlemen or employers. Moreover, virtually no state policies cover or protect these workers in any form.

Understanding and analysing the gender components of poverty is much more complicated (Buvinic et al., 1983; Cagatay, 1998, among others). Because of limited means available to estimate women–specific dimensions of poverty, the relative vulnerabilities of women–headed households as a proxy for the higher incidence of poverty faced by women have come to be commonly used. Nevertheless, as indicated earlier, it is not always the case that these households are the poorest of the poor. And yet some indicative issues can still be traced. The following section looks at FHHs more closely.

WOMEN-HEADED HOUSEHOLDS

The concept of women–headed households and its association with feminization of poverty occurred due to at least two sets of assumptions. The perceived strong link was an offshoot of observations made in the context of Western countries wherein increasing women–headed households, as a result of divorces or break–ups within families, were often seen to be more income poor compared to others (Chant, 1992; Masika et al., 1997). The absence of state support for divorced and single women by way of social security measures (Pearce, 1978) and the association of pauperization and welfare dependence as the price of independence also contributed to this understanding (McLanahan & Kelly, 1999). The changing family structure was blamed as the principal culprit for the feminization of poverty as it uncovers women's latent economic vulnerabilities (McLanahan et al., 1989).

Such observations may be extended to the social transition in family structures in the country from joint to nuclear families and the resultant exclusive responsibility of household work on women in latter households as compared to joint or extended families and the associated burden on them. This factor is certainly at play in terms of constraining the release of women for work in paid labour markets. It is also critical in terms of support structures for child care and domestic duties, activities that constrain women from labour market participation and enhance levels of stress faced by them.

The 61st round National Sample Survey Office (NSSO) data reveal an increase in the proportion of women-headed households from 9 per cent in 1999–2000 to 11 per cent in 2004–2005. The Census of India 2001 also generates a similar figure of 11 per cent for urban FHHs. The total FHHs estimated by NSS 61st round (2004–2005) reveal a slightly higher proportion of them in rural areas. However, it is in the urban areas that most of the FHHs are poor. This share of FHHs among the poor was higher earlier in 1993–1994 (Table 5.6). According to the 2004–2005 figures, the FHHs among the better-off sections of urban locations have registered an increase.

Most of the FHHs consist of widows as per the marital status classification. With improving educational levels, the possibilities of taking up compensatory jobs or pursuing one's own employment among the widows allow for improvements in their economic levels. This is also in part a reflection of the increasing tendencies of professional and

Table 5.6 *Women-headed Households by MPCE Quintiles*

MPCE Quintiles	2004–2005		1993–1994	
	Urban	Rural	Urban	Rural
Bottom 20 %	12.3	9.8	14.3	9.6
Q_2	11.6	9.9	10.3	8.7
Q_3	10.7	10.2	10.0	9.0
Q_4	10.3	11.4	10.4	9.8
Q_5	11.2	14.1	9.1	11.0
All	11.1	11.3	10.6	9.7

Source: Calculated from NSS unit records, 50th and 61st rounds.

working couples living separately in different locations pursuing their careers. In villages, on the contrary, there are more women-headed households among the relatively better-off sections. Although, over time, there seems to be an increase across MPCE categories among FHHs in rural areas.

Widows constitute nearly 70 per cent of all FHHs in urban areas, while they constitute 63 per cent in rural areas. Among FHHs, divorces or separated women constitute the smallest share, close to 3 per cent in both rural and urban areas. While 8 per cent of the FHHs are that of never married women, 20 per cent are that of currently married women as well in urban areas. The category of married women heads is relatively higher in rural areas, at 31 per cent, while the single women component for villages is less than 4 per cent (Table 5.7).

Table 5.7 *Marital Status of Women Heads within MPCE Quintiles: 2004–2005*

MPCE Quintiles	Never Married	Currently Married	Widowed	Divorced/ Separated	All
Urban					
Q^1 (bottom 20%)	8.9	13.6	74.3	3.1	100.0
Q$_2$	4.8	13.5	75.6	6.1	100.0
Q$_3$	3.5	15.6	77.9	3.1	100.0
Q$_4$	6.9	22.3	37.9	2.9	100.0
Q$_5$ (top 20%)	14.3	30.6	52.2	2.9	100.0
All	8.2	20.3	67.9	3.5	100.0
Rural					
Q^1 (bottom 20%)	6.0	37.6	54.8	1.6	100.0
Q$_2$	2.4	35.2	59.1	3.2	100.0
Q$_3$	1.2	28.4	67.6	2.9	100.0
Q$_4$	1.8	25.4	69.8	3.1	100.0
Q$_5$ (top 20%)	5.7	30.7	59.9	3.6	100.0
All	3.6	30.8	62.5	3.0	100.0

Source: Calculated from unit level employment–unemployment data of NSS 61st (2004–2005) round.

Overall, both urban and rural areas reflect declining work participation among women heads except among the two lower quintiles in urban areas. This depicts the compulsions of poverty as well as the availability of opportunities for women in urban locations. In rural areas, although women heads report a higher work participation rate compared to their urban counterparts, the distinctions across the poorer and better off households seem to be lower (Tables 5.8 and 5.9).

The absorption of women heads in regular employment is one major positive change over time, especially in urban areas whereby they are seen to be shifting from self-employment and casual employment to regular work in a significant manner (Table 5.10). The rural scenario is somewhat different, with only casual employment showing a decline over time. However, across MPCE quintiles, the lower quintiles which

Table 5.8 *Work Participation among Women Heads over Time: Urban–rural*

MPCE Quintile	Urban		Rural	
	1993–1994	2004–2005	1993–1994	2004–2005
Q_1	49.4	49.9	72.3	59.4
Q_2	52.5	52.7	74.1	60.8
Q_3	47.6	43.2	70.9	66.7
Q_4	37.8	35.6	68.6	61.1
Q_5	41.9	33.0	69.1	58.9
All	45.5	41.7	70.7	61.1

Source: Calculated from NSS unit records, 61st round.

Table 5.9 *Status of Employment of Women Heads*

Usual Principal and Subsidiary Status (UPSS) Workers	Urban		Rural	
	1993–1994	2004–2005	1993–1994	2004–2005
Self-employed	33.7	31.2	48.1	51.9
Regular	37.4	49.4	5.2	6.9
Casual	28.9	19.4	46.7	41.2

Source: Calculated from NSS unit records, 50th and 61st rounds.

Table 5.10 *Women Heads Employment Status across MPCE Quintiles: 2004–2005*

Self-employed		Regular	Casual	Total
			Rural	
Q^1 (bottom 20%)	41.1	7.0	51.9	100
Q_2	46.8	4.9	48.3	100
Q_3	48.6	4.5	46.9	100
Q_4	49.6	6.3	44.1	100
Q_5 (top 20%)	63.3	9.8	26.9	100
			Urban	
Q_1 (bottom 20%)	39.22	27.58	33.20	100
Q_2	33.13	42.18	24.69	100
Q_3	36.06	39.18	24.75	100
Q_4	28.52	58.58	12.90	100
Q_5 (top 20%)	19.60	78.70	1.70	100

Source: Calculated from NSS unit records, 61st round.

constitute the poorer households with women heads are dependent on casual employment and self-employment with a few variations across rural and urban locations. The major distinction is with regard to regular employment, which is gaining significantly in urban locations. Avenues for poor women in regular jobs seem to be available and this necessarily has to do with some improvements in their education attainments, even if only that of becoming literate.

CHANGES IN EDUCATIONAL ATTAINMENT

The general educational levels of all those across the country have been improving over time, but those of women are registering a higher rate of increase. It would be of interest to see if this improvement is reflected across women belonging to different economic classes. The proportion of women's population not literate in urban areas declined from 38 per cent to 31 per cent between 1993–1994 and 2004–2005 (Tables 5.11 and 5.12). In rural areas, illiteracy among women declined from 68 per cent to 55 per cent.

Table 5.11 *Distribution of All Women Persons across Educational Categories in 1993–1994*

MPCE Quintile	Not Literate	Literate & up to Primary	Middle	Secondary	Graduate & above	All
			Rural			
Q₁ (bottom 20%)	82.1	15.4	1.8	0.6	0.0	100
Q₂	75.2	20.2	3.3	1.2	0.1	100
Q₃	69.1	23.7	4.9	2.1	0.1	100
Q₄	61.2	27.4	7.5	3.6	0.3	100
Q₅ (top 20%)	50.9	28.8	10.7	8.3	1.2	100
All	67.9	23.0	5.6	3.1	0.3	100
			Urban			
Q₁ (bottom 20%)	61.1	28.6	6.5	3.4	0.4	100
Q₂	47.7	33.7	10.6	7.0	1.1	100
Q₃	35.8	35.3	13.8	12.6	2.5	100
Q₄	27.9	31.2	15.5	19.5	5.8	100
Q₅ (top 20%)	16.7	25.9	13.1	26.7	17.5	100
All	38.4	31.0	11.8	13.5	5.3	100

Source: Calculated from NSS unit records, 50th round.
Note: [a] Includes higher secondary, diploma/certificate.

Table 5.12 Distribution of All Women Persons across Educational Categories in 2004–2005

MPCE Quintile	Not Literate	Literate & up to Primary	Middle	Secondary	Graduate & above	All
			Rural			
Q_1 (bottom 20%)	67.8	26.4	4.3	1.4	0.1	100
Q_2	61.1	29.5	6.7	2.5	0.2	100
Q_3	56.8	30.6	8.3	4.0	0.3	100
Q_4	50.4	30.7	11.2	6.9	0.8	100
Q_5 (top 20%)	38.2	29.2	14.6	15.0	2.9	100
All	55.1	29.3	8.9	5.9	0.8	100
			Urban			
Q_1 (bottom 20%)	51.4	33.3	9.5	5.1	0.7	100
Q_2	40.0	33.9	14.3	10.0	1.9	100
Q_3	29.0	33.0	17.2	16.6	4.2	100
Q_4	20.2	27.5	17.9	24.9	9.5	100
Q_5 (top 20%)	10.9	18.8	13.3	31.2	25.7	100
All	30.7	29.4	14.4	17.3	8.2	100

Source: Calculated from NSS unit records, 61st round.
Note: [a] Includes higher secondary, diploma/certificate.

Across MPCE quintiles, the inroads of education are clearly visible, with even the households from the poorest quintile reflecting improvements in literacy rates from 39 to 49 per cent in urban areas and from 18 to 33 per cent in rural areas in little over a decade. Among the literates, most urban women have had schooling up to primary levels. The same is true for rural areas as well. While nearly 26 per cent of urban women have secondary or above levels of education, in rural areas, women with similar educational attainments are only 7 per cent (Table 5.12). Clearly, it is this last segment of women with secondary and above education whose labour market options are improved, more starkly noticeable for urban women than their rural counterparts.

The most significant aspect of women's education in urban areas is the increase in the graduates and above category from 5 to 8 per cent between 1993–1994 and 2004–2005. The households belonged mostly to the higher quintile households. Among the richest quintile, there were 40 per cent graduates and above in the workforce in 1993–1994, which increased to 50 per cent in 2004–2005 for urban areas, although there have been marginal increases even among the poorer households. Labour market benefits accruing to this category of graduates and above is clear from Tables 5.13 and 5.14.

In rural villages, the number of women workers with educational levels above secondary schooling has increased from 2.8 to 6.3 per cent between 1993–1994 and 2004–2005. Even among the poor women workers, the increase in the share of secondary and above educated is more than one percentage point during the same period. This reflects a slow and marginal albeit positive change.

Overall, however, the educational attainment among usual principal and subsidiary status workers clearly reveals the extent of deprivation and resultant vulnerabilities with which most urban poor women function within the labour markets. The detailed discussion on the work profiles of women and the poorest among them in rural and urban areas is undertaken in the next section.

WORK PROFILES OF WOMEN IN RURAL AND URBAN LOCATIONS

The work participation rate (WPR) of women in urban locations is far lower than that of rural women and different from it in certain ways.

Table 5.13 *Distribution of All Women Workers across Educational Categories in 1993–1994*

MPCE Quintile	Not Literate	Literate & up to Primary	Middle	Secondary/Higher Secondary	Graduate & above	All
Rural						
Q₁ (bottom 20%)	89.2	8.4	1.8	0.6	0.0	100
Q₂	84.5	12.0	2.5	0.9	0.1	100
Q₃	79.3	15.3	3.9	1.4	0.1	100
Q₄	73.4	18.3	5.3	2.7	0.2	100
Q₅ (top 20%)	63.0	20.5	8.3	6.6	1.5	100
All	78.2	14.8	4.3	2.4	0.4	100
Urban						
Q₁ (bottom 20%)	72.6	18.9	5.2	2.8	0.5	100
Q₂	60.8	24.1	8.1	5.1	1.8	100
Q₃	47.2	25.9	12.2	11.3	3.4	100
Q₄	34.7	22.2	11.1	19.9	12.2	100
Q₅ (top 20%)	14.0	11.4	6.8	27.8	40.0	100
All	49.1	20.4	8.3	12.0	10.2	100

Source: Calculated from NSS unit records, 50th round.

Table 5.14 *Distribution of All Women Workers across Educational Categories in 2004–2005*

MPCE Quintile	Not Literate	Literate& up to Primary	Middle	Secondary/Higher Secondary	Graduate& above	All
			Rural			
Q_1 (bottom 20%)	79.8	14.2	4.4	1.6	0.1	100
Q_2	73.1	17.2	7.1	2.5	0.2	100
Q_3	69.1	19.1	7.9	3.7	0.2	100
Q_4	61.7	21.6	10.3	5.7	0.7	100
Q_5 (top 20%)	47.8	22.7	13.3	13.0	3.1	100
All	66.0	19.0	8.7	5.4	0.9	100
			Urban			
Q_1 (bottom 20%)	61.7	24.1	9.1	4.6	0.5	100
Q_2	49.4	27.6	11.8	8.7	2.4	100
Q_3	35.9	25.7	16.4	15.3	6.8	100
Q_4	21.1	18.9	15.5	26.2	18.3	100
Q_5 (top 20%)	6.0	8.0	7.8	28.1	50.0	100
All	37.2	21.3	11.8	15.4	14.3	100

Source: Calculated from NSS unit records, 61st round.

The usual arguments proffered for this phenomenon are urbanization linked factors such as the better and higher earning profiles for men and the resultant dissuasion for women's entry into the labour markets; the higher educational attainment of women and the kind of formal sector employment they seek, especially by women belonging to relatively better economic backgrounds, and the burden of household work and other responsibilities which prevent them from supplying their labour in the market.

It is fairly well accepted that women, whether urban or rural, are not a homogeneous category, and therefore, their interaction with the labour market ought to expectedly vary across categories of women. The socially and economically marginalized women are found in the labour market out of compulsion and the level at which they work are often vulnerable, unprotected and inadequately remunerated. This is compounded by the fact that these women display low human capital endowments with poor educational levels if literate; without marketable skills, and inaccessibility to assets and economic resources, on the one hand. On the other extreme of this spectrum lie women who are highly educated, even professionally qualified, but only a few of them are in a position to exercise their right to work for different reasons. These reasons may range from sheer disinterest in taking up employment to conditions that disallow them from undertaking paid work. Apart from many women who are unable to work due to household responsibilities, there are women who are indeed involved in regular employment as salaried workers. This component stands out significantly in the case of urban women. It will be worthwhile to identify who these different women are and which consumption expenditure quintile they belong to, as a proxy indication for their broad household income status.

The work participation for women in urban areas is nearly half of what it is in rural areas. This is largely due to the nature of India's rural economy which depends critically on agriculture and animal husbandry that use substantial segments of unpaid family labour. This aspect remains the same even for the non-farm activities undertaken by rural households. In urban areas also, women undertake unpaid work in family enterprises or contract work as home-based workers in a host of manufacturing-related activities.

Do women in all categories of households participate equally in labour market activities? Is there a difference across income categories in women's work participation? An examination of these patterns is being undertaken here to elucidate the labour market participation of women in India. In villages, women's work participation rate has been around 33 per cent over the decade, while the male WPR has been close to 55 per cent. Women's work participation rate for urban locations was 17 per cent, while the male work participation rate was 55 per cent in 2004–2005 (Table 5.15). Thus, the male WPR is comparable across the rural-urban divide, whereas the female WPR varies quite significantly from rural to urban areas.

Rural areas have registered a slight decline in the WPR for both men and women, while the reverse holds true for the urban areas over the period 1993–1994 to 2004–2005. In a sense, two distinct patterns seem to be operational across rural and urban locations as far as women's work participation is concerned. The variations across income

Table 5.15 *Work Participation Rate (UPSS) for Women and Men*

MPCE Categories	Female Work Participation Rate		Male Work Participation Rate	
	1993–1994	2004–2005	1993–1994	2004–2005
Rural				
Bottom 20%	33.5	29.7	49.3	47.4
Q_2	33.1	32.3	53.3	51.4
Q_3	33.1	33.2	55.9	54.5
Q_4	32.3	33.9	57.6	58.1
Top 20%	31.8	34.5	60.1	61.3
All	32.8	32.7	55.3	54.6
Urban				
Bottom 20%	19.9	19.5	47.2	49.7
Q_2	16.1	18.4	50.1	53.7
Q_3	13.7	14.6	51.2	56.1
Q_4	12.7	14.2	54.4	57.4
Top 20%	14.6	16.1	57.0	57.2
All	15.5	16.6	52.1	54.9

Source: Calculated from NSS unit records, 50th and 61st round.

categories based on the MPCE classifications for women are more poignant, as can be seen in Table 5.15. The poorer women display a higher WPR compared to that of the better-off sections in urban areas, while the reverse is the case with rural women.

The WPR of the poorest women (that is the bottom most quintile group) in rural areas has declined from 34 per cent in 1993–1994 to 30 per cent in 2004–2005, while the better off women have registered an increase in their WPR from 32 per cent to 35 per cent over the same period. The male WPR has also registered a decline in rural areas except among the top two quintiles where a marginal increase is noted.

The urban women's work participation rate has increased from 15.5 to 16.6 during the period 1993–1994 to 2004–2005. The poorest women tend to have a higher WPR, and this holds across time. However, surprisingly, the women of the poorest households have recorded a slight decline in participation levels in the 61st round, 2004–2005 data. This is amidst an overall rise in urban women's work participation rates on the one hand (see Table 5.15). On the other hand, the male WPR among the bottom most quintile has increased from 47 to 50 per cent between 1993–1994 and 2004–2005. However, this increase is across the board for men in urban areas and not a feature of the poorest category of households alone. A look into other details on the status of employment, industrial and occupational categories of poor men and women may shed some light on the matter.

Large sections of women are self-employed in both rural and urban areas, with their share being higher in the villages, close to 64 per cent of women workers. Over time, the share of the self-employed has been rising, especially among women (Tables 5.16 and 5.17). While it may not be entirely clear whether involvement in self-employed activities is a survival-led residual option, an assessment of the HCRs of poverty among households dependent on different categories of employment will elicit some insight. Casual labour has been opted by far less proportion of urban women workers over time, from 26 per cent in 1993–1994 to 17 per cent in 2004–2005.

The sector that is less controversial and more indicative of a positive shift is that of the regular employment growth that too has registered an increase in both rural and urban areas except for urban men. The increase in regular employment across locations is much greater among

Table 5.16 *Distribution of Women Workers (UPSS) by Employment Status*

MPCE Quintiles	1993–1994			2004–2005		
	Self-employed	Regular	Casual	Self-employed	Regular	Casual
	Rural					
Q_1 (bottom 20%)	41.3	1.6	57.1	49.1	2.2	48.6
Q_2	51.6	1.7	46.7	57.4	2.0	40.6
Q_3	61.2	2.2	36.6	63.4	2.7	33.9
Q_4	66.9	2.5	30.6	70.5	3.7	25.8
Q_5 (top 20%)	75.1	5.5	19.4	76.5	7.7	15.8
All	58.8	2.7	38.6	63.7	3.7	32.6
	Urban					
Q_1 (bottom 20%)	43.1	13.4	43.5	52.4	18.0	29.6
Q_2	51.9	16.5	31.6	52.5	25.5	22.0
Q_3	50.4	25.1	24.2	54.9	30.7	14.4
Q_4	48.5	37.2	14.2	45.2	45.7	9.1
Q_5 (top 20%)	29.8	65.6	4.7	31.3	66.1	2.6
All	44.8	29.3	26.0	47.7	35.6	16.7

Source: Calculated from unit level data of NSSO, 61st and 50th round.

Table 5.17 *Employment Status of Men (UPSS) by MPCE Quintiles*

MPCE Quintiles	1993–1994			2004–2005		
	Self-employed	Regular	Casual	Self-employed	Regular	Casual
			Rural			
Q₁ (bottom 20%)	43.0	3.7	53.3	45.4	3.9	50.7
Q₂	52.7	4.8	42.5	53.0	4.9	42.1
Q₃	59.4	6.4	34.2	58.1	6.6	35.3
Q₄	63.8	8.8	27.4	64.7	9.0	26.3
Q₅ (top 20%)	65.8	17.1	17.0	65.6	18.0	16.4
All	57.6	8.5	33.8	58.1	9.0	32.9
			Urban			
Q₁ (bottom 20%)	44.1	21.8	34.1	47.2	22.0	30.9
Q₂	45.0	31.3	23.7	47.8	30.3	21.9
Q₃	44.2	41.1	14.7	46.2	39.6	14.3
Q₄	40.7	49.7	9.7	43.0	49.1	7.9
Q₅ (top 20%)	35.7	60.5	3.8	40.7	57.6	1.8
All	41.6	42.2	16.2	44.8	40.6	14.6

Source: Calculated from unit level data of NSSO, 61st and 50th round.

women in urban areas—from 29 per cent to 36 per cent between 1993–1994 and 2004–2005. However, a look at the employment status across MPCE quintiles is very revealing (Table 5.16). The major distinction is noted between the regular and casual employment, with a larger share of regular employment being concentrated at the top MPCE quintiles, while casual work is predominantly undertaken by poorer women. This pattern is noted in both rural and urban areas among men and women.

The share of regular employment in rural areas remains very low, both for women and men. The access of village women to regular employment remains at the low end, although moving from 3 per cent to 4 per cent over the decade, while rural men have increased their share from 8.5 per cent to 9 per cent over the same period. The better-off sections manage to benefit from such access to regular jobs much more than the poorer households. This leaves casual labour as the only livelihood resort for most of the poor. It is often lamented that the opportunities in the casual labour market are least desirable as they are not only low paying, but also offer insecure forms of employment. Hence, an over time decline in the share of casual workers as noted between the period 1993–1994 and 2004–2005 ought to be a matter for cheer. Certainly, for the segments who have made inroads into regular employment, this may be so. For others who depend on self-employment, the issue of whether such an occupation is a sign of betterment is not entirely clear. Given the fact that the bulk of the women who are self-employed constitute unpaid family workers, which is not necessarily economically empowering in as much as they are not paid as in the case of casual work, such a shift in these (helper) categories of work raises certain fundamental questions.

The decline in urban casual work seems to be a phenomenon which is prominent for women, and a shift into self-employment has been witnessed. From 26 per cent of urban woman casual workers in 1993–1994, the share declined to 17 per cent in 2004–2005. This is much more magnified among the poorest set of urban women, where the proportion of casual employment has declined from 44 per cent in 1993–1994 to 30 per cent in 2004–2005. Most of this decline is substituted by the self-employed category, whereas the share of urban poor women's employment has increased from 43 per cent to 52 per cent during the same period. What kind of work this involves and can there be any indication about whether this ameliorates or deteriorates their poverty situation is an issue that is discussed in the next few paragraphs.

Table 5.18 *HCR of Poverty and Share in Total Number of Poor by Household Type: Rural*

Household Type	HCR (%)		Share in Total Poor	
	1993–1994	2004–2005	1993–1994	2004–2005
Self-employed in non-agriculture	32.21	23.45	10.90	13.69
Agricultural labour	56.75	46.37	42.06	40.74
Other labour	39.69	30.40	7.82	11.20
Self-employed in agriculture	29.19	21.52	32.33	29.98
Others	17.57	14.12	3.75	4.38
All	37.21	28.29	100.00	100.00

Source: Calculated from the unit level data of Schh 1.0 from NSS 50th round (1993–1994) and NSS 61st round (2004–2005).
Note: Households are divided in different categories according to their principal source of earning. These categories are defined as 'household type'.

In order to examine the change in the poverty levels across different household types, the HCR and share of poor were calculated. In rural areas, the HCR is highest among the households dependent on agricultural labour, while in the urban areas it is predominantly the casual workers who report to have the highest HCRs (Tables 5.18 and 5.19). In terms of the share of the poor also, rural agricultural labour forms a substantial segment with 41 per cent. In urban locations, on the contrary, the bulk of the poor (46%) are among households dependent on self-employed activities. What is also noteworthy is that both the self-employed and the casual labour category of households are exhibiting an increase over time in the share of the urban poor (Table 5.19).

Among the self-employed, while the men are own account workers, the women tend to find themselves working as unpaid family workers. Across rural–urban areas, there are differences in the share of own account women workers and the unpaid family helpers. In the villages, three-fourths of the self-employed are unpaid family workers, while one-fourth are own account workers (Table 5.20). In urban towns and cities, self-employed women are one-half of own account workers

Table 5.19 HCR of Poverty and Share in Total Number of Poor by Household Type: Urban

Household Type	HCR (%)		Share in Total Poor	
	1993–1994	2004–2005	1993–1994	2004–2005
Self-employed	36.19	27.69	42.32	46.41
Regular salary/wage earning	20.93	15.29	26.93	23.52
Casual labour	62.64	57.04	24.49	26.04
Others	26.48	16.12	4.29	3.66
All	32.63	25.62	100.00	100.00

Source: Same as Table 5.18.
Note: Same as Table 5.18.

and one-half of unpaid family labour, with the share of the latter being higher among the poorer households in general.

One of the most striking variations is displayed among the regular salaried employees among the urban working women. The poorest women have also gained in terms of access to regular employment from 13 per cent in 1993–1994 to 18 per cent in 2004–2005. The share of gain in regular jobs increases as the expenditure quintiles move up. Women belonging to the affluent, very rich, higher quintile of MPCE households, if working, are mostly regular formal sector employees. Over time, however, there is not much change in the share of regular employment among the top quintile group. Nevertheless, more than two thirds of the working women among these rich households are among the secure salaried employment, while another 31 per cent of them are self-employed workers.

Industrial and Occupational Distribution

This section addresses the following questions: Where are the poor women working? What are the industries in which poor women workers are employed? What changes are witnessed over time? Also, are the labour market conditions facing poor households similar for men and women or are there any dissimilarities?

Table 5.20 *Self-employed Men and Women by Work Status: 1993–1994 and 2004–2005*

MPCE Quintile	1993–1994			2004–2005		
Rural Men	Own Account	Employer	Unpaid Family Worker	Own Account	Employer	Unpaid Family Worker
Q_1 (bottom 20%)	68.8	0.9	30.3	68.8	0.3	31.0
Q_2	67.2	1.8	31.0	70.8	0.7	28.5
Q_3	67.9	3.0	29.1	70.8	1.0	28.2
Q_4	68.0	4.4	27.6	71.6	1.8	26.7
Q_5 (top 20%)	66.9	8.5	24.5	71.9	5.7	22.5
All	67.7	4.2	28.1	71.0	2.2	26.8
Rural women						
Q_1 (bottom 20%)	22.5	0.4	77.1	20.6	0.2	79.2
Q_2	21.3	0.6	78.1	21.5	0.2	78.3
Q_3	24.4	0.8	74.8	23.7	0.4	75.9
Q_4	26.1	1.5	72.4	24.9	0.8	74.3
Q_5 (top 20%)	30.7	4.1	65.2	30.8	2.6	66.5
All	25.2	1.5	73.2	24.7	0.9	74.3
Urban men						
Q_1 (bottom 20%)	77.7	1.2	21.2	79.2	0.2	20.6
Q_2	76.4	3.3	20.3	78.7	1.5	19.8
Q_3	74.5	5.3	20.2	77.6	2.8	19.6

(Continued)

(Continued)

MPCE Quintile	1993–1994			2004–2005		
Rural Men	Own Account	Employer	Unpaid Family Worker	Own Account	Employer	Unpaid Family Worker
Q_4	72.0	8.6	19.4	75.2	7.5	17.3
Q_5 (top 20%)	68.9	17.3	13.8	65.0	20.3	14.7
All	73.9	7.2	19.0	75.2	6.4	18.4
Urban women						
Q_1 (bottom 20%)	50.5	0.4	49.1	46.5	0.1	53.4
Q_2	49.2	0.7	50.0	45.5	0.7	53.8
Q_3	50.9	1.4	47.7	48.3	1.4	50.3
Q_4	54.4	1.8	43.9	54.4	1.1	44.6
Q_5 (top 20%)	59.3	9.1	31.6	52.6	9.2	38.2
All	51.8	1.8	46.4	48.5	1.7	49.8

Source: Calculated from unit level data of NSSO, 61st and 50th round.

The bulk of the workforce in rural villages is involved in primary sector activities which include agriculture and related occupations based on animal and natural resources. The share of primary sector workers is, however, gradually declining over time, much more for men than among women (Table 5.21). In non-agricultural employment in rural areas, apart from manufacturing, construction, trade and hotels have registered an increase over time and yet almost three quarters of the rural workforce remains involved in the primary sector. It is urban areas employment and industrial distribution that display certain interesting patterns.

Primary sector activities have been on the decline in urban areas as well as both the men's and women's workforce. Urban women's employment has risen in manufacturing, trade, hotels and restaurants and to some extent in the services sector (Table 5.22). The increase

Table 5.21 *Industrial Distribution of Women and Men Workers (UPSS): 1993–1994 and 2004–2005 (Rural)*

Industry	1993–1994		2004–2005	
	Woman	Man	Woman	Man
Agriculture, hunting, forestry & fishing	86.2	73.9	83.3	66.5
Mining & quarrying	0.4	0.7	0.3	0.6
Manufacturing	7.1	6.9	8.4	7.9
Electricity, gas & water supply	0.0	0.3	0.0	0.2
Construction	0.8	3.2	1.5	6.8
Trade, hotels & restaurants	2.1	5.5	2.5	8.3
Transport, storage & communication	0.1	2.2	0.2	3.8
Finance, insurance, real estate & business	0.1	0.4	0.1	0.7
Community, social & personal services	3.3	6.7	3.8	5.1
Total	100.0	100.0	100.0	100.0

Source: Calculated from unit level employment–unemployment data of NSS 50th (1993–1994) and 61st (2004–2005) rounds.
Note: UPSS taken together.

Table 5.22 *Industrial Distribution of Women and Men Workers (UPSS): 1993–1994 and 2004–2005 (Urban)*

Industry	1993–1994		2004–2005	
	Women	Men	Women	Men
Agriculture, hunting, forestry & fishing	24.7	9.0	18.1	6.1
Mining & quarrying	0.7	1.3	0.2	0.9
Manufacturing	24.2	23.5	28.2	23.5
Electricity, gas & water supply	0.3	1.2	0.2	0.8
Construction	4.0	6.9	3.8	9.2
Trade, hotels & restaurants	10.1	22.0	12.2	28.0
Transport, storage & communication	1.3	9.8	1.4	10.7
Finance, insurance, real estate & business	1.9	3.8	3.3	5.9
Community, social & personal services	32.7	22.3	32.7	14.8
Total	100.0	100.0	100.0	100.0

Source: Calculated from unit level employment–unemployment data of NSS 50th (1993–1994) and 61st (2004–2005) rounds.
Note: UPSS: Usual principal and subsidiary status taken together.

in manufacturing activities is, however, not noted for the urban male workforce. Construction work has engaged urban men quite substantially, while the share of these activities in female employment has declined over time. Increasing mechanization and the use of prefabricated construction methods have witnessed the employment of men in this sector. The other sector where male employment is increasing is trade, hotels and restaurants, followed by the services sector.

An examination of the poorest MPCE quintile reveals that primary activities have registered a sharp decline even among the poorest households, both for men and women. From 36 per cent in 1993–1994, the share of women's employment in agriculture, hunting, forestry and fishing has declined to 26 per cent in 2004–2005. The industries where a substantial rise in women's employment has occurred are manufacturing, construction, trade, hotels and restaurants (Table 5.23).

Table 5.23 *Industrial Distribution of the Poorest (Bottom MPCE Quintile, Q1) of Women and Men Workers (UPSS): 1993–1994 and 2004–2005 (Urban)*

Industry	Woman		Man	
	1993–1994	2004–2005	1993–1994	2004–2005
Agriculture, hunting, forestry & fishing	36.0	25.7	19.2	10.5
Mining & quarrying	0.8	0.1	1.1	0.4
Manufacturing	26.9	35.0	20.0	22.4
Electricity, gas & water supply	0.1	0.1	0.5	0.3
Construction	4.8	5.9	10.5	16.9
Trade, hotels & restaurants	9.0	12.3	20.8	28.9
Transport, storage & communication	0.6	0.5	10.3	11.6
Finance, insurance, real estate & business	0.2	0.7	1.1	1.7
Community, social & personal services	21.4	19.8	16.5	7.4
Total	100.0	100.0	100.0	100.0

Source: Calculated from unit level employment–unemployment data of NSS 50th (1993–1994) and 61st (2004–2005) rounds.
Note: UPSS: Usual principal and subsidiary status taken together.

The poorest women seek employment in manufacturing and primary sector activities. The difference over time is that the former has been increasing, while the latter has been declining. Trade, hotels and eateries are other prominent activities employing women, mostly as self-employed and unpaid helpers. Construction activities among the urban poor constitute an important livelihood source employing women and men.

The occupational profile of the urban poor is given in Table 5.24 with over time changes. A bulk of the poor urban women (40%) and male workforce (55%) mostly undertake production-related manual labour. In spite of the declining share of primary activities even for the poorest quintile, 26 per cent of women continue to draw their

Table 5.24 *Occupational Distribution of the Poorest (Bottom MPCE Quintile, Q1) of Women and Men Workers (UPSS): 1993–1994 and 2004–2005 (Urban)*

Occupation	Woman		Man	
	1993–1994	2004–2005	1993–1994	2004–2005
Professional, technical & related workers	1.4	1.6	2.3	2.0
Administrative, executive & managerial workers	1.4	3.4	1.8	3.2
Clerical & related workers	0.7	0.4	3.3	2.1
Sales workers	7.6	9.7	17.3	19.2
Services workers	17.1	19.5	7.3	8.1
Farmers, fishermen, hunters, loggers & related workers	36.1	25.6	19.0	10.6
Production & related workers; Transport equipment operators & labourers	35.6	39.7	48.9	54.9
Workers (NEC)	0.1	0.0	0.1	0.0
Total	100.0	100.0	100.0	100.0

Source: Calculated from unit level employment–unemployment data of NSS 50th (1993–1994) and 61st (2004–2005) rounds.
Note: UPSS: Usual principal and subsidiary status taken together; NEC: Not elsewhere classified.

livelihood from working in these activities. Service work engages 20 per cent of poor women workers, while sales workers constitute 8 per cent. The situation of poor male workers is marginally different from that of their female counterparts. Sales work is relatively more prominent for poor men.

Given the concentration of self-employment, it is not surprising that, even for women workers, the proprietary segment constitutes a major bulk—57 per cent. The government sector of employment, most of which is likely to be in the organized sector, occupies 15 per cent of urban women workers, while private corporate employment only caters to 6 per cent of urban women employment as per the principal status

(Table 5.24). One major segment with 14 per cent of the principal workers employed is with private households as service providers, that is, domestic servants, cooks, drivers and gardeners, etc. Nearly one-fifth of the women workers from the two bottommost quintiles undertake such work. A further analysis of the regular workforce will elicit insights into the nature of poor women's participation as compared with the richer counterparts in urban areas.

Differential Access to Regular Employment in Urban Areas

The gains in employment for urban women in regular employment are distinct and reflect the education quotient clearly. While there remains a class-based inequality across MPCE quintiles, it is important to examine whether the returns earned by regular workers across consumption quintiles vary significantly. Also, what kinds of work do these regular workers among different classes of women undertake? And is the work poorer women undertake even with the regular employment mainly that of service providers for the relatively better-off sections of the population?

The analysis across the poorest and richest quintiles reveals the differences in labour market access for women across quintiles. Adopting a classification of any enterprise having 10 or more workers as organized and all others as unorganized, the regular workers have been divided into organized and unorganized sectors across MPCE quintiles. The bulk of the poorest women who are regular workers are employed in the unorganized sector, while the exact opposite picture is true for the richest quintile with 70 per cent women working in the organized sector (Table 5.25).

For regular workers, there is a substantial difference in the share of organized workers in the poorest and richest quintiles. The share of organized workers varies from 20 per cent in case of the poorest to 70 per cent in case of richest quintile regular workers (Table 5.26).

It can be seen that a staggering proportion of 53 per cent regular women workers is engaged in jobs with private households as maid servants, cooks, etc., in the poorest quintile (Table 5.27). The share of jobs in private households is also quite high in the next higher quintile of poor households. In the richest quintile, however,

Table 5.25 *Distribution of Women Workers (Principal Status) within MPCE Quintiles by Types of Enterprises: 2004–2005 (Urban)*

MPCE Quintiles	Proprietary	Govt/ Public Sector	Pvt. Corporate Sector	Pvt. HH.	Others
Q₁ (bottom 20%)	70.4	2.0	3.4	18.7	5.5
Q₂	67.6	4.5	3.1	18.8	6.0
Q₃	65.2	8.9	4.4	13.7	7.8
Q⁴	53.4	19.9	4.8	11.0	10.9
Q₅ (top 20%)	30.4	35.9	11.1	7.3	15.3
All	56.7	14.6	5.5	13.9	9.3

Source: Calculated from unit level employment–unemployment data of NSS 61st (2004–2005) round.

Table 5.26 *Distribution (%) of Regular Workers into Organized and Unorganized by MPCE Quintiles: 2004–2005 (Urban)*

MPCE Quintiles	Organized	Unorganized
Q₁ (bottom 20%)	19.1	80.9
Q₂	24.3	75.7
Q₃	37.6	62.4
Q₄	51.8	48.2
Q₅ (top 20%)	70.0	30.0
All	47.5	52.5

Source: Calculated from unit level employment–unemployment data of NSS 61st (2004–2005) round.

61 per cent of all regular workers are in government/public or large private organizations.

These differences in regular women workers between the poorest and the richest quintile are reflected in the nature of job contracts and social security benefits. In the poorest quintile, 91 per cent of jobs are based on verbal contracts (6% of jobs are based on written contracts) as opposed to 55 per cent of such contracts in the richest quintile,

Table 5.27 *Distribution (%) of Women Regular Workers (Principal Status) within MPCE Quintiles by Enterprise Types: 2004–2005 (Urban)*

MPCE Quintiles	Proprietary	Govt/ Public Sector	Pvt Corporate Sector	Pvt HH.	Others
Q$_1$ (bottom 20%)	24.8	6.5	10.4	52.7	5.6
Q$_2$	32.3	11.5	6.1	43.7	6.4
Q$_3$	29.2	19.5	10.0	27.2	14.1
Q$_4$	27.9	32.4	8.0	15.2	16.5
Q$_5$ (top 20%)	12.4	48.0	13.2	9.3	17.1
All	22.8	30.5	10.2	21.5	15.0

Source: Calculated from unit level employment–unemployment data of NSS 61st (2004–2005) round.

Table 5.28 *Distribution (%) of Women Regular Workers (Principal Status) within MPCE Quintiles by Types of Job Contract: 2004–2005 (Urban)*

MPCE Quintiles	No Written Job Contract	Written Job Contracts	
		More Than Three Years	Others
Q$_1$ (bottom 20%)	90.5	5.9	3.6
Q$_2$	84.9	12.0	3.1
Q$_3$	71.6	23.9	4.5
Q$_4$	55.5	37.6	6.9
Q$_5$ (top 20%)	37.8	54.5	7.7
All	60.4	33.7	5.9

Source: Calculated from unit level employment–unemployment data of NSS 61st (2004–2005) round.

whereas 38 per cent of jobs are based on unwritten contracts (Table 5.28). These contracts are for three or more years. In India, the practice of short-term written contract jobs is negligible.

In social security benefit also similar contrasting pattern can be observed. One gets full benefits in job or none. At the poorest quintile, only 3 per cent of regular women workers get all benefits and a huge 90 per cent gets no benefit. At richest quintile, 49 per cent of regular workers get full benefits and 30 per cent gets none (Table 5.29).

The average wage/salary received is as expected—higher for better-off quintiles, and there is a substantial disparity between men

Table 5.29 *Distribution (%) of Women Regular Workers (Principal) within MPCE Quintiles by Type of Social Security Benefits*

MPCE Quintiles	Not Eligible for Any Benefit	Only PF/ Pension	Eligible for PF/Pension, Gratuity Health & Maternity Benefit
Q_1 (bottom 20%)	92.2	2.6	2.9
Q_2	87.5	3.4	5.5
Q_3	72.9	5.2	13.1
Q_4	55.9	7.5	23.2
Q_5 (top 20%)	29.9	9.2	49.9
All	58.5	6.5	26.6

Source: Calculated from unit level employment–unemployment data of NSS 61st (2004–2005) round.
Note: Only major two types of social security benefits are given in the table. Rows will not add up to 100.0.

Table 5.30 *Average Wage/Salary Received (Rs.) by Regular Workers (Current Daily Status) by Gender and MPCE Quintiles (Age Group: 15–59 Years): 2004–2005 (Urban)*

MPCE Quintiles	Men	Women
Q_1 (bottom 20%)	79.49	33.31
Q_2	100.02	53.95
Q_3	135.06	76.49
Q_4	178.74	118.45
Q_5 (top 20%)	338.35	276.24
All	200.99	150.97

Source: Calculated from unit level employment–unemployment data of NSS 61st (2004–2005) round.

and women's average earnings (Table 5.30). The gender disparity declines among the higher MPCE quintile workers, reflecting the better educational qualifications and professional jobs that the women from better-off households enter as employees.

There are also women who do not opt for or cannot take up employment owing to the burden of domestic responsibilities. How many women are affected thus and what are the consequences of this for poor women both in rural and urban areas is what the next section looks at.

BURDEN OF DOMESTIC RESPONSIBILITIES

Does the burden of domestic responsibilities prevent women from opting for formal work and are the implications of the absence of other members to carry out domestic duties for the poor different from that of the richer women? The poorer women may be more constrained for hiring paid help, on the one hand, while the socio-religious constraints on using domestic assistance for certain domestic chores may be operative in certain households, on the other.

While certain women are bound by the regularity of domestic duties that take up most of their time, are there any variations across quintile groups? Of those women who are not spending most of their time on household duties, what are the reasons for their continuing to be principally involved in it? Is it non-availability of work or by own preference? Are there variations across MPCE categories in the work constraints faced by women in terms of non-availability?

The NSS data uses two codes for eliciting information on domestic duties (92 and 93).[2] Of all women, 89 per cent in urban areas and 87 per cent in rural areas are involved in domestic duties with little variation across the MPCE quintiles (Table 5.31). In other words, it would be appropriate to state that most women tend to have domestic responsibilities that occupy them throughout the year. This kind of domestic role is shared by women across cities, towns and villages. It is also more or less the same irrespective of the expenditure quintile-based class they belong to.

Among the women undertaking domestic duties, will they accept work if made available at home in spite of their preoccupation? Relatively more women in villages declared their willingness to accept

Table 5.31 *Share (%) Women Involved in Domestic Duties by MPCE Quintiles: 2004–2005 (Status: 92 and 93)*

MPCE Quintiles	Rural	Urban
Q$_1$ (bottom 20%)	85.9	87.6
Q$_2$	85.7	87.9
Q$_3$	88.0	89.7
Q$_4$	88.0	89.2
Q$_5$ (top 20%)	88.4	89.3
All	87.2	88.8

Source: Calculated from unit level employment–unemployment data of NSS 61st (2004–2005) round.

work—close to 33 per cent. In urban areas, around 27 per cent of the women were willing to take up work. In both instances, a majority of them seek regular part-time work. The proportion of poor women willing to accept work is higher than that of the richest quintile group (Table 5.32).

This is a reflection of the high potential for home-based work, developing of self-help group-based activities and training women in entrepreneurial activities which can be undertaken on a part-time basis.

Table 5.32 *Share (%) of Women Willing to Accept Work despite Their Preoccupation in Domestic Duties by MPCE Quintiles: 2004–2005*

MPCE Quintiles	% Willingness to Accept Work	
	Rural	Urban
Q$_1$ (bottom 20%)	36.4	35.4
Q$_2$	36.2	32.0
Q$_3$	32.7	29.3
Q$_4$	30.2	23.2
Q$_5$ (top 20%)	27.6	16.8
All	32.6	27.3

Source: Calculated from unit level employment–unemployment data of NSS 61st (2004–2005) round.

Policies for amelioration of poverty among women must be oriented towards and woven around such activities.

CONCLUDING REMARKS

Finally, some of the prominent findings based on the detailed analysis of rural and urban women's poverty, employment and well-being are highlighted in this section. Given the poverty line estimations provided by the Planning Commission Expert Group, the actual numbers of poor are increasing in urban areas, while they are clearly declining in rural areas. The compound growth rate of poverty estimated in actual numbers from 1993–1994 to 2004–2005 is higher for women than for men. Women in urban areas are also affected because of poverty as well as gender-based discrimination. Given the increasing incidence of poverty in terms of absolute numbers of poor women and the higher compound growth rate between the years 1993–1994 and 2004–2005, there is the need for specific focus on poor women in urban India. Also, the HCR of poverty among women-headed households is higher in urban areas compared to male-headed households.

Even the demographic composition or sex ratios among different expenditure quintiles reveal a higher or more equitable gender balance among the poorer households in both rural and urban locations. This also means that women bear the brunt of poverty much more as compared to men. Apart from this gender balance in the populations, the societal biases stemming from patriarchal values discriminate and assign undue burden on poor women who have to shoulder domestic responsibilities as well as economic work. Without adequate educational attainment, the employment avenues available to them remain informal, low paying and highly insecure. The lack of access to basic amenities and civil rights for the poor migrants who seek livelihood in urban areas makes their working and living conditions very vulnerable and women among the poor suffer most due to this. Women-headed households are also noted to be more among the urban poor compared to the rural poor.

It is noteworthy that although poorer women report a higher work participation rate compared to other categories, the female work participation rate has been registering a slight decline among the poorer households over time. Casual employment remains the major source for poor women in villages and urban locations in spite of the fact that, over time, there has been a substantial decline in the share of casual workers among the poorest households. A shift into self-employed activities and regular employment is noted.

An increasing trend of recourse to self-employment is noted, with the majority of poor women working as helpers in household enterprises. This could be a reflection of shifts in male employment patterns from casual to self-employed enterprises, wherein women also join in as helpers. The alternative argument of non-availability of work compelling poor women into self-employment as a residual activity may also be operative to some extent. In urban areas, the bulk of the poor households are dependent on this activity and the share of the poor in self-employment is increasing over time.

The positive shift in employment status noted among urban women is the increase in regular workers. While women belonging to the relatively better off sections of the population are increasingly entering the regular formal sector, poor women's opportunities are often a derivative of this increasing participation of the former set of women. The household responsibilities and services of working women in urban areas are increasingly being passed on to hired service providers. While women belonging to poorer households undertake these tasks, the returns they can manage improve with education and skill/training. Unless investments are made for women's education up to secondary and above levels, their entry into regular and relatively better paying jobs will continue to remain low. Given the compulsive participation of poor women in economic work, it is important to focus on measures that can assist them in accessing better avenues of work with scope for part-time regular work options.

NOTES

1. The child sex ratio (CSR), defined as the number of girls per 1,000 boys in the age group of 0–6 years for the slum population, is 919, which is significantly higher than the 904 recorded for non-slum urban areas. The CSR—an indicator which accounts for the noise factor of migration into urban cities and their seeking residence in slums—reflects an even clearer picture of the lower incidence of such gender-biased elimination or pre-birth selection being practised among poor urbanites.

    Inhuman murder is made technologically sophisticated when resorted to pre-birth sex determination-based abortion of woman's foetuses. The cost of these medical facilities cannot be afforded by the really poor; it is the non-poor who use these techniques. Also, the poor view any additional member as another working hand, and therefore a productive economic investment that will fetch returns. For the poor, the cost of investment into any child is relatively lower when compared to that of the non-poor. Additionally, the mortality rate of infants and children is higher owing to lower levels of nutrition and access to healthcare facilities. Slum dwellers tend to have a different approach to children and their protection. The survival of children—irrespective of gender—is a struggle that slum dwellers go through; hence, the reverse practice of killing any child would be against the grain of their existential philosophies (Rustagi, 2006).

2. While attending domestic duties only is Code-92, attending to domestic duties and also engaged in free collection of goods (vegetables, roots, firewood, cattle feed, etc.), sewing, tailoring, weaving, etc., for household use falls in Code-93.

REFERENCES

Agnihotri, S. B. (2000). *Sex ratio patterns in the Indian population: A fresh Exploration.* SAGE Publications.

Buvinic, M., Lycette, M. A., & McGreevey, W. P. (Ed.). (1983). *Women and poverty in the Third World.* The Johns Hopkins University Press.

Cagatay, N. (1998). Gender and poverty (Working Paper Series, No. 5). UNDP Social Development and Poverty Elimination Division.

Chant, S. (1992). *Gender and migration in developing countries.* Belhaven.

————. (2003). Woman household headship and the feminisation of poverty: Facts, fictions and forward strategies (New Working Paper Series, Issue 9). Gender Institute, LSE Gender Institute, London School of Economics, London. http://eprints.lse.ac.uk/574/1/femaleHouseholdHeadship.pdf

Gangopadhyay, S., & Wadhwa, W. (2003, November). Are Indian women-headed households more vulnerable to poverty. India Development Foundation, Delhi. https://citeseerx.ist.psu.edu/viewdoc/download?doi=10.1.1.541.1540&rep=rep1&type=pdf

Ghosh, J. (1998). Assessing poverty alleviation strategies for their impact on poor women: Study with special reference to India (Discussion Paper No. 97). United Nations Research Institute for Social Development, October. https://www.files.ethz.ch/isn/28922/dp97.pdf

GOI. (2007). *Poverty estimates for 2004–05.* Press Information Bureau, New Delhi, March 21. https://niti.gov.in/planningcommission.gov.in/docs/news/prmar07.pdf

Jackson, C., & Palmer-Jones, R. (2000). Rethinking gendered poverty and work. In S. Razavi (Ed.), *Gendered Poverty and Well-being* (1st ed., pp. 145–170). Wiley-Blackwell.

Kundu, A. (1993). *In the name of the poor: Access to basic amenities.* SAGE Publications.

Mahadevia, D., & Sarkar, S. (2004). Poverty, levels of living and employment structure in the small and medium size towns. Report submitted to CSO by Institute for Human Development, New Delhi.

Masika, R., De Haan, A., & Baden, S. (1997). Urbanisation and urban poverty: A gender analysis. Gender Equality Unit, Swedish International Development Cooperation Agency (SIDA), BRIDGE, IDS, Sussex. https://d1wqtxts1xzle7.cloudfront. net/52624585/Urbanisation_and_urban_poverty_A_gender_20170414-15748-1a05njm.pdf?1492217287=&response-content-disposition=inline%3 B+filename%3DUrbanisation_and_urban_poverty_a_gender.pdf&Expires=1 622376152&Signature=Wq--~nM6-T9RGs7ptE~IKAEGFMIEZLS84Z~b-~z2wPpTKbeJ1hk~y~KUFo2C8fxSd0dwV1oSyAgcqXGpDmSMBcbjta JzQ3Uc6LBuflmSmClHnLcOQ1EIt6pyoYjdOafz3DFD~JZ7IrllfqHtHU 9DSPMNkGiq28ohfcq~7hoyo~s68D0bb5jaz0RdCLapR2WoYKygKlr6 eEHgIto7YQlOYn3hj8eBMVDQzqUPMTCxC9jGdbz69AlBXf5qGx-ynKU-9LeiDXRCDc7iauNrf0T-dFrSepH~ucoX8inUCOdT4NRpPT6x-6-OCwe1OA~3bs8RcrDt8Z89lUPtwSPuKgfA~A__&Key-Pair-Id= APKAJLOHF5GGSLRBV4ZA

Mathur, O. P. (1994). Women, urban poverty and economic development. In N. Heyzer & G. Sen (Ed.), *Gender, economic growth and poverty: Market growth and state planning in Asia and the Pacific*, Kali for Women. International Books.

McLanahan, S., Sorensen A., & Watson, D. (1989). Sex differences in poverty 1950–1980. *Signs, 15*(1), 102–122.

McLanahan, S. S., & Kelly, E. L. (1999). The feminisation of poverty: Past and future. In J. Saltzman Chafetz (Ed.), *Handbook of the sociology of gender*. Kluwer Academic/Plenum Publishers.

Mitra, A. (2006). Labour market mobility of low income households. *Economic and Political Weekly, 41*(21).

Mitra, K., & Pool, G. R. (2000). Why women stay poor: An examination of Indian poverty in India. *Social Change, 30*(1/2).

NSSO. (2007). *Employment and unemployment situation in India 2004–05*. Report No. 515, 61st round. National Sample Survey Organisation, Ministry of Statistic and Programme Implementation, Government of India. http://mospi. nic.in/sites/default/files/publication_reports/515part1_final.pdf

Pearce, D. (1978). The feminisation of poverty: Women, work and welfare. *Urban and Social Change Review, 11*, 28–36.

Razavi, S. (2000). *Gendered poverty and well-being*. Institute of Social Studies, Blackwell.

Rodgers, G. (1989). Urban poverty and the labour market: Access to jobs and incomes in Asian and Latin American cities. World Employment Programme, ILO, Geneva.

Rustagi, P. (2006). The deprived, discriminated and damned girl child: Story of declining child sex ratios in India. *Women's Health and Urban Life: An International and Interdisciplinary Journal, 5*(1), 6–26.

World Bank. (1990). *World development report 1990*. Oxford University Press, June. https://openknowledge.worldbank.org/bitstream/handle/10986/5973/ WDR%201990%20-%20English.pdf?sequence=5

Chapter 6

Poverty and Disability in India*

Ambati Nageswara Rao

INTRODUCTION

Poverty has been described as a situation of 'pronounced deprivation in well-being' and being poor as

> To be hungry, to lack shelter and clothing, to be sick and not cared for, to be illiterate and not schooled.... Poor people are particularly vulnerable to adverse events outside their control. They are often treated badly by institutions of the state and society and excluded from voice and power in those institutions.
>
> (IBRD, 2001)

Using income as a measure of poverty, the *World Development Report* refers to the 'deep poverty amid plenty' in the world and states that a fifth of the world's people live on less than $1 a day, and 44 per cent of them are in South Asia.

Poverty and disability are closely linked and have a detrimental impact on the level of inclusion in society and its overall development. From the social perspective, both poverty and disability are products of capitalist development in a given society. Hence, this suggests society as the focal point of action to deal with both poverty and disability having created them in the first place. This is mainly through restructuring societal policies and provisions, including those of the economy.

* *Social Change* Vol 39, no. 1 (March 2009): 29–45.

According to the United Nations, 1 person in 20 has a disability. More than three out of four of these live in a developing country. Recent World Bank estimates suggest they may account for as many as one in five of the world's poorest (Elwan, 1999). Disability limits access to education and employment, and leads to economic and social exclusion (DFID, 2000). Poor people with disabilities are caught in a vicious cycle of poverty and disability, each being both a cause and consequence of the other. Therefore, it is argued that poverty alleviation is a key solution to prevent directly and indirectly. Breaking the chain of economic dependency of the poor requires the eradicator of poverty to help overcome the problems of social and economic deprivation. In this sense, poverty eradication can be regarded as a prerequisite to development.

Various measures can be considered as instrumental strategies in fighting widespread poverty amongst disabled people. This primarily includes different kinds of remunerated employment schemes as well as policies, legislation and welfare provisions. Together, these may facilitate the creation of an inclusive society, which allows disabled to people develop their economic potential and ultimately strengthen their independent life.

OBJECTIVES

The purpose of the study is to gain a deeper understanding of the relationship between poverty and disability.

1. First, it summarizes the current state of knowledge about disability and poverty.
2. Second, it discusses the relationship between disability and poverty.
3. Third, it explains the reason behind the lack of reliable information on disability and its impact.
4. Fourth, it describes the policy interventions aimed at greater inclusion of disabled people in the country's development process.

METHODOLOGY

Definitions of poverty and disability were searched on the Internet and in books and various publications. Google Scholar was used to trace articles and books and some articles. Several terms (poverty, disability, handicap, impairment, discrimination, exclusion, etc.) were used to search for articles on the link or definition. Articles used were first scrutinized on sources referring to a possible link between disability and poverty and sources that were seen as reliable.

DEFINITIONS

Before making any comparisons to existing data on incidence of poverty and disability, it is important to define what is understood by poverty and disability. There are many different definitions used in research studies that focus on disability and poverty.

Defining Poverty

In order to define poverty, it is important to realize that poverty has a multidimensional nature and to first consider which factors indicate poverty. In the different definitions that exist, many different factors are being mentioned, which makes it hard to indicate one specific definition as being the best or most accurate one. Mention is also made of two sorts of poverty, namely absolute poverty and relative poverty.

Absolute Poverty

If poverty is defined in absolute terms, needs are considered to be fixed at a level which provides for subsistence, basic household equipment and expenditure on essential services such as water, sanitation, health, education and transport (Wratten, 1995). The absolute definition is in common use by the World Bank and governments. However, it does not describe the extent of income inequality within society nor the fact that needs are socially determined and change over time. The absolute definition has to be adjusted periodically to take account of technological developments such as improved methods of sanitation.

Relative Poverty

The concept of relative poverty is more flexible and allows for minimum needs to be revised as standards of living in society alter.

It reflects the view that poverty imposes withdrawal or exclusion from active membership of society: People are relatively deprived if they cannot obtain 'the conditions of life, that is, diets, amenities, standards and services, which allow them to play the roles, participate in the relationships and follow the customary behaviour which is expected of them by virtue of their membership of society.

The United Nations describes poverty as 'the denial of opportunities and choices most basic to human development to lead a long, healthy, creative life and to enjoy a decent standard of living, freedom, dignity, self-esteem and the respect of others' (United Nations Development Programme, 1997).

The Chronic Poverty Research Centre states in its report on chronic poverty that there is no objective way of defining poverty. Many countries have defined their own poverty lines, which would represent the level of income or consumption necessary to meet the minimum requirements, such as clothing, housing and healthcare. Most countries use the minimum amount of nutritional intake needed in order to measure poverty, but different nutritional norms are used. When every country adopts its own poverty line, it becomes impossible to make cross-country comparisons with regard to poverty, and someone defined as poor in one country might not be poor according to standards used in other countries.

INCIDENCE OF POVERTY IN INDIA

The Planning Commission estimates the incidence of poverty in India on the basis of household consumer expenditure surveys conducted by the National Sample Survey Organization. Table 6.1 shows that the incidence of poverty expressed as a percentage of people below the poverty line declined continuously from 51.3 per cent to supposedly 19 per cent.

However, the pace of reduction in poverty varied considerably during this period, with a large decline in the percentage of the population in poverty throughout the 1980s, a slowdown in the pace of poverty reduction in the early 1990s and a reported but contested sharp 10 per cent decline in poverty in the second half of the 1990s. The decline in poverty after Independence, particularly in the 1970s,

Table 6.1 Poverty in India after the 1970s

Year	Poverty Ratio Percentage		
	Rural	Urban	Combined
1977–1978	53.1	45.2	51.3
1983	45.7	40.8	44.5
1987–1988	39.1	38.2	38.9
1993–1994	37.3	32.4	36.0
1999–2000	27.1	23.6	26.1
2007	21.1	15.1	19.3

Source: The Tenth Five-year Plan.

is attributed to the various poverty alleviation programmes started by governments in various states of the country (Sooden and Kumar).

The most important of these programmes which have a direct attack on poverty included the Twenty Point Programme (1975); public distribution system which had been revamped in 1975; blocks in remote and backward areas to increase the supply of essential consumer items at cheaper rates for the poor in 1775; Food for Work and Antyodaya Yojana (1977–1978); Training Rural Youth for Self-employment (1979); Jawahar Rozgar Yojana (1989); Ganga Kalyan Yojana (1997–1998); Swarna Jayanti Gram Swarozgar Yojana (1999); Pradhan Mantri Gramodaya Yojana (2000); Pradhan Mantri Gram Sadak Yojana (2000); National Food for Work Programme (2004), and National Rural Employment Guarantee Act (2005).

The National Rural Employment Guarantee Act was launched in Bandlapalli village of Anantapur district in Andhra Pradesh on 2 February 2006. This step has been viewed as historic and revolutionary in the history of independent India because the act will create a new rural infrastructure and improve road connectivity, school buildings and water supply to the villages. The Act guarantees 100 days of wage employment in a year to every rural household in 80,000 villages in 200 districts across the country.

CONCEPT OF DISABILITY

According to the 2001 Census of India, people with disability are 21,906,769 in India, which constitute more than 2 per cent of total population.[1] There are several definitions in use to describe persons with disabilities, and most of them reflect an understanding that disability is an individual pathology, a condition grounded in the physiological, biological and intellectual impairment of an individual. According to the Persons with Disabilities (Equal Opportunities, Protection of Rights and Full Participation) Act, 1995, of the Government of India, a person with disability is defined as a person suffering from not less than 40 per cent of any disability as certified by a medical authority. The conditions of disability include blindness, low vision, hearing impairment, locomotor disability, mental retardation leprosy and mental illness which have been listed as disability in the National Trust Act of 1999 (Singh, 2005).

Disability is a complex phenomenon to measure for a number of reasons. People's understanding of definitions of disability and the concept of disability itself vary: It is possible for one person to define themselves as disabled when another person with an identical condition would not. One reason for this can be a perception that 'disabled' is a stigmatizing label (Tibbie, 2004). Over the past century, the concept of disability has evolved significantly. The terms most frequently used by professionals are impairment, disability and handicap, and although there are differences of opinions over definition and usage, there is a measure of consensus over the need to divide or categorize the disabled population as an aid to interdisciplinary communication. In 1980, the World Health Organization (WHO) commissioned Philip Wood (Oliver, 1990) to devise a classification system for disability. The resulting definitions are shown below.

Impairment

Impairment has been defined as an 'anatomical, pathological or psychological disorder' which is defined and described symptomatically or diagnostically. Impairments may affect locomotion, motor activities, sensory systems and be medically based or of psychological origin. A more concise definition is 'any loss of psychological, physiological or anatomical structure or function'. Impairments may be permanent or temporary, be present from birth or acquired adventitiously. It is appropriate to regard the term impairment as a neutral or objective description of the site, nature and severity of loss of functional capacity.

Disability

Disability refers to the impact of impairment upon the performance of activities commonly accepted as the basic elements of everyday living—walking, negotiating stairs, getting in and out of bed, feeding, using the lavatory, bathing, holding down a job or just being able to carry on a conversation. Disability can be used when an impairment, objectively defined, constitutes a hindrance to mobility, domestic routines or occupational and communication skills.

Handicap

Handicap is a term that has come to represent the more profound effects of impairments and disabilities that implicate the whole person rather than just selective incapacities. Handicap has been seen as an impairment or a disability that 'for a substantial period or permanently, retards, disturbs or otherwise adversely affects normal growth, development and adjustment to life' in children and 'constitutes a disadvantage for a given individual in that it limits or prevents the fulfilment of a role that is normal (depending on age, sex and social and cultural factors)' in adults. Handicap is therefore an evaluator concept in which the interaction of impairment and disability with an individual's psychological make-up, the resources available and social attitudes affects adversely the performance of ordinary roles. Handicap is a value judgement applied by others to an impaired disabled person on the basis of failure to perform customary social roles, and of course, the impaired-disabled person may apply or vigorously reject this value judgement to himself/herself. To move from impairment to handicap is to cover the distance from symptoms to social role. It is also to move from objectivity to subjectivity.

Figure 6.1

Impairment (intrinsic situations: exteriorized as functional limitations)
Disability (objectified as activity restriction)
Handicap (socialized as disadvantage)

Source: Thomas (1982).

The presence of impairment does not necessarily imply disability and neither does disability imply handicap (Thomas, 1982). On the other hand, it is possible for impairment to lead to disablement or handicap because two people with broadly similar functional limitations may face objectively similar activity restrictions, but one may retain his/her conventional social roles (albeit somewhat modified), while the other, with different resources (personal or community), may cast himself/ herself or be cast as a handicapped person. Some people in wheelchairs succeed in working and maintaining a high level of independence, while others require a high degree of nursing care. Disability is, therefore, to some extent 'self-defined' as with a handicap.

THEORETICAL FRAMEWORK

Over the last 20 years, there have been substantial challenges towards dominant perceptions of and attitudes to disabled people. Such challenges, mainly articulated by disabled people themselves and the organizations which they have formed, have focused primarily on questioning the notion of disability as an individual, a tragic occurrence that classes a person as sick or incapacitated in some way and thus dependent on the good will and care of others. There are two main approaches to disability which are as follows.

Medical Model of Disability

This model is one of the dominant ways of understanding disability and the associated attitudes and responses to disabled people. It is most often referred to as the medical discourse on disability or, in more popular language, the medical model of disability. It has tended to focus attention on the nature of the person's impairment and the degree to which this impairment may or may not prevent the person from carrying out various tasks or participating in activities in ways regarded as normal (Shakespeare, 2006). Such definitions focus on the physiology of the impairment and the perceived deficits of the individual person rather than on the barriers in society that prevent him/her from doing these things. They focus, for example, on the nature of a person's spinal injury rather than on the physical barriers that limit his or her mobility as a wheelchair user, or on the degree of a person's deafness rather than on accommodating the use of sign language as the language of communication and instruction for that person.

Social Model of Disability

This kind of approach to disability derives from social and political understandings of disability, where the focus is on the nature and organization of society and its response to people with impairments rather than on the nature and extent of the individual's impairment. The following is a definition of disability according to the social model:

> Disability refers to the disadvantage or restriction of activity caused by the way society is organized which takes little or no account of people who have physical, sensory or mental impairments. As a result such people are excluded and prevented from participating fully on equal terms in mainstream society. Disability is thus imposed on people with impairments who, as a result, become disabled not by their impairments, but by society. (Terzi, 2005)

From the perspective of the social model, disability can therefore be understood only by focusing on the relationship between persons with impairments (or perceived impairments) and the society of which they are part. One fundamental consequence of applying the social model of understanding disability is that shifting attention from the individual and the nature of his/her impairment to the relationship that exists between that person and the society in which he/she lives makes it more difficult to categorize people as disabled or non-disabled. The nature of that relationship and the experience of disability are always dependent on how that society is structured and functions. A social model perspective forces us to turn our attention away from defining who is or is not disabled to identifying and addressing the barriers which in a given society restrict disabled people's participation in 'normal' life. In this social view, people with disabilities are seen as being restricted in performing daily activities because of a complex set of interrelating factors, some pertaining to the person and some pertaining to the person's immediate environment and social/political arrangements.

THE PREVALENCE OF DISABILITY IN INDIA AND THE LACK OF RELIABLE INFORMATION AND ITS IMPACT

Information on disability has been collected in India for a long time through sample surveys and censuses. For conducting nationwide large-scale socio-economic sample surveys on a regular basis, the Government of India set up the National Sample Survey (NSS) in 1950. The survey focuses on various socio-economic aspects in different years. The survey period of National Sample Survey Office (NSSO) is identified as round, and it varies from six months to one year. As far as complete enumeration is concerned, the Office of Registrar General of India has conducted population censuses at an interval of 10 years since 1881. The Indian population census has been providing some useful data on the physical infirmities from its inception. The census questionnaire of 1872, called 'House Register', included questions on the physically disabled such as the blind, the deaf and the dumb. But owing to constraints in enumeration, the quality of data collected through the population censuses was not satisfactory, and thus, the practice was discontinued after 1931. No attempt was, therefore, made to collect information on disability through censuses of 1951, 1961 and 1971. Collection of certain important information on physically handicapped persons was again taken up in the 1981 census. The declaration of the year 1981 as the international year for disabled persons by the United Nations was also a reason for taking up the aspect of disability in the 1981 population census. The enumeration of disabled persons was again taken up along with the Population Census of India conducted in 2001. According to the 2001 Census of India, people with disability are 21,906,769 in India which constitute more than 2 per cent the total population. But according to NSSO surveys, in India people with disabilities are 18,491,000, which constitutes less than 2 per cent of the total population.

First, this conclusion is misleading because the definitions adopted by the two organizations are different. Second, if we look at the types of disabled people in India as estimated by two organizations, according to the Census of India, the proportion of seeing disabled in the total disabled population is 48.55 per cent, whereas according to NSSO, their proportion is 15 per cent. Similarly in the case of people with movement disabled, the Census estimates at 27.87 per cent of total disabled population, whereas NSSO estimates them at 57.51 per cent.

Table 6.2 *Estimates of Disability in India by Census and NSSO*

Sr. No.	Types of Disabilities	Census 2001	Total Number of Disabled (%)	NSSO 2002	Total Number of Disabled (%)
1.	Seeing	10,634,881	48.55	2,826,700	15.29
2.	Speech	1,640,868	7.49	2,154,500	11.65
3.	Hearing	1,261,722	5.76	3,061,700	16.56
4.	Movement	6,105,477	27.87	10,634,000	57.51
5.	Mental	2,263,821	10.33	2,097,500	11.34
6.	Total	21,906,769	100.00	18,491,000	100.00

Source: Census of India 2001 and NSS 58th Round 2002 as reported in and Bhanushali, K. (2005) World Bank Report (2009).

Thus according to Census of India, disabled with seeing disabilities are leading in number in India, whereas according to NSS, disabled with locomotor disability are leading. Similarly, there are differences in estimates in the case of other disabilities as well.[2]

If we compare these two definitions, the definitions adopted by the Census of India are wide in coverage compared to NSSO. The definition adopted by NSSO includes persons either with no light perception or blurred vision. Whereas the Census includes, apart from these two categories, people with proper vision in one eye and also people who may have blurred vision and had no occasion to test whether their eyesight would improve by using spectacles. Because of vide definition, the Census of India estimates of people with seeing/visual disabilities are more as compared to NSSO estimates. In the case of disabled with speech disability, the Census of India estimated that, in India, there are 1,640,868 (7.49% of total disabled) persons with such disabilities, whereas NSSO estimated them at 2,154,500 (11.65% of total disabled). Here also, variation is due to definitional aspects.

Consequently, the needs of disabled people are often poorly served by development agencies. Disability issues are often viewed as outside the mainstream of development theory, policy and practice. All too often, governments and NGOs fail to recognize disability for what it really is—a central and vitally important issue in global poverty, not a minor irritant on the margins.

Disability is a major cause of poverty, social exclusion and inequality throughout the world, on a par with gender discrimination and the denial of human rights. Disability as a cause and consequence of poverty now needs to be brought to centre stage, and the development community needs to reorder its priorities to put disability in the mainstream and need proper data on disability. Till this is achieved, disabled people will continue to be relegated to the margins of society, but once it is done, agencies will begin to better meet the needs of millions of impoverished people.

DISABILITY AND POVERTY

The connection between poverty and disability is complex and multidirectional. In 1996, the United Nations estimated that as many as 300 million people in the world are severely or moderately disabled and, according to the World Bank, as many as two-thirds of those individuals live in poverty. With such overwhelming numbers of disabled individuals living in poverty, one cannot help but wonder whether one causes the other.

It is relatively simple to make the causal connection between disability and poverty. Individuals with disabilities are often excluded from the labour market. Fears of increased costs, inflexibility in

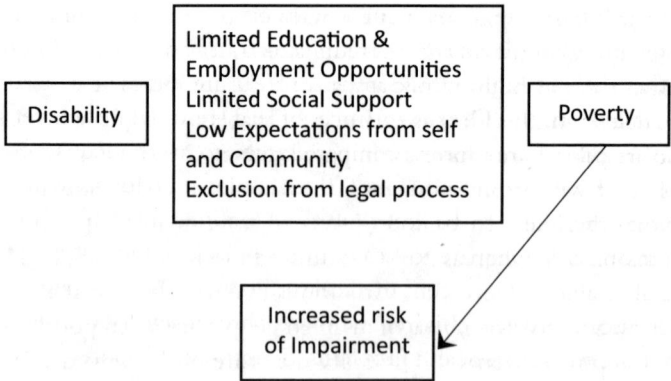

Figure 6.2 *Disability and Poverty Cycle*

Source: Census of India 2001 and NSS 58th Round 2002 as reported in Sophie Mitra & Sambamoorthi, U. (2006).

considering necessary accommodations and outright prejudice contribute to an artificially small job market for people with disabilities. Even when included, people with disabilities often work fewer hours and in lower-paying or lower-skilled positions. In some instances, individuals with disabilities are unable to work in the competitive marketplace. For those who are so disabled that competitive work is impossible, Social Security Disability Insurance and Supplemental Security Income are most often relied upon. However, federal benefits do not provide a living wage, making poverty inevitable. The extent to which people with disabilities are segregated also contributes to their marginalization.[3] For people with disabilities living in the community, the array of options is similarly limited. People with physical disabilities may only be able to access a fraction of the housing that people without disabilities may access. People with cognitive disabilities are often congregated in group housing, or supervised apartments, where their only neighbours are others with similar disabilities.

The trail from poverty to disability may not be as clear as the road from disability to poverty. However, a critical examination of the issue demonstrates that those living in poverty are exposed to a variety of risk factors that increase the possibility of impairment and disability (Beckles, 2004). Poverty almost necessarily leads to insufficient nutrition, sub-standard or crowded housing and inadequate physical and mental healthcare. These factors alone or in combination lead to an increased risk of impairment, which in turn may lead to disability. The WHO estimates that one hundred million people worldwide have impairments which are caused by malnutrition and poor sanitation. For example, children living in low-income housing disproportionately are exposed to lead paint. The deleterious health consequences of lead are well known, yet people who are poor do not have meaningful access to more adequate housing.

Let's take chronic hunger. For example, individuals who live in poverty are likely to be food insecure (defined as having limited or nutritionally inadequate food as a result of lack of money or resources to gain access to it). Recent medical studies have demonstrated a strong association between children who are chronically food insecure and physical and mental health problems. School-aged children with severe hunger were more likely to have low birth weights, chronic health problems and stressful life events.

They were also more likely than non-hungry children to have developmental delays, emotional problems including anxious and depressive symptoms, and learning disabilities. The authors also postulated that hunger may have had a negative impact on children's psychosocial functioning, increasing the risk of behavioural problems. This relatively simple example of inadequate nutrition demonstrates the profound impact of poverty on child development and the resulting increased risk of impairment and disability.

The incidence of disability is often seen as a natural phenomenon, one beyond the control of the individual. We don't often blame individuals for being born cognitively disabled or developing a chronic health condition. However, when one considers the causal connection between poverty and disability, blame could be attributed if we wanted to do so. We could, with considerable evidence, point a finger at ourselves for not paying living wages, for not providing a truly open and accommodating labour market, for not providing safe and affordable housing and for not providing adequate and affordable healthcare for all our fellow citizens, even those with physical or mental disabilities.

As many as 50 per cent of disabilities are preventable (DFID, 2000). For example, the WHO currently estimates that, worldwide, there are 1.5 million blind children, mainly in Africa and Asia. In developing countries, up to 70 per cent of blindness in children is either preventable or treatable. The WHO also estimates that around 50 per cent of disabling hearing impairment is also preventable. In 1995, this affected a total of 120 million people worldwide (including seven million children).

A large proportion of disability is preventable. Achieving the international development targets for economic, social and human development will undoubtedly reduce the levels of disability in many poor countries. However, general improvements in living conditions will not be enough. Specific steps are still required, not only for prevention, but also to ensure that people with disabilities are able to participate fully in the development process. Disability and poverty reinforce one another, contributing to increased vulnerability and exclusion. The majority of people with disabilities find their situations affecting their chances of going to school, working for a living, enjoying family life and participating as equals in social life. It is estimated that only 2 per cent of people with disabilities in developing countries have access to rehabilitation and appropriate basic services.

POLICY INTERVENTIONS

The Indian Persons with Disability (Equal Opportunities, Protection of Rights and Full Participation) Act, 1995, was a landmark in that it was the first major piece of disability legislation based largely on the United Nations Standard Rules.[4] It provided disabled people, in the second largest population in the world, with constitutional recognition. The main provisions of the Act are:

1. Prevention and early detection of impairment
2. Integration of disabled students into mainstream state education
3. Reservation of at least 3 per cent of government and public sector vacancies for disabled people—1 per cent each for persons with visual impairment, hearing impairment and physical impairment
4. Identification of jobs which can be held by disabled people
5. Job protection for people who have become disabled during service
6. Local authorities should, within their economic limits, make adjustments to the physical environment to take account of the access needs of disabled people (e.g., install sound signals at traffic lights, create curb cuts and slopes in pavements, build ramps in public buildings and install Braille systems in lifts)

The Act is currently being revised. The amendment committee published their final report in March 1999 with over 50 amendments. These proposed amendments are now being considered by a government sub-committee. However, there has been little sign of progress since the final report was produced. The problems with the Act include the following:

- Disability is defined in this legislation by a list of only seven impairments. People with other impairments are technically not eligible for support under this Act. There is, for example, no provision for sign language use.
- Many disabled people are not aware of their rights under the Act. In a country with 15 major languages and low levels of literacy, dissemination of information is a problem.
- There has been a lack of political will and excessive bureaucracy in implementing and monitoring the legislation.

- Only 0.14 per cent of disabled people in India have had regular employment since 1960 (Mohan, 1999, cited by Moll, 2001). Therefore, the section on preventing dismissal or demotion of disabled people in employment is only relevant to a small minority.
- The Act is not integral to other legislation; for example, provision for disabled people's education is under the Ministry of Social Justice and Empowerment rather than the Department of Education and is therefore separate from other legislation on education.
- Each state is obliged to establish a commission for disability to promote and monitor implementation of the Act. Of the 29 states, 4 have independent commissions under the Ministry for Social Justice and Empowerment. Most states put disability work as an appendage to another department, reflecting the significance attributed to it. In Karnataka, for example, the person responsible for disability is also the Secretary for Women and Child Welfare.

This Act was obtained through lobbying by disability activists and non-governmental organizations. Work was done to educate and mobilize public opinion as well as to influence government officials. Consultation meetings, protest marches and press conferences continue to be held to increase awareness and encourage enforcement (Yeo, 2001). The International Day of the Disabled Persons is a focal point for this work. In areas where there are active organizations of disabled people, for example, Karnataka, Tamil Nadu and Andhra Pradesh, the legislation has been used to help raise awareness of disabled people's rights. Most importantly, the Act helps to put the responsibility on society to make adjustments to include disabled people.

Disabled people's needs, however, still remain peripheral to the government's agenda in terms of resource planning and allocation. There is no provision for representation of disabled people in the national Parliament or local government. It has been left to non-governmental organizations to promote awareness of the Act, translating it into local languages.

There are several other pieces of legislation and programmes of work, which refer specifically to disabled people. The government also has programmes providing assistance for poor people in general. Individual states then decide whether or not to include disabled people in this work or to consider disability separately.

CONCLUSION

People with disabilities tend to be among the most socially and economically marginalized populations wherever they exist. Disability and poverty tend to go together, forming a cycle of cumulative causation. Disabled people are more likely to become disabled than those who are not. In official reports and literature, data on disability in developing countries is largely ignored. Due to the lack of accurate data on disability, the needs of disabled people are often poorly served by development agencies. Disability issues are often viewed as outside the mainstream of development theory, policy and practice. Disability is a major cause of poverty, social exclusion and inequality throughout the world, on a par with gender discrimination and the denial of human rights. It is already known that living in poverty increases the likelihood of getting an impairment; disabled people generally experience higher rates of poverty as a result of being disabled, and when people living in poverty become disabled, they are often more severely marginalized than wealthier people. The existing legislation needs to be effectively implemented. The amendments that have been suggested to the Act should be tabled and passed in Parliament. Disability should become an integral part of all national policies. Poverty reduction can never be met unless persons with disabilities are included. Developing countries must strive to ensure that they accept their responsibilities of the policy agenda, particularly the empowerment of the poor, of which persons with disabilities form a part.

NOTES

1. https://www.censusindia.gov.in/Census_Data_2001/
2. http://www.disabilityindia.org/nsso-census.cfm
3. www.ecomod.org/files/papers/181.pdf
4. For the complete Act see www.disabilityactindia.org

REFERENCES

Beckles, B. (2004). Poverty and disability: Advocating to eliminate social exclusion. National Centre for Persons with Disabilities. Trinidad and Tobago. November 2004.

DFID (Department for International Development). (2000). *Disability, poverty and development*. Department for International Development. https://hpod.law. harvard.edu/pdf/Disability-poverty-and-development.pdf

Elwan, A. (1999). Poverty and disability: A survey of the literature. December 18. https://documents1.worldbank.org/curated/en/488521468764667300/pdf/multi-page.pdf

IBRD. (2001). World Development Report: *Attacking Poverty*, OUP, Delhi.

Moll, K. (2001). Disabled people in development; moral obligation or socio-economic imperative. (unpublished).

Oliver, M. (1990). *The politics of disablement*. Macmillan.

Rust, T., & Robert, M. (2007). Poverty and Disability: Trapped in a Web of Causation. https://ecomod.net/sites/default/files/document-conference/ecomod2007-rum/181.pdf

Shakespeare, T. (2006). *Disability rights and wrongs*. Routledge.

Singh, J. (2005). *Disability and development in India*. Rehabilitation Council of India.

Sooden, M., & Kumar's paper presentation. Poverty and human development after globalization in India. Department of Economics, Himachal Pradesh University, Summerhill, Shimla, HP.

Terzi, L. (2005). A capability perspective on impairment, disability and special needs: Towards social justice in education. *Theory and Research in Education*, 3(2), 197–223.

Thomas, D. (1982). *The experience of handicap*. Methuen & Co.

Tibbie, M. (2004). User's guide to disability estimates and definition. Department for Work and Person, Social Research Division, London, March. www.dwp.gov.uk/

United Nations Development Programme. (1997). *Human development report 1997: Human development to eradicate poverty*. Oxford University Press.

Wratten, E. (1995). Conceptualizing urban poverty. *Environment and Urbanization*, 7(1), 11–38.

Yeo, R. (2001). Chronic poverty and disability. Chronic Poverty and Research Centre, Action in Disability and Development. http://www.chronicpoverty.org/uploads/publication_files/WP04_Yeo.pdf

Chapter 7

Children Toiling at a Tender Age*

Helen R. Sekar and Manju Khurana

Globally, out of an estimated 211 million children between the ages of 5–14 who are engaged in some form of economic activity, 186 million children fall within the accepted International Labour Organization (ILO) definition of child labour.[1] Another 59 million children are child labourers in the age group of 15–17. The Asian Pacific region harbours the largest number of child workers in the 5–14 age group—127 million—constituting 19 per cent of the total population of children (ILO 2002). An estimated 171 million children between the ages of 5–17 work in hazardous conditions. Overall, more than two-third of child labourers are still in hazardous activities. In addition, it is estimated that about 8.4 million children are engaged in forms of child labour such as trafficking (1.2 million), forced and bonded labour (5.7 million), armed conflict (0.3 million), prostitution and pornography (1.8 million) and illicit activities (0. 6 million; ILO 2002). According to the 1991 Census, there were 11.28 million child workers out of the total 209.99 million children in the age group of 5–14. As per census data, child workers form 5.37 per cent of all the children in the age group of 5–14. This proportion is higher in the rural areas— 6.56 per cent of all the children in the workforce, as against only 2.04 per cent in urban areas. Around 90.87 per cent of the child workers were concentrated in rural areas and the remaining 9.13 per cent in urban areas. Of the 6.18 million male child workers in the

* *Social Change* Vol 34, no. 1 (March 2004): 52–65.

country, 88.2 per cent were main workers, and the rest are marginal workers.[2] Of the 5.1 million female child workers, nearly 94 per cent were main workers. The work participation of female children was thus more than that of male children (GOI 1991).

CAUSES AND IMPACT

Child labour is a symptom of the underlying problems of widespread poverty and inequality in society. It is also a cause of poverty; children who join the workforce at an early stage do so without any formal education or skills that will help them to be upwardly mobile. In most cases, they are involved in monotonous and laborious tasks. They grow up as illiterates devoid of any skills for further development. Consequently, they get into low-paid unskilled work when they become adults. As adults, when they marry and have children, they are already in a poor economic condition and are forced to send their children to work. Therefore, this forms the cycle of child labour–poverty–illiteracy–child labour (Sekar 1993).

Take the case of the beedi industry spread in different parts of the country. It is one of the main sources of livelihood for people associated with this occupation and is known for its large-scale employment of children. Studies on child labour in the beedi industry show that a vicious cycle of child labour–poverty–child labour is operating in these areas, where child labour has been prevalent for more than three generations. Thus, child labour has perpetuated poverty and child labour again and again (Vidyasagar 2000).

This vicious cycle is strengthened by adult unemployment owing to the large number of children competing for jobs with adults. Moreover, not only does child labour increase labour supply and result in increasing underemployment and unemployment of adult workers, but it also makes labour cheap and depresses the general wage level as well (Vidyasagar 2000).

Another often quoted factor that forces children into work is the state of the basic education system. The existing educational policy continues to be fairly insulated from the sociocultural and economic ground realities in which the child and his/her family are situated. In most parts of the country, access to education is very limited, especially in the rural and tribal areas. Even in places where it is available, parents may not be able to afford the investment. Moreover, schools where the curriculum is unattractive cannot be an instrument for attracting children away from the labour market. In spite of substantive achievements, particularly in higher enrolment rates in the last decades, the primary education system remains dysfunctional because of low retention and high dropout rates, and class, gender and regional disparities in access to education (Sekar and Mohammad 2001).

Child labour is not a supply side phenomenon alone; it is also a creation of demand side factors thriving on the seedbed of poverty. In the unorganized sector of the Aligarh lock industry, artisans are totally dependent on middlemen for credit to buy raw materials and tools. Since most artisans are illiterate, they are unaware of the trends in the market and end up incurring losses. Moreover, the artisans are not in a strong bargaining position in regard to the price of the output; they have to sell their locks to middlemen at less remunerative prices. Therefore, the only way to survive in the competitive business of lock production is to rely heavily on cheap labour (Sekar and Mohammad 2001).

A census survey conducted in December 1994 revealed that 33 per cent of the labour force in match production were children of less than 14 years old (21% female children and 12% male children). Around 55 per cent were female adults. Thus, women and children constitute about 88 per cent of the total labour force in the handmade match industry (Vidyasagar 1994). Children are used more because they are docile, uncomplaining and obedient. While explaining the prevalence of child labour, one of the studies has concluded that it exists because of the demand side factors that create a selective market for cheap child labour, which is then serviced by poorer, but not necessarily poverty-stricken households. Given the nature of organization of production in the hand-made match industry and the comparative labour cost advantage that the industry has, demand side factors play a primary role in the persistence of child labour (Chandrasekher 1997).

CONSEQUENCES FOR THE CHILD

In many occupations, children join the labour force at a very early age. One of the studies of the Markapur slate industry reveals that the minimum age of workers in the industry is eight for boys and seven for girls. The data reveals that about 21 per cent of the child workers identified started working when they were below 8 years old. A majority of the child workers (61%) joined the workforce when they were in the age group of 9–10. In all, only about 18 per cent of child workers started working after the age of 11 (Chandra 2000).

Labouring at a young age has many adverse consequences for children. Children employed in carpet weaving, match and fireworks, glass and bangles, stale/pencils, diamond cutting and polishing, abattoirs/slaughterhouses, lock-making, etc., are continuously exposed to various hazards, including, at times, physical, social, sexual and psychological abuses. Children can be seen working underground, under water, at dangerous heights or in confined spaces, handling dangerous machines, equipment, tools and, sometimes, heavy loads. There is continuous exposure to hazardous substances or extreme temperature or noise levels. They also work for long hours or during the night. Through child labour, the child's potential is put to improper use for the employers' benefits (Singh and Sekar 2003).

HEALTH HAZARDS

The adverse consequences of children working in hazardous occupations are many. First, it poses a challenge to the safety of the workers. Second, health hazards have more long-term implications in terms of making the person invalid for any work at an early age. Various studies have shown that the impact of hazardous work begins to show in its severe form only after 2–3 years in terms of morbidity, fever, cold, cough, dysentery, body ache and weakness, tuberculosis and other respiratory problems (Bimal 2000). Another study in Andhra Pradesh reveals that those who work in lime kilns and slate mines from their childhood are prone to respiratory diseases at an early age. It is estimated that one in every three child labourers does not even reach the age of 18 (Vishwanathan 1987).

A study in Markapur slate mines shows that the average age of workers is only about 30–35. These people are forced to push their children into work for their living, as they become invalid workers at an early age (Chandra 2000). The study by Sekar and Mohammad (2001) on child labour in the home-based lock industry of Aligarh gives a very clear indication of the impact on children. The most hazardous work in lock making and in other metal works are polishing, electroplating and spray painting. In polishing work, child workers inhale powder and metal dust continuously. This leads to respiratory and other lung-related diseases. In electroplating, chemicals such as hydrochloric acid are used, and the limbs of children get affected when they regularly dip the cross-section of the locks in these chemical solutions for electroplating. In most of the units, children work without wearing any footwear or gloves. The other hazardous impact of this work relates to the inhaling of noxious fumes, emitted from the chemical solutions when a current is passed through it. It affects both the lungs and eyes. In one study, breathing trouble was found to be rampant among workers engaged in electroplating work. Besides, there always remains a possibility of receiving electric shocks because most of the electroplating units have illegal connections and open wiring. In spray painting units, children inhale paint and paint thinner, which also leads to lung related diseases after continuous inhaling for long hours. Another occupational hazard is pneumoconiosis, for which there is no cure. The only remedy is to prevent secondary infection and to remove the person from the place of work.

The ILO report of the Director General in the 68th Session of the International Labour Conference, 1983, observed that the vulnerability of working children to health hazards is increased by the high incidence of malnutrition and undernourishment, in contrast to their increased requirement for energy utilization to perform heavy work activities. The incidence of communicable diseases is always higher among these children. Children come into close contact in work situations with infective cases of tuberculosis and other similar diseases. Severe malnutrition, anaemia, hard labour, fatigue and inadequate sleep make them more susceptible to infectious diseases. Such an impact on working children was also reflected in the findings of a study on girl child labour in the match industry of Sivakasi by Helen R. Sekar in 1993. Long working hours, unhygienic and unsafe surroundings, less than subsistence wages and hazardous tasks are the characteristic features of child labour scenario in the Sivakasi match industry. The risk from fire is always present because all chemicals used in the manufacturing of matches—ammonium phosphate, potassium chlorate, sulphur, manganese and phosphorus—are inflammable. There is a high risk of fire and explosion in the raw materials store and in the paste making, match head coating and box filling processes. Certain match manufacturing processes, such as paraffining and the preparation of chemical coating mix, expose workers in that section to continuous heat.

Enquiries about physical ailments of child labourers showed that 96 per cent of girl child workers in a sample of 115 suffered from body aches, fever, cough, cold, headache, stomach ache or itching in the hands. So great is the hazard to the lives and safety of children that they become unemployable for life, and so great is the degree of desperation of some of the parents at the predicament of their children that they sometimes vow never to send their children to work again; one parent is quoted to have said: 'So long as I am alive, I will never let my children work, look at my condition. I cannot even breathe easily' (Bimal 2000).

PSYCHOLOGICAL CONSEQUENCES

Many psychologists believe that childhood is the critical period for later development of personality and the exploitative situations of child labour exert strong influence on the child's self-concept and self-esteem. Children growing up in such a negative atmosphere feel incompetent, rejected and unwanted. It leads to deficits in their physical, mental, social and emotional development. At times, street children and self-employed children are charged with vague offences such as vagrancy or loitering. They are often arbitrarily rounded up and detained simply because they are on the streets and appear to be homeless. These children are subjected to physical and emotional abuse. Emotional abuse may take a number of forms, such as verbal assault, including threats of sexual or physical abuse, close confinement such as locking a child in a room, and withholding of food (Magill 1996).

Abused children exhibit significantly more fantasy aggression, overt aggression, lower feelings of belongingness, self-reliance and lower verbal intelligence than normal children. Such children were rated more aggressive and inadequate (Thomas and Joshep 1976). They were also found to be significantly lower on measures of empathy and higher on measures of emotional maladjustment (Straker and Jacobson 1981). Children in this category are at increased risk of developing a variety of psychological problems, including low self-esteem, anxiety, depression, behavioural disorders, educational difficulties and distorted relationships with peers and adults.

Another consequence of child labour is an anti-social personality, generally seen among self-employed and street children, especially ragpickers. To increase the feeling of independence and project pseudo maturity, they start using abusive language, incur extravagant expenses and indulge in bad habits such as smoking and gambling. They are also exposed to social evils and sometimes crimes such as drug trafficking and prostitution. The characteristics of anti-social personality are very much manifested in these children. When they grow up, many of them do not abide by the usual rules of society. They do not follow through on promises or obligations; they are perfectly willing to deceive and defraud. They feel no close bonds with others but are often remarkably apt at convincing other people to help and trust them. Research studies have clearly indicated that most of the time it is street children who stand in court as juvenile delinquents (Pandey 1993). Early work also confines a child's vision. He hardly knows about the professions beyond his territory, and thus, lack of education limits his aspirations to a great extent. The child is forced to do what he/she does not personally like doing. He/she is the victim of the fight against hunger and poverty (Bimal 2000).

FUTURE PROSPECTS

Deprivation of education and vocational training also has a telling effect on working children. The future of a working child is endangered, as he/she cannot go to school or is bound to leave school prematurely or is unable to coordinate the two activities. He/she lacks fundamental general and professional knowledge, which is required for normal mental and intellectual development and for making the child into a skilled worker and enabling him/her to prosper in social and occupational fields. Children, thus, find themselves locked in unskilled, low-paying, unpleasant and unsafe working situations and permanently disadvantaged in the labour market. Ennew (1986) is of the opinion that as adults they are not only unemployed but also unemployable.

CONCLUSIONS

Child labour is a violation of a range of child rights. Children are deprived of their right to education; they are deprived of their right to play, leisure and healthy growth and of free mental, physical, psychological and spiritual growth. Being future assets of any country, their arrested growth affects the country as a whole in the long run. Societies with large numbers of working children will be producing more and more illiterate citizens, devoid of skills that a country needs for development. This also adversely affects national development.

Although there are different welfare programmes to address the child labour problem, there is a general mismatch between the programmes. The sheer magnitude and the complex nature of the problem calls for more intensive and cost-effective approaches to its elimination. There is a need for a concerted and well-coordinated effort among different government departments on the one hand and different sections of the civil society on the other.

The most enduring steps towards eradicating child labour would be to improve the economic conditions of the families from where the child labourers are drawn into the workforce. The provision of assistance in the form of income generating assets under different rural development and poverty eradication programmes needs to be provided to such families. An improvement in the economic condition of the family also brings about a significant change in the attitude with an inclination towards sending the children to schools. Apart from legislative measures, there is an urgent need to give importance to supportive measures for child labour.

NOTES

1. According to the ILO,

    Child Labour includes children prematurely leading adult lives, working long hours for low wages under conditions damaging to their health and to their physical and mental development. Sometimes separated from their families, frequently deprived of meaningful education and training opportunities that would open for them a better future.

    The definition of the Encyclopaedia of Social Science also has a similar emphasis: 'When the business of wage earning or of participation in self or family support conflicts directly or indirectly with the business of growth and education, the result is child labour.'

2. According to the census definition, 'main workers' are those who have worked for the major part of the year (for 183 days or six months), preceding the date of enumeration, and whose main activity was in either cultivation or as agricultural labourer or in household industry or in other work. Marginal workers are those who have not worked for the major part (for 183 days or six months) of the preceding year but nevertheless have done some work during any time in the reference period.

REFERENCES

Aggarwal, R. 1999. *Street Children*. New Delhi: Shipra Publications.

Bhan, S. 1991. *Child Abuse. An Annotated Bibliography*. New Delhi: Institute of Peace Research and Action.

Bimal, K. 2000. *Problems of Working Children*. New Delhi: APH Publishing.

Browne, K., and C. Davis. 1989. *Early Prediction and Prevention of Child Abuse*. New York, NY: John Wiley & Sons.

Corby, B. 1987. *Working with Child Abuse*. Philadelphia, PA: Open University Press.

Cornelia, B. 1984. 'Multiple Personality and Child Abuse: An Overview.' *Psychiatric Clinics of North America* 7, no. 1: 3–7.

Daley, M. 1982. 'Child Abuse and Delinquency: Are There Connections between Childhood Violence and Later Deviant Behaviour?' *International Sociological Abstracts*, 3788.

Georgopoulou, Helen Agathonos. 1993. 'Third European Conference on Child Abuse and Neglect, Prague, Czechoslovakia, June 23–26, 1991.' *Child Abuse and Neglect: The International Journal* 17, no. 2: 191–196.

Gomango, S. P. 2001. *Child Labour. A Precarious Future*. New Delhi: Author Press.

Harold, G. E. 1990. 'Childhood Sexual Abuse: Long-term Effect on Psychological and Sexual Functioning.' *Journal of Child Abuse and Neglect* 14, no. 4: 503–515.

Harold, P., and Martin, D. 1979. 'Child Abuse and Development.' *Journal of Child Abuse and Neglect* 3, 415–421.

Magill, Frank N. 1996. *International Encyclopedia of Psychology* (Vol. 1). London: Routledge.

International Encyclopedia of Psychology (Vol. 2).

Mendelievich, Elias. 1979. *Children at Work*. Geneva: ILO.

Mhatre, S. L. 1995. 'Child Labour Legislation in South Asia, 1881–1995: A Documentation & Analysis.' UNICEF, Kathmandu.

Mishra, L. 2000. *Child Labour in India*. New Delhi: Oxford University Press.

Morgan, Clifford T., Richard A. King, John R. Weisz, and John Schopler. 1986. *Introduction to Psychology*. New York, NY: McGraw Hill.

Nangia, P. 1987. *Child Labour: Cause-effect Syndrome*. New Delhi: Janak Publishers.

Naidu, S. 1984. *Child Labour and Health: Problems & Prospects*. Mumbai: Tata Institute of Social Science.

Oates, R., F. Kim, and A. Peacock. 1985. 'Self-esteem of Abused Children.' *Child Abuse and Neglect* 9, no. 2: 159–163.

Pandey, R. 1993. *Street Children of Kanpur: A Situational Analysis*. Noida: V. V. Giri National Labour Institute.

Panicker, R., and K. Desai. 1992. *Working and Street Children of Delhi: A Situational Analysis*. Noida: V. V. Giri National Labour Institute.

Reddy, N. 1992. *Street Children of Banglore: A Situational Analysis*. Noida: V. V. Giri National Labour Institute.

Rosenhen, L. D., and M. Seligman (eds). 1989. *Abnormal Psychology* (2nd ed.). New York, NY: WW Norton & Company.

Sekar, H. R. 1993. *Girl Child Labour in the Match Industry of Sivakasi: No Light in Their Lives*. Noida: Child Labour Cell, V. V. Giri National Labour Institute.

Sekar, H. R., and N. Mohammad. 2001. *Child Labour in Home Based Lock Industries of Aligarh*. Noida: V. V. Giri National Labour Institute.

SPARC International. (1999). *The Worst Form of Child Labour Convention 1999*. SPARC International (Society for the Protection of the Rights of the Child). http://www.org/compaigns/crp/promises/ police.html

Vidyasagar, R., and G. Kumarababu. 2000. *Child Labour in the Match Industry of Sivakasi*. Noida: V. V. Giri National Labour Institute

Yates, A. 1981. 'Narcissistic Traits in Abused Children.' *American Journal of Orthopsychiatry* 51, no. 1: 55–62.

Chapter 8

Industrial Pollution and Health Hazards in Jharkhand*

Bijay Sarkar

INTRODUCTION

In ecology, the environment means all factors which affect the survival and reproduction of the living organism in the general sense. The affront to the environment by frenzied industrialization manifests itself in three major ways: (a) by uneven distribution of the supply of substances necessary for life (undernutrition), (b) by changes in the mode of life (hypokinesis), (c) disturbances in the equilibrium between organism and environment (pollution and diseases).[1] This chapter will deal with the third aspect only as a menacingly growing problem for the life and health of the people of the Jharkhand region.

The Jharkhand region on account of its richness in some key ores and minerals and its abundance in cheap labour, thanks to its backwardness, otherwise, has been the site of a good many industrial establishments since pre-Independence days, and industrialization has brought with it concomitant ill effects, the worst of which is the devastation of its environment. In the name of development, large forests have disappeared, tracts of inhabited land have gone under water and air and water in the region around industrial areas have been polluted to an extent far exceeding the prescribed safety level. In fact, polluted water carried down by streams and rivers spreads mischief in distant areas also. Industrial pollution is not a danger of the future but

* *Social Change* Vol 29, no. 3 and 4 (December 1999): 220–232.

is already playing havoc with the life and health of the people of the region. Not only should immediate steps to check and control this pollution from industries be taken but also there must be an attempt to evolve the means and ways to alter the strategy of development that is being pursued now.

INDUSTRIES IN JHARKHAND

The Jharkhand region since the days of British rule had its coal and mica mines. It had also mines of iron and copper ores. Jamshedpur had a pioneering iron and steel industry. The industrialization spurt during the last two decades made many more additions to the industrial map of the region, namely iron and steel industries in Ranchi, Rourkela and Bokaro, fertilizer industries in Sindri and Rourkela, cement factories in Sindri, non-ferrous metal extraction and refineries in Ghatsila, scores of thermal power plants. Added to it were soap, rubber, chemical, refractory and other ancillary industries. On the trail of this industrialization, there has been urbanization of the population. As an example, the percentage of the urban population to the total population of Dhanbad district in 1951 was 8.59, while in 1981, it was 50.61. The demographic distribution is now intensely clustered around industrial cities and townships, thereby the problem of treatment of human wastes adds up to the problem of industrial wastes.

HOW INDUSTRIES MARAUD ENVIRONMENT

Charak Samhita warns us 'when air, water and other elements of nature are polluted, seasons start working against the routine of cycles, vegetations begin to get ruined, excruciating sufferings plunge mankind.' These are the very evils which industries, as they are today, spill in the name of development. Industrialization attacks on four major fronts. First, it discharges dust, smoke and toxic wastes into the ground, air and water. Second, it forces people out of hamlets and villages sparsely scattered all over the country and industrial centres. The townships so formed, as a rule, do not have proper human waste disposal infrastructure, thereby causing grave water pollution. Third, it makes a heavy demand for sources of power from nature and undertakes power projects disastrous for the people (deforestation, dams uprooting people and submerging green tracts, giant thermal power plants belching ashes and smoke, nuclear reactors threatening holocaust). Fourth, it exposes its workers in the work place to a physicochemical environment which slowly pushes them to disease and death.

This chapter does not purport to be a compendium of all aspects of the pollution problems arising from industries in Jharkhand for two simple reasons. First, that is not possible in the space of the chapter. The more cogent second reason is that published data are scarce because very little systematic exhaustive work in the concerned field has been encouraged. This chapter will glean some representative data only from published sources and from one unpublished work by the author himself to appraise the readers of the gravity of the problem.

DRINKING WATER SUSTAINS LIFE OR DEATH?

Ground Water Pollution

The idea that the soil mantle acts as a filter and removes the harmful substance is not always true. The sources of contamination are (a) industrial wastes, (b) domestic wastes, (c) mine spills, (d) agricultural wastes and (e) waste water treatment lagoons. Domestic waste is partly incorporated into soil. It leaches into the aquifer below, and there is a danger of contaminated water being drawn up—the main contaminant being pathogenic organisms.[2] Industrial wastes contaminating ground water are mainly inorganic chemicals and heavy metals. The problem of ground water (as also river water) pollution manifests itself in an annual spate of acute enteric diseases taking a heavy toll on human life, especially on children. The problem is very serious because of the fact that drinking water facilities are limited and that many townships, if not all, in Jharkhand have no developed sewerage system. Table 8.1 depicts the state of sewerage, sanitation and drinking water system in some townships in Jharkhand.

The growth of the urban population in the Dhanbad region as compared to that in the whole of Bihar is shown in Table 8.2.

Table 8.1 *Profile of Sanitation Facilities*

Name of Town	Population	System of Sewerage	No. of Latrines			Night Soil Disposal	Source of Water Supply
			Water Borne	Service	Other		
Bokaro Steel City	224,099	S	4,500ᵃ		–	ST	T, W
Chas	40,381	OSD	3,000	1,000	500	HL, ST	T, TW
Dhanbad urban agglomeration:							
Dhanbad	120,221	OSD	6,447	1,000	553	ST, HL	T, TW
Kerkend	75,186	OSD	–	1565	185	HL, ST	T
Jorapokhar	65,156	OSD, Pt	1725	225	–	ST, HL	T
Sindri	70,645	OSD	8600	20		HL, ST	T
Jharia	57,496	OSD	947	2,450	64	WB, ST	T
Kumardhubi urban agglomeration:							
Kumardhubi	53,692	OSD	1677	1,468	307	HL, ST	T, W

Source: 1981 Census.

Notes: ᵃ Fifty adult people per latrine.

Abbreviations: System of sewerage: S = Sewer, OSD = Open surface drains, Pt = Pit system.

Disposal of night soil: ST = Septic tank latrine, S = Sewerage, HL = Head load.

WB = Wheel barrow.

Water supply source: TW = Tube well, T = Tap water, W = Well water.

Table 8.2 *Growth of Urban Population*

(A) Growth of Urban Population in Dhanbad District			
Year	Total Population	% Urban	Density of Population per Sq. Km
1951	924,764	8.59	1,565
1981	2,115,000	50.62	2,423

(B) Growth of Urban Population in Bihar			
Year	Total Population	% Urban	Density of Population per Sq. Km
1951	38,782,271	6.77	2,320
1981	69,914,734	12.47	2,727

Source: Murty, *Sc. Rep.* 1977.

River Water Pollution

The two main sources of pollution of river water in Jharkhand are industrial effluents and city sewages. A survey of an 18 km stretch of the Subarnarekha River between Hatia Dam and Namkum vis-à-vis critical evaluation of two water supply 'systems at Ranchi' has been conducted by S. Rajgopalan et al.[3] The study indicates that the city receives effluents and sewage from Heavy Engineering Corporation, Hindustan Steel, high-tension insulator factories and many other outfalls of treated and untreated sewage (2.5 million gallons per day domestic and 2.3 million gallons per day industrial) from different townships of the city. The study shows that the coliform content of water at two intake stations of MES at Khojatoli and Namkum is dangerously high (5,000 MPN/100 ml). The authors have suggested that the effluents need immediate predischarge treatment to ensure safety from hazards to the health of the community.

Fertilizer factories rank high among other water polluting agents. FCI (Sindri) and HSL (Rourkela) fertilizer factories discharge effluents in the Damodar and South Koel rivers, respectively. The wastes are mainly (a) oil-bearing wastes from compressor houses of ammonia and urea plants, (b) ammonia-bearing wastes from ammonia plants and (c) ammonia and urea wastes from urea plants. Arsenic is one of the very toxic inorganic constituents of the effluents discharged. Toxicity values of ammonia and ammonium salts are very high even at pH values below 9. The toxic effect of arsenic is cumulative. N in river water for pisciculture, and for AS, ISI has prescribed a limit of 1.0 mg/1.[4]

Another type of toxic substance in fertilizer factory effluent is fluoride content in drinking water of 1.5 mg/1; it causes dental fluorosis. Oil-bearing wastes degrade water by reducing the dissolution of oxygen in water. Kumar et al.[5] have carried out ecological studies on algae isolated from the effluents of Sindri fertilizer factory. They report that 6–8 million gallons of waters are discharged per day as composite effluent from the factory which along with the township sewage is discharged into the River Damodar through a 16 km long stream which also receives the effluent from a cement factory located

Table 8.3 *Range of Chemical Characteristics of Raw Factory Effluent: Sindri*

pH	8.9–9.2
TDS	2,100–2,260
Ammoniacal nitrogen	800–850
Nitrate nitrogen	100–105
Organic nitrogen including area	135–200
Sulphate as SO_4	1,610–1,670
Phosphates as PO_4	0.1–2.1
Phenol	140–156
COD	470–5,375
Dissolved oxygen	Nil
Chlorides as Cl	60–80
Calcium as Ca++	85
Magnesium as Mg ++	15
Total alkalinity as $CaCO_3$	125
Suspended solids	211–232

Note: All results except pH are in mg/litre.

Table 8.4 *Common Toxins and Their Sources*

Toxins	Sources
Acids mainly inorganic but some organic causing pH < 6	Acid manufacture, battery manufacture, chemical industry and steel industry
Alkalis causing pH > 9	Brewery wastes, food industries, chemical industry and textile manufacture
Ammoniacal nitrogen	Coke manufacture, fertilizer and rubber industry
Chromium, mainly hexavalent	Metal processing and tanneries
Cyanide	Coke production and metal plating
Detergents	Detergent manufacture and textile manufacture
Herbicides and pesticides	Chemical industry and agricultural waste
Metals mainly, Cu, Cd, Co, Pl, Ni, Hg and Zn	Metal processing and plating chemical industry
Phenols	Coke production
Solvents (e.g., benzene, acetone, CCl_4, alcohols, etc.)	Chemical and pharmaceuticals industry

Source: R. M. Harrison, ed., *Pollution: Causes, Effects and Control* (London: Royal Society of Chemistry, 2015), 52.

nearby. Table 8.3 shows the chemical characteristics of the raw effluent inside the factory.

The above two cases are only typical examples. There are many more toxins in industrial effluents polluting river water, which ultimately forms the source of drinking water for a large section of people in Jharkhand. Sources of some common toxins are given in Table 8.4.

BREATHE WE MUST BUT WHAT?
Air Pollution

Primary pollutants in air are smoke, ash, sulphur dioxide, carbon oxides, nitrogen oxides, lead, chlorine and fluorine compounds, offensive odours, aerosols and solid particles. Sources of pollution are mainly fuel burning chambers and processes—burning of coke, coal or oil—in industries, thermal power stations, domestic stoves or automobiles. Gases from chemical works, radiation from nuclear reactors, cigarette smoking, etc., also add up to the list of pollutants which are produced by atmospheric chemistry from the primary soup, for example, oxidation of NO to NO_2.

No published data of air quality survey for the cities and industrial areas in Jharkhand could be procured by the author. A study was conducted by the present author Jamshedpur for one month in 1978 from materials collected by deposit gauge. The unpublished data of that study along with corresponding data for residential and extreme industrial areas in Great Britain[6] are given in Table 8.5 for comparative evolution.

To get an idea about the state of air pollution in areas around thermal power stations, we reproduce the standard estimate of release of pollutants from a 400 MW plant (Table 8.6). Table 8.7 gives maximum ground level concentration around a 400 MW coal-based plant and the accepted tolerance limit.

There is very little published work on pollutants in the air from fertilizer industries in India. R. Haty R. and K. S. Chary[7] only enumerates the pollutants but no quantitative data are presented. The pollutants are dust, coming from material handling, crushing, grinding,

Table 8.5 *Study of Materials by Deposit Gauge*

_Material Collected at Jamshedpur	Great Britain	Residential Areas	Extreme Industrial Areas
Rainfall	38 mm/month	–	–
pH value	7.1	–	–
Insoluble matter:	All quantities in kg/100 m²/month		
Combustible	1.00	0.16	1.20
Ash	4.5	0.20	4.40
Soluble matter:			
Chloride	0.10	0.08	0.16
Sulphate	0.60	0.08	0.44
Calcium	0.03	0.03	0.40

Table 8.6 *Annual Release (Pounds) from a 400 MW Plant*

Pollutants	Annual Release Using		
	Coal	Oil	Natural Gas
Aldehydes	4.6×10^4	1.03×10^4	2.72×10^4
Oxides of nitrogen	1.84×10^7	1.91×10^7	1.06×10^7
Oxides of sulphur	1.22×10^8	4.64×10^7	1.08×10^4
Carbon monoxide	4.6×10^5	7.36×10^3	Negligible
Hydrocarbons	1.84×10^5	5.88×10^3	Negligible
Particulates	3.96×10^6	6.4×10^5	4.08×10^5

Source: Terrill et al. *Journal of Surgery and Medicine* 36, 42 (1967).

Table 8.7 *Concentration of Pollutants from a Fertiliser Plant*

Pollutant	Maximum Concentration (ppm)	Concentration Standard (ppm)
Aldehydes	1.9×10^{-1}	Unknown
Oxides of nitrogen	79	1
Oxides of sulphur	240	0.1
Carbon monoxide	2.08	1
Hydrocarbons	1.47	Unknown
Particulates	3.6×10^{-2}	Unknown

Source: Terrill et al., *Journal of Surgery and Medicine.*

etc., oxides of sulphur, oxides of nitrogen, fluorides and ammonia, leaking from pipes. Raman et al.[8] published some data after a field survey in a fertilizer industry but kept the name of the factory a secret, presumably not to incur the wrath of the men in power.

HOW SAFE IS THE LIFE OF YOUR CHILDREN?

If one culls newspaper reports (since no worth believing health bulletins are published) for the past 10 years, one will find that killer diseases are running rampant in Purulia, Singhbhum, Giridih, Mayurbhanj in every district of Jharkhand as well as in adjoining districts. Wellpath health experts label these diseases as Japanese encephalitis, unknown viral fever, and so on and so forth. But the helpless Jharkhandi children continue to fall victim to these diseases. Jharkhahdi people are paying dearly with their and their children's lives for the devastation of environment, especially pollution of water, and paying they are since the days of British rule. Report on Labour Conditions in the Mica Mining and Mica Manufacturing Industry (1946)[9] revealed that silicosis, diarrhoea, dyspepsia, bronchitis, rheumatism plagued the Jharkhandi working people in mica mine areas. High rate of incidence of dysentery and diarrhoea was attributed to water pollution and bronchitis and silicosis to air pollution in the mining area. The then colonial government at least took up a systematic study of the conditions of health of a section of Jharkhandi people. That task is still grossly neglected by apparently benevolent national governments. But the risk to health has augmented because of the proliferation of the number and volume of toxic substances released into the atmosphere now.

WATER THAT KILLS YOUR THIRST AND LIFE

Pollutants from sewage introduce a host of pathogenic bacteria, including those which cause cholera, typhoid, diphtheria and streptococcal infection. With increased biochemical oxygen demand, such water is also harmful for aquatic lives. The occurrence of nitrates, chloroform and other tetrakis hydroxymethyl-phosphonium sulphate (THPS), alkylating agents, dichlorodiphenyltrichloroethane, polychlorinated biphenyls, fluorides, sodium and polynuclear hydrocarbons above a certain limit is hazardous to health. The WHO prescribes for 'wholesome' drinking water certain standards,[10] which are not at all adhered to even in Jharkhand cities. Excess nitrate level cause deadly methemoglobinemia in children and gastric cancer. The WHO standard is 50 mg/1 (as NO3). The extra softness of water has certainly some connection with cardiovascular mortality. THPS and polycyclic aromatic hydrocarbons (PAHs) are carcinogens, whereas phenol is a promoter. There are a host of carcinogenic and mutagenic chemicals making their way to drinking water from sewage or industrial effluents which cause cancer of gastrointestinal and genitourinary tracts. Metal pollutants also pose considerable hazards, as vindicated in the Minamata Bay case of mercury poisoning in Japan in the 1950s.

POISONOUS GAS THAT IS AIR

Dusts in mines or adjoining places regularly inhaled cause pneumoconiosis, including silicosis, a progressive inflammation of the lung tissues, and chronic bronchitis is also attributed to dust and SO2 in air. The noxious gases from industrial plants, namely oxides of nitrogen and organic compounds, including PAH, are harmful to humans, plants and animals.

- **SO$_2$:** SO$_2$ is oxidized to H$_2$SO$_4$. When absorbed in minute quantities, it penetrates deep into the lungs and causes damage.[11] Around 1 ppm of SO$_2$ for 1 hour or 0.3 ppm for 8 hours[12] is considered considerably adverse.
- **NO$_X$:** NO is converted into NO$_2$ which breaks up to give atomic oxygen, which in turn combines to give ozone. Around 2 ppm of nitrogen oxides can cause chronic fibrotic changes. At higher concentrations, these gases cause pulmonary oedema. They also cause smog.
- **CO:** Exposure for 1 hour to a concentration of 120 ppm of CO causes inactivities of about 5 per cent of the body's haemoglobin.
- **Pb:** Lead from vehicular emission and other sources accumulates in the body. According to different blood levels of lead, it causes anaemia and neurological damage in children, gastro-intestinal and encephalopathic symptoms, coma and death. The maximum safe level for a child is 30/ug/dl.

WHAT IS TO BE DONE?

It would be far from truth to assert that industrial pollution is a problem specific to the Jharkhand region only. Actually, it is a global problem with different degrees of intensities and levels of initiatives from governmental authorities, on one hand, and industrialists, on the other, to check and ameliorate it. It is in this plane of initiatives from concerned authorities, in response to the men who matter, in the attitude to recognizing the gravity of the problem, that the scenario here has a touch of peculiarity. Governmental authorities are apathetic; industrialists are non-cooperative, and bureaucrats are servile to the powerful industrial lobby. The pollution problem in Jharkhand has its origin, as in other places of the globe, in the wrong concept of development, that is, taking the volume of production as the single yardstick of development. The peculiar absence of any regulatory or reformative initiative in Jharkhand emanates from the fact that the Jharkhandi people have no political power to wield, no state of their own to influence their decisions about planning, execution of planning or redressal of any imposed event, whatever traumatic influence that it may exert on the people who suffer. It will not be irrelevant if we quote a passage from the inaugural address of the orientation seminar on India's policy on the environment.[13] The inaugural address was given by P. R. Dubhasi, Director of the Indian Institute of Public Administration, New Delhi. Professor Dubhasi stated,

> You start a paper factory. The Marwari families go there and start investing in the paper mills.... And they cut the bamboo and they cut the other forests and thus develop more paper. But they are not responsible for replanting. And therefore the whole rich forest there is getting sacrificed at the altar of this kind of prosperity.

Why blame Marwaris alone? But Professor Dubhasi has hit the nail on the head. In Jharkhand, Jharkhandi people are relegated to acting as coolies and labourers, and it is they who lay the pillars of industrial establishments, whereas the milk and honey flows elsewhere. In return, their land, forest and air and water are surreptitiously but irrevocably done away with. Nobody should know the truth behind Professor Dubhasis's assertion than the Jharkhandi people, and it is high time that this wanton destruction should be resisted successfully. A successful resistance needs a comprehensively new theory of development, on the one hand, and well-knit people's movement to translate into practice that theory, on the other.

A NEW PATH TO TREAD

The error in the present economic theory of development is the identification of production growth with economic growth. This outmoded conception has its roots in the 18th and 19th centuries and was fathered by Adam Smith and his followers. In Adam Smith's opinion, marketable goods only form the wealth of nations. Even services, considered 'immaterial', fall from grace, as does the environment. This concept was replaced in the late 19th century. The concept of wealth was replaced by the concept of welfare, and the distinction between material goods and 'immaterial' services went. In this way, production acquired a more modest place. This theory is now to be rejuvenated and taken up so that increasingly high levels of welfare, that is, satisfaction of wants, replace the aim of increased production. Welfare depends on a number of factors of which production is only one. One should, in the new theory, take into account the costs for prevention, restoration and compensation for losses of environmental function (as deterioration of the environment leads to an individual's debilitation or death) and to deduct it from the amount of goods and services produced. The difference is only considered for the cost efficiency of an industrial project.[14] Baba Amte has shown in a parallel and independent way that the Narmada Valley Project is not cost-efficient.[15] One should estimate on this basis the cost efficiency of the Koel Karo Project.

As a corollary to this theory—instead of heavy technology, inter-mediate technology; instead of colossal dams, intermediate sized dams and dykes; instead of fertilizer, insecticide-propelled agriculture—eco-farming becomes an obvious choice. As the welfare of people becomes the pivot of this theory of exploitation of man by man, the plunder of the earth below and man above either by foreign or Indian mega giants loses its social sanction.

As regards the application aspect of this theory, the author would like to exhort JMM leaders or prominent individuals of Jharkhand to set up an environmental army and demand that industrial planning in the area must be weighed against the prospective loss of environment and that the existing industrial establishments must conform to WHO standards for treatment of effluxes and to ILO standards of workplace environments. A separate Jharkhand state will go a long way to remove the dichotomy of the interests of the state-level bureaucrats and the interests of the Jharkhandi people, but unless the struggle for the environment is taken to people at grassroot level, very little will be achieved. So people must be assiduously educated about the causes, effects and prevention of pollution.

NOTES

1. Wolanski Hapolson, in *Man and his environment* (Xth ICAES, Series No. 2), eds. I. P. Singh and S. C. Tiwari (New Delhi: Concept Publishing Company, 1980).
2. Murty, *Sc. Rep. 14*, 109, 1977.
3. S. Rajgopalan et al., *Environment Health* 12, 246 (1970).
4. G. J. Mohan Rao and P. V. R. Subrahmanyam, *Indian Journal of Environmental Health* 15, 4 (1973).
5. Kumar et al., *Indian Journal of Environmental Health* 16, 247 (1974).
6. A. R. Meetham, D. W. Bottom, and S. Cayton, *Atmospheric Pollution: Its Origins and Prevention* (Oxford: Pergamon Press, 1964).
7. R. Haty, and K. S. Chary, *Indian Journal of Environmental Health* 15, 189 (1973).
8. V. Raman et al., *Indian Journal of Environmental Health* 15, 283 (1973).
9. The report was prepared by the Department of Labour, Government of India (1946). Similar reports on the conditions of labour in iron and coal mining were prepared by B. P. Adarkarj (1945) and S. R. Deshpande (1946), respectively.
10. WHO, *International Standards for Drinking Water* (3rd Ed.), Geneva, 1971, http://apps.who.int/iris/bitstream/handle/10665/39989/9241540249_eng.pdf;jsessionid=285848543EDA58CBFF72C2CA89664087?sequence=1
11. P. Abraham, *Environment Health* 12, no. 297 (1970).
12. Bull. New York. *Academic Medicine* 41, 310 (1965).
13. Shekhar Singh, *Environment Policy in India*, 1984, http://shekharsinghcollections.com/content/Environment/Policy/1984-Environmental-Policy-in-India.pdf
14. R. Heuting, and C. Leipart, *The Environmentalist* 10, 25 (1990).
15. N. Haldar, ed., *Baba Amte, Narmadar Kanna* (In Bengali).

Chapter 9

Some Cognitive and Motivational Concomitants of Poverty*

Durganand Sinha

In April 1974, an interdisciplinary seminar in Hyderabad was held to discuss who are the poor. Most of the social scientists who had come as participants had travelled by air and were staying in reasonable comfort in the University Guest House. In the preparation for the seminar, a good deal of money had been spent. Many journalists, scholars and student leaders questioned the very wisdom of holding such a conference when the amount spent could have been more gainfully utilized in ameliorating the lot of some who were poor. It was, with considerable justification, contended that the phenomenon of poverty was so widespread that one did not require a theory or need to discuss the methodology for its study. This reminds one of the reactions of Karl Marx to the publication of Proudhon's two-volume treatise on economic inequality entitled *Philosophy of Poverty*. Marx was so enraged that he wrote a rejoinder and called it *Poverty of Philosophy*. More recently, in 1967, when Allen was editing the papers presented during a conference held in Madison on *Psychological Factors in Poverty,* Pearl was so provoked that he wrote a paper called 'Poverty of Psychology: An Indictment' which Allen (1970) included in his book. There is considerable justification for decrying purely academic exercise on

* *Social Change* Vol. 10, no. 1–2 (March-June 1980): 3–8.

Largely based on the theme paper presented to the All India Conference on 'Poverty, Ecology, Cognitive and Motivational Factors in Adolescents,' Zakir Husain College, University of Delhi, 30 and 31 March 1979.

poverty. It is such a widespread as well as a national problem. Its psychological cost is so great and its concomitants and consequences so harmful that merely an academic analysis of the phenomenon would be a futile exercise representing a deplorable ivory-tower attitude. It necessitates an attitude which is avowedly problem-oriented with the explicit objective of doing something about the phenomenon and evolving some intervention strategies for its solution. Pearl (1970) is right in lamenting that, as a group, psychologists have been guilty of refusing to accept the challenge that poverty has presented to society, not simply in countries with unparalleled affluence but even in those that are underdeveloped. Moscovici's (1972) contention that most psychological researches contains no reference at all to the real society in which people live is very true of most psychological studies conducted in India. With about 40 per cent of the rural and 50 per cent of the urban population living below the poverty line (Dandekar and Rath 1971), what could be a more socially relevant topic for research? There is, however, a healthy trend visible as reflected in distinct effort to plan and conduct studies with the specific purpose of utilizing the results for dealing with some aspects of the problem of poverty by developing intervention programmes for moderating and compensating for its negative consequences.

Poverty is a phenomenon of multiple determination. It is true that the economic system and social structure mainly underlie its existence. But it has inevitable psychological concomitants which have a detrimental influence on the general functioning of the individual, rendering him/her less capable of overcoming poverty by his/her personal effort. It would be wrong to suggest that one is poor because of one's psychological limitations and thereby providing a psychological justification for his/her poverty. The poor are certainly the victims of the socio-economic system. But it is also true that a life of poverty, in its torn, produces many psychological ill effects rendering the individual incompetent to cope with his/her problems. A kind of vicious circle is created; economic and social factors generate poverty, which in turn makes the individual incapable of coping with poverty. What is emphasized is that rather than being its cause, psychological consequences accentuate the condition of poverty. It is contented that a unidisciplinary approach to the problem is not adequate to combat the phenomenon because it gives only a lop-sided view of a very complex social problem. As it has rightly been observed, any diagnosis and programme of eliminating it 'have a significantly greater likelihood of success if relevant systems at all levels of analysis are brought to bear in a concentrated fashion (Allen 1970). In this respect, it is to be noted that psychology as a discipline is most competent to deal with behavioural dimensions of poverty. While other aspects are not ignored or their importance minimized, it is emphasized that ignoring the psychological variables may lead to ameliorative programmes with unexpected and undesirable consequences. Understanding the psychological characteristics of the poor is as important as the analysis of the system that brought about the condition of poverty.

For psychology, the phenomenon can best be viewed from an ecological perspective. The economic and sociocultural environment of the poor is characterized by low income, inequality, sociocultural disadvantage due to their position in the class and caste hierarchy, familial deprivation, early separation from family, illiteracy and exposure to inadequate schooling, low-educational level of parents, inadequate housing and residence in slums or remote rural areas have all cumulatively produced a phenomenon of extreme deficit or disadvantage. Following Bronfenbrenner (1974), it is advantageous to conceptualize these in ecological terms as it helps to understand better the psychological factors of poverty (Sinha 1977). A two-tiered concentric layer of factors has been proposed. The upper or more visible layer contains the immediate socio-physical environment of the child (such as home, school and peer groups), each providing three dimensions of physical space and materials, social roles and relationships and his/her activities. The second concentric layer is the 'supporting or surrounding' one, embedding the former as provided by the physical and geographical environment, institutional setting of the individual in terms of social class, caste and so on, and the general services and amenities available to him. As Sinha (1977) puts it, the psychological problems of what we call the 'weaker sections of society,' the underprivileged, backward classes, the Scheduled Castes and Tribes, which usually constitute the poor, can be viewed in terms of these concentric layers of ecology. For example, general poverty and the attendant congestion of the locality to which people belong, the limitations and roles enjoined by caste, and the facilities provided by the civic authorities to the areas where people reside can be viewed as the surrounding layer of ecology. Again, the conditions and facilities prevalent in the home, the role relationships prevalent therein, and the activities encouraged or discouraged would constitute the outer and visible layer of ecology. Similarly, the conditions of the school and the nature and quality of schooling, as well as the nature of peer groups to which the child belongs, would be regarded as other factors of outer layer ecology. The contrast in ecologies in both the layers is easily visible in comparing children from caste-Hindu families with those from the Scheduled Castes or the so-called 'untouchables.' For centuries, the Scheduled Castes have been living under conditions of intense social disadvantages and prevented from sharing in the mainstream of sociocultural and economic life of the Hindu society. The sociocultural disadvantages under which they exist are often referred to by Indian psychologists as cultural deprivation. Whiteman and Deutsch (1968) have observed that 'social deprivation implies that the association between social grouping and specific environmental factors is not directly causal, but is mediated by more basic societal conditions such as unemployment, poverty, and inequality of opportunity in various areas.' Misra (1977) remarks that these ecological factors provide the source and variety for sensory stimulation and thereby enrich or impoverish the experiential content of the individual. Within this ecological framework, the salient causative factors producing significant psychological consequences can be conceptualized and understood. These factors, it is felt, would affect the psychological functioning of the individual at their own level as well as interacting with each other and with factors at the other level, so that sometimes one observes extremely complex reactions to poverty on the level of the individual. The author (Sinha 1977) has used this model for his own studies related to poverty and has found it useful for generating problems and analysing its psychological concomitants.

From the point of view of a psychologist, we can group poverty research under five broad headings, namely (a) effects of poverty on cognitive, perceptual and linguistic skills, (b) motivational and personality dimensions, (c) personal style including self-concept, success and failure orientation, time perspective and coping strategies developed by the poor, (d) nutritional, sensory, motor and physiological factors related to poverty and (e) mental health, crime and delinquency as related to poverty. I would only deal with one or two research relating to the cognitive and motivational spheres, with which I have been personally associated or indirectly involved.

Most of the studies dealing with the cognitive aspects of poverty have been conceptualized within the broad framework of deprivation effects. In one of our studies, we (Shukla and Sinha 1974a; Sinha and Shukla 1974b) investigated the effects of familial deprivation on child's proficiency in utilizing different pictorial depth cues. It was observed that the pattern of development of the efficacy, with which various depth cues such as interposition, relative size, shading, texture gradient, linear perspective and aerial perspective were used, was similar in children who had been brought up in families as well as in those suffering from parental deprivation or separation due to being institutionalized. But though the *pattern of emergence* of this skill was similar, the two groups differed regarding the *level of competence* in using these cues. Even when children were pair-matched for intelligence, the deprived group was significantly lower in competence than the normal group.

We have been conducting a number of studies on perceptual skills by comparing some socially disadvantaged groups with more advantaged groups. The indices of disadvantage that we have used are socio-economic and caste status, nature of schooling facilities and rural/urban background. Using measures of pictorial skills where certain positional cues have to be arranged in their proper sequence and extracting a story from them, it has been observed that while both the advantaged and disadvantaged groups of children distinctly showed a developmental trend, the effects of schooling and caste were significant. Children from higher castes and exposed to better schooling facilities consistently performed better than those from the Scheduled Castes and those exposed to inadequate schooling or no exposure to schools. Another interesting result which we have observed is that when the trends of development of these skills are compared among children from different types of schools, it was observed that in case of the ordinary schools, the higher caste or Scheduled Caste differences tended to get levelled off with increase in years of schooling. But in the so-called superior schools, the reverse seemed to be the case. In the lower age groups, the scores of higher castes and the Scheduled Caste were similar if not slightly in favour of the Scheduled Caste.

But with advancing age and years of schooling the differences got reversed and accentuated in favour of higher castes, producing a kind of 'broomstick effect' or 'torchlight effect.' It indicated that in spite of the fact that the underprivileged had been provided with excellent schooling facilities, its effect was not towards reducing the higher caste–Scheduled Caste disparity in these skills. On the contrary, the disparity was getting more accentuated with advance in age and schooling. It indicates that the problem is not simply a matter of providing belter schooling facilities or opportunities. The roots of the malaise lie deeper and operate in a very complex manner.

Many other studies on cognitive and intellectual consequences of poverty have indicated that, apart from economic deprivation, the poor are also the victims of many sociocultural disadvantages whose psychological consequences are harmful. As it has been suggested, all these deficiencies are not due to lower intelligence but due to the eco-cultural factors that surround the poor.

Before passing on to the motivational dimensions, I would like to refer to one of the important consequences of poverty in the shape of restriction of language and linguistic modes of communication. I need not deal at any length with the brilliant and extensive studies of Bernstein (1960, 1962, 1964), who has demonstrated the interfacing of language with other forms of social behaviour and the association of class differential with linguistic skills. There is a wealth of evidence which shows that the linguistic code developed by the poor is restricted, relatively undifferentiated, simplex, lacking in modifiers, implicit and aimed at reinforcing and implementing the social structure rather than conveying information. In contrast, the linguistic code of the middle upper-class strata is elaborated. Bernstein's work has been criticized. Whatever may be the criticism, it is clear that the linguistic skills developed by the poor as also the cognitive-perceptual skills render them less capable of performance on the kind of academic tasks with which educational institutions confront them. They encounter failure and frustration and, due to poor academic attainments, are rendered less capable of combating their poverty. The total effect is that their condition, which was already bad due to poverty, is made worse. Due to the limitations suffered from poverty, they do not easily acquire such skills that would enable them to counter poverty.

It has been suggested that poverty produces some motivational and personality characteristics that result in various kinds of inadequacies in behaviour for successfully coping with the problems that are created by it. The roots can probably be traced to parental interaction and the general process of socialization which the child experiences in his/her impoverished environment. Hess (1970) rightly describes it as the 'socialisation of apathy and under-achievement.' Professor Rath (1972, 1974) in his studies has reported significantly low aspiration levels for income, occupation and education of the poor and underprivileged tribal students in comparison to those of higher castes. There was also a high and significant positive correlation between the low aspirations of the parents and their school going children of lower caste and tribal groups. It was contended that 'aspirations of children were nothing but the internalized projections of similar aspirations of their parents (Rath 1973). Others have commented upon low self-concept and low self-esteem among the poor and the underprivileged, while some have pointed to the lower need for achievement among lower class individuals (Gokulnathan and Mehta 1972). The general description of the poor from the motivational side that can be gathered from various psychological studies is that they are low in motivation and aspiration, apathetic, fatalistic and resigned to their lot. My own studies among the residents of highly backward and undeveloped villages indicate that, when compared to those from the advanced villages, they were overwhelmingly concerned with immediate needs of subsistence and had a static level of aspiration. They frequently construed their hopes and aspirations in fanciful and unrealistic terms and were unable to conceptualize the needs under the wider frame of reference of a village community or a country. Their behaviour was characterized by extreme caution, absence of risk-taking and failure avoidance. They tended to underestimate their performance and displayed an attitude of apathy and resignation. While conceptualizing what constituted a happy life, they were significantly vague and frequently fantasy-oriented (Sinha 1969). All these cumulatively indicate that the condition of poverty had produced a motivational syndrome which made it extremely difficult for him to cope with the problems created by poverty. Professor Udai Pareek (1970) defines poverty psychologically in terms of deprivation and helplessness and elaborates the motivational pattern induced by it.

Apart from orientation to helplessness and feeling of powerlessness, he suggests a paradigm of culture of poverty, that is, poverty as a structural component produces a threefold motivational pattern characterized by low need for achievement, low need for extension and high need for dependency. He contends that dependency motivation is expressed through lack of initiative, avoidance syndromes, excessive fear of failure, seeking favours from superiors, over-conformity and aggressive rejection of authority. This dependency is often reflected in over-dependence on governmental and other external agencies and almost total lack of self-help.

Recently, we have been concerned with analysing the coping strategies of poor underprivileged students coming to universities from families with no tradition of education. We have been struck by the reactions which many of these students display towards success and failure. While the findings are still tentative, it appears that they have a strong tendency to refer success to 'external' factors such as kindness of teachers, God and fate. They are thankful for their beneficence rather than ascribe success to their own efforts and thus take pride in their accomplishment and experience a sense of fulfilment, which would be reinforcing to their behaviour. This externalization of the success factor reduces its reinforcing value. The mediating mechanism that they adopt of ascribing success to external agencies frequently leads to superstitious behaviour, perpetuation of fatalistic outlook and produces superstitious ritualism, that is, performing the same rites before undertaking a big task. It also sometimes leads to the ingratiation of significant others.

While success factors are externalized, failure is often ascribed to oneself. Along with harsh self-criticism and less favourable self-concept, one has rigid and stringent standards for evaluating one's performance which are dysfunctional. One frequently displays an internalized mechanism of self-discouragement. Instead of ascribing failures to others as one does in case of success, one views it as due to one's own inadequacies. Thus, the motivational characteristics of the poor and the underprivileged that we have observed seem to be low or unrealistic motivation, external locus for success and personal inadequacies for failure, harsh and rigid self-evaluation and extreme anxiety about the outcome of one's performance. The inevitable result is discouragement. The effect of one's coping strategy for dealing with success and failure seems to be that while one's success is not reinforcing as it should have been, the failure is extremely discouraging. One experiences a state of uncertainty and wonders whether all the external forces are working in the right direction or not—a state of doubt which motivationally is damaging. Further, since the failure is ascribed to internal causes, one does not have an outside scapegoat for it but begins to blame oneself, thereby lowering one's own self-image.

The general direction of the findings relating to cognitive and motivational components of poverty indicates that some of the effects that poverty produces in these two areas are damaging to the individual and undermine his/her competence for coping with the problems of poverty. In conclusion, it may be pointed out that these psychological dimensions of poverty require careful analysis to help forge adequate intervention strategies so that economic and other programmes of combating poverty do not get distorted and run into unexpected and sometimes harmful directions.

REFERENCES

Allen, V. L. 1970. *Psychological Factors in Poverty*. New York, NY: Free Press.

Bernstein, B. 1960. 'Language and Social Class.' *British Journal of Sociology* 11, no. 3: 271–276.

———. 1962. 'Linguistic Codes, Hesitation Phenomena and Intelligence.' *Language and Speech* 5, no. 2: 31–46.

———. 1964. 'Elaborated and Restricted Codes: Their Social Origins and Some Consequences.' *American Anthropologist* 66, no. 6 (Part 2): 55–69.

Bronfenbrenner, U. 1974. 'Development Research, Public Policy, and Ecology of Childhood.' *Child Development* 45, no. 1: 1–5.

Dandekar, V. M., and Rath, N. 1971. 'Poverty in India.' *Economic & Political Weekly* 6, no. 2: 25–48: 106–146.

Gokulnathan, P. P., and Mehta, P. 1972. 'Achievement Motive in Tribal and Non-tribal Assamese Secondary School Adolescents.' *Indian Educational Review* 7, no. 1: 67–90.

Hess, R. D. 1970. 'The Transmission of Cognitive Strategies in Poor: The Socialisation of Apathy and Underachievement.' In *Psychological Factors in Poverty*, edited by V. L. Allen. New York, NY: Academic Press.

Misra, G. 1977. 'Cognitive Functioning and Ecological Factors.' Paper presented to the symposium on 'Ecological Factors in Cognitive Development', Annual Convention of U. P. Psychological Association, Kanpur, February.

Moscovici. S. 1972. 'Society and Theory in Social Psychology.' In *The Context of Social Psychology*, edited by J. Israel and H. Tajfel. New York, NY: Academic Press.

Pareek, Udai. 1970. 'Poverty and Motivation: Figure and Ground.' In *Psychological Factors in Poverty*, edited by V. L. Allen. New York, NY: Academic Press.

Pearl, A. 1970. 'The Poverty of Psychology: An Indictment.' In *Psychological Factors in Poverty*, edited by Vernon L. Allen. New York, NY: Academic Press.

Rath, R. 1972. 'Cognitive Growth and Classroom Learning of Culturally Deprived children in the Primary Schools.' Paper presented at the East-West Centre for Cross-Cultural Studies, Honolulu.

————. 1973. 'Teaching-learning Problems of Primary School Children: A Challenge to Indian Psychologists and Educationists.' Presidential Address, 11th Annual Conference of the Indian Academy of Applied Psychology. University of Calcutta, December 27–29.

————. 1974. 'Teaching and Learning Problem of the Disadvantaged Tribal Children.' Presidential Address, 12th Annual Conference of the Indian Academy of Applied Psychology, Utkal University Bhubaneswar. December 28–30.

Shukla, P., Sinha, D. 1974a. 'A Developmental Study of the Relative Efficacy of Different Cues in Depth Perception.' *Indian Journal of Psychology* 49, no. 3: 220–230.

————. 1974b. 'Deprivation and Development of Skill for Pictorial Depth Perception.' *Journal of Cross-cultural Psychology* 5, no. 4: 434–450.

Sinha, D. 1969. *Indian Villages in Transition: A Motivational Analysis*. New Delhi: Associated Publishers.

————. 1977. 'Some Psychological Disadvantages and Development of Certain Perceptual Skills.' *Indian Journal of Psychology* 52, no. 2: 115–132.

Tripathi, L. B., and Misra, G. 1975. 'Cognitive Activities as a Function of Prolonged Deprivation.' *Psychological Studies* 20, no. 3: 54–61.

Whiteman, M., and Deutsch, M. 1968. 'Social Disadvantages as Related to Intellective and Language Development. In *Social Class Race, and Psychological Development*, edited by M. Deutsch, I. Katz, and A. R. Jensen. New York, NY: Holt, Rinehart.

Section III
Disparities

Sectional Introduction

K. B. Saxena

Poverty indicates not only the mean income but also conveys how income is distributed among various economic classes and social groups. The latter reflects the level of inequality which influences the relationship between growth and poverty and determines the share that the poor will obtain from the growth process. A high level of existing inequality will reduce this share and adversely affect the pace of poverty reduction (Kapoor, 2013). This can only be countered by significant redistributional measures.

Inequality has shown a declining trend in rural and urban area until the 1980s. Thereafter, there has been a steady rise in inequality and an increasing trend in rural–urban disparity. Rural growth largely benefitted the poor between 1983 and 1993–1994. It turned distribution neutral between 1993–1994 and 2004–2005. In urban areas, it has moved from being distribution neutral to being pro-rich and has increased rural–urban disparity. This explains the overall rise in national inequality (World Bank, 2012). This assessment based on consumption surveys does not, however, reflect the increase in income and wealth in the top bracket of the economic divide between rich and poor. Rich Indians have cornered the bulk of the gains from the higher economic growth post-reforms in the 1990s, which has also increased wealth inequalities.

Inequality in incomes across states also rose substantially, with rich states having an average income four times those of the poor states (World Bank, 2011). But the inequalities are much higher when education, healthcare and so on are taken into account.

Rising inequality is a disturbing trend as it leads to lower human capital development and excludes the poor, particularly Scheduled Castes (SCs)/Scheduled Tribes (STs)/minorities and women from the development process. This exclusion further entrenches structural inequality based on caste, ethnicity, religion and gender. Inequalities in the labour market in terms of wages, earning, quality of work, access to jobs between the organized and unorganized sector and segmentation based on occupational skills affect not merely poverty reduction and human development but also the sustainability of growth itself (Dev, 2016a). It signals the possibility of further accentuation in disparities (Deaton & Dreze, 2002). A failure to arrest this trend and achieve equity not only in the nature and composition of growth, but also across social and economic groups, between states and regions within them through strong redistributive measures will not merely jeopardize the prospects of growth but would also lead to social instability (Kapoor, 2013).

This section highlights some of the disparities mentioned above through the inclusion of three papers. One highlights disparities in asset holding across economic and social groups, while the other brings out disparities in access to civic amenities. The remaining two papers shift the focus on disparities across regions and social groups within the states of Uttar Pradesh and Odisha.

Arjun Kumar's paper has investigated rural households' access to basic amenities and shown the extremely high levels of the unavailability of basic amenities in rural India. While there is a gradual improvement in access to amenities in proportional terms, the rural poor continue to face high levels of deprivation. He highlights appalling socio-economic disparities and exclusion. Households belonging to weaker sections have been the most deprived, neglected and excluded. The disparities have increased in access to these amenities between poor and non-poor, between STs and SCs and between SC and other households. The gap and differences are on account of caste, ethnicity based discrimination. The highest level of discrimination in access occurs in areas where weaker sections live.

Prashant Kumar Trivedi's paper examines intrastate inequities in development outcomes in Uttar Pradesh based on available information in respect of poverty, land ownership, employment, access to social services and consumer expenditure. He also captures the differentiation that exists at regional, rural–urban, caste, class and gender levels. He notes that despite some improvement in respect of a few dimensions of development, Uttar Pradesh still has a large poor population, and disparities among social groups are substantially high. The process of development excludes a substantial part of the population, and the pattern of economic development does not exactly coincide with social development. This situation is related to the dominant caste and class structure. Political mobilization of dalits and backwards has brought few gains for the poorer sections.

Satya Prakash Dash's paper highlights the failure of economic reforms to generate a positive impact on the toiling masses living in rural areas. This he does with reference to the tribal concentration districts of Koraput, Balangir and Kalahandi (KBK) districts. People living in these areas are deprived of basic social services, and a high level of poverty still exists notwithstanding that a special area development programme focused on these districts has been implemented for a long time. Socio-economic indicators present a depressing picture. The backwardness of the area is multifaceted. The health status of the SC/ST population is very low and morbidity level, and nutritional deficiencies are very high. Access to health services is very poor and health services suffer from an urban bias. Landless labourers with virtually no assets comprise 81 per cent of the SCs/STs segment. Migration, scarcity of food and starvation deaths are among other problems. Besides poverty, people face the burden of social isolation. The failure to address these problems has given rise to a Left extremist movement. The state's response to it is to crush the movement with militarization of the area rather than tackling people's grievances and giving them a voice in decision-making.

Chapter 10

Rural Households' Access to Basic Amenities in India*
Deprivation and Socio-economic Exclusions

Arjun Kumar

INTRODUCTION

Basic amenities such as water, sanitation, electricity and drainage are essential for a secure, dignified and healthy human life. Delivery of such amenities in India has been inadequate, which is reflected in the pitiable standard of living and widespread poverty, especially in rural areas. Very often, such deprivations vary spatially and across socio-economic sections of society, leading to abysmal exclusions. The excluded sections, deprived of basic amenities, are also deprived of their capacity to benefit from the opportunities and developmental efforts provided by the government. This has led to the creation of a vicious cycle of deprivation and destitution for the rural poor.

While the delivery of basic amenities was one of the key objectives of the Millennium Development Goals (MDGs), expiring in 2015, it continues to remain the central objective of the Sustainable Development Goals for ending extreme poverty and multiple deprivations, especially in developing and underdeveloped countries.

Over the last two decades, the government has launched a host of programmes and schemes to improve and ensure access to basic amenities in rural areas with special provisions for the poor, excluded

---

* *Social Change* Vol 45, no. 4 (December 2015): 561–586.

and marginalized groups. Some of these include the Indira Awas Yojana, National Rural Drinking Water Programme under Rajiv Gandhi National Drinking Water Mission, Rajiv Gandhi Grameen Vidyutikaran Yojana and Total Sanitation Campaign renamed as the Nirmal Bharat Abhiyan under the umbrella of Bharat Nirman and Provision of Urban Amenities in Rural Areas (PURA; Kumar, 2012, 2014a, 2015). These efforts have been supplemented with region-compatible, state-level policies and schemes. Even the Twelfth Five-year Plan (2012–2017) recognized that an 'inclusive growth' approach would yield benefits for all, particularly the marginalized sections of society (Dubey & Thorat, 2012).

These efforts have, however, fallen short of achieving the desired results; large-scale deprivation in accessing basic amenities in rural India continues with visible cases of extreme impoverishment amongst vulnerable social groups, particularly the Scheduled Caste (SC) and Scheduled Tribe (ST) households and other classes, including agricultural labourers (ALs) in rural areas (Bhagat, 2013; Dreze & Sen, 2013; Kumar, 2012, 2014a, 2014b, 2014c).

Consequently, the need to promote the interests of economically and socially weaker sections in rural areas has been reiterated by several reports of the United Nations and the World Bank, as well as by experts studying discrimination. For instance, in 2012, Dubey and Thorat in their study, *Has Growth Been Socially Inclusive during 1993–94—2009–10?*, observed that the insights from the experience of poverty and consumption expenditure changed during the periods from 1994–2005 to 2005–2010, particularly during the latter period, which stressed the need for a more broad-based, pro-poor policy, further supplemented by group-specific—social, religious and economic—policies being made an integral part of the overall planning strategy.

DATABASE AND METHODOLOGY

This study is based on the database on basic amenities in the Census of India and National Sample Survey Organisation. The indicators of access to basic amenities used here are deprivation measures, including the unavailability of drinking water, sanitation, electricity and drainage arrangements in the house.

Census of India

Data on Houses, Housing Amenities and Assets, House Listing and Housing Census Data, 2001 and 2011

1. *Households without drinking water available within the premise.* This refers to households with drinking water available near or away from the premises.
2. *Households without a latrine facility within the premise.* This refers to households with public and open latrines for use but no latrine facilities within the premise.
3. *Households without electricity in the house as a source of lighting.* This refers to households with kerosene and other sources of lighting in the house but no electricity.
4. *Households without closed drainage connectivity for waste water outlet.* This refers to households with open drainage and no drainage connectivity for waste water outlet.

National Sample Survey (NSS) Housing Conditions Round Data, 1993 and 2008–2009

1. *No facility of drinking water in the house.* This refers to the community use of drinking water facilities available to the household.
2. *No latrine facility in the house.* This refers to the public or community use of latrine facilities and non-availability of such a facility within the house.
3. *No electricity used for domestic purposes.* This refers to the non-availability of electricity to the household for domestic use.
4. *Open katcha and no drainage arrangement.* Here, underground and *pucca* arrangements for drainage are excluded.

For the analysis, proportions in percentages and absolute levels of deprivation in accessing basic amenities by households in rural India have been calculated. Changes in levels of deprivation have been measured using a compounded annual growth rate.

The analysis of the levels of and changes in deprivation in accessing basic amenities—water, sanitation, electricity and drainage—has been done for rural households in India and also by disaggregation into households belonging to the poor and non-poor, caste and ethnic groups and religious groups and economic groups-livelihood categories. To tackle the issue of sufficient sample sizes for the analysis from the NSS, while making minute enquiries, sample sizes have been checked and reported in Annexure A for every unit of analysis, and only the minute enquiries with sufficient and appropriate sample sizes have been reported in the chapter. To overcome the limitations of the NSS, since it is based on sampling and not the whole universe, data from the Census for household information have also been referred to.

The disparities in deprivation of basic amenities among various groups have been measured using the Modified Sopher's Disparity Index (Modified Sopher's Disparity Index = Log (X2/X1) + Log [(200-X1)/(200-X2)]), where X1 and X2 are percentage values of the indicators (deprivation of basic amenities) for Groups 1 and 2, respectively; the ideal value for the Index for having no disparity is 0; a higher value of the Index shows that the extent of disparity is higher and vice versa. A positive value suggests that the situation is in favour of Group 1 (less deprived of basic amenities), and a negative value suggests that the situation is in favour of Group 2. The changes in the index values, over time, were also captured and analysed.

The determinants of households with access to basic amenities in the house have been estimated using the probit[1] model on household unit record data, NSS Housing Conditions round (using the sample (probability) weights), 2008/2009, to identify the factors that affect the likelihood of households to have access to basic amenities in the house. The dependent variables in the model are households with the facility of drinking water in the house, households with latrine facilities in the house, households having electricity for domestic purposes and households with closed drainage arrangements in the house, and the explanatory variables are households' affiliation to monthly per capita expenditure (MPCE) quintile class categories, household types (livelihood categories), social groups and religious groups (with one sub-category of a variable referred to as the 'reference category' for that variable).

To study the contribution of caste-based factors to the difference in the accessibility rate of basic amenities among various social groups in rural India, the difference between the mean probability of access to basic amenities by upper caste (others) households (or the reference group) and households belonging to group X (or STs, SCs or Other Backward Classes [OBCs]) has been decomposed into 'attributes' contribution' (contribution of non-caste-based factors) and 'coefficient's contribution' (contribution of caste-based factors), using the method[2] of extension of the Blinder–Oaxaca decomposition technique to Logit and Probit (discrete choice) models (Borooah et al., 2014; Fairlie, 2006; Sinning et al., 2008). The dataset used here is from NSS Housing Condition Round 2008/09 and the estimates are based upon the sample (probability) weights provided by the NSS household-level unit record data (for 8,130 villages and 97,144 households[3]).

The attributes' contribution (explained differences) was computed by asking what the difference between others households and households from Group X, in their proportions accessing basic amenities in the house, would have been if the difference in attributes between them had been evaluated using a common coefficient vector. The coefficients' contribution (the unexplained differences) was computed as a residual, that is, the observed difference minus the attributes' contribution, and this could be ascribed to the 'structural advantage/disadvantage' that the households from the others group enjoyed over those from Group X. It must be pointed here that the source of this structural advantage/ disadvantage cannot be ascribed, which has also been pointed out by Borooah et al. (2014). The coefficient's contribution is regarded as caste-based factors' contribution to the differences in probabilities of accessing basic amenities between two groups.

SUMMARY OF FINDINGS

Aggregate

According to the data from the latest Census of 2011 (Table 10.1), the levels of deprivations in accessing basic amenities in rural India are found to be deplorably high. There is no contesting the fact that the developmental policies of the government, especially from 2001 to 2011, have helped in improving the rural households' access to drinking water within the premise, latrine facilities within the premise, electricity in the house and closed drainage connectivity for waste water outlet, as is shown in the decline in the percentage of households not having these amenities.

Table 10.1 Access to Important Basic Amenities in Rural India, 2001 and 2011 (Numbers Are in Millions)

	Levels			2001–2011 (Changes)	
	2011	2001	Numbers (Millions)	As Proportion of Total Households (HHs) During 2001 (in %)	Annual Compounded (in %)
Number of HHs (in millions)	167.83	138.27	29.56	21.37	
In %					
Number of HHs not having availability of drinking water within the premise (near the premise and away; in millions)	109.09	98.59	10.50		
As proportion of total HHs (in %)	65.00	71.30		10.65	−0.92
Number of HHs not having latrine facility within the premise (public and open latrine use; in millions)	116.30	107.99	8.31		
As proportion of total HHs (in %)	69.30	78.10		7.70	−1.19
Number of HHs not having electricity in the house (kerosene, other sources and no lighting; in millions)	75.02	78.12	−3.10		
As proportion of total HHs (in %)	44.70	56.50		−3.97	−2.32
Number of HHs not having closed drainage connectivity for waste water outlet (open drainage and no drainage; in millions)	158.18	132.87	25.31		
As proportion of total HHs (in %)	94.25	96.09		19.05	−0.19

Source: Author's calculation using tables on houses, household amenities and assets, house listing and housing data, Census of India, 2001 and 2011.

Note: Annual compounded growth rate is calculated based upon proportion of HHs in 2011 over proportion of HHs in 2001 of levels of deprivation.

However, despite the improvement in percentage terms, the absolute number of deprived households rose during this period, except in the case of accessing electricity. This absolute rise is a cause of concern for policymakers. The reason for this trend is the low rate of improvements (or decline in the compounded annual rate) of deprivation in the case of accessing drinking water, sanitation and draining facilities in the house.

In rural India, 65 per cent of households did not have drinking water available within their premises in 2011. This was an improvement over the 71.3 per cent deprived households in 2001, but the absolute number of rural households with no drinking water facility within the premises rose by 10.50 million during the decade, thereby marking a decadal growth of 10.7 per cent.

The percentage of households not having a latrine facility within the premise fell from 78.1 per cent in 2001 to 69.3 per cent in 2011. However, the absolute number of households without a latrine facility within the premises rose by 8.3 million, thereby marking a decadal growth of 7.7 per cent (Kumar, 2014c, 2015).

Access to electricity, on the contrary, showed an improvement in both percentage and absolute terms. The percentage of households in rural areas not having electricity in the house fell from 56.5 per cent in 2001 to 44.7 per cent in 2011, and correspondingly, the absolute number of households in rural areas not having electricity in the house fell by 3.1 million over the period, thereby marking a decadal growth of −3.9 per cent.

The percentage of households not having closed drainage connectivity for waste water outlets fell from 96.1 per cent to 94.3 per cent. However, the absolute number of households in rural areas not having closed drainage connectivity for waste water outlet rose by 25.31 million from 2001 to 2011, thereby marking a decadal growth of 19.1 per cent.

The difference in the decadal growth of and an absolute rise in deprivation among the various indicators of basic amenities is explained by their rates of improvement or compounded annual rates of decline during the period. The rates were as low as 0.9 per cent, 1.2 per cent and 0.2 per cent, respectively, for the percentage of households not having access to drinking water, latrine facilities within the premise and closed drainage connectivity for waste water outlets in the house. Only access to electricity in the house improved faster at 2.3 per cent—fast enough to fill the wide gap of deprivation in its access in rural areas during 2001–2011.

Table 10.2 Access to Basic Amenities by Poor–Non-poor Households in Rural India, 1993 and 2008–2009 (in Percentage Points)

	Non-poor	Poor	Total		Modified Sopher's Disparity Index (Poor, Non-poor)
No Facility of Drinking Water in the House					
Levels in 1993	69.83	78.00	73.48	Changes in index value	−0.08
Levels in 2008–2009	52.17	68.98	56.90		−0.17
Changes during 1993–2008/2009 (annual compounded)	−1.83	−0.78	−1.61		−0.10
No latrine facility in the house					
Levels in 1993	84.01	91.65	87.83	Changes in index value	−0.07
Levels in 2008–2009	59.83	83.80	66.46		−0.23
Changes during 1993–2008/2009 (annual compounded)	−2.13	−0.57	−1.75		−0.16
No Electricity Use for Domestic Purposes					
Levels in 1993	56.71	71.08	63.04	Changes in index value	−0.14
Levels in 2008–2009	27.57	50.93	33.99		−0.33
Changes during 1993–2008/2009 (annual compounded)	−4.48	−2.09	−3.85		−0.19

Open, Katcha and No Drainage Arrangement in the House				
Levels in 1993	88.39	92.67	90.43	Changes in index value
Levels in 2008–2009	72.09	84.03	75.32	
Changes during 1993–2008/2009 (annual compounded)	–1.29	–0.62	–1.15	

				Changes in index value
				–0.04
				–0.11
				–0.07

Source: Author's calculation using National Sample Survey, Housing Conditions Round, unit record data for the respective years, Planning Commission and Ministry of Labour, GoI.

Notes: Poverty line has been calculated based on old official poverty line method used by the Planning Commission.
Poverty line has been updated from 1993 and 2004–05 poverty estimates of Planning Commission using consumer price index for agricultural labourers (base year 1986–1987 = 100) for rural areas.

NSS data from 1993 to 2008/2009 in Table 10.2 also shows the same improvement in rural areas, that is, a decline in the proportion of deprived households, with the annual rates of decline in deprivation of facility of drinking water, latrine facilities, electricity and *pucca* drainage arrangement in the house being 1.61 per cent, 1.75 per cent, 3.85 per cent and 1.15 per cent, respectively, where higher rates in the decline of deprivation of basic amenities led to lower levels of deprivation.

Acceleration in improvement was observed in the decline in the deprivation in access to basic amenities by households during 2002–2008/2009, as per the NSS data (Kumar, 2012, 2014a), showing that the policies adopted in 2005, under Bharat Nirman, did speed up the development process and delivery. However, the pace needs to be further improved in order to achieve the MDGs and a decent standard of living for all.

Economic Groups: Poor and Non-poor

Poor households in rural India witnessed a low annual rate of decline in deprivation in access to basic amenities as compared to non-poor households from 1993 to 2008/09, resulting in high levels of deprivation faced by the poor in 2008/09 (Table 10.2). Also, the disparities in access to basic amenities by the poor and the non-poor (as measured by the Modified Sopher's Disparity Index) were observed to have increased substantially during the same period.

Economic Groups: Livelihood Categories

ALs' households were found to be the most deprived of all amenities, followed by other labourers (OLs). Households of the self-employed in agriculture, self-employed in the non-agriculture sector and Others were slightly better off than ALs and OLs (Table 10.9).

Caste and Ethnic Groups

In rural India, centuries of caste-based social organizations have left a legacy of inequalities and led to the process of exclusion, discrimination and deprivation (Thorat, 2008; Thorat & Mahamallik, 2006; Thorat & Newman, 2010). Historical inequalities continue in the current system and society: Present-day biases on the basis of caste, ethnicity and classes further aggravate a weak implementation system designed to rectify the dismal state of the marginalized sections.

ST and SC households in rural India have witnessed a low annual rate of decline in deprivation in accessing basic amenities as compared to others households, during 2001–2011, as per census and during 1993–2008/2009 as per NSS data (Tables 10.3 and 10.4), resulting in high levels of deprivation of ST and SC households in the concluding periods. The levels of deprivation in accessing basic amenities in the house were found to be very high for STs and SCs, followed by OBCs and then the others households in 2008–2009 by NSS data (Table 10.9; Kumar, 2012).

There are high disparities in deprivation in accessing basic amenities between ST and SC households and between SC and Others households, and these disparities rose marginally, as per the values of the Modified Sopher's Disparity Index from 2001 to 2011 (census data) and from 1993 to 2008/09 (NSS data).

Religious Groups

Households belonging to other religious minorities (ORMs) witnessed the lowest levels of deprivation in accessing basic amenities, followed by Muslims and then Hindus (Table 10.9). Hindus experienced the highest levels of deprivation in accessing drinking water and sanitation facilities in the house, whereas Muslims experienced the highest levels of deprivation in accessing electricity and drainage arrangements.

Economic Groups and Caste and Ethnic Groups

Changes in the percentage levels of deprivation in accessing drinking water, latrine facilities, electricity use and *pucca* drainage arrangements in the house have been analysed across an interface of households belonging to poor–non-poor (MPCE quintiles) and various social groups for 1993–2008/2009 in Tables 10.5, 10.6, 10.7 and 10.8.

Table 10.3 Changes in Levels of Deprivation of Few Important Basic Amenities by Social Groups Households in Rural India, 1993 and 2008–2009 (in Percentage Points and Annual Compound Growth Rate)

	ST	SC	Others	All		Modified Sopher's Disparity Index	
						(SC, ST)	(SC, Others)
No Facility of Drinking Water in the House							
Levels in 1993	84.66	77.89	69.84	73.25	Changes	0.06	−0.08
Levels in 2008–2009	77.26	67.83	49.58	56.82	in index	0.09	−0.19
Changes during 1993–2008/2009 (annual compounded)	−0.58	−0.87	−2.15	−1.60	value	0.03	−0.12
No Latrine Facility in the House							
Levels in 1993	90.83	91.09	85.37	87.24	Changes	0.00	−0.05
Levels in 2008–2009	76.52	77.43	60.92	66.41	in index	−0.01	−0.16
Changes during 1993–2008/2009 (annual compounded)	−1.08	−1.03	−2.12	−1.72	value	−0.01	−0.11
No Electricity Use for Domestic Purposes							
Levels in 1993	69.86	67.42	60.11	62.80	Changes	0.02	−0.07
Levels in 2008–2009	42.67	40.54	30.21	33.95	in index	0.03	−0.15
Changes during 1993–2008/2009 (annual compounded)	−3.08	−3.18	−4.27	−3.83	value	0.00	−0.08
Open, Katcha and No Drainage Arrangement in the House							
Levels in 1993	95.23	91.96	88.81	90.21	Changes	0.03	−0.03
Levels in 2008–2009	89.09	79.35	71.71	75.39	in index	0.09	−0.07
Changes during 1993–2008/2009 (annual compounded)	−0.42	−0.93	−1.35	−1.13	value	0.06	−0.04

Source: Author's calculation using National Sample Survey, Household Conditions Rounds, unit record data for the respective years.

Notes: ST—Scheduled Tribe, SC—Scheduled Caste, Others—Forward Castes and also OBC—Other Backward Castes

Table 10.4 Access to Basic Amenities by Various Social Groups' Households in Rural India, 2001 and 2011

	ST	SC	Other	Total	Modified Sopher's Disparity Index	
					(SC, ST)	(SC, Other)
Households						
2011						
Number (in million)	20.1	32.9	114.8	167.8		
Share of households in %	12.0	19.6	68.4	100.0		
2001						
Number (in million)	15.9	27.9	94.4	138.3		
Share of households in %	11.5	20.2	68.3	100.0		
2001–2011 (changes)						
Decadal growth in %	26.8	17.8	21.5	21.4		
Annual exponential in %	2.4	1.6	1.9	1.9		
Households Not Having Availability of Drinking Water within the Premise						
2011						
Number (in million)	17.30	23.70	68.08	109.07		
As proportion of total HHs (in %)	85.9	72.0	59.3	65.0	0.13	–0.13

(Continued)

(Continued)

	ST	SC	Other	Total		Modified Sopher's Disparity Index	
						(SC, ST)	(SC, Other)
2001							
Number (in million)	14.21	22.09	62.27	98.57		0.09	−0.12
As proportion of total HHs (in %)	89.4	79.1	65.9	71.3			
2001–11 (changes)					Changes in index value		
Number (in million)	3.09	1.61	5.80	10.50		0.03	0.00
Decadal growth in %	21.7	7.3	9.3	10.7			
compounded annual in %	−0.4	−0.9	−1.1	−0.9			

Households Not Having Latrine Facility within the Premise

	ST	SC	Other	Total		(SC, ST)	(SC, Other)
2011							
Number (in million)	16.96	25.40	73.89	116.25		0.06	−0.12
As proportion of total HHs (in %)	84.2	77.2	64.4	69.3			
2001							
Number (in million)	14.13	23.72	70.12	107.97		0.04	−0.10
As proportion of total HHs (in %)	88.9	84.9	74.2	78.1			

					Changes in index value	
2001–2011 (changes)						
Number (in million)	2.84	1.67	3.77	8.28	0.03	–0.02
Decadal growth in %	20.1	7.1	5.4	7.7		
Compounded annual in %	–0.5	–1.0	–1.4	–1.2		

Households Not Having Electricity in the House

2011						
Number (in million)	10.84	16.64	47.54	75.02	0.04	–0.11
As proportion of total HHs (in %)	53.8	50.5	41.4	44.7		
2001						
Number (in million)	11.1	18.1	48.9	78.1	0.05	–0.14
As proportion of total HHs (in %)	69.6	64.9	51.8	56.5		

					Changes in index value	
2001–2011 (changes)						
Number (in million)	–0.22	–1.50	–1.35	–3.07	–0.01	0.03
Decadal growth in %	–2.0	–8.3	–2.8	–3.9		
Compounded annual in %	–2.5	–2.5	–2.2	–2.3		

Households Not Having Closed Drainage Connectivity for Waste Water Outlet

2011						
Number (in million)	19.80	31.73	106.66	158.18	0.02	–0.03
As proportion of total HHs (in %)	98.3	96.4	92.9	94.3		

(Continued)

(Continued)

	ST	SC	Other	Total	Modified Sopher's Disparity Index	
					(SC, ST)	(SC, Other)
2001						
Number (in million)	15.66	27.28	89.93	132.87		
As proportion of total HHs (in %)	98.6	97.6	95.2	96.1	0.01	–0.02
2001–11 (changes)					Changes in index value	
Number (in million)	4.14	4.45	16.73	25.31	0.01	–0.01
Decadal growth in %	26.4	16.3	18.6	19.1		
Compounded annual in %	0.0	–0.1	–0.2	–0.2		

Source: Author's calculation using tables on houses, household amenities and assets, house listing and housing data, Census of India, 2001 and 2011.

Notes: ST—Scheduled Tribe, SC—Scheduled Caste, Other—Other than ST and SC.

Table 10.5 No Facility of Drinking Water in the House by Social Groups and MPCE Quintile Categories in Rural India, 1993 and 2008–2009 (in Percentage Points)

CEC	ST	SC	Others	All	Modified Sopher's Disparity Index (SC, ST)	(SC, Others)
Levels in 1993					1993	
0–20	87.62	81.32	75.83	79.10	0.06	–0.05
20–40	83.79	78.73	73.15	75.71	0.05	–0.05
40–60	83.29	74.45	72.32	73.79	0.08	–0.02
60–80	81.86	76.23	66.05	69.40	0.05	–0.10
80–100	82.59	68.02	58.92	61.64	0.14	–0.09
Total	84.66	77.89	69.84	73.25	0.06	–0.08
Levels in 2008–2009					2008–2009	
0–20	84.94	74.98	62.38	70.02	0.09	–0.12
20–40	79.28	72.16	56.90	63.52	0.07	–0.15
40–60	75.09	68.27	52.50	58.42	0.06	–0.16
60–80	71.34	60.51	47.53	52.30	0.11	–0.14
80–100	60.35	53.42	32.90	37.64	0.07	–0.27
Total	77.26	67.83	49.58	56.82	0.09	–0.19
Changes in Levels during 1993 to 2008–2009, Annual Compounded					Changes in Index Value	
0–20	–0.20	–0.51	–1.23	–0.77	0.03	–0.07
20–40	–0.35	–0.55	–1.58	–1.11	0.02	–0.10
40–60	–0.66	–0.55	–2.01	–1.47	–0.02	–0.14
60–80	–0.87	–1.46	–2.07	–1.78	0.06	–0.05
80–100	–1.97	–1.52	–3.63	–3.08	–0.06	–0.18
Total	–0.58	–0.87	–2.15	–1.60	0.03	–0.12

Source: Author's calculation using National Sample Survey, Household Conditions Rounds, unit record data for the respective years.
Notes: MPCE—monthly per capita expenditure. Consumption expenditure classes (CEC) MPCE quintile classes are in percentages.

Table 10.6 No Latrine Facility in the House by Social Groups and MPCE Quintile Categories in Rural India, 1993 and 2008–2009 (in Percentage Points)

CEC	ST	SC	Others	All	Modified Sopher's Disparity Index (SC, ST)	(SC, Others)
Levels in 1993					1993	
0–20	94.65	93.63	90.99	92.26	0.01	–0.02
20–40	91.73	92.03	88.68	89.82	0.00	–0.03
40–60	88.32	90.13	86.93	87.73	–0.02	–0.03
60–80	87.31	88.92	83.18	84.62	–0.01	–0.05
80–100	80.79	82.47	73.57	75.20	–0.02	–0.08
Total	90.83	91.09	85.37	87.24	0.00	–0.05
Levels in 2008–2009					2008–2009	
0–20	91.07	89.12	80.09	84.63	0.02	–0.08
20–40	79.14	82.79	73.93	76.85	–0.03	–0.08
40–60	71.36	76.62	65.78	68.86	–0.05	–0.10
60–80	66.07	70.97	56.40	60.19	–0.05	–0.15
80–100	47.82	52.17	35.05	38.38	–0.05	–0.22
Total	76.52	77.43	60.92	66.41	–0.01	–0.16
Changes in Levels during 1993 to 2008–2009, Annual Compounded					Changes in Index Value	
0–20	–0.24	–0.31	–0.81	–0.55	0.01	–0.06
20–40	–0.93	–0.67	–1.15	–0.99	–0.03	–0.05
40–60	–1.34	–1.03	–1.75	–1.53	–0.03	–0.07
60–80	–1.75	–1.42	–2.44	–2.14	–0.03	–0.10
80–100	–3.27	–2.87	–4.60	–4.18	–0.04	–0.14
Total	–1.08	–1.03	–2.12	–1.72	–0.01	–0.11

Source: Author's calculation using National Sample Survey, Household Conditions Rounds, unit record data for the respective years.
Note: MPCE—monthly per capita expenditure. Consumption expenditure classes (CEC) MPCE quintile classes are in percentages.

Table 10.7 No Electricity for Domestic Purposes by Social Groups and MPCE Quintile Categories in Rural India, 1993 and 2008–2009 (in Percentage Points)

CEC	ST	SC	Others	All	Modified Sopher's Disparity Index (SC, ST)	(SC, Others)
Levels in 1993					1993	
0–20	74.83	73.35	71.46	72.48	0.01	–0.02
20–40	71.26	70.58	64.88	66.97	0.01	–0.06
40–60	74.31	63.95	62.01	63.56	0.10	–0.02
60–80	60.83	59.41	55.01	56.36	0.01	–0.05
80–100	56.56	50.68	41.37	43.57	0.07	–0.11
Total	69.86	67.42	60.11	62.80	0.02	–0.07
Levels in 2008–2009					2008–2009	
0–20	52.76	56.05	49.95	52.20	–0.04	–0.07
20–40	43.18	45.02	41.55	42.64	–0.02	–0.04
40–60	37.83	36.73	31.12	33.09	0.02	–0.09
60–80	37.75	29.72	22.67	25.46	0.12	–0.14
80–100	24.14	19.44	11.51	13.46	0.11	–0.25
Total	42.67	40.54	30.21	33.95	0.03	–0.15
Changes in Levels during 1993–2008/2009, Annual Compounded					Changes in Index Value	
0–20	–2.19	–1.69	–2.25	–2.06	–0.05	–0.05
20–40	–3.13	–2.81	–2.79	–2.83	–0.03	0.01
40–60	–4.20	–3.46	–4.28	–4.06	–0.08	–0.07
60–80	–2.98	–4.30	–5.47	–4.92	0.11	–0.09
80–100	–5.26	–5.90	–7.80	–7.19	0.04	–0.13
Total	–3.08	–3.18	–4.27	–3.83	0.00	–0.08

Source: Author's calculation using National Sample Survey, Household Conditions Rounds, unit record data for the respective years.
Note: MPCE—monthly per capita expenditure. Consumption expenditure classes (CEC) MPCE quintile classes are in percentages.

Table 10.8 *Open, Katcha and No Drainage Arrangement in the House by Social Groups and MPCE Quintile Categories in Rural India, 1993 and 2008–09 (in percentage points)*

CEC	ST	SC	Others	All	Modified Sopher's Disparity Index (SC, ST)	(SC, Others)
Levels in 1993					1993	
0–20	95.63	93.35	93.34	93.68	0.02	0.00
20–40	95.53	92.98	89.04	90.73	0.02	–0.03
40–60	95.46	91.80	89.78	90.73	0.03	–0.02
60–80	94.57	91.58	87.91	89.21	0.03	–0.03
80–100	93.48	83.08	82.68	83.44	0.09	0.00
Total	95.23	91.96	88.81	90.21	0.03	–0.03
Levels in 2008–2009					2008–2009	
0–20	93.75	85.21	81.69	84.85	0.08	–0.03
20–40	86.95	80.74	78.23	79.92	0.06	–0.02
40–60	89.29	79.98	73.86	76.82	0.08	–0.06
60–80	89.59	75.09	68.47	71.72	0.13	–0.06
80–100	77.37	68.89	59.60	62.07	0.08	–0.09
Total	89.09	79.35	71.71	75.39	0.09	–0.07
Changes in Levels during 1993 to 2008–2009, Annual Compounded					Changes in Index Value	
0–20	–0.13	–0.58	–0.84	–0.63	0.06	–0.03
20–40	–0.60	–0.89	–0.82	–0.80	0.03	0.01
40–60	–0.42	–0.87	–1.23	–1.05	0.05	–0.04
60–80	–0.34	–1.25	–1.57	–1.38	0.10	–0.03
80–100	–1.19	–1.18	–2.06	–1.86	–0.01	–0.09
Total	–0.42	–0.93	–1.35	–1.13	0.06	–0.04

Source: Author's calculation using National Sample Survey, Household Conditions Rounds, unit record data for the respective years.
Note: MPCE—monthly per capita expenditure. Consumption expenditure classes (CEC) MPCE quintile classes are in percentages.

The results show that STs and SCs experienced higher levels of deprivation and lower rates of improvement in accessing basic amenities in the house as compared to others households, in every MPCE quintile class category, during 1993–2008/2009. However, as we move from the lower quintiles to the higher ones, the levels of deprivation in accessing basic amenities seem to decrease and the annual rates of decline in deprivation seem to improve for all the social groups, but the order among social groups remains the same, as discussed for rural India as a whole. Disparities in accessing basic amenities across social groups were also seen to have increased in every MPCE quintile class. It indicates that even if the same economic conditions prevail, there is a variation in accessing amenities by different social groups and this further reiterates that there are factors based on social affiliations, acting as constraints, that lead to the denial of access to basic amenities.

Economic Groups: Poor–Non-poor by Caste and Ethnic Groups, Religious Groups and Livelihood Categories

It was found that disparities in accessing basic amenities among social groups, religious groups and economic groups (livelihood categories) had similar patterns across the economic category, poor–non-poor, as that in rural India as a whole (Table 10.9). It suggests that there are factors beyond poverty criterion—social groups, religious groups and economic groups (livelihood categories)—that play an important role in attaining access to basic amenities in the house in rural areas. Households of STs, SCs and wage labourers (ALs and OLs) belonging to lower MPCE quintiles (poor) were found to be the most deprived in accessing basic amenities in the house.

DETERMINANTS OF HOUSEHOLDS WITH ACCESS TO BASIC AMENITIES IN THE HOUSE

The results (estimated marginal effects) of the econometric exercise (Probit model) that was carried out to examine the determinants of access to basic amenities in the house by rural households in India during 2008/2009 are reported in Table 10.10.

Table 10.9 Access to Basic Amenities among Social Groups, Religious Groups and Household Types across Poor and Non-poor Households in Rural areas, in 2008–2009 (in percentage points)

	ST	SC	OBC	Others	Hindu	Muslims	ORM	SEinNA	AL	OL	SEinA	Others	Total
No Facility of Drinking Water in the House													
Non-poor	72.7	64.0	50.1	39.9	55.1	39.1	33.9	46.4	70.4	58.5	46.1	37.2	52.2
Poor	83.8	74.7	62.4	59.3	70.6	56.7	67.2	63.7	77.2	76.1	59.3	56.9	69.0
Aggregate	76.8	68.0	53.3	43.2	59.5	44.2	38.3	50.5	73.1	63.7	49.3	40.0	56.9
No Latrine Facility in the House													
Non-poor	67.6	72.0	65.2	40.2	63.7	43.5	32.2	46.6	78.9	61.5	60.2	36.4	59.8
Poor	89.2	88.4	85.9	65.0	86.1	67.9	76.6	74.4	89.4	85.2	80.9	71.8	83.8
Aggregate	76.3	77.4	70.4	44.5	70.0	50.6	38.2	52.8	83.1	68.2	65.3	41.4	66.5
No Electricity Use for Domestic Purposes													
Non-poor	36.7	33.3	26.5	21.9	27.0	39.5	14.0	22.1	37.4	23.9	28.2	16.7	27.6
Poor	51.1	54.6	49.7	47.5	49.7	62.6	40.6	49.6	54.1	54.0	46.6	48.0	50.9
Aggregate	42.5	40.7	32.5	26.3	33.4	46.2	17.5	28.4	44.0	32.1	32.5	21.1	34.0

Open, Katcha and No Drainage Arrangement in the House

Non-poor	86.5	77.0	71.7	64.6	72.2	76.6	63.2	66.7	82.6	75.8	70.7	59.2	72.1
Poor	92.8	84.3	81.2	82.7	83.7	85.8	86.6	78.8	88.3	85.0	80.9	78.7	84.0
Aggregate	88.7	79.4	74.0	67.7	75.4	79.4	66.4	69.6	84.9	78.8	73.2	62.3	75.3

Source: Author's calculation using National Sample Survey, Housing Conditions Round, unit record data for the respective years, Planning Commission and Ministry of Labour, GoI.

Notes: ORM—other religious minorities, SEinNA—self employed in non-agriculture, AL—agricultural labour, OL—other labour and SEinA—self employed in agriculture.

Table 10.10 Results of Maximum Likelihood Probit Model for Access to Basic Amenities in Rural India, 2008/2009

Dependent Variable:	Households Having Facility of Drinking Water in the House dF/dx	Households Having Latrine Facility in the House dF/dx	Households Having Electricity Use for Domestic Purposes dF/dx	Households Having Closed Drainage Arrangement in the House dF/dx
CEC MPCE Quintile Categories				
Quintile 1 (0–20)*	−0.207	−0.301	−0.370	−0.131
Quintile 2 (20–40)*	−0.175	−0.247	−0.294	−0.098
Quintile 3 (40–60)*	−0.143	−0.193	−0.209	−0.081
Quintile 4 (60–80)*	−0.101	−0.138	−0.133	−0.047
Household Types				
Self-employed in Non-agriculture*	−0.081	−0.048	−0.024	−0.041
Agricultural labourers*	−0.237	−0.259	−0.128	−0.149
Other labourers*	−0.168	−0.145	−0.042	−0.098
Self-employed in agriculture*	−0.051	−0.160	−0.089	−0.071
Social Groups				
ST*	−0.254	−0.177	−0.144	−0.164
SC*	−0.127	−0.189	−0.130	−0.065
OBC*	−0.037	−0.180	−0.055	−0.036

Religious Groups				
Hindus*	**-0.214**	**-0.251**	**-0.126**	**-0.067**
Muslims*	**-0.104**	**-0.101**	**-0.333**	**-0.121**
Number of observations	97,135	97,135	97,135	97,135
Pseudo R2	0.0908	0.1652	0.0862	0.0573

Source: Estimated using unit record data from the National Sample Survey on Housing Conditions during 65th round (2008/2009).

Notes: Reference categories—MPCE: Quintile 5 (80–100); Household types: Others; Social groups: Others; Religious groups: Other Religious Minorities.

Df/dx are marginal effects, that is, the change in probability of having basic amenities in the house with a one unit change in the right side variable (discrete change of dummy variable from 0 to 1)

Significant marginal probabilities are in bold (at 1% level of significance). z and $P > |z|$ correspond to the test of the underlying coefficient being 0. * implies that the variable is dichotomous.

The results reveal that across economic groups—MPCE quintiles, as we move towards bottom quintiles, the probability for households having access to basic amenities in the house lowers as compared to the top quintiles' (reference category) households, controlling other factors. The pattern across household types shows that AL and OL households were found to be in the worst situations with lesser probabilities of accessing basic amenities as compared to others (livelihood categories) households. The pattern across caste and ethnic groups suggests that ST and SC households were found lagging with lesser probability of accessing basic amenities, followed by OBCs as compared to households belonging to Others social groups. Across religious groups, Hindu households, followed by Muslim households, were found to have lesser probabilities of access as compared to ORM households.

These results on determinants of access to basic amenities in the house by rural households reiterate the fact that there are vast socio-economic exclusions in rural India.

DECOMPOSITION BY SOCIAL GROUPS OF THE PROBABILITIES FOR ACCESSING BASIC AMENITIES IN THE HOUSE

The structural probabilities for the various social groups show that if the entire sample had comprised respective social groups, the probability of accessing basic amenities in the house was lower for STs, SCs followed by OBCs as compared to the reference group of others households (Table 10.11). It also demonstrates that the observed difference of probabilities (gap) or differences in the sample means that access rates of basic amenities in the house were very high between others and ST households, others and SC households, followed by others and OBC households.

The decompositions are obtained by using the others (upper caste) coefficient estimates (that is, the estimates obtained when the equation was estimated over the observations pertaining to others households) as the common coefficient vector. The results of the decomposition of the differences in the probabilities for accessing basic amenities in the house, into attributes and coefficient contribution, indicates the significant presence of coefficient contribution (or the contribution of caste-based factors) in the observed differences for STs and SCs (along

Table 10.11 Decomposition Results (Observed Differences, Attribute and Coefficient Contributions to Differences) between Upper Caste and Other (STs/SCs/OBCs) Caste Households in their Respective Proportions in Access to Various Basic Amenities in the House in Rural India, 2008/2009

Community X↓	Px	Po	Observed Difference/Sample Average (Px−Po)	Explained Difference (due to Endowments)	Attributes Contribution[a] (%)	Coefficient Contribution[b] (%)
Households Having Facility of Drinking Water in the House						
ST	0.228	0.568	−0.341	−0.090	26	74
SC	0.322	0.568	−0.247	−0.134	54	46
OBC	0.467	0.568	−0.101	−0.068	67	33
Households Having Latrine Facility in the House						
ST	0.235	0.555	−0.320	−0.121	38	62
SC	0.226	0.555	−0.329	−0.123	37	63
OBC	0.296	0.555	−0.259	−0.069	27	73
Households Having Electricity Use for Domestic Purposes						
ST	0.573	0.736	−0.163	−0.024	15	85
SC	0.595	0.736	−0.142	−0.023	17	83
OBC	0.676	0.736	−0.060	−0.006	11	89

(Continued)

(Continued)

Community X↓	Px	Po	Observed Difference/Sample Average (Px−Po)	Explained Difference (due to Endowments)	Attributes Contribution[a] (%)	Coefficient Contribution[b] (%)
Households Having Closed Drainage Arrangement in the House						
ST	0.109	0.323	−0.214	−0.052	24	76
SC	0.206	0.323	−0.117	−0.065	56	44
OBC	0.259	0.323	−0.064	−0.027	41	59

Source: Estimated using unit record data from the National Sample Survey on Housing Conditions during 65th round (2008/2009).

Notes: Decompositions were computed using upper (others) caste (non-ST/SC/OBC) coefficients/Community X attributes evaluated using others coefficients.

[a]Difference in households proportions in access to basic amenities due to inter-group differences in attributes as a percentage of the overall difference.

[b]Difference in households proportions in access to basic amenities due to inter-group differences in coefficients as a percentage of the overall difference.

with a high gap), and OBCs as compared with the reference category of others households.

Therefore, the decomposition or break-up of the average gap amongst the probabilities to access basic amenities between different social groups illustrates that caste-based factors and discrimination are the significant major reasons for these differences besides attributes (factors such as endowment) contribution.

CONCLUSION AND POLICY IMPLICATIONS

The above study underscores the fact that access to these basic amenities can guarantee a minimum standard of living in rural India: a part of the country that presents a stark picture of deprivation and socio-economic exclusion. This lacuna, it can be argued, is one of the dominant reasons that is hindering the development of the country and it spells out an urgent need to formulate and implement policies from which the hitherto deprived, excluded and discriminated sections of society can actually benefit.

This study demonstrates extremely high levels of unavailability of basic amenities in rural India. For instance, in 2011, 65 per cent, 69.3 per cent, 44.7 per cent and 94.3 per cent of rural households had no drinking water within the premise, latrine facilities within the premises, electricity in the house and closed drainage connectivity for waste water outlet, respectively. However, the effect of policies like Bharat Nirman, adopted in 2005, seemed to have contributed to a decline in the percentage of households deprived of basic amenities, as is shown by census data, 2001–2011 and NSS data, 1993–2008/2009.

But, the improvement in percentage terms is, however, not reflected in absolute terms during 2001–2011. In fact, there was a marginal increase in the absolute number of households deprived of drinking water within their premises, of latrine facilities within their premises and of closed drainage connectivity for waste water outlet, due to the low rates of improvement during the period. This absolute rise is a cause of concern for policymakers. Only access to electricity in the house showed an improvement in absolute terms, as this indicator experienced a decent annual rate of improvement.

This shows that policies adopted for providing basic amenities in rural India did create some movement in the development process and delivery. However, that speed needs to be enhanced in order to achieve the MDGs and a decent standard of living for all.

The weaker sections of rural society such as poor households vis-à-vis non-poor households and ST and SC households vis-à-vis others households, have witnessed a low annual rate of decline in accessing basic amenities, resulting in high levels of deprivation, as is seen in the concluding periods of this study. The disparities in accessing basic amenities have increased between poor and non-poor households, between ST and SC households and between SC and Others households.

Even in identical MPCE quintiles (poor and non-poor), ST and SC house-holds have lagged behind Others households in their levels of accessing basic amenities and the corresponding rates of improvement, besides disparities have also increased. The results suggest that there are factors based on social backgrounds (caste and ethnicity) that act as constraints and lead to the denial of accessing basic amenities.

The decomposition of the differences between the access rate of basic amenities in the house of households belonging to others (upper caste) and weaker sections (ST, SC and OBC) shows that the majority of these gaps/differences is explained by significant caste-based factors, establishing the presence of caste-based exclusion and discriminations in accessing basic amenities in rural India.

Overall, poor households belonging to STs, SCs and wage labourers (ALs and OLs) were lagging the most in accessing basic amenities in the house in the rural India. The results on the determinants of households having access to basic amenities in the house further support these findings.

The overall situation in rural areas and a study of available literature also suggest that the highest level of deprivation in accessing basic amenities and services like roads occurs in areas where weaker sections of village society live, highlighting the issue of socio-spatial situatedness in rural areas. The need for a more focused, targeted delivery of such facilities in areas occupied by margi-nalized and excluded communities then becomes all the more apparent.

Thus, there is clearly a need to chart out group-specific (economic and social) policy measures to tackle severe deprivation in rural India and to provide safeguards to its marginalized sections for equal access to basic amenities, as has been noted in the inclusive growth agenda of the Twelfth Five-year Plan of the Government of India (Planning Commission, 2011) and suggested by the World Bank (2013) and United Nations (2013).

ACKNOWLEDGEMENTS

This chapter is an abridged version of research studies undertaken by the Indian Institute of Dalit Studies under its Think Tank Initiative programme, International Development Research Centre. It has benefited substantially from constructive comments by anonymous referees in an earlier draft of this chapter. The author would like to acknowledge Professor Sukhadeo Thorat, Professor Amitabh Kundu, Professor P. M. Kulkarni, Professor Amaresh Dubey, Dr Himanshu, Ajaya Kumar Naik, Dr Nitin Tagade, Khalid Khan and the Indian Institute of Dalit Studies Research team for their insightful comments on earlier version of this chapter.

ANNEXURE A

Table 10A.1 *Number of Sample Sizes and Household Details for Social Groups and Poor–Non-poor by NSS Rounds during 1993 and 2008–2009 in Rural India*

	ST	SC	Others	All	Non-poor	Poor	Total
1993							
Sample size	11,915	16,051	47,287	75,253	46,460	28,793	75,253
Number of households (millions)	12.74	25.42	77.27	115.43	66.34	49.09	115.43
Share of households	11.04	22.02	66.94	100.00	57.47	42.53	100.00
2008–2009							
Sample size	16,159	21,142	59,821	97,122	72,219	24,925	97,144
Number of households (millions)	17.65	35.95	104.54	158.14	114.97	43.19	158.16
Share of households	11.16	22.73	66.11	100.00	72.69	27.31	100.00

Source: Author's calculation using National Sample Survey, Housing Conditions Round unit record data for the respective years, Planning Commission and Ministry of Labour, GoI.

Notes: ST—Scheduled Tribe, SC—Scheduled Caste, Others—Forward Castes and also OBC—Other Backward Castes.
Poverty line has been calculated based on old official poverty line method used by Planning Commission. Poverty line has been updated from 1993 and 2004–2005 poverty estimates of Planning Commission using consumer price index for agricultural labourers (base year 1986–1987 = 100).
Weights as given by NSS have been used for household analysis.

Table 10A.2 Number of Sample Sizes and Household Details for Social Groups and MPCE Quintiles by NSS Rounds during 1993 and 2008–2009 in Rural India

CEC	1993				2008–2009			
	ST	SC	Others	Total	ST	SC	Others	Total
	Sample Sizes				Sample Sizes			
0–20	3,109	5,186	9,619	17,914	3,882	5,324	10,220	19,426
20–40	3,153	4,837	12,366	20,356	2,866	4,966	11,613	19,445
40–60	1,264	1,604	5,038	7,906	3,021	4,373	12,010	19,404
60–80	2,383	2,756	10,360	15,499	3,249	3,746	12,516	19,511
80–100	2,006	1,668	9,904	13,578	3,141	2,733	13,462	19,336
Total	11,915	16,051	47,287	75,253	16,159	21,142	59,821	97,122
	Households Details				Households Details			
0–20								
Number (millions)	4.42	8.43	17.32	30.17	6.02	9.63	18.01	33.65
in %	14.65	27.95	57.40	100.00	17.88	28.60	53.52	100.00
in %	34.70	33.17	22.41	26.14	34.08	26.78	17.23	21.28
20–40								
Number (millions)	4.06	8.26	22.58	34.90	3.94	8.55	20.55	33.04
in %	11.63	23.66	64.71	100.00	11.93	25.88	62.19	100.00
in %	31.85	32.49	29.23	30.23	22.33	23.79	19.66	20.90

(Continued)

(Continued)

	1993				2008–2009			
	ST	SC	Others	Total	ST	SC	Others	Total
40–60								
Number (millions)	1.13	2.53	8.46	12.12	3.09	7.25	20.74	31.07
in %	9.34	20.88	69.78	100.00	9.93	23.33	66.74	100.00
in %	8.88	9.96	10.94	10.50	17.48	20.16	19.84	19.65
60–80								
Number (millions)	2.11	4.15	16.27	22.53	2.76	6.03	21.38	30.16
in %	9.36	18.42	72.22	100.00	9.15	19.98	70.87	100.00
in %	16.55	16.33	21.06	19.52	15.63	16.76	20.45	19.07
80–100								
Number (millions)	1.02	2.04	12.64	15.71	1.85	4.50	23.86	30.20
in %	6.51	13.02	80.48	100.00	6.12	14.89	78.99	100.00
in %	8.02	8.04	16.36	13.61	10.47	12.51	22.82	19.10
Total								
Number (millions)	12.74	25.42	77.27	115.43	17.65	35.95	104.54	158.14
In %	11.04	22.02	66.94	100.00	11.16	22.73	66.11	100.00
In %	100.00	100.00	100.00	100.00	100.00	100.00	100.00	100.00

Source: Author's calculation using National Sample Survey, Housing Conditions Round unit record data for the respective years, Planning Commission and Ministry of Labour, GoI.

Note: MPCE—monthly per capita expenditure. Consumption expenditure classes (CEC) MPCE quintile classes are in percentages.

Table 10A.3 Number of Sample Sizes and Household Details among Social Groups, Religious Groups and Household Types across Poor and Non-poor by NSS Rounds during 2008–2009 in Rural India

	ST	SC	OBC	Others	Total	Hindus	Muslims	ORM	Total	SEinNA	AL	OL	SEinA	Others	Total
Sample Sizes															
Non-poor	11,397	14,399	27,822	18,587	72,205	55,835	7,904	8,472	72,211	10,505	15,492	9,014	27,575	9,613	72,199
Poor	4,762	6,743	9,203	4,209	24,917	20,796	3,012	1,114	24,922	2,816	9,826	3,126	7,726	1,417	24,911
Total	16,159	21,142	37,025	22,796	97,122	76,631	10,916	9,586	97,133	13,321	25,318	12,140	35,301	11,030	97,110
Households details															
Non-poor															
Number (millions)	10.32	23.87	49.12	31.65	114.95	96.72	11.70	6.54	114.96	16.51	27.02	13.07	43.95	14.40	114.95
in %	8.97	20.76	42.73	27.53	100.00	84.13	10.18	5.69	100.00	14.36	23.50	11.37	38.24	12.53	100.00
in %	58.45	66.40	74.25	82.45	72.69	72.13	70.89	86.66	72.69	77.11	60.03	72.94	77.04	86.08	72.70
Poor															
Number (millions)	7.33	12.08	17.04	6.73	43.18	37.38	4.81	1.01	43.19	4.90	17.99	4.85	13.10	2.33	43.16
in %	16.98	27.97	39.45	15.60	100.00	86.54	11.13	2.33	100.00	11.35	41.67	11.23	30.35	5.40	100.00
in %	41.55	33.60	25.75	17.55	27.31	27.87	29.11	13.34	27.31	22.89	39.97	27.06	22.96	13.92	27.30

(Continued)

(Continued)

	ST	SC	OBC	Others	Total	Hindus	Muslims	ORM	Total	SEinNA	AL	OL	SEinA	Others	Total
Total															
Number (millions)	17.65	35.95	66.15	38.38	158.14	134.10	16.51	7.54	158.15	21.41	45.00	17.91	57.05	16.73	158.11
in %	11.16	22.73	41.83	24.27	100.00	84.79	10.44	4.77	100.00	13.54	28.46	11.33	36.08	10.58	100.00
in %	100.00	100.00	100.00	100.00	100.00	100.00	100.00	100.00	100.00	100.00	100.00	100.00	100.00	100.00	100.00

Source: Author's calculation using National Sample Survey, Housing Conditions Round unit record data for the respective years, Planning Commission and Ministry of Labour, GoI.

Notes: ORM—other religious minorities, SEinNA—self-employed in non-agriculture, AL—agricultural labour, OL—other labour and SEinA—self-employed in agriculture.

Poverty line is used here to distinguish between non-poor and poor and is based on old official Planning Commission methodology. Poverty line has been updated from 2004–2005 poverty estimates of Planning Commission using consumer price index for agricultural labourers (base year 1986–1987 = 100) were used for rural areas.

Table 10A.4 Access to Numbers of Few Important Basic Amenities (Comprising of Six Indicators) of the Household in Rural Areas by Social Groups and Poor–Non-poor (MPCE Quintiles) during 2008–2009 (in percentage points)

	ST	SC	OBC	Others	0–20	20–40	40–60	60–80	80–100	Total
No amenities	4.57	7.16	4.00	2.82	8.46	5.87	4.14	2.36	1.06	4.49
Only one amenity	13.59	13.21	8.78	6.03	15.69	12.28	8.95	6.97	3.49	9.66
Only two amenities	25.51	20.52	16.06	10.65	25.49	19.55	16.66	13.71	7.42	16.82
Only three amenities	29.89	26.86	25.70	19.28	27.59	28.51	27.52	23.96	16.07	24.87
Only four amenities	15.46	17.97	20.91	20.88	14.44	19.77	21.73	23.07	19.64	19.63
Only five amenities	7.88	9.89	16.86	23.14	6.08	10.41	14.72	20.43	29.00	15.80
All the amenities	3.10	4.40	7.69	17.19	2.25	3.62	6.28	9.50	23.32	8.73

Source: Author's calculation using National Sample Survey Household Conditions Rounds unit record data, 2008–2009.

Notes: Six indicators of basic amenities used here are: facility of drinking water, latrine facility, electricity use for domestic purposes, pucca drainage arrangement, good or satisfactory condition of structure and pucca roof type in the house.
ST—Scheduled Tribe, SC—Scheduled Caste, OBC—Other Backward Castes and Others—Forward Castes. MPCE: monthly per capita expenditure. Consumption expenditure classes quintiles are in percentages.

Table 10A.5 Access to Numbers of Few Important Basic Amenities (Comprising of Six Indicators) of the Household in Rural Areas by Household Types and Religious Groups during 2008–2009 (in percentage points)

	SEinNA	AL	OL	SEinA	Others	Hindu	Muslims	ORM	Total
No amenities	3.48	8.24	4.70	2.21	3.30	4.56	5.52	0.99	4.49
Only one amenity	7.31	16.17	11.21	6.18	5.36	9.73	11.37	4.62	9.66
Only two amenities	12.13	23.68	18.06	14.91	9.43	17.27	15.77	10.99	16.82
Only three amenities	20.86	27.53	24.70	27.30	14.76	25.95	20.29	15.85	24.88
Only four amenities	22.34	15.84	19.47	22.41	17.04	19.94	17.43	18.83	19.63
Only five amenities	20.51	6.95	16.02	17.57	27.32	14.55	20.32	28.00	15.80
All the amenities	13.37	1.60	5.84	9.41	22.79	7.99	9.30	20.72	8.73

Source: Author's calculation using National Sample Survey Household Conditions Rounds unit record data, 2008–2009.

Notes: Six indicators of basic amenities used here are: facility of drinking water, latrine facility, electricity use for domestic purposes, pucca drainage arrangement, good or satisfactory condition of structure and pucca roof type in the house. ORM—other religious minorities, SEinNA—self-employed in non-agriculture, AL—agricultural labour, OL—other labour and SEinA— self-employed in agriculture.

NOTES

1. Probit estimation is done using dprobit stata command, vce (robust) command and sample weight.
2. Decomposition estimation is done using the Fairlie Stata command, using sample weight based on the probit model.
3. The shares of rural households among social groups in the sample were 16.6 per cent (ST), 21.8 per cent (SC), 38.1 per cent (OBC) and 23.5 per cent (Others).

REFERENCES

Bhagat, R. B. (2013). Conditions of SC/ST households: A story of unequal improvement. *Economic and Political Weekly, 48*(41), 62–66.

Borooah, V. K., Diwakar, D., & Sabharwal, N. S. (2014). Evaluating the social orientation of the integrated child development services programme. *Economic and Political Weekly, 49*(12), 52–62.

Drèze, J., & Sen, A. (2013). *An uncertain glory: India and its contradictions*. New Delhi: Penguin Books.

Dubey, A., & Thorat, S. (2012). Has growth been socially Inclusive during 1993–94–2009–10? *Economic and Political Weekly, 47*(10), 43–53.

Fairlie, R.W. (2006). *An extension of the Blinder–Oaxaca decomposition technique to Logit and Probit models*. Institute for the Study of Labor (IZA), IZA Discussion Paper No. 1917 & Economic Growth Center, Yale University, Discussion Paper No. 873.

Kumar, A. (2012). *Access to basic amenities: Aspects of caste, ethnicity, religion, livelihood categories and poverty in rural and urban India during 1993 to 2008–09*. Working Paper No. 53, Indian Institute of Dalit Studies (under Think Tank Initiative programme, IDRC), New Delhi.

———. (2014a). Access to basic amenities: Aspects of caste, ethnicity and poverty in rural and urban India—1993 to 2008–2009. *Journal of Land and Rural Studies, 2*(1), 127–148.

———. (2014b). Estimating rural housing shortage, review of rural affairs. *Economic and Political Weekly, 49*(26–27), 74–79.

———. (2014c). Sanitation in rural India: An analysis of households' latrine facility. *Journal of Studies in Dynamics and Change, 1*(6): 231–246.

———. (2015). Discrepancies in sanitation statistics of rural India. *Economic and Political Weekly, 50*(2), 13–15.

Planning Commission. (2011). *Faster, sustainable and more Inclusive growth: An approach to the twelfth five year plan (2012–17)*. New Delhi: Planning Commission, Government of India.

Sinning, M., Hahn, M., & Bauer, T. K. (2008). The Blinder–Oaxaca decomposition for nonlinear regression models. *The Stata Journal, 8*(4): 480–92.

Thorat, S. (2008). *Dalits in India—Search for common destiny*. New Delhi: SAGE Publications.

Thorat, S., & Mahamallick, M. (2006). *Chronic poverty and socially disadvantage groups: Analysis of causes and remedies*. Working Paper 33, Chronic Poverty Centre, London and Indian Institute of Public Administration.

Thorat, S., & Newman, K. (2010). *Blocked by caste: Economic discrimination in modern India*. New Delhi: Oxford University Press.

United Nations. (2013). *Inequality matters: Report of the world social situation 2013*. New York: Department of Economic and Social Affairs, United Nations.

World Bank. (2013). *Inclusion matters: The foundation for shared prosperity. New Frontiers of Social Policy*. Washington, DC: The World Bank.

Chapter 11

Disparity and Development in Uttar Pradesh[*]

Prashant Kumar Trivedi

INTRODUCTION

Uttar Pradesh (UP) is the most populous state in India, having a population of more than 166 million, and if compared in terms of population with other countries in the world, it stands only after China, India, Indonesia, Brazil, Russia and the USA. In terms of population, it may stand ahead, but as far as human development is concerned, it ranks in 138th position as a separate political entity among world countries on the United Nations Development Programme (UNDP) list (Dreze and Gazdar 1997). An estimated 8 per cent of the world's poor live in UP alone (Kozel and Parker 2003). Compared to other Indian states after Independence, UP has slipped down on the development ladder; its per capita income is the lowest among the states, except for Bihar. UP performs badly in terms of other indicators as well (Shanker 2002).

Traditionally, economic growth was considered as the only parameter of development. This understanding has been challenged in a big way and concepts such as human development and social development have gained currency in recent years. Human development is interpreted in different forms by several scholars. It is a process of increasing people's choices and the *UNDP Human Development Report* puts it as an end, while economic growth as a means (Shariff and National Council for Applied Economic Research 1999). Human development is also seen

[*] *Social Change* Vol 37, no. 1 (March 2007): 162–178.

as an investment for economic development. Amartya Sen and Jean Dreze (1995) are of the opinion that the central goal of development is to expand human capabilities. Although social development and human development cover a common area regarding development of human beings with reference to education, health, employment, drinking water, food, habitation, etc. However, the former is a much broader concept that, as Dubey (2005) defines, also covers 'analyses of social processes, social attitudes and institutions'.

Social development has a relation with economic development as growth in per capita income, land access, assets and employment opportunities support the process of social development. Dreze and Gazdar (1997) have a different understanding regarding this point, and in a study of UP, they argue that figures of below the poverty line population for India and UP are not much different, but on social parameters, UP's performance is way below. Another point is important to mention here that the discussion regarding social development should be carried out keeping in mind the differentiation that exists at several levels, including caste, class, gender, rural–urban and region.

POVERTY

Many scholars have defined poverty purely in economic terms. However, recent studies contradict this position and argue that 'well-being encompasses a multitude of both economic and non-economic dimensions and is therefore difficult to define and quantify.' Conventional income or consumption-based measures, while essential to poverty monitoring, may fail to capture many of its critical dimensions (Kozel and Parker 2003). On the same lines, Dreze and Gazdar (1997) refer to Amartya Sen's concept of poverty as a failure of basic capabilities.

As Table 11.1 suggests, during the period of 1993–1994 to 1999–2000, a sharp decline was seen in the poverty in UP from 41.0 per cent to 32.9 per cent, but even after the progress made during the whole period of the 1980s and 1990s, nearly one-third of the population is compelled to remain deprived. In absolute numbers, those below the poverty line in UP are as high as 55 million.

Table 11.1 *Trends in Poverty: UP*

Year	Round	Urban	Rural	Overall
1983	38th	51.0	47.4	48.1
1987–1988	43rd	45.0	42.3	42.8
1993–1994	50th	35.4	42.3	42.8
1999–2000				
Official	55th	30.9	31.2	31.1
Corrected	55th	30.4	33.7	32.9

Source: Kozel and Parker (2003).

REGIONAL VARIATIONS IN POVERTY

On the account of several historical, social and economic factors, presently UP is divided into four regions, namely Harit Pradesh (western), Avadh (central), Purvanchal (eastern) and Bundelkhand (southern). Poverty varies in different regions of UP, least in the western, higher in central and eastern and highest in the southern region. Valerie Kozel and Barbara Parker (2003) have discussed this phenomenon at length in their comprehensive article on poverty in UP. The article notes that even poverty reduction is not equally distributed; the southern region lags way behind other regions in this aspect too. For a comparative study of different regions, these scholars take the poorest quartile of the whole state's rural population and study its regional distribution at two junctures, 1993–1994 and 1999–2000. This study notes some shift in regional distribution of rural poverty and underlines the fact that the eastern and central regions still house a disproportionate number of the poorest population of UP. This study further notes that 'relative to their population shares, there has been a decrease in the percentage of 'poor' individuals living in the eastern and southern region' and 'a concomitant increase in the percentage of poor living in the western and central regions'. The study correlates changes in poverty pattern with a shift in the regional trend of agriculture wages.

CASTE DIFFERENTIATION

Poverty, like all other development indicators, varies with the caste hierarchy. As we move towards the lower strata, the incidence of poverty increases. Kozel and Parker (2003) note that caste is linked to poverty in a number of ways, playing the role of a deterrent for occupational mobility, which creates conditions for low-paid jobs. Banerjee and Knight (1991, quoted by Thorat) observe that the pro-elite economic function which the caste system performs, suggests that the discrimination is based 'on economic interest, so making prejudice more difficult to eradicate'. Poverty, inequality and caste go simultaneously with each other. On the one hand, inequality creates material conditions for the survival of the caste system and caste perpetuates and reproduces poverty, on the other.

Besides this discussion, Tables 11.2 and 11.3 reveal a great deal about the relationship between caste and poverty. Data provided by the 61st round of the National Sample Survey Office (NSSO) reveals that caste categories that find a lower position in the caste hierarchy are much more concentrated in lower per capita monthly expenditure class. In rural UP, 10.8 per cent of scheduled tribe (ST) households comes into the category of less than ₹235 category as compared to 0.9 per cent households of other category. The same trend is confirmed by the numbers in highest class, 9.3 per cent of households of other category have more than ₹1,155 per capita consumer expenditure, and none of ST households appears in this category. Only 1.5 per cent of scheduled caste (SC) households have made their place in this elite category.

Differentiation on the basis of caste is not only a feature of rural society but is similarly influential in urban settings. Table 11.3 reveals the same sad story of poverty in urban UP: The lower the position in the caste hierarchy, the higher the incidence of poverty. About 67.9 per cent of SC households have monthly per capita consumption expenditure (MPCE) up to ₹410 as compared to 34.6 per cent of other category households. Almost 36.4 per cent of households of the other category find place in more than ₹580 class against 9.7 per cent SCs. In this way, we see that the so-called lower castes are over represented among the poor and under-represented among the upper strata of society.

Table 11.2 Percentage Distribution of Households by Household per Capita Consumer Expenditure in Rural UP

Social Category	< 235	235–270	270–320	320–365	365–410	410–455	455–510	510–580	580–690	690–890	890–1155	1,155>
ST	10.8	0.0	1.0	11.7	12.6	10.6	12.2	9.4	22.8	8.5	5.0	0.0
SC	2.7	4.5	10.3	13.4	12.5	12.1	11.7	11.3	9.7	7.0	3.3	1.5
Other Backward Class (OBC)	2.0	2.8	9.0	9.8	10.8	11.2	12.2	12.3	12.0	9.9	4.7	3.3
O'rs	0.9	1.6	3.8	5.9	7.3	9.0	9.7	13.6	13.6	13.6	11.7	9.3
All	2.0	3.0	8.3	10.1	10.5	11.0	11.6	12.3	11.7	9.8	5.7	4.0

Source: NSSO, 61st round, 2004–2005.

Table 11.3 Percentage Distribution of Households by Household per Capita Consumer Expenditure in Urban UP

Social Category	<235	235–270	270–320	320–365	365–410	410–455	455–510	510–580	580–690	690–890	890–1155	1155>
ST	26.8	7.1	17.4	17.0	12.8	6.6	1.4	5.8	1.4	0.0	2.9	0.0
SC	12.7	9.2	15.2	19.2	11.6	8.7	8.2	5.5	2.0	4.5	1.7	1.5
OBC	6.2	9.5	13.3	10.9	14.3	8.7	10.3	7.6	12.2	3.6	1.7	1.6
O'rs	3.6	2.4	8.4	12.0	8.2	9.5	10.2	9.3	12.4	8.4	8.2	7.4
All	6.1	6.5	11.5	12.4	11.4	9.0	9.9	8.0	11.0	5.7	4.4	4.0

Source: NSSO, 61st round, 2004–2005.

RURAL-URBAN

The comparison between Tables 11.2 and 11.3 also indicates the rural–urban pattern of poverty. Here, we can see that, as compared to rural areas, a greater number of urban households are nearer the bottom. In less than ₹235 category, 61 urban households are placed against 20 rural households, and in up to ₹320 MPCE, 133 rural households find their place against nearly double, that is, 241 households. This data shows that the proportion of the poor population is much higher in urban settings than in rural, though the absolute number of poor may be higher in the latter area.

EMPLOYMENT SCENARIO

Employment opportunities in UP are as dismal as reflected in the above discussion about poverty. Unemployment, underemployment and low-paid casual jobs have created conditions for a huge migration of the UP's workforce. Casualization of the workforce is on the rise in UP, and this casual labour constitutes a bigger part of the poor. During 1993–1994 and 1999–2000, the share of casual labour in the rural population reached 31 per cent from 23 per cent, registering a growth of 8 per cent only in seven years. In the same period, 5 per cent growth has been registered in urban settings. Casual jobs and poverty are interrelated to each other. Data provided by NSSO reveals that in 1999–2000, more than half of the casual agricultural labour was below the poverty line, and 43.9 per cent of the non–agriculture casual labour in rural areas were poor. Poverty incidence among urban casual labour is much higher: Around two-third of them are compelled to remain below the poverty line. Field studies suggest that agriculture labour get far less wages than the minimum wage declared by the government.

In UP, the largest proportion of employment comes from agriculture, but this employment scope is also losing its strength. A large number of self-employed workers, that is, cultivators in agriculture, have been thrown out of this occupation. NSSO data reveals that, in 1983, 61 per cent rural population was occupied in agriculture as compared to 58 per cent in 1993–1994 and only 54 per cent in 1999–2000.

Employment conditions also have a caste dimension. Workers from the SC background are much more concentrated in low-paid casual jobs in both rural and urban areas. Sukhdeo Thorat (2004) notes,

> Since more than 60 per cent of the Scheduled Caste workers in rural and urban areas depend on wage labour for employment, their earnings are determined by the level of wage earning, daily or regular. Scheduled Caste workers seem to suffer from possible discrimination both in employment and wage earning in the labour market.

Data provided by NSSO reveals that, in 2004–2005, 40.3 per cent of rural SC households were-dependent on wages earned as casual labour against only 9 per cent of other category household. On the same lines, the proportion of wage dependent urban SC households is as high as 24.6 per cent compared to only 3.8 per cent of other category households.

LAND POSSESSION

Land is the most important asset in rural UP, and poverty is directly related to it. Kozel and Parker (2003) note that poverty falls as land ownership rises and many of the poorest households own little or no land. They quote NSSO data to show that the share of the population has very small land, and the corresponding number of poor is growing. In 1983, 27 per cent of the population had less than a half hectare of land. This population composes 30 per cent of the rural poor. The share of the population having less than a half hectare of land reached 43 per cent in 1993–1994, and this section was 54 per cent of the rural poor. The situation further worsened in 1999–2000, when nearly two-third of the rural population owned less than a half hectare of land, composing 61 per cent of the rural poor. Table 11.4 also reveals that, in rural UP, 54.9 per cent of households owned up to 0.4 hectares of land. Another source confirms the trend of unequal distribution of land in UP. In 1995–1996, nearly 90 per cent of the landholdings were small and marginal, owning an area of less than 58 per cent of the total land, and the remaining 10 per cent had more than 40 per cent of total land (Planning Commission and Government of India 2007).

Land possession in UP is also related to caste. The lower castes have far less land possession than others. Table 11.4 shows that 70.7 per cent

Table 11.4 *Percentage Distribution of Households by Size Class of Land Possessed for Rural UP*

Social Category	Landless	0.001–0.004	0.005–0.40	0.41–1.00	1.01–2.0	2.01–4.0	4.01 and above
ST	0.0	28.2	37.8	8.6	17.1	6.3	2.0
SC	1.9	11.3	57.5	20.1	7.1	1.8	0.3
OBC	1.3	7.1	42.5	27.9	13.5	6.0	1.7
Others	1.4	8.9	32.8	24.0	18.2	10.6	4.2
All	1.5	8.7	44.7	24.9	12.7	5.8	1.8

Source: NSSO, 61st round, 2004–2005.

of SC households have up to 0.4 hectare of land against 43.1 per cent of others. Similarly, only 0.3 per cent of SC households find their place in the highest category of more than 4 hectare of land, compared to 4.2 per cent of others.

EDUCATION

Education is one of the most important indicators and components of social development and is closely related to other development indicators. Table 11.5 shows that though UP is a success story in

Table 11.5 *Literacy Rates of India and Selected States (%)*

State 1 Union Territory	1991		2001	
	Male	Female	Male	Female
India	64.13	39.29	75.3	53.7
Andhra Pradesh	55.13	32.79	70.3	50.4
Kerala	93.62	86.17	94.2	87.7
UP	55.73	25.31	68.8	42.2
West Bengal	67.81	46.56	77.0	59.6
Maharashtra	76.56	52.32	86.0	67.0

Source: Census of India, Registrar General and Commissioner, Census Operations Government of India, New Delhi, 1991 and 2001.

increasing its female literacy rate by more than 16 per cent and male literacy rate by around 13 per cent within a time span of 10 years, it still lags behind other major states of different regions. As far as female literacy is concerned, UP is way behind than even average all-India literacy. In the same period, Andhra Pradesh achieved a 15 per cent increase in male literacy and 18 per cent in female literacy rate.

CASTE VARIATIONS

SCs have a very low literacy percentage as compared to the total population of UP. Rural SC women that are marginalized on various levels, including caste, class and gender, have only 28.3 per cent of the literacy rate in UP. If we compare Table 11.5 and Table 11.6, the caste differential for both males and females is enough to explain the impact of caste on access to education. Even an 8 per cent and 12 per cent differential between males and females of total and SC population is not a real indicator of ground reality because, in total population, SC constitute 21.15 per cent portion and their low literacy rate brings down the total literacy rate thus diluting the appearance of difference between SC and other category.

Caste differential can be better understood with the NSSO data of 2004–2005. It shows that, in rural UP, 78.9 per cent of ST, 72.1 per cent of SC and 40.3 per cent of other category households

Table 11.6 *Sex-wise Rural–Urban Literacy Rates of SCs in UP (%)*

Year	Male	Female	Gender Difference
1991			
Rural	38.86	8.47	30.39
Urban	54.79	27.35	27.44
Total	40.79	10.68	30.11
2001			
Rural	59.0	28.3	30.7
Urban	69.1	45.5	23.6
Total	60.3	30.5	29.8

Source: Census of India, Registrar General and Census Commissioner, Government of India, New Delhi, various reports.

have no literate adult female member. The rural–urban divide is also reflected in this data which reveals that in rural areas, 61.5 per cent of total households do not have any female adult members as compared to 31.0 per cent of urban households. In rural UP, the other category men with most rewarding social status have four times chances of being literate than SC women with the lowest social status.

Apart from literacy, access to formal education is another important component that needs our attention. Here too, we find all kinds of variation, including gender, caste and rural–urban. Tables 11.7 and 11.8 are also based on NSSO data collected in the 61st round during 2004–2005. It reveals the pathetic situation of literacy among rural SC and ST women. Around 87.2 per cent of ST and 80.3 per cent of women in rural areas of UP are still illiterate. None of these ST women and only 0.4 per cent of SC women have attained a degree. Besides this, only 12.5 per cent of ST and 17.8 per cent of SC women in rural UP have attained education up to secondary level. Another point is worthwhile to note that, in rural areas, the gap between the male and female literacy of the same caste category widens with the rising position in the caste hierarchy. This trend supports the earlier observation of many scholars that women are better placed in the so-called lower castes than in the so-called higher castes. This trend may not be so explicitly seen in urban settings because traditional values are much more influential in rural areas.

The comparison between Tables 11.7 and 11.8 gives us the rural–urban divide. The situation in urban settings is better than in rural areas. In urban areas, only 10.9 per cent of other category males and 21.5 per cent of females are illiterate, as compared to 21.1 per cent and 48.8 per cent of rural area, respectively. Even the weaker sections are in a better position in urban settings. Urban SC women have nine times the chances of having a degree than their counterpart in rural areas. This data suggests that the impact of urbanization can help in overcoming handicaps imposed by caste. Among urban SC women, 3.6 per cent have a degree that is comparable with 3.4 per cent of rural other category women.

EDUCATION AND POVERTY

As stated earlier, education, being the most crucial component and indicator of social development, is directly related to other indicators, including poverty incidence. In urban settings, this relationship is more

Table 11.7 Percentage of Persons (15 Years and above) by Level of General Education for Rural UP

Caste	Not Category Literate		Literate & Primary		Middle		Secondary		Higher Secondary		Diploma/ Certificate		Graduate & above	
	Male	Female	Male	Female	Male	Female	Male	Female	Male	Female	Male	Female	Male	Female
ST	48.5	87.2	22.1	3.3	14.6	9.0	0.2	4.4	4.3	0.3	0.0	0.0	6.1	0.0
SC	46.3	80.3	22.1	8.9	19.6	6.7	2.2	5.6	3.9	1.3	0.1	0.1	2.3	0.4
OBC	37.2	72.5	22.6	12.3	19.7	8.2	3.6	10.4	6.2	2.6	0.3	0.0	3.5	0.6
O'rs	21.1	48.8	19.2	20.2	20.3	13.2	7.9	16.3	12.6	6.5	0.7	0.1	9.7	3.4

Source: NSSO, 61st round, 2004–2005.

Table 11.8 Percentage of Persons (15 Years and above) by Level of General Education for Urban UP

Caste	Not Category Literate		Literate & Primary		Middle		Secondary		Higher Secondary		Diploma/ Certificate		Graduate & above	
	Male	Female	Male	Female	Male	Female	Male	Female	Male	Female	Male	Female	Male	Female
ST	22.0	53.9	46.4	15.1	16.2	18.4	4.9	4.4	5.2	2.0	0.0	0.0	5.3	6.1
SC	28.7	60.1	27.7	17.2	21.2	11.2	9.1	4.8	6.7	2.7	0.4	0.5	6.2	3.6
OBC	27.6	51.1	27.7	19.6	16.2	13.4	10.3	7.1	8.2	4.9	1.5	0.1	8.1	3.8
O'rs	10.9	21.5	12.8	14.1	15.4	12.3	16.2	14.8	15.8	14.6	2.0	0.5	27.0	22.0

Source: NSSO, 61st round, 2004–2005.

pronounced than in rural areas, but this trend is changing, and in rural areas also, the relation between formal education and poverty is coming to the surface. In 1993–1994, 59 per cent of illiterate-headed urban households were poor as against only 7 per cent of households whose head had completed tertiary education.

The picture was slightly different in rural areas, where 51 per cent illiterate head, and 20 per cent of households whose head had attained tertiary education were below the poverty line. By 1999–2000, this trend changed to a limit when 52 per cent of households with an illiterate head, and 9 per cent of households whose head completed tertiary education were poor (Kozel and Parker 2003).

HEALTH

Like education, health is also an indicator as well as an important component of social development. It also contributes to other development indicators, including poverty, education, employment, water supply and access to health facilities. The relationship between these factors is 'complex, multifaceted and multidirectional'. Poverty may manifest itself in the form of food deprivation and thus have a direct bearing on the health of a person. Conversely, economic and educational attainment helps to sustain a better health status. Enhanced purchasing power attained through better employment opportunities may lead to nutritional adequacy and food security (Nanda and Ali 2005).

AGE AT FIRST MARRIAGE

It is an important indicator of health, especially for women. For women, marriage means that there may be chances of pregnancy that can be harmful at an early age. Table 11.9 shows the median age at marriage and age of women at first cohabitation with the husband. These can be termed as social and biological marriages, and both are important in a different context. Although the age of marriage has risen with the passage of time, the National Family Health Survey (NFHS–3) reveals that 53 per cent of women got married even before 18 years of age, the legal age of marriage but it is lower than 64.3 per cent in 1998–1999. Urban–rural variation is also seen in this aspect:

Table 11.9 *Age at Marriage of Women*

	Median Age at First Marriage	Median Age at First Cohabitation with Husband
UP	14.7	16
India	16.4	17

Source: NFHS–2, 1998–1999, quoted by Mehrotra (2006).

30 per cent of women in urban areas, compared to 61.1 per cent of rural areas in 2004–2005.

TOTAL FERTILITY RATE

In a very interesting comparative study of UP and Tamil Nadu, Mehrotra (2006) notes that the total fertility rate in UP is nearly double that of Tamil Nadu and one child higher than in the rest of India. Another important point to note is that upward movement in the caste hierarchy is accompanied by a fall in the fertility rate. In 1998–1999, the total fertility rate of SC women in UP was 4.44 as compared to 4.12 of OBC and 3.77 of others. In India, Kerala and Tamil Nadu have achieved the crucial fertility rate of 2.1 that is important to stabilize the population, but UP lags far behind. Unmet need for family planning is also responsible for this situation because SC women of UP want only three children as OBC and other category women too want at least one child less than they have (Mehrotra 2006). Fertility is also related to agrarian relations, as self-cultivating small farmers and labour have a tendency of high fertility to get the maximum number of working hands.

Education and fertility are also related. With the rise of educational standards, the fertility rate goes down, and it can be seen conversely as well. Data provided by NFHS–3 shows that illiterate women have a fertility rate of 4.61, in contrast to 2.36 of women having completed 10 years of education. Within seven years of the time span of 1998–1999 and 2005–2006, the total fertility rate has also fallen slightly to 3.82 from 4.1.

PLACE OF BIRTH

It is another important indicator that reveals access to health facilities. In 1998–1999, three-fourth of all pregnant women in UP delivered their babies at home, compared to Tamil Nadu where three-fourth deliveries took place at a health facility. Only 17.1 per cent of all pregnant SC women could get the help of trained health professionals, compared to 29.7 per cent women of other category (Mehrotra 2006). Medical help for delivery also depends upon habitation and education. Urban women (50.5%) have more than double the chances of getting the help of trained professionals in UP than rural women (23.8%). Similarly, 68.8 per cent of women having completed 10 years of education got the help of trained health professionals for the delivery in 2005–2006 against only 19.2 per cent of illiterate women.

INFANT MORTALITY AND CHILD MORTALITY

As compared to Tamil Nadu, twice the number of babies die in UP in the first week of their birth. The infant mortality rate (IMR) for UP is much higher than the all India average. The IMR of other category of UP is comparable to all India SC IMR. It indicates that the health condition of the so-called upper castes in UP is poorer than in other states SCs because, on all-India average, UP contributes maximum and lowers the average to a lower level. Table 11.10 shows that babies of illiterate women have much higher IMR than total women. So the contrast between babies of literate and illiterate mothers would be much higher. NFHS–3 provides the data regarding the health of children below the age of 3 in 2005–2006. It indicates that even today,

Table 11.10 *IMR and Child Mortality Rate (MR) in UP and India*

	UP	India		
_	IMR	Under-5 Mortality Rate (USMR)	IMR	USMR
Illiterate	104.7	146.3	86.5	122.8
SC	110	158.1	83.0	119.3
ST	83.3	124.5	84.2	126.6
OBC	105.7	142.2	76.0	103.1
Others	82.3	112.1	61.8	82.6
Total	86.7	122.5	67.6	94.9

Source: NFHS-2, 1998–1999, Quoted by Mehrotra (2006).

46 per cent of children are too short for their age; 11 per cent are very thin for their height, and 47 per cent are too underweight for their age. Although it can be claimed that on this front, UP has improved a little, even then, these figures are capable enough to reveal the pathetic situation of child's health.

The poor condition of children's health is also due to poor performance of the immunization programme. The latest NFHS reveals that only 23 per cent of babies aged between 12 and 23 months could get all the recommended vaccines in UP. The situation is even worse in rural areas where this number stands at only 21 per cent. The pace of progress is also very slow, only a 3 per cent increase in the last seven years.

NUTRITIONAL STATUS OF WOMEN

Women below a height of 145 cm and a body mass index below 18.5 kg are considered undernourished. On this criterion, 16.4 per cent of UP women are short statured, and for SC women, this percentage goes even higher to 18.4 per cent. Similarly, 48.7 per cent of all women in UP are anaemic, which includes 51.9 per cent of anaemic women from SC background. Besides this, 34.2 per cent of other category women have low body mass index against 41.6 per cent of SC women.

MORBIDITY AND HEALTH FACILITIES

The number of persons reporting ailments (PAP) and reporting commencement of ailments (PPC) is given in Table 11.11. It also gives the MR that stands at 83 and 58 for rural and urban areas respectively. In contrast, Kerala has MRs of 11 and 8 for both rural and urban areas. The availability of health facilities is also very poor in UP as compared

Table 11.11 *Per 1,000 Distribution of Persons Reporting PAP and PPC along with MR*

PAP	PPC	MR	
Rural	100	55	83
Urban	108	55	58

Source: NSS, 60th round.

to other states. In UP, the population per bed is as high as 2,647, in contrast with Kerala where this number is only 325. Even other bigger states like Maharashtra and Gujarat have only 920 and 709 population per bed.

The quality of government hospitals is so poor that people in the state prefer private hospitals that are much costlier. Although the total number of beds available in government hospitals is 72 per cent of all available beds, only 26.9 per cent of cases in rural areas and 31.4 per cent of cases in urban areas were treated in government hospitals.

STRUCTURE OF DWELLINGS

Around one-fifth of rural households in UP still live in kaccha houses and a quarter of all households are compelled to remain in semi-pucca ones. Only slightly above the half of all households (56.1%) have possession of pucca house. The situation is better in urban settings where the proportion of kaccha and semi-pucca is only 4.4 per cent and 8.8 per cent only. The NSSO 60th round shows that the rural–urban divide is still very wide, and in 2004, there was more than 30 per cent difference between the proportion of households living in pucca houses in rural and urban areas. The NFHS–3 provides data supporting trend manifested in NSS data and informs that 71.9 per cent of urban and only 12.2 per cent of rural households live in pucca houses.

DRINKING WATER, ELECTRICITY AND SANITATION

The major source of drinking water in rural UP is still tube wells or hand pumps that fulfil the needs of 88.3 per cent of people. In urban areas, tap water and hand pumps supply water to 40.7 per cent and 58.5 per cent of households. NSSO 60th round data reveals that 56.3 per cent of rural households and 41.2 per cent of urban households treat water before drinking. NFHS–3 shows that 34.8 per cent of urban and 2 per cent of rural households have access to piped drinking water. The same survey also shows that 16.3 per cent of urban and 84 per cent of rural households still lack toilet facilities. Besides this, 14.6 per cent of urban and 71.7 per cent of rural households do not have access to electricity.

CONCLUSION

With the above discussion, it is clear that some development has taken place in UP in terms of access to education, health, land, etc., but if we compare UP with other states, its backwardness comes to the surface. In the same period, many other states have done far better than UP. For these social failures, economic reasons are not the only reason but 'aborted land reforms, the displacement of healthcare by family planning programmes, the decay of public schooling system, the widespread corruption in poverty alleviation programmes, the suppression of women's informed agency in the society and the fragile basis of local democracy' are other major factors (Dreze and Gazdar 1997).

There has been a massive mobilization of dalits and OBCs in UP like Tamil Nadu, but in UP, it failed to garner few gains for the poorer section of society. Although both the states have large SC and OBC populations, one of the reasons for the different experiences of these two states is related to understanding of political parties representing these sections (Mehrotra 2006). In the coming elections also, the Samajwadi Party that represents OBCs and the Bahujan Samaj Party that represents dalits are the major forces, and it is interesting to see whether they are keen to pick up the issues that are important not only for their own following but also for the whole state.

It is also clear that the process of development in UP excludes a substantial part of the population. This exclusion breeds poverty in 'its various economic and non-economic dimensions' (Kozel and Parker 2003). The poor population of UP is not only marginalized in terms of access to material gains but is also deprived of social development. This leaves them incapable of taking advantage of any opportunity if they have any. Someone may leave a sigh of relief noting that in some dimensions disparities have come down, but still inter-group disparities are very high. It is due to the coincidence of caste and class. A large section of the population marginalized on the basis of class also faces caste handicaps. It reveals that the development of UP faces stiff challenges from the caste-class structure.

The study of the process of development in UP poses many interesting questions for researchers as well. One should note that the pattern of economic development does not coincide exactly with social development. It gives an opportunity for researchers to identify the relationship between these two important aspects of development. Apart from that, it is not the case that this pathetic situation is only due to politics. Politics itself is related to other social, cultural and economic entities. So to find out the reasons behind this situation in UP, the task that remains in the hands of researchers is to go into deeper study of the complex relationship between development, its various dimensions and sociological categories.

REFERENCES

Banerjee, and Knight. 1991. 'Quoted by Sukhadeo Thorat,' 2004, 'Caste, Exclusion and Poverty.' In *Unquiet Worlds, Dalit Voices and Visions*, edited by Mukul Sharma. New Delhi: Heinrich Boll Foundation.

Dreze, Jean, and Haris Gazdar. 1997. 'Uttar Pradesh: Burden of Inertia.' In *Indian Development-Selected Regional Perspectives*, edited by World Institute for Development Economics Research. New Delhi: Oxford University Press.

Dubey, Muchkund. 2005. 'Foreword.' In *India Social Development Report*, edited by Council for Social Development. New Delhi: Oxford University Press.

Kozel, Valerie, and Barbara Parker. 2003. 'A Profile and Diagnostic of Poverty in Uttar Pradesh.' *Economic and Political Weekly* 38, no. 4. Available at: https://www.epw.in/journal/2003/04/special-articles/profile-and-diagnostic-poverty-uttar-pradesh.html (accessed on 31 May 2021).

Mehrotra, Santosh. 2006. 'Well-being and Caste in Uttar Pradesh: Why UP Is Not Like Tamil Nadu.' *Economic and Political Weekly* 41, no. 40. Available at: https://www.epw.in/journal/2006/40/special-articles/well-being-and-caste-uttar-pradesh.html (accessed on 31 May 2021).

Nanda, A. R., and Almas Ali. 2005. 'Health Sector: Issues and Challenges.' In *India: Social Development Report*, edited by Council for Social Development. New Delhi: Oxford University Press.

Sen, Amartya, and Jean Dreze. 1995. *India: Economic Development and Social Opportunities*. Oxford/Delhi: Oxford University Press.

Shanker, Kripa. 2002. 'Development of UP: Tasks for the New Government.' *Economic and Political Weekly* 37, no. 22. Available at: https://www.epw.in/journal/2002/22/commentary/development.html (accessed on 31 May 2021).

Shariff, Abusaleh, and National Council for Applied Economic Research. 1999. *India Development Report: A Profile of Indian States in the 1990s*. New Delhi: Oxford University Press.

Thorat, Sukhdeo. 2004. 'Caste, Exclusion and Poverty.' In *Unquiet Worlds, Dalit Voices and Visions*, edited by Mukul Sharma. New Delhi: Heinrich Boll Foundation.

Planning Commission and Government of India. 2007. *UP Development Report*. New Delhi: Academic Publications.

Chapter 12

Development and Poverty in an Indian State[*]
A Study of KBK Districts of Orissa

Satya Prakash Dash

> The ambition of the greatest man of our generation has been to wipe every tear from every eye.
>
> —Jawaharlal Nehru

The word 'development' is a holistic concept. It has varied implications and multifarious dimensions. Development cannot and should not be restricted to a narrower meaning but assumes a wider connotation. Development may not only mean tangible things but is also intangible, such as clean environment, civic life, literacy and social capital. In a sense, development has no limits, but it should also be remembered that development should only be in a positive direction and which is good for society and humankind. In the name of development, one should not attempt to do things which may bring sorrow and misery to the people at large. Development should always have a moral and ethical angle and should always aim at the welfare and upliftment of the people. For this, the government implements various developmental policies and programmes which also serve a dual purpose, that of the welfare of people and also securing a mandate in the election so as to retain power. Interpreted in this way, development may be said to be both altruistic and selfish. Development is such a vast and varied

---

[*] *Social Change* Vol 37, no. 2 (June 2007): 76–98.

concept that it cannot be achievable in a unidirectional manner; it has to be treated in small bits. Justifying this argument, Partha Chatterjee (2000, 121) writes,

> Development implied a linear path, directed towards a goal, or a series of goals, separated by stages. It implied the fixing of priorities between long-run and short-run goals, and conscious choice between alternative paths. It was premised, in other words, upon a *rational* consciousness and will, and in so far as 'development' was thought of as a process affecting the whole of society, it was also promised upon *one* consciousness and will that of the whole. Particular interests needed to be subsumed within the whole and made consistent with the general interest.

Analysing the inequitable concentration of wealth and the ethics of development in reducing such phenomenon, Amartya Sen (2000), in *Development as Freedom*, is of the view that, in the world today, we live both with 'unprecedented opulence' and 'remarkable deprivation, destitution and oppression'. According to him, the central exercise of development is to overcome these problems, and to achieve this, the 'various types of un-freedoms' have to be removed. It concentrates particularly on the roles and interconnections between certain crucial instrumental freedoms, including economic opportunities, political freedoms, social facilities, transparency guarantees and protective security (Sen 2000, xii). Development, today, is a multidimensional process and is interdependent on various parameters. It is not to be based purely on economic parameters, only promoting the earlier concept of 'growth', by the transfer of finance, technology and experience from the developed countries, but encompasses within itself a whole range of social, economic, institutional, environmental, cultural and other parameters.

> From being a purely economic phenomenon, today it is an all round transformation of a country. It is holistic. It encompasses advancement of output and income, as well as radical transformation of institutional, social and administrative structures: and finally changes in popular attitudes, customs and beliefs. (Sebastian 1997, 329)

With one objective of accelerating the pace of development and to evenly distribute it over the people, at large, economic reforms were introduced and implemented in India with a cautious approach. The economic reforms brought with it the liberalization era of the Indian economy. The Preamble to the Constitution of India defines it, among other things, as a socialist state, and the economy of India was a 'mixed' economy with the coexistence of both the public and private sector. Nehru (1989, 137), though, was not very critical of capitalism, but at the same time, he did not much appreciate it. Nehru was of the following view,

> Capitalism increased the wealth of the world tremendously. It increased the food of the world, it increased the standard of the world a great deal. We must not simply think that capitalism has always been bad. But it has served its purpose, it does not any more fulfil a purpose. The good points of capitalism should be retained but fitted to a new structure so that it may give society the benefit of the new methods. The problem of production of wealth was solved by capitalism but not the problem of distribution of wealth.

In order to mitigate the inherent problems of capitalism, Nehru sought the mid-course so as to reap the benefits from both capitalism and socialism. During the period beginning from 1950 and compared with to the colonial period, this economic policy brought successes in certain fields such as industrial and agricultural growth. There was diversification of industrial production and also the export of some manufactured goods, replacing the old phenomenon of primary commodities. There was some sort of domestic self-sufficiency in agricultural production. It is for this reason, Baidyanath Mishra (1998) said, 'India's development strategy and economic policy since independence were guided by the objectives of accelerating the growth of output and employment but with social justice and equity'. However, the outcomes of the economic policy, which was so arduously followed, did not bring the desired results. The public sector undertakings were established with a view to increase production and employment opportunities, but it was found that except the *Navratnas* in the public sector, all the others were rather a liability than assets. There were several disadvantageous positions in managing the public sector undertakings, such as political and bureaucratic interventions, corruption and financial mismanagement, and this led to the untimely closure of these undertakings. Again, in 1990, there was a crisis in the balance of payments. In order to solve the multidimensional crisis and to accelerate the development process, it was necessary to implement certain economic reforms which would act as a buoyant on the economic policy. While analysing the 'mixed' economy of India, Jayati Ghosh (1998, 169) writes,

> Related to this is the unfortunate reality that four decades of planned development have not created a situation in which state and market aspirations combine to provide basic needs to the bulk of the population. This inadequate provision to the masses of essential items of survival including both goods such as food, clothing the minimally acceptable housing, and services such as universal primary education, adequate health care and sanitation, must be counted as the single-most damaging aspect of the development process. Not only is the availability deficient in aggregate terms, but access to such basic minimum goods and services is very unequally distributed, and is determined not only by wealth and asset positions, but by a complex system of patronage and clientelism in both rural and urban India.

One of the basic aims of the economic reforms, leading to a free-market economy, was the removal of poverty along with emphasis on micro-economic policies in some important areas such as agriculture, infrastructure and social development. It can be said with a certain degree of certainty that development/improvement in the above-mentioned areas can, to an extent, lead to poverty alleviation. Implementation of poverty alleviation programmes alone cannot eliminate poverty, and it has to be supplemented with other micro-economic policies and programmes which can also ensure social justice. Economic reforms, if pursued in the right direction and with a humane approach, can ultimately result in the removal of poverty and thereby can bring betterment in the living standards of the toiling mass. For that, we need a government which can govern and carry on with reforms but reorient those reforms towards uplifting the poor, promoting social justice and stability (Sengupta 2001, 248). However, this seems to be a distant dream and the case of the poor is nowhere visible to be in a good position. Economic reforms have brought in the major capitalist players, and this class, as usual, is thriving by exploiting the poor and the rural masses.

STATE OF ORISSA

As per the 2001 Census, the total population of Orissa is 36,804,660, and this is 3.57 per cent of the total population of India. The percentage of rural population is 85.03 per cent and the percentage of Scheduled Castes (SCs) and Scheduled Tribes (STs) population to the total population of Orissa is 16.50 per cent and 22.21 per cent (2001 Census), respectively. The literacy rate of rural and urban areas in Orissa is 59.8 per cent and 80.8 per cent, respectively. Orissa has a total of 30 districts out of which the undivided districts of Kalahandi, Balangir and Koraput (KBK) are the most backward and underdeveloped districts with perpetual poverty. After the distinct reorganization in 1993, the three districts have been divided into eight districts. However, in order to develop the districts, a Special Area Development Programme is being implemented in all the eight districts of undivided KBK districts.

Even though the state of Orissa is endowed with rich natural resources and fertile land, the economic condition of the people of Orissa is not good.

> According to a household census done by the State Government in 1992 and 1997, the percentage of rural family below the poverty line (BPL) was 78.6 per cent and 66.23 per cent respectively. In the sample survey conducted by the Government of India in 1999–2000, the percentage of rural persons living below the poverty line was 47.15 per cent. The State Government again did a survey of the people living below the poverty line in 2002 but its results have not been made public as the Supreme Court has stayed it on a writ petition filed by the People's Union for Civil Liberties (PUCL). According to the Planning Commission estimation of poverty in Orissa based on the Quinquennial Consumer Expenditure survey, in 1999–2000, 47.15 per cent of population lived below the poverty line. The rural and urban proportion was 48.01 per cent and 42.83 per cent respectively. During the same period, the national level data was 26.10 per cent and the corresponding rural and urban proportion was 27.09 per cent and 23.62 per cent respectively. (Dash 2004, 438)

It is pertinent to mention that in the undivided KBK districts, the percentage of families living below the poverty line (BPL) is 82.60 per cent and 71.97 per cent as per the 1992 Census and 1997 Census conducted by the Panchayati Raj Department (2005b), Government of Orissa.

From Table 12.1, it is evident that compared with the national level, the position of Orissa is not encouraging. However, in both, with the progress of years, the rate of poverty has declined. If a comparison is made between the years 1993–1994 and 1999–2000, it can be said that even though the rate of decline of poverty at the national level was significant, in Orissa, it was marginal, and in the urban area of Orissa, the rate of poverty has, in fact, increased during the same period. Broadly, it can be presumed that even though the economic reforms of 1991 had a positive impact at the national level, Orissa did not benefit much from it. Supplementing to this is the fact that 71.97 per cent of the rural families of undivided KBK districts live BPL. The total rural population in the undivided KBK districts and in Orissa as per the 2001 census is 6,554,537 and 31,287,422 persons respectively, which is 20.95 per cent. The incidence of poverty in Orissa vis-à-vis other major states is detailed in Table 12.2.

The *Economic Survey 2003–2004* of Orissa enumerates several special features of poverty in Orissa. It can be analysed from the special features of poverty in Orissa that there are regional variations and disparities leading to unbalanced growth and development. The position of the SCs and STs is highly vulnerable and precarious even though many programmes and policies are being implemented for their welfare. There is a phenomenal lack of infrastructural development in Orissa, and this is one of the major causes of perpetual poverty and underdevelopment.

Table 12.1 *Percentage of People BPL (Orissa and India)*

	Orissa			India		
Year	Rural	Urban	Total	Rural	Urban	Total
1973–1974	67.28	55.62	66.18	56.44	49.01	54.88
1977–1978	72.38	50.92	70.07	53.07	45.24	51.32
1983–1984	67.53	49.15	65.29	45.65	40.79	44.48
1987–1988	57.64	41.53	55.58	39.09	38.20	38.36
1993–1994	49.72	41.64	48.56	37.27	32.36	35.97
1999–2000	48.01	42.83	47.15	27.09	23.62	26.10

Source: Government of Orissa (2004, 8/1).

Table 12.2 *Incidence of Poverty in Orissa vis-à-vis Other Major States: 1973–1974 to 1999–2000*

State	People BPL (%)					
	1973–1974	1977–1978	1983–1984	1987–1988	1993–1994	1999–2000
Andhra Pradesh	48.86	39.31	28.91	25.86	22.19	15.77
Bihar	61.91	61.55	62.22	52.13	54.96	42.60
Gujarat	48.15	41.23	32.79	31.54	24.21	14.07
Haryana	35.36	29.55	21.37	16.54	25.05	08.74
Karnataka	54.47	48.78	38.24	37.53	33.16	20.04
Kerala	59.79	52.22	40.42	31.79	25.43	12.72
Madhya Pradesh	61.78	61.78	49.78	43.07	42.52	37.43
Maharashtra	53.24	55.88	43.44	40.41	36.86	25.02
Orissa	66.18	70.07	65.29	55.58	48.56	47.15
Punjab	28.15	19.27	16.18	13.20	11.77	06.16
Rajasthan	46.14	37.42	34.46	35.15	27.41	15.28
Tamil Nadu	54.94	54.79	51.66	43.39	35.03	21.12
Uttar Pradesh	57.07	49.05	47.07	41.45	40.85	31.15
West Bengal	63.43	60.52	54.85	44.72	35.66	27.02
All India	54.88	51.32	44.48	38.36	35.97	26.10

Source: Government of Orissa (2004, 8/2).

Infrastructural development is most required in different areas of Orissa, and its inadequacy results in various negative spill–over effects. In addition to this, Orissa is prone to natural calamities, and it would not be incorrect to say that this has become an annual phenomenon. Although the state government is implementing various poverty alleviation programmes with a view to providing livelihood support and ensuring food security to the needy people, lack of infrastructural development is hampering the yields from such programmes.

KBK DISTRICTS

In order to develop the most backward and poverty-stricken districts, the state government is implementing the Special Area Development

Programme in KBK districts. The main objective of this programme is to accelerate the developmental targets and remove the regional disparities. In addition to general grants, these underdeveloped and backward districts are given special grants with specific thrust on development and welfare of the people. The state government, in consultation with the Government of India, has formulated a Revised Long-term Action Plan (RLTAP) for expeditious development of the KBK districts. The RLTAP project envisages an integrated approach for speeding up the socio-economic development of this region by synergizing developmental activities and schemes under implementation.

The KBK districts account for 20.85 per cent of the total population of Orissa and are tribal dominated districts. The tribals constitute 38.4 per cent of the total population of these districts and this also includes some of the primitive tribal communities such as Bondas, Dadai, Langia Souras and Dangaria Kandhas. The tribal population of the undivided Koraput district is 23.37 per cent of the total tribal population of Orissa. The SC papulation to the total population of KBK districts is 16.26 per cent. The demographic and literacy rate is detailed in Table 12.3.

From Table 12.4, it is self-explanatory that overall poverty has declined over a period of five years from 1992 to 1997, as the data presents a comparative figure after the economic reforms of 1991. However, the effective decline in poverty is more prominently marked in the divided Kalahandi, Balangir, Nabarangpur and Rayagada districts. The first two districts are located in the relatively developed areas of the undivided Kalahandi and Balangir districts and the last two districts are the industrial belt of the undivided Koraput district. In all the other four districts of KBK, poverty has moreover remained stagnant or has increased. From this, it may be presumed that the benefit of economic reforms has not really reached the poor or that effective development processes have not been properly initiated and implemented.

The socio-economic indicators of the KBK districts present a gloomy picture of development. The literacy rate and female literacy rate is 42.72 per cent and 28.8 per cent, respectively, compared to the state average of 63.1 per cent and 50.5 per cent as per the 2001 Census. Prevalence of use of family planning methods is low, that is, 38.73 per cent in KBK, compared to the national average of 48 per cent. This again is strengthened due to the fact that 48.23 per cent of all children born are the

Table 12.3 *Demographic and Literacy Indicators in the KBK Districts: 2001*

District	Population Indicators				Literacy Rate			
	Popu-density	Total (000)	Female %	Rural %	ST %	SC %	Total %	Female %
1	2	3	4	5	6	7	8	9
1. Koraput	134	1,178	49.96	83.18	49.6	13.0	35.7	24.3
2. Malkangiri	83	480	49.91	92.79	57.4	21.4	30.5	20.09
3. Nabarangpur	192	1,018	49.81	94.18	55.0	14.1	33.90	20.70
4. Rayagada	116	823	50.71	85.98	55.8	13.9	36.10	24.60
5. Balangir	203	1,336	49.56	88.45	20.6	16.9	55.70	39.50
6. Sonepur	231	541	49.13	92.59	23.6	9.8	62.80	46.20
7. Kalahandi	168	1,334	50.00	92.49	28.6	17.7	45.90	29.30
8. Nuapada	138	531	50.15	94.34	34.7	13.6	42.00	25.80
KBK districts	152	7,241	49.91	89.89	38.4	16.3	42.72	28.81
Orissa	236	36,707	49.29	85.03	22.21	16.50	63.10	50.50

Source: Census 2001.
Note: Popu-density: population density (persons/sq. km).

Table 12.4 *Census of Families BPL in KBK Districts (in Lakhs)*

Districts	1992 Census			1997 Census		
	Total	BPL	%	Total	BPL	%
Kalahandi	2.41	2.07	85.77	3.08	1.93	62.71
Nuapada	0.94	0.79	83.64	1.27	1.09	85.70
Balangir	2.39	1.81	75.82	3.30	2.01	61.06
Sonepur	0.92	0.57	62.29	1.10	0.80	73.02
Koraput	1.88	1.63	86.59	2.65	2.22	83.81
Malkangiri	0.80	0.63	84.81	1.09	0.89	81.88
Nabarangpur	1.52	1.38	90.56	2.15	1.59	73.66
Rayagada	1.42	1.22	86.04	1.88	1.36	72.03
Total	12.28	10.14	82.60	16.52	11.89	71.97

Source: Government of Orissa (2004, 18/2).

third or succeeding higher births in the family. Girls marrying below the age of 18 years constitute as high as 60.60 per cent in KBK districts in comparison to the national average of 36.80 per cent. The districts also suffer from high morbidity on account of under nutrition, endemic malaria and other local diseases. There is also depletion of forest area. Migrations, scarcity of food and starvation deaths are other features of KBK districts, particularly during the drought period and lean seasons.

The *Economic Survey 2003–2004*, Government of Orissa (2004) states that, According to the Report of the Committee on the Constitution of Separate Development Board in Orissa, 96 per cent of the Community Development (CD.) Blocks in these districts are either 'very backward' or 'backward'. To be specific, 49 CD. Blocks and 28 CD. Blocks are considered as very backward and backward respectively. Only 3 CD. Blocks are treated as 'developing' blocks and none are considered to be 'developed'. Therefore, backwardness of this region is multi-faceted, (i) tribal backwardness, (ii) hill area backwardness, (iii) backwardness due to severe natural calamities, and (iv) backwardness due to depletion of natural resources.

The RLTAP has been operational in these districts since 1998 with a total outlay of ₹6,251.06 crore fund over a period of nine years from 1998–1999 to 2006–2007. The programme aims at (a) drought proofing, (b) development saturation and poverty alleviation and (c) improving quality of life of the people of this region. Projects for the RLTAP based on the regional sub-plan mode are prepared by the district administration, and according to the projects, additional/special central assistance is sanctioned. The strategical approach to achieve the aims and objectives of RLTAP leading to development are (a) building rural productive infrastructure (e.g., roads, bridges, tanks, godowns, etc.), (b) income generation on sustainable basis (e.g., poverty alleviation programmes), (c) mobilizing and energizing the rural poor (e.g., self-help groups, water-users associations, etc.) and (d) restructuring and energizing social security system (e.g., education, health, food security, etc.). The projected outlay for RLTAP in KBK districts under different schemes from 1998–1999 to 2006–2007 is given in Table 12.5.

The additional/special central assistance to KBK districts from the year 1998–1999 to 2003–2004 is given in Table 12.6. All this assistance was spent under different programmes/schemes of the various departments of the state government. A total of eighteen different departments are implementing various developmental and welfare-oriented programmes/schemes for the development of the KBK districts. These programmes/schemes include watershed development projects, rural electrification, infrastructure/institutional development, health, rural development, tribal development, etc. *The Indian Express,* in a news report, dated 21 February 2004, published a news item under the caption 'Low Utilisation of RLTAP Funds in KBK'. It reported, 'it appears that the State Government is yet to put an effective mechanism in place'. It also contained excerpts of a press release by the then chief secretary, the Government of Orissa, that the state government had been able to spend only ₹111 crore out of a total allocation of ₹377 crore under RLTAP. The expenditure is less than one-third of the total allocation for the financial year 2003–2004. Secretaries of administrative departments concerned were requested to ensure that at least ₹300 crore of the total allocation had to be used in the financial year 2003–2004.

The National Bank for Agriculture and Rural Development (NABARD) is also extending assistance and loans to the state government for development of rural infrastructure out of the Rural Infrastructure Development Fund (RIDF). The programmes

Table 12.5 *Projected Outlay for RLTAP in KBK Districts (1998–1999 to 2006–2007)*

| | | | Projected Outlay (Rupees in Crores) | | | | |
| | | | Centrally Sponsored Plan Shares | | | | |
Sl No.	Scheme	Central Plan	Central	State	Total Central Share	Total State Share	Grand Total (Rupees in Crores)
1.	Agriculture	44.74	30.19	10.01	74.93	10.01	84.94
2.	Horticulture	66.17	6.35	1.62	72.52	1.62	74.14
3.	Watershed development	601.90	194.96	81.42	796.86	81.42	878.28
4.	Afforestation	347.83	14.11	14.11	361.94	14.11	376.05
5.	Rural employment	–	2,235.05	558.76	2,235.05	558.76	2,793.81
6.	Irrigation	812.11	–	–	812.11	–	812.11
7.	Health	150.95	–	–	150.95	–	150.95
8.	Emergency feeding	88.50	–	–	88.50	–	88.50
9.	Drinking water supply	–	67.74	67.74	67.74	67.74	135.48
10.	Rural connectivity	–	534.70	65.00	534.70	65.00	599.70
11.	Welfare of ST/SC	257.12	–	–	257.12	–	257.12
	Total	2,369.32	3,083.10	798.66	5,452.42	798.66	6,51.06

Source: Government of Orissa (2004, 18/4–5).

Table 12.6 *Demand and Sanction of Additional/Special Central Assistance to KBK Districts (Rupees in Crores)*

Year	Allocation	Expenditure[a]	Submission of UC[b]	Demand by State Government
1998–1999	46	10.51	–	307.19
1999–2000	57.60	55.91	–	307.34
2000–2001	40.35	57.14	–	341.74
2001–2002	100	61.37	–	355.93
2002–2003	200	131.99	192.77	NA
2003–2004	250	318.54	111.63	NA
2004–2005	250	279.11	NA	NA
Total	943.95	914.57	304.40	

Source: Government of Orissa (2005a, 18/5–6).
Notes: [a] Expenditure includes the unspent balance of the previous year.
[b] State government started furnishing utilization certificate (UC) from 2002–2003 against ACA/SCA received from 1998–1999.

Table 12.7 *Utilization of RIDF Programmes for KBK Districts (Rupees in Lakhs)*

Programmes Year	Roads & Bridges	Irrigation	Wells
2000–2001	265.87 (5.74%)	– (0%)	–
2001–2002	740.65 (10.02%)	146.40 (10.53%)	3.26 (0.56%)
2002–2003	373.86 (6.02%)	– (0%)	35.36 (32.91%)
2003–2004	359.70 (6.44%)	– (0%)	41.92 (8.40%)
Total	1740.08 (7.31%)	146.40 (3.64%)	80.54 (6.75%)

Source: http://www.orissa.gov.in/finance/ index.htm

sanctioned and utilization of funds for the last four financial years under NABARD assisted RIDF projects for KBK districts in detailed in Table 12.7. The percentage of funds for KBK districts to the total is given in parenthesis.

Table 12.8 *Functioning of MHUs*

Sl. District No.	No. of Block	No. of MHU	No. of MHU Functioning in Institutional Vehicle		No. of MHU Functioning in Hired Vehicle
			Four-wheeler	Two-wheeler	
1 Koraput	14	15	5	–	10
2 Rayagada	11	12	10	–	2
3 Nabarangpur	10	11	4	–	7
4 Malkangiri	7	10	1	2	7
5 Kalahandi	13	14	6	–	8
6 Nuapada	5	6	4	–	2
7 Balangir	14	15	4	–	11
8 Sonepur	6	7	3	–	4
Total	80	90	37	2	51

Source: Directorate of Health Services, Government of Orissa, 2006.

HEALTH STATUS IN KBK DISTRICTS

Human rights, in a sense, are very 'general' and not special and are universal, inalienable and inherent. Every person is born with certain rights, and this includes the rights to life, liberty, equality and dignity. The very basis of human rights lies in the inherent dignity and worth of human beings so as to receive respect and protection. The United Nations Centre for Human Rights defines human rights as 'those rights that are inherent in our nature and without which we cannot live as human beings'. The Constitution of India in Article 21 includes protection of life and personal liberty as a fundamental right and states, 'no persons shall be deprived of his life'. The Supreme Court of India has also proclaimed and interpreted the right to life to include 'right to health' (State of Punjab v. Mohinder Singh Chawla AIR 1997 SC 1225) and 'right to timely medical treatment in government hospital' (Paschim Bangal Khet Mazdoor Society v. State of West Bengal AIR 1996 SC 2426). In spite of these provisions and rights, the issue of health still remains a controversial subject in the right's perspective. This assumes a greater proportion in the context of the poor, *Dalits*, tribals and other deprivileged and disadvantaged sections of the population. For the poor, health remains as an unaffordable need, and this increases manifold times in rural and inaccessible villages even though, 'the development of health is a holistic process related to the overall growth and development of social, cultural, economic, educational, political and environmental factors' (Mukhopadhyay 1997, 36).

'Health policy is broadly defined as goals and means, policy environments and instruments, processes and styles of decision-making, implementation and assessment. It deals with institutions, political power and influence, people and professionals, at different levels from local to global' (Leppo 1997). The policy enumerates the guidelines to proceed in a positive direction with a result-oriented approach. With this aim and objective, the State of Orissa formulated a new health policy, namely Orissa State Integrated Health Policy 2002 (Government of Orissa 2003). The objectives in the policy states, 'steps are being taken to make improvements in the health care system in the State to cater to the health needs of the people in the rural areas, particularly in the tribal and backward regions of the State'. It also states, 'to ensure greater access to primary health care by bringing medical institutions as close to the people as possible or through mobile health units, particularly in the under-served and backward districts' and 'to improve health care in the KBK districts of the State' among others. The state government has also formulated a health Orissa Vision 2010 document for better delivery of health services.

The Vision 2010 document includes, 'the overall goals of the health systems are to reduce mortality and morbidity, ensure equity in health status, protect the poor and disadvantaged from financial costs of illness and increase public satisfaction'. It also contains, 'the health status of SC/ST populations, facing the double burden of social exclusion and poverty, can serve as a sensitive indicator for inequities.' The status of the SC/ST with regard to health services and utilization is very low, and this is mainly due to poverty and lack of awareness of general health services. They suffer from many of the preventable and curable diseases and are afraid to go to the health centre for varied reasons. Almost 81 per cent of ST/SC groups are landless labourers with practically no assets (Health and Family Welfare Department 2003). They have consistently worse health outcomes and low access to healthcare facilities. Disadvantaged groups carry a larger burden of disease.

It is observed that the state allocates resources for delivery of better health services, but it remains confined to the speciality and super-speciality health services available in the three medical colleges and in the district headquarter hospitals. This is done as the number of persons treated in these institutions is higher compared to their capacity for treatment. This is for the simple reason that urban centres are more densely populated than the rural areas, where the population is dispersed over a larger geographical area and that too inaccessible and interior area. Health institutions in urban areas also have a number of doctors and para-medical staff and so their salaries also increase the budgetary allocation. All this is intended to serve a more quantified number of patients, which will suo moto lead to a better health status for the entire state. The cost of healthcare has grown enormously with an adverse effect on the health and economic status of disadvantaged groups. On average, they spend 12 per cent of their annual income on healthcare, as opposed to only 2 per cent spent by the rich. However, the richest 20 per cent enjoy three times the share of public subsidy for health compared to the poorest quintile (Health and Family Welfare Department 2003). Hospitalized ST/SC people spend more than half of their total annual expenditure on healthcare, while 45 per cent borrow money/sell assets to cover expenses and 35 per cent fall BPL (Peters et al. 2002, 288–289). Out of pocket medical costs alone may push 2.2 per cent of the population to BPL in one year. The number of disadvantaged poor, who did not seek treatment because of financial reasons, increased from 15 per cent to 24 per cent in rural areas and doubled from 10 per cent to 21 per cent in urban slums in the decade 1986–1996.

The State of Orissa, in order to provide basic health services, has 183 community health centres/upgraded primary health centres (PHCs), 142 block PHCs, 1,165 single doctor PHCs (new), 90 mobile health units (MHUs) in the Koraput, Balangir and Kalahandi (KBK) districts, 109 area hospitals and 5,927 sub-centres (auxiliary nurse midwife centres). Existing data reveal that there is no shortage of primary healthcare outlets such as PHCs if the population norm is applied to the state's population as a whole. However, when assessed block-wise, there is a shortage of PHCs, particularly in tribal areas. There are 1,165 single-doctor PHCs or PHC (N) in the state. Taking into account the norms for establishing PHCs at the rate of one per

30,000 populations in general and one for 20,000 in tribal areas, there is a need for an additional 39 single-doctor PHCs in tribal areas alone. However, the benefits of establishing single doctor PHCs are somewhat doubtful. Doctors are reluctant to stay in these institutions and the services offered are consequently uncertain. Doctor absenteeism is a recurrent problem in rural medical institutions, particularly in the KBK districts. It is therefore a better strategy to strengthen block level and community health centres.

Since July 2001, the state government started the Panchabyadhi Chikitsa Scheme which guarantees free treatment, including free medicine for five common communicable diseases, namely malaria, leprosy, diarrhoea, acute respiratory infections and scabies. These five diseases constitute approximately 70 per cent of the patient load in the primary health institutions and affect a large number of poor people (Health and Family Welfare Department 2004).

The 90 MHUs serve the inaccessible and remote villages in the underdeveloped tribal districts of Koraput, Balangir and Kalahandi (KBK). The MHUs are provided with a doctor, pharmacist, health worker (female), attendant along with a vehicle and driver (Table 12.8). All these staff are purely on an annual contractual basis. These MHUs meet the health needs and provide service to those people who find it very difficult to go to the PHC or any health institution due to inaccessible communication and transportation. The MHUs, apart from rendering health services, also undertake various national health programmes and organize health camps. The MHUs in this process also generate awareness about health needs, medicines and other preventive measures in case of epidemics in remote areas. The funding for the MHU was provided by the RLTAP of the central government from 1998 to 2007, among other health programmes such as retinal capillary hemangioblastoma, tuberculosis and malaria control programmes. As the term of the programme is now going to end, the central government has agreed to continue the programme. In addition to that, the state government has also launched a Biju KBK programme in line with the central government scheme from 2007. This has been done to counter the central government programme, with similar aims and objectives. Whatever the name may be, the objectives of development must reach the poor tribal people and they must also feel it. It is only with the funds received from the central government that the MHU units are being made operational in the KBK districts. In the health sector, the central plan under RLTAP for the entire period of 1998–2007 is ₹150.95 crore.

Tribal persons face a double burden of social isolation and poverty. Orissa has a tribal population larger than the national average. They constitute 8 per cent of the country's population and 22.21 per cent of the state's population. Tribal persons have worse health outcomes and less access to healthcare. The tribal people suffer disproportionately more from pretransition diseases, such as malaria, sexually transmitted diseases and tuberculosis. Genetic diseases, nutritional deficiency diseases, and sickle cell anaemia are specific to them. When hospitalized, they spend more than half of their annual expenditure on healthcare services: 45 per cent of them borrow money or sell assets to cover the expenses and 35 per cent fall BPL (Health and Family Welfare Department 2003). Low awareness of ill health and health-seeking behaviour are important barriers to maintaining health. The tribal people rely mainly on unqualified doctors/quacks and traditional healing systems. Alienation from forest resources for livelihood, exploitation by the non-tribal, deforestation and various 'development' works further deteriorates their health status.

The presence of unqualified doctors/quacks is rampant in tribal and remote villages. Untrained practitioners, faith healers, traditional birth attendants, priests and local medicine women and men largely cater to the rural areas (Peters et al. 2002, 47). They visit these villages on a weekly basis and administer medicines and injections to people suffering from various ailments. They also charge high fees and inflated costs for medicine. The innocent villagers are compelled to pay the high price for the sake of getting health services on their doorstep. In the process also, they did not have to abandon their day's work/labour. Again, unqualified doctors/quacks are also available whenever they are given a call by these villagers, as they reside in a neighbouring village. The social network of the villagers is also good enough to pass on the call to the unqualified doctors/quacks. However, in this process, they remain unaware of the amount of risk they are undertaking for the very cause of health which is dear to them. Such instances were observed during a field visit to some of the villages in Rayagada district. In spite of the availability of health institutions and public transport, the tribals do not opt for it for the simple reason of losing a day's work. Again, they are also not sure of the availability of doctors in such health institutions. Another reason for their preference for these unqualified doctors/ quacks is the fact that they administer injections which the health centres do not give unnecessarily and if given, then they have to pay for it. When the payment factor is common, then why should they not opt for treatment in their home rather than come to the health institution? One fact which is certain from this observation is that the tribals have gained awareness of allopathic treatment rather than the traditional system of healing. However, it cannot be said with certainty without a thorough study. Greater penetration of public medical institutions is hence required to mitigate this problem, and here the role of the MHUs is massive. Studies in rural primary healthcare reveal that though the infrastructure exists in most areas, it is grossly underutilized because of poor facilities, inadequate supplies, insufficient effective person hours, poor managerial skills among doctors, faulty planning of the mix of health programmes and the lack of proper monitoring and evaluating mechanism (Mukhopadhyay 1997, 38).

Development does not mean only official policies and programmes, but it must be physically reflected in the human development indices, such as health, literacy, safe drinking water and redistribution of assets and incomes. The following health indicators focus on the precarious health status of the tribals in Orissa. These indicators supplement what has been discussed above and the challenge it poses in the context of economic reforms and development.

> The health indices of the tribal population are worse than the national average: Infant mortality rate: 84.2: under-five mortality rate: 126.6: children underweight: 55.9 per cent: anaemia in children: 79.8 per cent: children with recent acute respiratory infection: 22.4 per cent: children with recent diarrhoea: 21.1 per cent: women with anaemia: 64.9 per cent. A high incidence of malnutrition is seen in Phulbani, Koraput (undivided) and Sundergarh districts. (Health and Family Welfare Department 2003)

As per the National Sample Survey Organisation (2006), Government of India, press note issued in March,

Nationally, the average medical expenditure per hospitalisation during a period of last 365 days was estimated as ₹5,695 in the rural and ₹8,851 in the urban areas. The average expenditure in the case of hospitalisation of male member was a little more (rural—₹5,946: urban—₹9,535) than those on females (rural—₹5,406: urban—₹8,112).

The average medical expenditure in the case of non-hospitalised treatment during a period of the last 15 days had been ₹257 in the rural and ₹306 in the urban areas. This expenditure was higher in the case of males (rural—₹275: urban—₹322) than that in the case of females (rural—₹240: urban—₹291).

These average medical expenditures indicate another ill effect of economic reforms and may be attributed due to the increasing reliance on private healthcare services rather than public health institutions.

LEFT EXTREMISM

In the context of fragility, the KBK districts exhibit a strong case in its favour. The Department for International Development, UK, defines 'fragile states' as 'those states where the government cannot or will not deliver core functions to the majority of its people, including the poor'. Fragile states include various categories such as weak states, conflict areas, post-conflict environments and states that have strong capacity but are unresponsive to the international community and the needs of their citizens. The State of Orissa in India falls under the last category. It has the capacity to perform well for the upliftment and development of the people in the KBK districts, particularly the disadvantaged groups (SCs and STs), but for some reason or the other, such as lack of dedication, sincerity, integrity, on the part of the officials and official/staff absenteeism, the state government is failing to deliver the services it is supposed to deliver. In this sense, it can be presumed that the institutional mechanism of the state government has to be re-energized and overhauled for effective delivery of public services and welfare-oriented policies. The range of problems associated with weak or ineffective states is broad and includes poverty, conflict and humanitarian crisis, human rights violations, global security threats and weakened international systems (Torres and Anderson 2004).

It is due to the ineffectiveness of the state government in the KBK districts that the problem of Left-extremism (Maoists) movement is acute in these districts, particularly in the undivided district of Koraput. The KBK districts account for 89.95 per cent of people still living in villages. Lower population density (152 persons/sq. km) compared to 236 for Orissa indicates difficult living conditions and an underdeveloped economy. Tribal communities dominate this region. As per the 2001 Census, about 38.4 per cent people of these districts belong to the ST communities, including four primitive tribal groups. The undivided district of Koraput (Koraput, Rayagada, Nabarangpur, and Malkangiri) comes under the scheduled area, with each individual district having 49.6 per cent, 55.8 per cent, 55 per cent and 57.47 per cent of the tribal population respectively, as per the 2001 Census.

The lack of proper developmental initiatives, policies and programmes and exploitation of the poor and disadvantaged group of people at the hands of the rich feudal class and officials is attributed to be the main cause of this problem. Supplementing this, the state government and also the Indian government, consider Left extremism more to be a 'law-and-order' problem than a 'socio-economic' issue. Instead of vigorous and expeditious implementation of developmental programmes, the state government is focusing on police and paramilitary forces to curb the menace of Left extremism. But are the police and paramilitary forces sufficient to wipe out the activities and plans of Left extremists? Owing to their justified action, the Left extremists have gained the trust, support and sympathy of the local tribal population. These people are all in favour of the Left extremists. They are pretty aware that the left extremists are fighting for their cause and welfare and also protecting them from further exploitation. The threat of the Left extremists is so high that even government officials and elected representatives also fear going to the areas which are densely infested with Left extremists. Government officials are also hesitant to be posted in these districts for the fear of the Left extremism, and if posted, many remain on long leave. In this context, the developmental and welfare programmes are seriously jeopardized and hampered, and for which reason, unscrupulous elements take an advantage, leading to the exploitation of the innocent tribals. The Left extremism thrives due to the presence of a weak and unresponsive state governance and administrative system.

CONCLUSION

As the socio-economic indicators, mentioned earlier, present a very dismal picture of KBK districts, special focus is required on the part of the government to achieve an all-round development of this area. There is a decline of forest areas, concentration of land in the hands of a few, repeated drought and drinking water problems, etc., in the KBK districts. By the self-employment scheme of Swarnjayanthi Gram Swarozgar Yojana of the Government of India, in 2003–2004, 13,404 self-help groups were formed and ₹2,203 crore were given as loans to beneficiaries. Disbursement of loans is not the only solution. There is a lot of follow-up action like creation of a market for distribution, proper supervision and care for its effective utilization and other ancillary requirements which are not effectively implemented by the state government. For which reason, the self-help groups are facing problems and hence loan repayment is declining and success rate is low. Health and medical care is abysmally low in KBK districts and many medical and health posts remain vacant as government doctors are trying their best not to be posted in KBK districts. KBK districts are malaria-prone and the people here also suffer from water-borne diseases. Malnourishment and anaemia are other major health-related problems in KBK districts.

The Panchayati Raj institution is another instrument for the development and welfare of the people. It is based on decentralization of power and bringing people directly to the participatory process of growth and development. The twin governmental policies of liberalization and decentralization in the 1990s provide the new panchayats space to function by both reducing the role of bureaucracy and increasing grassroots participation, while at the same time maintaining the support of the state (Pai 1996, 79). However, in KBK districts, though due to reservations, SCs and STs and women are being elected, there is a prevalence of gender-based discrimination. Again, due to the low literacy rate, there is a lack of awareness, for which reason, the elected grassroots members become victims of unscrupulous elements. In actual practice, however, the Panchayati Raj system has not yet gathered the momentum it should have and, therefore, has not yet been able to arrest the waste or misuse of resources that has become typical (Sengupta 2001, 42). Kothari (1990, 277) is of the opinion that decentralization, not only economic but also political, is essential in order to challenge the rich and elite by the lower and much more numerous castes, and only then will destitution and poverty and illiteracy come to an end.

The *World Development Report 2000–2001* (World Bank 2000) presented a three-pronged strategy for poverty alleviation. These are, (a) promoting opportunity, (b) facilitating empowerment and (c) enhancing security. As per the report, there should be creation of institutional growth for the economic and all-round development opportunity of poverty-stricken people. Second, the administration in the poverty-stricken countries should be more accountable and responsive. It should ensure that the real poor participate in the political process and local decision-making process. This can only be possible when discrimination based on caste, class, gender and groups is eliminated. Third, the social safety nets are strengthened and people are brought within the safety nets. The World Bank's three-pronged strategy may be relevant for poverty alleviation but it certainly requires commitment and dedication on the part of the administrators who are its implementers.

Due to the development initiative in KBK districts, Kalahandi district is now contributing a fourth of Orissa's rice production. In the year 1993–1994, Kalahandi provided 24,000 tonnes of rice and it reached 37,700 tonnes in 1995–1996. However, this has not evaded the problem of poverty and the tribals still suffer and are compelled to eat poisonous mango kernels in order to satiate hunger. 'The paradox of plenty is not confined to Kalahandi. Much of India is faced with the Kalahandi syndrome—food stocks piling up to unmanageable levels at a time when more than 320 million do not have the means to purchase it' (Chatterji 2004).

Development is a process of growing up in a positive direction in a continuum. Economic development is certainly the means to achieve the goals of general development and ushering in social justice. Rajni Kothari (1990, 268) is of the opinion that economic development does not lead to curbing of civil liberties and dictatorial state in order to remove poverty and inequity, and to strengthen it. He gives evidence from India and a number of third world countries. Most of these countries present a picture of a high level of economic mismanagement accompanied by an increase in disparities and deterioration in the conditions of the poorer sections of the people. With regard to development being an instrument of social justice, Kothari writes, 'the point is that once the logic of development gets overpowered by the logic of technology, once the nature and direction of development becomes dependent on a given technological package instead of being its determinant, development ceases to be an instrument of social justice' (1990, 396). If such a situation arises, then the condition of the poor remains unaltered, whereas the rich get the benefits of such development. Kothari concludes by writing, 'development has been hijacked by corporate capitalism in the garb of high technology and 'democracy' has become a playground of the corrupt, communal and criminalised sectors of the polity and the economy' (1990, 396).

Economic reforms may have created opportunities for people living in urban areas and have facilitated the entry of multinational companies, but the poor living in the rural areas still remain neglected and suffer. Implementation of development policies alone is not sufficient: it needs proper and appropriate follow-up action. Added to this, there is also a lack of awareness of the development and welfare objectives of the government. Special emphasis should be given to the generation of awareness, and this could be possible through increasing levels of 'functional' literacy and educational opportunities. Studying development problems involves identifying and analysing the difficulties people encounter in their efforts to make—on the basis of their varied interests and ideas—the best possible use of the potential of their country, region or sector of society (Tornquist 1999, 7). A cautious approach is also required to be followed as our economy belongs to the developing category, thereby contrasting it to the developed one, as there is every chance of being dominated by the latter. This late development has led to great suffering and adjustment difficulties for extremely large numbers of people, even in cases where the successes have been and are considerable (Tornquist 1999, 7). 'The central issue in economic development is to expand the social opportunities open to the people. The expansion of markets has a crucial role to play in this transformation' (Sen 1997, 62).

In conclusion, it would be noteworthy to mention what Arjun Sengupta (2001, 87) writes:

In an economy like India no reform can succeed that does not take care of the problems of poverty alleviation and social development and where substantial sectors such as infrastructure, agriculture and employment would call for a major involvement of the government. Economic reforms no doubt facilitate the realization of development objectives, but they do not obviate the active role of the government. A plan for development policies will therefore have to build on the policies for economic reforms, and then go much beyond to address specific problems.

REFERENCES

Chatterjee, Partha. 2000. 'Development Planning and the Indian State.' In *Politics and the State in India*, edited by Zoya Hasan. New Delhi: SAGE Publications.

Chatterji, Shoma, A. 2004. 'Problems of Distribution.' Kolkata, *The Statesman*, December 8, 2004.

Dash, Satya Prakash. 2004. 'State Administration.' *Indian Journal of Political Science* 65, no. 3: 435–456.

Ghosh, Jayati. 1998. 'Development Strategy in India: A Political Economy Perspective.' In *Nationalism, Democracy and Development*, edited by Sugata Bose and Ayesha Jalal. New Delhi: Oxford University Press.

Government of Orissa. 2003. *Orissa State Integrated Health Policy-2002*. Bhubaneswar.

———. 2004. *Economic Survey 2003–2004*. Bhubaneswar: Planning and Coordination Department.

———. 2005a. *Economic Survey 2004–2005*. Bhubaneswar: Planning and Coordination Department, Bhubaneswar.

———. 2005b. *Panchayati Raj Dept. Activities Report 2004–2005*. Bhubaneswar: Government of Orissa.

Health and Family Welfare Department. 2003. *Orissa Health Vision 2010: A Health Strategy*. Bhubaneswar: Government of Orissa. Available at: https://health.odisha.gov.in/PDF/vision2010.pdf (accessed on 31 May 2021).

———. 2004. *Orissa Health Activities Report 2003–2004*. Bhubaneswar: Government of Orissa.

Kothari, Rajni. 1990. *Politics and People* (vol. 1 and 2). New Delhi: Ajanta Publications.

Leppo, K. 1997. 'Introduction.' In *Making a Healthy World: Agencies, Actors, and Policies in International Health*, edited by M. Koivusalo and E. Ollila. London: Zed Books.

Mishra, Baidyanath. 1998. 'Fifty Years of India's Economy.' Fourth Professor. Shreeram Chandra Dash Memorial Lecture. Bhubaneswar: Utkal University.

Mukhopadhyay, Alok. 1997. *Report of the Independent Commission on Health in India*. New Delhi: Voluntary Health Association of India.

National Sample Survey Organisation. 2006. *Morbidity, Health Care and Condition of the Aged*. Ministry of Statistics and Programme Implementation, Government of India. Available at: http://mospi.nic.in/sites/default/files/publication_reports/507_final.pdf (accessed on 31 May 2021).

Nehru, J. 1989. *Selected Readings*. Compiled by Arjun Dev. New Delhi: National Book Trust.

Pai, Sudha. 1996. 'Panchayats and Grassroot Democracy.' Agora Project. Sweden: Uppsala University.

Peters, Davis, H., Abdo S. Yazbeck, Rashmi R. Sharma, G. N. V. Ramana, Lant H. Pritchett, and Adam Wagstaff. 2003. *Better Health Systems for India's Poor*. New Delhi: The World Bank and Hindustan Publishing Corporation.

Sebastian, M. 1997. 'India's Search for Appropriate Development Model.' In *Political Economy of Reforms and Liberalisation* (vol. 1 and 2), edited by V. S. Mahajan. New Delhi: Deep and Deep.

Sen, Amartya. 1997. 'Beyond Liberalisation: Social Opportunity and Human Capability.' In *Political Economy of Reforms and Liberalisation* (vol. 1 and 2), edited by V. S. Mahajan. New Delhi: Deep and Deep.

———. 2000. *Development as Freedom*. New Delhi: Oxford University Press.

Sengupta, Arjun. 2001. *Reforms, Equity and the IMF*. New Delhi: Har-Anand Publications.

Tornquist, Olle. 1999. *Politics and Development*. New Delhi: SAGE Publications.

Torres, Magui M. and Anderson, Michael. 2004. 'Defining difficult environments for poverty reduction', PRDE Working Paper, UK Department for International Development, http://www.oecd.org/dataoecd/30/62/34041714.pdf, undated.

World Bank. 2000. *World Development Report 2000–2001: Attacking Poverty*. New York, NY: Oxford University Press. Available at: https://documents1.worldbank.org/curated/en/230351468332946759/pdf/226840WDR00PUB0ng0poverty0200002001.pdf (accessed on 31 May 2021).

Section IV

Programmes for Poverty Alleviation

Sectional Introduction

K. B. Saxena

India's policy establishment has consistently held the view, as reflected in all plan documents, that the large incidence of poverty can only be solved through rapid economic growth which would not only provide employment and raise per capita income but also increase state revenues which would permit larger resources to be allocated for social sector expenditure (Sen, 2011). But poverty has persisted, particularly in the hardcore, because growth-oriented strategies have bypassed historically marginalized social groups and backward regions where poverty is concentrated. Therefore, the state has resorted to a direct attack on poverty through wide-ranging programmes targeting the poor besides other development interventions, which would also benefit the poor along with others.

These poverty alleviation programmes fall into four categories. First, the category of programmes that provide wage employment and financial support for creating productive assets, credit and skill development support for self-employment, food grains, nutritional, supplements, housing and opportunities for participation in the development process for the targeted vulnerable groups. The second category consists of general development programmes with universal coverage such as education, health, drinking water, sanitation and rural infrastructure, which also benefit the poor directly or indirectly. The third category encompasses welfare programmes targeting the most vulnerable groups—Scheduled Castes (SCs)/Scheduled Tribes (STs), women and lately minorities—to combat social discrimination and exclusion. The fourth category focusses on area-based development programmes targeting backward regions characterized by specific disadvantages.

The strategy of poverty eradication has evolved over time, resulting in changes in the nomenclature of programmes, their design, coverage and institutional mechanisms for the delivery of services based on the feedback gathered from implementation, with some of the programmes in the first category converted into right-based statutory entitlements. But the number of poor is still very large, which indicates inadequacies whether of insufficient funding or design flaws or errors of targeting or weaknesses in implementation (ICPR, 2011). This section brings together four papers that have examined some of these programmes. While two papers deal with a single programme each, the other two cover a wider range of programmes and draw lessons from them.

Kamta Prasad in his paper has critiqued the strategy of growth, which was viewed as too low to produce any perceptible impact on the poor. While the industrial sector did not absorb surplus labour from agriculture, the capital intensity of technology in agriculture has tended to slacken the demand for labour. The major development projects of irrigation, mineral and industrial development and transportation produce adverse effects on the poor through displacement from land and habitat. Resources for agriculture development were concentrated in the better-off states rather than areas with a high incidence of poverty. Schemes of welfare for SC/STs suffered from a meagre allocation of resources. Commercial exploitation of forest resources has hit the tribal economy hard and land reforms failed to redistribute land due to the limited quantity of land declared surplus. Drastic land reforms are not feasible in the socio-political context. Poverty alleviation programmes suffered from strategic deficiencies as well as meagre allocation, weak delivery system and wrong selection of beneficiaries. The author recommends some policy changes, including making a rehabilitation policy an integral part of development, the integration of poverty alleviation progarmme with area-based development programmes, development of small towns and a 'cafeteria' approach whereby blocks are given funds with the freedom to choose from a menu of national and state schemes rather than uniform standard and programmes for all. This would require careful micro-level planning and functional integration of various schemes.

T. Haque's paper deals with the flagship rural employment guarantee programme (MGNREGA). He highlights its positive impact in terms of higher crop yields, raising income, an increase in market wage rates, improved agricultural productivity in some places and a decline in the incidence of migration in several places. However, the programme implementation suffers from several inadequacies, such as less than 50 days of employment provided; the failure to provide one-third of the employment to women workers as mandated by law; resistance to social audit, and poor implementation in areas affected by the Left-extremist movement. He also identifies key challenges which include bridging the entitlement gap in the provision of employment, the creation of awareness; the correct and timely payment of wages; the utilization of assets created for productivity enhancement; a people-centric social audit, capacity building of Panchayati Raj Institution (PRI) functionaries and government officials, and addressing the issue of social inclusion. He recommends that the additional cost of production due to MGNREGA linked rise in wage should be compensated by a proportionate increase in the minimum support price.

Ratnawali's paper on the working of anganwadis (childcare centres) in the tribal areas of Gujarat highlights the very limited success in achieving its objective. This was due to the services delivered being poorer in more backward and distant hilly areas. Only one-fourth of the targeted population has benefited from food supplements. A very low number of children are registered and available for food due to the inaccessibility of anganwadis to the dispersed habitations where children are more impoverished. The infrastructure barriers, such as a lack of toilets, potable water, inadequate space, poor ventilation and the lack of playing materials, were also factors. Inadequate effort and the negligence of anganwadi workers to undertake home visits to motivate families to attend and low awareness among beneficiary households has further restricted the flow of services and accounts for their poor functioning. A strong participation of people is recommended to make the programme a success. The paper recommends that the panchayat should be engaged in the following: procuring of produce from local farmers to reduce transportation costs, mandatory social auditing and proper monitoring and supervision of anganwadi workers and supervisors.

Chapter 13

Planning for Alleviation of Rural Poverty in India*
Experience and Lessons

Kamta Prasad

Alleviation of poverty, in one form or the other, has been an important—quite often, a very important—stated objective of our five-year plans from the beginning. Yet the problem of poverty, whether conceived in terms of size, spread or complexity, has remained as severe as ever before (Prasad, 1985, pp. 49–52). The achievement of our plans, if that can be said, lies in preventing the problem from becoming more acute despite the rapid growth of the population. But the experience of dealing with the problem that the country has acquired is so rich and varied as well as unique that it is quite rewarding to examine it, especially for deriving lessons for the future. This is what I propose to do in this chapter. And while doing so, I would concentrate on poverty in rural areas, not only because it is more pervasive and acute than that in urban areas but also because the latter is an overflow of the former.

The main components of the strategy adopted so far for alleviation of rural poverty have been (a) reliance on overall growth rate through the trickle-down mechanism, (b) distribution of land to the landless in rural areas, investment in human capital through education and training and (d) creation of additional employment opportunities through specific schemes for the weaker sections such as the Small Farmers Development Agency (SFDA), the Integrated Rural Development Programme

* *Social Change* Vol 16, no. 2 and 3 (June–September 1986): 68–75.

(IRDP), the National Rural Employment Programme (NREP), the Rural Landless Employment Guarantee Programme (RLEGP) and the Employment Guarantee Scheme (EGS). In view of the constraint of space, it is not possible to go into the details of these measures.[1] Instead, attention will be focused on the issues involved.

TRICKLE-DOWN STRATEGY

The earlier five-year plans, more particularly the first three ones, hoped to tackle the poverty problem through programmes of overall development. But questions related to the magnitude of the required growth rate and its feasibility were not examined. And the growth rate of 3–5 per cent actually achieved turned out to be too low to produce any perceptible impact on the condition of the rural poor. The gross domestic product from agriculture increased at the rate of 2.1 per cent per annum from 1961–1962 to 1976–1977 (Planning Commission, 1978 p. 35), while the number of agricultural labourers increased from 31.33 million in 1861 to 47.04 million in 1971, that is, at the rate of about 4.2 per cent per annum (Srivastava, 1971). The urban industrial sector also did not grow at a rate sufficiently high to absorb the surplus labour force from the rural agricultural sector. At the same time, the increasing capital intensity of technology in agriculture tended to slacken the demand for labour still further. The resulting decline in the number of days of wage employment in agricultural operations and the average daily earnings in real terms has been confirmed by the findings of the Rural Labour Enquiry 1974–1975. It can be said that the plans, as formulated, postulated higher rates of growth. Even these, however, did not visualize any marked reduction in the volume of unemployment. At the same time, major development projects, such as those of big irrigation, power, mineral development, large-scale industry and transportation, have adverse effects on the poor through displacement of their land and settlements and through undermining the competitive position of their traditional sources of employment. Moreover, resources set apart for agricultural development were concentrated not in areas suffering from higher incidence of rural poverty such as the backward states and districts of Assam, Bihar, Eastern Uttar Pradesh (UP) and Orissa but in areas such as Western UP, Punjab and Haryana which were relatively better off.

WELFARE OF SCHEDULED CASTES AND TRIBES

Schemes for the upliftment of the Scheduled Castes and the Scheduled Tribes, who constitute the hard core of the poor, have been in operation since the beginning of the planning era. These are comprised of programmes of education, training and job reservations. However, the amount allocated has been quite meagre, namely ₹90 crore in the Second Plan, ₹114 crore in the Third Plan, ₹171 crore in the Fourth Plan, ₹327 crore in the Fifth Plan and ₹1,560 crore in the Sixth Plan. And there has been no policy to give preference to the poor among the Scheduled Castes and the Scheduled Tribes. As a result, most of the concessions, limited as they are, have been cornered by the better off among them. The inadequacies of several facilities, such as the rates of pre- and post-matric scholarships and training facilities, have been repeatedly pointed out in the annual reports of the commissioner for the Schedule Castes and Tribes but with no effect.

The tribal economy depends mostly on agriculture and forestry. The main problem in tribal agriculture is inadequate irrigation. The level of irrigation in tribal areas has been less than 1 per cent (Government of India, 1977, Part I, p. 98) as against 25 per cent in the country as a whole. Yet no strategy has been designed to rectify this. Barring Maharashtra and Gujarat (Government of India, 1977, Part I, p. 98), there is no policy in other states to ensure that a certain percentage of the total water in each river basin is reserved for use only in the upper reaches, usually inhabited by the tribals. Forestry, another basis of the tribal economy, has been losing ground on account of commercial exploitation of forests by government and non-government agencies and competition from crop cultivation. Hence, the two main props of the tribal economy have either been left unattended or led to be affected adversely by the policies pursued so far.

LAND REFORMS

Income to individuals flows from ownership of assets and from employment. The basic reason why the rural poor have low income is that they possess little or no cultivable land, which is the most important productive asset in rural areas. The provision of land to the rural poor would, therefore, be a direct and one of the most effective means of raising their living standard. Accordingly, the government undertook measures related to ceiling on holdings and distribution of surplus land to the poor. But the scope for land transfers within the framework of the existing ceiling limits is constrained by the limited quantity of surplus land available for distribution. There is scope for rehabilitating at most between 7.86 and 15.59 lakh families through this measure if each family is provided 0.63 hectare of land, which is the average for the past several years. (Prasad, 1985, pp. 137–138). The amount of land to be allotted to each landless family should be higher so that the resulting holdings are economically viable and these provide sufficient income to the poor so as to enable them to go above the poverty line. This would, however, further reduce the number of the poor who can be thus rehabilitated. It is possible to overcome this constraint by a drastic reduction in the ceiling level. But the feasibility of bringing this about in the next few years is doubtful in view of the prevailing socio-political context. Alleviation of poverty, however, is an urgent problem. Hence, given the present context, one cannot rely on land redistribution as the only or even a major policy element for alleviation of rural poverty, at least for the time being. Within its limited scope, the policy of land transfer can, however, be made more effective by giving land to marginal farmers rather than landless labourers and concentrating initially on very large landholders while enforcing ceiling measures. In addition, the poor may be provided funds (say, through the IRDP) to acquire land out of the normal exchange transactions in land. In addition, consolidation of landholdings should be completed immediately so that small and marginal farmers are in a position to derive maximum advantage from modern agriculture.

SFDA, IRDP, NREP AND RLEGP

The failure of the trickle-down strategy along with the recognition of the limited scope for transfer of land (whose supply is also fixed) to the poor forced the government to rely more and more on transfer of different forms of capital goods (whose supply is elastic) such as livestock, pump sets and small industries to the poor and on provision of employment opportunities to them. This is a unique experiment started in India and would, therefore, be discussed in slightly greater detail.

It started with the establishment of the SFDA in the Fourth Plan. These agencies were, however, not designed to tackle the problem of the landless labourers, rural artisans and others who constitute the poorest section. This deficiency was sought to be rectified under the Sixth Plan which introduced the IRDP throughout the country. This programme is supposed to help the poorest of the poor in rural areas so as to bring them above the poverty line. The programme is to continue during the Seventh Plan as well and may possibly continue thereafter also.

The programme, good in several respects and implemented reasonably satisfactorily, is, however, based on a few unrealistic assumptions which tend to reduce its effectiveness. It is basically a copy of the SFDA model based on self-employment. It may, however, be asked whether the poorest of the poor have the necessary resources, tradition, inclination and initiative to undertake self-employment ventures as a primary occupation. They would be inclined to use the IRDP funds for subsidiary employment like animal husbandry, which, incidentally, has been the most popular activity under the programme. That the very poor, like the landless labourers in rural areas, are interested primarily in wage employment is well known. (See, for example, Srivastava et al. 1981; the findings of a recent survey of the poor in the Ballia district of UP made by the State Planning Institute, UP Government). The Planning Commission also realized this, though belatedly. While discussing the Training of Rural Youth for Self-employment (TRYSEM) programme, the Mid-term Appraisal of the Sixth Plan admitted that it appears too optimistic to expect rural youth from poor families to set up industry, business or service ventures on their own. A more practical and modest objective of the programme would be to enable trainees to get wage employment in small and village industries and under artisans after giving them the necessary training (Planning Commission, 1983, p. 52).

Self-employment, no doubt, is a laudable objective, but it is more difficult. Here, one is reminded of the French queen who advised her subjects on the verge of starvation to eat cake if they do not have enough bread. The provision of remunerative jobs of a continuing nature would be more useful. Yet another problem relates to the grant of institutional credit on an individual basis. One is not sure whether our credit institutions are well equipped to do this to the desired extent, even if they disregard the usual considerations and profit which may not be met in many cases. The experience of the last five years shows how difficult it has been to mobilize bank credit despite concentration of effort from top to bottom. With respect to credit, there is one more problem. Apart from production credit, which is provided under the IRDP, an overriding need of the poorest section is for consumption credit for meeting the requirements of deficit budgets and essential social functions. Quite often, credit taken ostensibly for productive purposes is diverted to meet such consumption requirements. The Expert Committee on Consumption Credit, 1976 (Chairman B. Sivaraman), had recommended the supply of such credit to this section, but the progress achieved has been disappointing. The committee had estimated the consumption needs of the weakest sections at ₹170 crore for 1976–1977. The target fixed for cooperatives in June 1976 was ₹115 crore. However, they could provide only ₹2.28 crores for this purpose by the end of December 1976 (Reserve Bank of India, 1977, p. 18). And more than 90 per cent of Farmers' Service Societies had not issued consumption loans, though it was thought of as an essential service. The performance of the regional rural banks was no better (Reserve Bank of India, 1977, p. 18).

Taking up petty individual schemes in an isolated manner without regard to integrated production programmes for the areas as a whole is not an economically viable proposition. The success of the IRDP would depend much upon the linkages that it is able to establish with other sectoral development programmes and supporting infrastructure and back-up services. A beneficiary can derive full benefit from a newly acquired asset out of IRDP assistance if he can get supporting help from various related agencies. This is possible only if the selected schemes are enmeshed into the normal developmental programmes of various departments/agencies of the government. To cite a familiar example, the flow of final benefit from the purchase of milch cattle would be contingent upon the availability of veterinary services, fodder and feed and arrangements for the marketing of milk.

Being a source of wage employment, NREP, introduced in the Sixth Plan (1977–1978, if account taken of the Food for Works Programme which was its predecessor), has potential, especially for landless labourers. But its scope has been restricted because it is 'mandated to provide opportunities during the lean agricultural period' (Planning Commission, 1980). And even that is not guaranteed. Further, because of the small outlay set aside for this programme, it has been able to touch only a fringe of the problem of rural poverty and unemployment/underemployment. Even this gets diluted because

> Adequate matching funds are not always provided for this programme in a number of States. Normal funds of departments like P.W.D., Irrigation etc., are sometimes shown as matching contribution from the States. That NREP is an additional programme for generating additional employment over and above what could be achieved through normal departmental activities is often overlooked. (Planning Commission, 1983, p. 51)

Such a programme can produce a lasting effect on the condition of the unemployed/underemployed in rural areas only if it can help in providing a permanent source of employment or at least guarantee the availability of jobs. Further, the activities should be so designed that the level of productivity is higher than the wage rate, which in turn should be high enough to lift the workers above the poverty line.

RLEGP, introduced in August 1983, has been a welcome addition. Its aim is to guarantee the availability of jobs during the lean period for those (from landless families) seeking them. But it is still far short of a permanent source of employment for the vast mass of the rural poor. And the administrative mechanism through which this programme is operated does not ensure that its benefits will always go to the eligible families. Moreover, the running of this programme, along with the NREP but with cent per cent central assistance, may create some problems. The programme is likely to develop at the cost of the NREP.

MINIMUM NEEDS PROGRAMME (MNP)

The Fifth Five-year Plan introduced MNP which aimed at providing free or subsidized services through public agencies so as to improve the consumption levels of those living below the poverty line. The programme, which continued during the Sixth Plan, covered eight items, namely elementary education, rural health, rural water supply, rural roads, rural electrification, housing assistance to rural landless labourers, environmental improvement of urban slums and nutrition for small children. The programme will continue during the Seventh Plan period. It has been proposed to integrate it with other rural development and anti-poverty programmes.

A comment that can be offered is that the advantage of certain components of this programme such as rural roads and rural electrification may be derived more from the better-off sections. On the other hand, the programme, during the Fifth and Sixth Plan, did not take account of such basic needs as those for food, fuel and clothing as well as employment. There has been a public distribution system (PDS), no doubt, but there is no link between this and the MNP. The PDS is effective only in urban areas for a limited range of commodities and is accessible to both the rich and the poor alike. The Seventh Plan has proposed to include domestic cooking energy, public distribution and rural sanitation as additional components to the MNP. But the details are yet to be worked out. Several people regard gainful employment as the cornerstone of a basic needs approach. Without remunerative jobs, most poor people will not have enough income to fulfill their basic needs. As regards health and education, the measures taken so far have failed to reach the poor majority, particularly those in rural areas, possibly due to limited funds set aside for them.

FUND AVAILABILITY

Apart from the strategic deficiencies of the poverty alleviation programmes described earlier, a common drawback of all of them has been meagre allocation of funds for each of them. The amount spent on the SFDA/Marginal Farmers and Agricultural Lobourers Scheme from the period 1970–1971 to 1979–1980 amounted to ₹231.64 crore giving an average of ₹290 per beneficiary during the above period. The programme was able to reach only a very small fraction of the rural poor. As regards the IRDP, the planned outlay per block for the Sixth Plan period was ₹35 lakh, which could at most assist only 3,000 out of 10,000–12,000 poor families in a block. As regards the NREP, a provision of ₹980 crore has been made in the Sixth Plan in the central sector with matching contributions to be obtained from the states. At this scale, the NREP could be expected to raise the income of those below the poverty line by ₹50 lakh per family. This would, at best, make a small dent in the colossal problem of mass poverty. The same problem of meagre allocation confronts us whichever anti-poverty programme we take up. Even the total of plan outlay under all such programmes has been extremely meagre. During the period up to the Fifth Plan, only 3–5 per cent of the national plan outlay had been set apart for beneficiary-oriented schemes for the rural poor who constituted about 40 per cent of the total population. The position improved during the Sixth Plan when about 9 per cent was allocated. (Prasad, 1985, p. 96). Such a situation is the direct consequence of the capital-intensive model of development followed so far, resulting in a residual approach to allocation of funds for the programmes dealing with poverty alleviation and employment generation.

How can a programme, even if it is sound and is effectively implemented, produce a significant effect at the macro level, if its coverage is limited and investment is meagre? It follows that the scale of effort in terms of allocation of resources and building up of administrative and technical support should match up with the extent of the problem.

The funds (as well as the necessary complement of physical resources) required for the benefit of the poor should be provided on a priority basis. This amounts to a complete reversal of the prevailing practices whereby a residual approach is followed for the poverty-alleviation-oriented programmes. This is not possible without assigning the highest priority to the objective of poverty alleviation in the real sense of the term with the necessary commitment of political will. Given the overall shortage of resources, this would entail a diversion of resources from other fields and sectors to programmes of poverty alleviation. Further, in case of resource constraint, priority should be given to poverty concentration areas. Spreading the limited resources thinly over wider areas, as has been the case so far, reduces their effectiveness and should be avoided.

DELIVERY SYSTEM

Finance by itself is not enough. Proper utilization of funds is equally important. There has been considerable evidence of flaws in the implementation of poverty alleviation programmes on account of a weak delivery system. There is no separate delivery system for the weaker section except for credit. The banks are under obligation to provide credit to approved schemes of the IRDP beneficiaries. The effectiveness of this is determined to a large extent by the strength and coverage of the banking system. The position in this respect is far from satisfactory despite concerning efforts made by the government during the past few years. Patches of unbanked areas lie scattered through-out the country, especially in the deep interior. And the so-called banked areas suffer from several limitations. There is considerable evidence that the weaker sections tend to be neglected in projects or programmes that provide common services such as extension, input supplies and technical assistance to the rich and the poor alike. There is said to be an elitist bias at all levels of local administration, and this is not conducive at all to the successful implementation of programmes for the benefit of the poor. Institutions of local government like the panchayats are also dominated by richer sections. What has also been noticed is the continued neglect of the poor in programmes designed specifically for them. This is reflected in the wrong selection of beneficiaries on which there are several studies. Many times, even the properly identified beneficiaries fail to receive the whole of the sanctioned amount of benefit due to prevailing corruption. There is, therefore, a need for strengthening the implementation machinery for improving the delivery and receiving systems and for reducing the scope for leakages. A more effective system of periodic monitoring and follow-up action should be established. Norms of personnel performance based on the impact of programmes in terms of their objectives should be evolved and enforced. In order to ensure coordinated implementation, there should be a combined agency to execute all multi-sectoral development programmes at the district level such as the IRDP, the NREP, the RLEGP, the MNP and the Drought Prone Area Programme.

POVERTY ALLEVIATION AND GROWTH

Assigning top priority to poverty alleviation does not and should not imply reducing the growth rate. Growth is necessary for reducing poverty and should be in-built into programmes of poverty alleviation. This can be done by a careful selection of projects and programmes fulfilling the following conditions. First, all projects must satisfy the basic condition of an excess of benefits over costs so as to generate a surplus for growth. Second, the wage rate as well as income from self-employment ventures should be high enough to raise the worker's family above the poverty line. Third, the level of productivity must be higher than the wage rate so that a surplus is generated and the growth process continues. Fourth, technologies selected should have the potential to absorb the mass of the poor. Products using labour-intensive techniques of production should, therefore, have preference over others. Fifth, the activities selected for employing the poor should be such that they have a high growth potential. This would provide expanding opportunities for both wage employment and self-employment to take care of the fast growing labour force. Products whose income elasticity of demand is more than one and those with high forward and backward linkages would satisfy this condition. Sixth, the commodities considered necessary for the welfare of the poor, that is, the so-called wage goods should be made available in adequate quantity and at reasonable prices. Seventh, activities should also result in strengthening of the basis of the economy necessary for further growth. More attention needs to be given to the development of infrastructure in background areas/states where the incidence of poverty is also higher.

REHABILITATION POLICY

A suitable rehabilitation policy should form an integral part of the developmental policy to take care of the adverse effects of developmental projects on the poor. For example, the establishment of a paper mill reduces the availability of free supply of bamboo to basket makers and others who depend on it. Similarly, the construction of a reservoir results in the uprooting of villages and settlements. Modern industries force poor artisans to close their business and join the ranks of the unemployed. Persons adversely affected by a developmental project should be adequately rehabilitated in terms of land and jobs so as to prevent them from joining the ranks of the poor.

INTEGRATION WITH AREA DEVELOPMENT PROGRAMMES

Programmes formulated to make a direct attack on the problem of rural poverty through the target group approach such as the IRDP and NREP should form an integral part of the area development approach. The growth of the area provides a framework as well as an opportunity for the development of the poor. The selective approach of a beneficiary-oriented programme like the IRDP would not be very useful in areas where there is heavy concentration of poverty or where there are no infrastructural facilities worth the name. Here, development can be accelerated if an area approach is adopted. (This has now been realized by the government as can be inferred from various statements made in the Seventh Five-year Plan recently brought out). First, a list of developmental activities in an area may be drawn and their interlinkages explored. Then these can be allocated to the poor by appropriate policy measures. Imbalances, if any, between the skill composition of the labour force, and the skill requirements of planned activities should be taken care of by short term training of the TRYSEM type supplemented by on-the-job training. Some of the areas are extremely backward and would need special measures for their growth and diversification. A policy of graded incentives is suggested for this purpose. This implies that incentives for attracting industries to more backward areas should be higher than those for less backward ones. In addition, area specific targets for small scale and household industries should be fixed so as to facilitate their dispersal in rural areas.

PROGRAMME CONTENT

Agriculture is the predominant activity in rural areas with the potential for further development and absorption of manpower. It should, therefore, receive priority in any scheme of rural development. Moreover, an increase in production of food grains is necessary for meeting the additional consumption requirements of the poor arising out of the rise in their income. Improved agriculture also facilitates growth of secondary and tertiary activities which provide an additional source of employment for the poor and thereby raise their income further.

However, agriculture, by itself, is not expected to raise the income levels of all the rural poor. The benefits of improved agricultural productivity flow primarily to those who have land. But the rural poor are either landless or own tiny pieces of land. Hence, the extent of the benefit derived from them is determined by the effect of agricultural development on employment and wage rate. The scope for further development of agriculture, especially in poverty concentration areas, in the near future is not wide enough to absorb all the surplus labour (Prasad, 1985, pp. 164–165). Hence, there is a need for a deliberate policy of bringing about occupational diversification by encouraging rural industries and support services. Since secondary and tertiary activities have a natural tendency to be concentrated in urban areas, it will be desirable that the development of small towns should form an integral part of the strategy for rural development. Further, the development of secondary and tertiary sectors should be so designed as to enable the weaker sections to derive maximum benefits from them. This would require giving preferential treatment to them, including reservation of schemes of production and distribution of inputs in their favour in some cases.

CAFETERIA APPROACH

Of late, there has been a proliferation of beneficiary-oriented national schemes, each of which run in every block in the country. Is it desirable to follow such a uniform approach in different parts of the country? In view of wide variations in techno-economic and socio-economic conditions, it is better to follow a more flexible or a cafeteria approach whereby the blocks are given not a fixed menu of schemes but a menu of their choice out of the available national or State schemes. Rather than launching national programmes and running them on a uniform pattern throughout the country irrespective of regional and local differences, the government should announce its firm commitment to attainment of specific objectives and allocate enough physical and financial resources to district level administration to enable them to formulate and execute appropriate schemes. The emphasis should be on the attainment of specific objectives which may be uniform across the nation, such as giving full employment to every work-seeker or eradicating poverty by a certain percentage and not on any specific programme. The performance of local level administration should be judged with respect to their success or failure in attaining objectives rather than in meeting the targets of a programme: What this implies is that the central or the state government may evolve and offer specific schemes, such as the IRDP, NREP, RLEGP, MNP, but they should leave it to the blocks to adopt one or more of these, depending upon their local requirements, administrative capabilities and other relevant factors. For example, some of the blocks may opt for IRDP and some for NREP and some for a combination of the two in varying proportions. Incidentally, this would also provide a real test of the popularity of different schemes and create an environment for their improvement, The present pattern results in too much of an imposition which is not in the best interests of the poor.

The above consideration is especially relevant to the choice between wage employment and self-employment. It is doubtful whether the IRDP pattern of assistance relying on self-employment is suitable for all the poor, particularly those in the more backward areas. The poor are less interested in self-employment ventures as full-time occupations because of the risk involved in production and marketing, absence of traditions of entrepreneurship and lack of training. They may welcome opportunities for self-employment more as a part-time venture than as full-time ones. The current popularity of the milch animal programme among the poor, which has so far been the most important component of the IRDP throughout the country, is presumably due to the fact that it can be accommodated as a part-time occupation or can be looked after by house-wives or children, leaving the male members free to attend to some other full-time occupations.

PLANNING MACHINERY

The implementation of the suggestions given in the preceding paragraphs would require more careful micro-level planning. Adequate attention should be given to functional integration of various schemes which is not done at present. It is necessary to have a unified planning team working at the district level to prepare an integrated district plan. The plan of the District Rural Development Agency as well as other agencies should form part of it. Satisfactory local-level planning would also require identification and demarcation of fields of activities to be planned at different levels, access to adequate funds and availability of reliable data.

CONCLUSION

Poverty alleviation is possible in the next 10 years or so if concerted efforts are made in terms of changes in the objectives and strategy of planning and adoption of a set of interrelated policy measures of the type suggested here.

NOTE

1. Interested readers may get the details from the author's recent book *Planning for Poverty Alleviation*.

REFERENCES

Government of India. (1977). *Report of the commissioner for Scheduled Castes and Scheduled Tribes, 1977–78*.

Planning Commission. (1978). *Draft Five Year Plan 1978–83*. Government of India.
———. (1980). *Sixth Five-year Plan*. Government of India. http://niti.gov.in/ planningcommission.gov.in/docs/plans/planrel/fiveyr/6th/welcome.html
———. (1983). *Sixth Five-year Plan 1980–85: Mid-term appraisal*. Government of India. http://14.139.60.153/bitstream/123456789/1584/1/Sixty%20Five%20 Year%20Plan%201980-85%20MID-Term%20Appraisal%2c%20Govt%20 of%20India%20Planning%20Commission%20August%201983%2cG-0748.pdf

Prasad, K. (1985). *Planning for poverty alleviation*. Agricole Publishing Academy.

Reserve Bank of India. (1977). *Regional rural banks: Report of the Review Committee*. https://rbidocs.rbi.org.in/rdocs/PublicationReport/Pdfs/CR440_19776E6C 93F2847B4D41AD0BCDED1752F412.PDF

Srivastava, S. C. (1971). Census of India 1971. http://lsi.gov.in:8081/viewer/ common/split_document.jsp?viewType=single&doc=46253_1971_CCM. pdf123456789/371/1/

Srivastava, S. C. et al. (1981). *People below poverty line: Identification and strategy for Development*. (A diagnostic case study of Ballia district, Lucknow, UP, Perspective Planning Division, States Planning Institute, Planning Department, Government of Uttar Pradesh).

Chapter 14

Supplementary Nutrition to Women and Children*

A Situational Analysis of Anganwadis in
Tribal Areas of Gujarat

Ratnawali

INTRODUCTION

India ranks way below many of the developing countries in the nutritional
status. It has the highest prevalence of underweight children in
the world which is double that of Sub-Saharan Africa (Gragnolati
et al., 2005). Although the country had achieved food security in
the 1970s, a substantial proportion of the population still belongs
to the malnourished status. In order to strengthen the nutritional status,
the Integrated Child and Development Services (ICDS) programme
was started in 1975 to provide supplementary nutrition to pregnant
and lactating women as well as children below the age of 6 years. It
was believed that improvement in nutritional status was also likely to
thwart the health impairment caused by under nutrition. Although
supplementary nutrition was the focus of the programme, nonetheless
it aimed at providing a package of services incorporating pre-school
education and health monitoring of the targeted population through
its anganwadi centres (AWC).

In order to ensure effective implementation of this programme, each
anganwadi was assigned to serve a population of 1,000 in the rural area

---

* *Social Change* Vol 40, no. 3 (September 2010): 319–343.

and of 700 in tribal areas, keeping in mind the scattered habitation of the latter. Each anganwadi was supported by an anganwadi worker (AWW) and a helper to implement the programme of ICDS. Till date, 649,000 anganwadis are functioning across the states through 4,200 projects, of which 740 are located in the tribal areas.

Under the scheme, supplementary nutrition to the extent of 300 calories and 10 grams of protein for each normal nourished child, 500 calories and 20 grams of protein to pregnant and nursing mothers and 600 calories and 20 grams of protein to each severely malnourished child was the goal set up by the government to achieve the desired success. It also included preschool education for children in the 3–6 year age group, proper information to the expectant and nursing mothers regarding healthy feeding practices, weaning food, breast feeding and balanced nutrition in the early years of the child. Care of women during pregnancy and after child birth were also the components of the scheme.

Though the programme is a well conceived one, its implementation fell short of the desired outcome. A number of reasons were identified for the low performance, which, among others, also included caste discrimination, distant location as well as the mismanagement of available resources (Mander & Kumaran, 2006; Ramchandran, 2005; Saxena, 2004). It even varies between the states with regard to their monetary allocation per beneficiary. In a report, submitted by commissioners appointed by the Supreme Court (2004), it was pointed out that monetary allocation per beneficiary was highest in Tamil Nadu (₹1.69) and lowest in Bihar (15 paise). A field survey conducted in six states by FOCUS (2006) found good performance of the ICDS scheme in Tamil Nadu where 90 per cent of the mother utilized the service and expressed their satisfaction with the functioning of anganwadis. However, states such as Chhattisgarh, UP, Maharashtra, Rajasthan and Himachal Pradesh lagged far behind in accessing and utilizing the services. The success in Tamil Nadu was attributed to good governance and willingness on the part of the state government to combat the scourge of malnutrition and hunger. In a study by FORCES (2007) and social audit undertaken at Ratakhandi, Orissa (Adhar, 2008) irregularities in the functioning of Anganwadis with respect to weighing of children, difference in registered and actual attendance of children, immunization, non-enrolment of pregnant women, migrating women and disabled children and poor health monitoring services were reported. On a positive note, some studies (Chaturvedi et al., 1986; Tandon, 1989) have highlighted the improvement in the nutritional status of the children covered by the ICDS scheme. The observation of the National Nutrition Monitoring Bureau (2002) is an eye opener in this regard. According to its estimate (2001–2002), about half of the rural children below the age of 5 years suffer from malnutrition, and 40 per cent of adult suffer from chronic energy deficiency. The nutritional status of the tribal population is worse. Nearly 55 per cent tribal children and half of the tribal adults still suffer from malnutrition (IIPS, 2007), despite the fact that 740 out of 4,200 ICDS projects are operational in the tribal area.

Considering the poor nutritional status and its bearing on the workforce, the projected figure of the population (GOI, 2006) in the year 2026 presents a worrisome picture. According to the projection, 60–65 per cent of the population will be constituted of people between the age group 15–59 years. This will also be the group from where the main workforce would be drawn. Given the poor nutritional status of the children in the 0–6 age group, the future workforce is expected to be undernourished with a considerable health burden (Gragnolati et al., 2005). It implies that the working potential of a large proportion of the workforce will remain underutilized. The situation will be alarming for the tribal population considering their poorer nutritional and economic status. A colossal loss of unutilized human potential and an ailing population seems to be in the offing.

In the above context, the relevance of the ICDS programme increases manifold, and it is thus imperative to take stock of the situation. This article, therefore, presents the situational analysis of the anganwadis and the services rendered by them in providing supplementary nutrition to women and children in the tribal regions of the State of Gujarat.

THE ICDS PROGRAMME AND NUTRITIONAL STATUS OF TRIBES IN GUJARAT

The economic growth of the states does not necessarily ensure a better nutritional status of its population. Gujarat is a case in point.

Economy-wise, the state is one of the leading states of India, but malnutrition prevails at all stratum of the population, especially among women and children. The state has implemented the ICDS programme since its inception at the national level. With a sizable tribal population of 15 per cent, its Chhotaudepur taluka of Vadodara district was the one among the 33 blocks that were initially chosen to implement the programme in 1975. It now covers the entire state with a total of 225 operational ICDS blocks. The state has 37,100 functioning anganwadis catering to 1,921,300 beneficiaries (www.wcd.gujarat. gov.in). According to NFHS-2, 90.2 per cent of the rural population have at least one anganwadi within their village (IIPS, 2001), and 84 per cent of the children under six are covered by anganwadis (IIPS, 2007). The tribal population of the state comprises 7.4 million people (GOG, 2004) and are well served with anganwadis. All 46 ICDS project and 7,737 anganwadis within the tribal area are functional. However, the health status of the tribal population does not reflect the desired achievement expected of the ICDS programme even though it has been in operation for three decades. As per NFHS-3 (IIPS, 2007), nearly 83 per cent of tribal children under the age of five years suffer from some form of anaemia with a substantial proportion of 59 per cent belonging to the moderate category. Around 23.8 per cent are wasted, 61 per cent stunted and 64.5 per cent suffer from chronic and acute under nutrition. The situation for tribal women is equally appalling. Around 62 per cent are undernourished, while 74.2 per cent suffer from anaemia. It appears that the ICDS projects have made limited inroads into improving the health status of the target group. The gap between delivery and outreach services to women and children is thus evident.

In order to understand the ground realities and the factors that impede the utlization of service offered by anganwadis, a survey was carried out in the tribal-dominated district of Valsad.

STUDY AREA AND THE METHODOLOGY

Valsad is situated in the southern part of the state and is inhabited by a number of tribal communities, constituting more than 60 per cent of its total population. The Dharampur and Kaprada talukas of the district were chosen for their preponderance of tribal population. Dhodia,

Kukna, Varli, Kolcha and Bhil are major tribes, constituting more than 90 per cent of the total population of these areas. Topographically, these talukas have plain and hilly landscapes of the Sahyadri and Satpura ranges and have substantial forest area covering 90,859 hectares of land.

According to Census 2001 (GOG, 2006), the household size of all the villages of Dharampur and Kaprada (where selected anganwadis were located) averages around 5.2 and 5.8, respectively. The hilly areas of both the talukas have shown higher family size compared to the plain areas. Similar is the trend for the 0–6 year age group population, which has registered a higher proportion in hilly areas in both the talukas. The proportion therefore averages 11.36 and 15.07 for the plain area, whereas 20.77 and 22.7 have been recorded for hilly areas of Dharampur and Kaprada respectively. Kaprada, however, has registered higher proportions of the 0–6 year age group, both on the plains as well as in the hilly areas. The greater household size and higher proportion of the 0–6 age group population in the hilly areas, in general, and Kaparada, in particular, highlights the unmet reproductive health needs of the population who are also at a locational disadvantage in accessing such services. Use of spacing methods among the tribal women in the age group of 18–30 years is very low (Kumar & Joshi, 2008), which also contributes to the greater family size. The literacy status of the study area is much below the District's average (62.5). It is 45.01 for Dharampur whereas Kaprada accounts for 34.48 per cent literates from among its population.

METHODOLOGY

A sample of 10 per cent of the anganwadis was selected from each of these talukas. Thus, 20 anganwadis from Dharampur (out of 185) and 20 from Kaprada (out of 197) were selected in proportion to their geographical spread in relatively plain and hilly/forested areas. Samples were drawn randomly. Thus, in Dharampur, where anganwadis are distributed roughly in equal number over plain and hilly/forested areas (88 and 97, respectively), 10 anganwadis from each area were selected. Similarly, from Kaprada, 6 and 14 anganwadis were selected from each of the plain and hilly areas (53 and 144), respectively.

Data was collected through detailed schedules prepared for AWWs and helpers to record their responses pertaining to their work and functioning of the anganwadis. Interviews and group discussions in each of the selected village/anganwadi were undertaken to obtain views and perceptions of women and men regarding access and utilization of services from these centres. Secondary data were also collected from the office of the Child Development Project Officer (CDPO) and AWWs.

ANGANWADIS/AWCS: POPULATION DISTRIBUTION AND COVERAGE

Depending upon the population size, most of the villages had one or more anganwadis in their vicinity. Tables 14.1 and 14.2 show the anganwadis and their population coverage. Although the average population covered by an anganwadi was less than 1,000 persons, they vary considerably even within the same village in terms of the population they were assigned to look after. Some anganwadis had to cater to a disproportionately large population, whereas the others had to cover a smaller proportion of the population. Thus, the village Bamti, with a population of 4,665, was served by two anganwadis only. The one that we visited covered just 541 persons. The second one obviously could not cover the remaining population effectively. Such a disproportionate distribution of population was found in many places in both the talukas. As shown in the table, a number of anganwadis were not in conformity with the population norms (700 in tribal areas), and sometimes, their coverage exceeded far beyond the specified norm in both the talukas. We found that sometimes, even an anganwadi allotted for the whole village did not serve the entire population of the village, and it was explained by the ICDS functionaries that when the population is dispersed over a wide area, it becomes difficult to provide services; hence some of them are not taken into anganwadi fold. Thus, a part of the population stayed deprived of services offered by anganwadis.

Anganwadis located in the plains and hilly areas show an interesting pattern. In both the talukas, anganwadis in the hilly areas had lesser population coverage, higher household size and more women and children registered with them than with the anganwadis in the plain areas. It may further be noted that among the two talukas, the average figures for all the variables mentioned above were higher for Kaprada.

Table 14.1 *Demographic Profile of Selected Anganwadi in Dharampur*

S. No.	Name of the Village	Total Population of the Village	Total no. of Anganwadi in the Village	No. of Households	Total Population Covered	Household Size	No. of Women Registered with Anganwadi	No. of Children Registered with Anganwadi	Percentage of Children in 0–6 age Population
							Selected Anganwadis		
	Plain area								
1.	Amba Talat	5,033	3	109	777	7.12	17	91	11.7
2.	Bamti	4,655	2	118	541	4.58	3	42	7.7
3.	Barolia	3,892	3	95	740	7.78	11	49	6.6
4.	Bhambha	1,400	2	106	762	7.18	12	52	6.8
5.	Bhensdara	4,195	3	250	1,389	5.55	12	67	4.8
6.	Bilpudi	8,336	2	103	750	7.28	14	74	9.9
7.	Dasherapati	4,288	–	139	816	5.87	8	67	8.2
8.	Khatana	2,251	3	133	767	5.76	6	76	9.9
9.	Maraghmal	1,368	2	90	759	8.43	11	57	7.5
10.	Zariya	1,453	2	137	719	5.24	14	49	6.8
	Subtotal			1,280	8,020	–	108	624	–
	Average			128	802	6.26	11	62	7.78

	Hill area								
11.	Ambosi Bhavthan	1,882	2	92	560	6.08	16	71	12.6
12.	Avdha	2,390	3	85	907	10.7	17	54	5.9
13.	Bopi	2,364	3	120	860	7.16	21	86	10.0
14.	Hedri	717	1	102	717	7.02	16	128	17.8
15.	Jagiri	1,413	1	109	940	8.62	10	76	8.08
16.	Khadki	708	1	111	708	6.37	8	64	9.0
17.	Mankadban	3,835	–	134	914	6.82	10	68	7.4
18.	Mor Dahad	433	1	72	433	6.01	10	85	19.6
19.	Nani Korval	876	1	154	876	5.68	14	66	7.5
20.	Nani Vahiyal	4,036	2	130	738	5.67	10	73	9.8
	Subtotal			**1,109**	**7,653**	**–**	**132**	**771**	**–**
				111	**765**	**6.9**	**13**	**77**	**10.07**
	Total			**2,389**	**15,025**	**–**	**240**	**1,255**	**–**
	Average			**119**	**751**	**6.29**	**12**	**63**	**8.35**

Source: Anganwadi Records, 2005.

Table 14.2 *Demographic Profile of Selected Anganwadi in Kaprada*

S. No.	Name of the Village	Total Population of the Village	Total no. of Anganwadi in the Village	No. of Households Covered	Total Population Covered	Selected Anganwadis		
						Household Size	No. of Women Registered with Anganwadi	No. of Children Registered with Anganwadi	Percentage of Children in 0–6 age Population
Plain area									
1.	Ambheti	7,371	3	400	707	1.76	11	80	11.3
2.	Dhodhad kuva	2,134	2	144	992	6.88	10	63	6.3
3.	Kaprada	4,368	2	126	800	6.34	29	134	16.7
4.	Mota Pondha	8,618	2	90	725	8.05	12	65	8.96
5.	Nana Pondha	3,524	2	151	681	4.5	13	100	14.7
6.	Sukhala	4,192	3	113	789	6.98	9	62	7.8
	Subtotal			1,024	4,694	–	84	504	–
	Average			171	782	6.00	14	84	10.74
Hill area									
7.	Amba Jungle	3,194	4	104	715	6.87	12	67	9.3
8.	Astul	1,888	2	91	777	8.53	12	89	11.4
9.	Bhavada Jagiri	1,144	1	62	922	14.9	24	114	12.3

10.	Chandvegan	1,997	1	138	812	5.88	15	62	7.6
11.	Eklera	3,940	1	120	899	7.49	12	101	11.3
12.	Huda	1,703	2	65	458	7.04	9	72	15.7
13.	Mendha	2,573	1	100	714	7.14	14	94	13.2
14.	Moti Palsan	3,339	3	82	817	9.96	15	82	9.9
15.	Tiskari jungle	1,775	2	77	588	7.63	11	81	13.7
16.	Vadoli	3,348	3	60	526	8.76	11	106	20.2
17.	Valveri	906	1	133	777	5.84	17	84	10.8
18.	Vardha	944	1	118	944	8.0	16	85	9.0
19.	Varoli Jungle	1,904	2	87	642	7.37	12	87	13.5
20.	Virsetra	3,375	4	153	1,068	6.98	23	78	7.3
	Sub total			1,390	10,659	–	203	1,200	–
	Average			99	761	7.66	15	86	11.26
	Total			2,414	15,353	–	287	1,706	–
	Average			121	768	6.36	14	85	11.11

Source: Anganwadi Records, 2005.

The pattern therefore confirms that even within a backward region (Dharampur–Kaprada combine in this case), a relatively more backward area (Kaprada in this case) registers a higher need for the mother and child care services. Villages in Kaprada generally had larger average household size, higher registration of children and women and a higher percentage of 0–6 population. Within Kaprada also, anganwadis in the hilly area had higher values for both the variables.

The survey record maintained by anganwadis concerning the 0–6 year age group is low in reliability. While the proportion of this age group was substantially lower than the Census figures (2001), household size was much higher for most of the villages. The differences between the census and survey figures were conspicuous. However, the survey recording were also doubted as greater average family size calculated out of anganwadi survey book did not conform to the relatively low proportion of children registered in the 0–6 year age group. Thus, population enumeration at village level by the AWWs appears to be less than satisfactory and it assumes significance as allocation of food supplements and further calculation of nutritional status is based on these figures.

ANGANWADIS: THE FUNCTIONAL ASPECTS

The functioning of anganwadis, as the focal point for providing supplementary food to women and children, are examined in the following section by looking at the infrastructure facilities and services they provide.

Physical State of Anganwadis

Since adequate space and proper infrastructure are necessary conditions for efficient working of the anganwadi, it was noted that 20 per cent of anganwadis at Dharampur did not have their own building. In Kaprada, 35 per cent of anganwadis were functioning from rented premises or from the residence of AWWs. Such situations are more common in the hilly areas than in the plains. Due to the lack of adequate space and proper building, it was difficult to accommodate women and children and also to store the food stocks safely.

Poor ventilation and lack of toilet facilities were the common features in most of the anganwadis. Toys, games and teaching aids were also missing. Except for a few charts depicting mother and child care, other educative material to keep the children's interest were conspicuously absent. In most of the places, the mats were tattered while they were missing at other anganwadis and children were made to sit on the floor. It was reported that requests for these things had been made to the CDPO office several times but the requirements had not been met. On probing the issue, the CDPO was guarded in her response. She claimed that the mats have been replaced at many places and other playing materials have also been provided to anganwadis. But as she has to depend on allotments by the government, requirements at certain places are yet to be fulfilled. However, most of the anganwadis lacked these materials during our survey. In some places, the cooking space or hearth was located in the same room, partitioned by a low wall, resulting in smoke and indoor pollution. Besides causing suffocation, it could be detrimental to the health of women and children.

Hand pumps or wells were the only source of potable water in most of the anganwadis. During summer, as the ground water level goes down, water has to be brought from a distance of 1–3 km. The problem was more acute in Kaprada than in Dharampur taluka as also more in the hilly areas than in the plains. This impacts the maintenance of hygiene and cleanliness in the anganwadi. Children were neither asked nor were seen washing their hands before a meal. At some places (Vadoli, Dhodhad Kuva, Mota Pondha, Virstra, Zariya), garbage was also found littered around the anganwadis which reflected little concern of AWWs in maintaining proper hygiene and health upkeep of the children in these places.

Profile of Anganwadi Worker (AWW) and Helper

As the performance of any institution is dependent on its functionaries, the experience, educational achievements, regularity and the availability of anganwadi workers and helpers reflect their functional capabilities in managing the anganwadis. Barring a few (15% anganwadis in Dharampur and 25% in Kaprada), all AWWs were residing in the same village; all the anganwadi helpers also lived in the same village where they worked. The arrangement thus helps in the timely opening of anganwadi and carrying out regular activities.

Most of the AWWs have been working for a long time in their respective anganwadis. On average, they were serving their respective villages for 12.8 years in Dharampur and 13.5 years in Kaprada. Among anganwadi helpers, 47 per cent were working for more than 10 years while 35 per cent had experience of less than 5 years. All but 15 per cent of AWWs in each of the talukas were trained, though only a few among them attended training programmes at regular intervals. Most of them had training at the time of joining, which dates back to 10–13 years. With the long serving record of AWW and helper, it is expected that, apart from having good rapport in the community, they would have enough understanding of women's and children's needs in general and supplementary food in particular. This, however, could not be corroborated by our findings, which we will discuss later.

Literacy-wise, all AWWs had at least six years of school education. Nearly half of all AWWs had studied between 7th to 9th grades. Among them, 84 per cent of AWWs were from the hilly areas. Around 35 per cent had been educated up to Class 10th and 12th and were evenly distributed in both geographical regions of the selected talukas. Educational attainment was particularly higher in Dharampur, where 25 per cent of AWWs had studied beyond Class 12th while only 10 per cent of Kaprada belonged to this category. Literacy among the helpers is quite low. Nearly 65 per cent of them were illiterate. The proportion at Kaprada was a little higher, with 70 per cent having not received any education.

Timings and Attendance of Children at Anganwadi

The official timing of the anganwadis is 11.00 a.m. to 3.00 p.m. Normally, anganwadis open at 11.00 a.m. but the closing time varies considerably between the two talukas. Around 70 per cent of the AWCs at Kaprada reported closing at 2.00 p.m while it was 3.00 p.m. at all centres in Dharampur. However, we did not find strict adherence to timing on our visits, neither did we find that it was working beyond 1.30 or 2.00 p.m. Starting hours also differed from the stated timing and at many places it was reported by the villagers that the anganwadi did not function for more than two hours. The short working hours thus adversely impacted other activities, like pre-school education, which was found compromised to a great extent.

By and large, AWCs maintained regularity with the exception of a few that were located in the distant and hilly terrain (10% and 15% for Dharampur and Kaprada, respectively). These were also the places where AWWs were irregular and AWCs were run by helpers. Normally, anganwadis function for 25–26 days in a month.

Attendance of children at anganwadis was found to be much lower than the registered numbers (Tables 14.3 and 14.4). Most of the children did not come on their own. Although helpers were expected to bring children from distant hamlets, most of the people reported otherwise. Probably, such services were provided to those households having locational proximity to the anganwadis. Very few persons brought their children to the anganwadi by themselves. Most prioritized their work over bringing children to the centre. In fact, many people reported that children did not show interest in visiting anganwadis. Our observations reveal that AWWs did not make much effort to engage children in playing or other activities. Once children are in, they are not attended to with care and affection. The distant location of anganwadi was the other reason, cited by the parents for not sending their children to the centre. However, parents expressed their willingness to send their ward if the helper would come to take them. Thus, a majority of potential service users living at considerable distance from the anganwadi remained deprived of anganwadi services.

Across the surveyed areas, AWWs acknowledged that the actual number of children attending the anganwadis was much lower than the registered number of children. On a random visit, we observed low attendance, which was even lower than the figures given by AWWs for normal daily attendance. However, in the case of women beneficiaries, the attendance on random visits was more in conformity with the figures given by AWWs. Overall, the average number of daily attendance as reported by AWWs, was nearly 40 per cent of the registered number, but in actuality, it was found to be less than one-fourth of the total registered beneficiaries. Low attendance thus leaves out a sizeable proportion of the eligible population from availing food from the anganwadi. However, in the hilly areas of Kaprada, the stated figures for approximate daily attendance were more realistic as they matched the actual attendance. If seen from the aspect of the poor economic condition of the people of hilly areas, the nutritional support from anganwadis thus appears crucial for the food requirements of the population who otherwise have little to support them.

Provision and Availability of Supplementary Food

As improvement in the nutritional intake of children is the main aim of the ICDS programme, all anganwadis are supplied with cereals and pulses so that cooked meals may be provided to children and women as per the stated norms. According to the norms, a normal nourished child is given 60 grams of cereal whereas those in the 3rd and 4th grade of under-nourishment are supplied with double the normal quota. Women are eligible to get 120 grams of cereals. As per government specification, food should be provided at least 300 days in a year.

However, knowledge about the quantity of food to be provided to the beneficiaries was quite low among the AWWs. Around 32.5 per cent of AWWs did not know about the actual quantity of food to be given to the eligible women and children. A large proportion (84%) of them belonged to Kaprada. While the lack of this vital information calls for quality training for AWWs, it also raises doubt about the adequate quantity of food being provided to the beneficiaries.

In both talukas, most of the anganwadis (78%) were regularly providing food to the children and women except for a few located in the distant hilly region. As we have mentioned earlier that the economic condition of these areas are generally poor and a substantial proportion of children are regularly attending the anganwadis, irregularity in food supply adversely impact the nutritional security of the targeted population. It not only hampers the effectiveness of the programme but also deprives the neediest section of the population of some kind of food security available to them.

Food was generally served to the children after 12.30 or 1.00 p.m. in order to retain them longer for educational activities. However, such activities were generally not found and most of the children came to the centre at the time when food was served. Obviously, activities such as playing and pre-school education were not the usual part of AWCs.

The actual turnout of beneficiaries during meals was much lower than what is reported by the AWWs. As already presented in Tables 14.3 and 14.4, hardly 25 per cent of the registered number of children and women turned out to consume supplementary food. During group discussions, women expressed the view that distant location of anganwadi is a big deterrent in availing food by the beneficiaries. It should be noted that houses in the tribal villages are scattered far and wide; hence, covering long distances could be difficult for women and small children. Further, the burden of domestic work load and ignorance about their eligibility for supplementary food were also some of the often mentioned reasons. There were frequent complaints about the poor quality and taste of the food. It was found that many a time, supply of oil and spices were not received along with other ration stocks and AWWs had to procure them from the market by paying the amount themselves. Although the money was reimbursed, the delay in the procedure made expenses difficult to sustain on the meagre salary received by AWWs. Therefore, they preferred not to purchase the materials and prepare meals without spices, leaving it tasteless.

In the plain areas of Dharampur, where people were comparatively better off, receiving or eating food at anganwadi was perceived as lowering one's social status, hence attendance at these places was much lower. Ignorance among women about their eligibility was also common, whereas in some places, they expressed anguish over differential treatment as they felt that AWWs ignored visiting them because of their poor economic condition. In their opinion, information about the anganwadi activities was selectively disseminated, and often, eligible women outside the chosen group were deliberately left out even for supplementary food. Home visits by AWWs were not a regular feature, which could be the reason for their poor rapport in the community and low awareness among women about their eligibility for the services offered by anganwadis. Thus, social status, ignorance and personal relations too appeared to contribute towards low turnout at AWCs.

Normally, anganwadis receive their stock of rations from the ICDS office every two or three months. There was usually a regular supply of wheat, grams and cooking oil. Surprisingly enough, the same quantity of cereals like 250 kg of wheat, 60 kg of grams and 15 kg of cooking oil

Table 14.3 Registered Numbers of Children and Women, Reported and Observed Attendance in Anganwadis: Dharampur

Village	Total Registered Numbers		Reported Daily Attendance				Attendance during Random Visit			
	No. of Children	No. of Women	Children		Women		Children		Women	
			No.	%	No.	%	No.	%	No.	%
Plain area										
Amba Talat	91	17	20	21.9	6	35.2	3	3.2	5	29.4
Bamti	42	3	20	47.6	3	100.0	8	19.04	2	66.6
Barolia	49	11	25	43.8	9	81.8	14	28.5	4	36.3
Bhambha	52	12	15	28.8	12	100.0	7	13.4	2	13.3
Bhensdara	67	12	25	37.3	5	41.6	–	–	–	–
Bilpudi	74	14	25	33.7	5	35.7	15	20.2	9	64.2
Dasherapati	67	8	30	44.7	4	50.0	–	–	–	–
Khatana	76	6	30	39.4	5	83.3	17	22.3	5	83.3
Maraghmal	57	11	25	51.0	6	54.5	20	35.0	4	36.3
Zariya	49	14	17	34.6	4	28.5	17	34.6	4	28.5
Hilly area										
Ambosi Bhavthan	71	16	22	30.9	8	50.0	15	21.1	6	37.5
Avadha	54	17	35	64.8	9	52.9	15	27.7	4	23.5
Bopi	86	21	35	40.6	5	23.8	30	34.8	6	28.5
Hedri	128	16	55	42.9	16	100.0	35	27.3	11	68.7

Jagiri	76	10	30	39.4	4	40.0	35	46.0	4	40.0
Khadki	64	8	40	62.5	5	62.5	12	18.7	3	37.5
Mankadvan	68	10	40	58.8	5	50.0	35	51.4	5	50.0
Mor dahad	85	10	20	23.5	4	40.0	20	23.5	2	20.0
Nani Korval	66	14	45	68.1	7	50.0	–	–	–	–
Nani Vahiyal	73	10	25	34.2	5	50.0	12	16.4	4	40.0

Source: Field Survey.

Table 14.4 Registered Numbers of Children and Women, Reported and Observed Attendance in Anganwadis: Kaprada

Village	Total Registered Numbers		Reported Daily Attendance				Attendance during Random Visit			
	No. of Children	No. of Women	Children		Women		Children		Women	
			No.	%	No.	%	No.	%	No.	%
Plain area										
Ambheti	80	11	35	43.7	5	45.4	–	–	–	–
Dhodhad kuva	63	10	15	23.8	5	50.0	10	15.8	4	40.0
Kaprada	134	29	40	29.8	5	17.2	25	18.6	4	13.7
Mota Pondha	65	12	32	49.2	7	58.3	14	21.5	6	50.0
Nana Pondha	100	13	25	25.0	4	30.7	17	17.0	4	30.7
Sukhala	62	9	20	32.2	4	44.4	12	19.35	6	66.6
Hilly area										
Amba Jungle	67	12	25	37.3	8	66.6	20	29.8	6	50.0
Astul	89	12	70	78.6	10	83.3	50	56.1	9	75.0
Bhavada Jagiri	114	24	35	30.7	9	37.5	19	16.6	4	16.6
Chandvegan	62	15	30	48.4	8	53.3	25	40.3	5	33.3
Eklera	101	12	55	54.4	11	91.6	30	29.7	9	75.0
Huda	72	9	60	83.3	9	100.0	35	48.6	5	55.5
Kaprada	134	29	40	29.8	5	17.2	25	18.6	4	13.7

Mendra	74	14	30	31.7	4	26.5	30	31.7	4	26.5
Moti Palsan	82	15	40	48.7	8	53.3	35	42.6	7	46.6
Tiskari Jungle	81	11	60	74.0	8	72.7	40	49.3	10	90.9
Vadoli	106	11	35	33.3	11	100.0	20	18.8	10	90.9
Valveri	84	17	35	41.6	9	52.9	25	29.7	5	29.4
Vardha	85	16	35	41.1	10	62.5	27	31.7	6	37.5
Varoli Jungle	87	12	60	68.9	4	33.3	50	57.4	6	50.0
Virshetra	78	23	35	44.8	15	65.2	35	44.8	12	52.1

Source: Field Survey.

were supplied by ICDS to all anganwadis, even though the requirement of anganwadis is supposed to vary with the number of beneficiaries registered with them. Considering the fact that cereals were allotted to each anganwadi after assessing their requirement by periodic checking of the food stock by the supervisor, one cannot but doubt the sincerity with which such assessments were undertaken. Further, contrary to the record (annual report) of CDPO which mentioned shortage in cereals and oil supplies in some of the anganwadis in the study area, we did not come across such a shortage in the AWWs record. While shortage of oil is sometimes reported, deficit of wheat and gram was not reported by AWWs. Moreover, they mentioned internal arrangements like borrowing from nearby surplus anganwadis which help to tide over the crisis if at all occurs. Although the CDPO report registered a substantial deficit of grams in various months for a considerable number of anganwadis, we did not find such a shortage in our study areas. It thus seems that either the records were poorly maintained or demands were exaggerated apprehending shortage by the officials. However, a thorough look into the food requirement of anganwadis and the judicious supply of the same is needed to avoid the wastage or misuse of the precious resource.

As mentioned earlier, anomalies exist in the actual number of food recipients and the regular recipients reported by AWWs. It is significant as the quantity of cereals to be cooked is assessed on the basis of the attendance of children and women on the previous day. Here, we found a mismatch between the quantity of cereals cooked and the number of beneficiaries receiving the food on a random day. Table 14.5 reveals this difference. It shows that food was cooked in excess of the number of expected regular visitors. With the actual number of beneficiaries visiting anganwadis being lower than the expected number, the difference would be much higher even on a single day. Month-wise disparity in cooked and required food assumes significance as the excess cereal amounts to 20–28 kg per anganwadi per month (for details see Ratnawali & Iyengar, 2005). In some villages, it even exceeded beyond that. It can be put to proper utilization if attendance of the recipients is ensured by motivating the eligible group to avail of the food.

Table 14.5 Quantity of Food Required and Cooked at Anganwadis per Day as per Number of Beneficiaries

Villages/Taluka	Quantity of Food Required as per Total Registration (in Kg.)	Quantity of Food Required as per Daily Attendance (in Kg.)	Quantity of Food Cooked Daily (in Kg.)	Villages/Taluka	Quantity of Food Required as per Total Registration (in Kg.)	Quantity of Food Required as per Daily Attendance (in Kg.)	Quantity of Food Cooked Daily (in Kg.)
Dharampur				*Kaprada*			
Bhambha	4.56	2.34	2.8	Amba Jungle	5.40	2.40	2.9
Amba Talat	7.50	1.92	3.7	Ambheti	6.12	2.70	4.0
Ambosi Bhavthan	6.18	2.28	3.5	Astul	6.78	5.40	4.0
Avdha	5.28	3.18	3.0	Bhavada Jagiri	9.72	3.18	4.2
Bamti	2.88	1.56	2.8	Chandvegan	5.52	2.76	4.0
Barolia	3.60	2.58	3.8	Dhodhad Kuva	4.98	1.50	2.9
Bhensdara	5.46	2.10	2.8	Eklera	7.50	4.62	4.4
Bilpudi	6.12	2.10	4.0	Huda	5.40	4.65	4.5
Bopi	7.68	2.70	3.5	Kaprada	6.78	3.00	4.1
Dasherapati	4.98	2.28	3.0	Mendha	7.32	2.28	6.0
Hedri	6.60	5.22	6.5	Mota Pondha	5.34	2.76	3.4
Jagiri	5.76	2.28	3.5	Moti Palsan	6.72	3.36	5.7
Khadki	4.80	3.00	4.0	Nana Pondha	7.56	1.98	3.0

(Continued)

(Continued)

Villages/Taluka	Quantity of Food Required as per Total Registration (in Kg.)	Quantity of Food Required as per Daily Attendance (in Kg.)	Quantity of Food Cooked Daily (in Kg.)	Villages/Taluka	Quantity of Food Required as per Total Registration (in Kg.)	Quantity of Food Required as per Daily Attendance (in Kg.)	Quantity of Food Cooked Daily (in Kg.)
Khatana	5.28	2.40	3.0	Sukhala	4.80	1.68	3.0
Mankadban	5.28	3.00	3.75	Tiskari Jungle	6.18	4.56	5.34
Maraghmal	4.74	2.22	2.0	Vadoli	7.68	3.42	5.43
Mor Dahad	6.30	1.68	2.5	Valveri	7.08	3.18	5.4
Nani Korval	5.64	3.54		Vardha	7.02	3.30	4.5
Nani Vahiyal	5.58	2.10	2.0	Varoli Jungle	6.66	4.00	5.5
Zariya	4.62	1.50	2.0	Virstra	7.44	3.90	4.4

Source: Field Survey.

Assessment of Nutritional Status

Periodic weighing of children is one of the important functions of anganwadis for assessing the nutritional status of the children. It detects growth faltering and allows for subsequent measures, like providing adequate nutritional supplement, to check further damage to the child's health. All anganwadis were supplied with weighing scales to weigh children. Across the village, weighing of children was reported to be done once a month. However, responses to weighing the new borns differed considerably. At most of the places AWWs as well as women reported that weighing of newborns never takes place prior to the completion of one month for fear of attracting the evil eye. In some places, it was reported to be done only once or twice up to the age of six months of the child. While it shows the inability of AWWs to convince people, it also fails to register the birth weight, an important parameter to monitor infants' growth. Weighing of children even in the subsequent age group is also limited. Since many children are not regular to anganwadis, it can be assumed that most of the children in the age group 0–6 are not weighed and their growth is not monitored by AWWs. Though the AWWs asserted that such children were weighed at their home, the same was never confirmed by mothers and women of the village. However, the children who paid regular visits were weighed periodically, a fact confirmed by women. It therefore, appeared that children who were not regular to anganwadi were in all probability not being weighed. Either this service was provided to the houses located near the anganwadi or probably for personal relations. Thus, a large number of children (as more than half were not regular) were left out of nutritional assessment and the actual growth status of many children remained under-assessed. Mothers of children who were weighted were not aware of the nutritional status of their child, which suggests that the matter was not discussed by the AWWs with the parents of the children.

Plotting of a growth chart provides useful information about a child's growth. While it was found updated at most of the anganwadis, in some places, growth charts were seen plotted after taking three or four readings over a period of three-four months. Such lapses negate the actual assessment and monitoring of nutritional status as also the timely intervention to be taken for the severely malnourished child. The laxity in the assessment also finds echo in the annual report prepared by the CDPO office. It shows figures regarding percentage of children falling under various grades of malnutrition with conspicuous regularity over the period of time. Data from 3 April to 4 March show a consistent figure of 46–47 per cent in Grade I, 21 per cent in Grade II and 1 and less than 1 per cent in Grade III and IV, respectively. The consistency of these figures makes one ponder whether there has been any impact of supplementary food on children. Either these are entered without looking into actual figures or other factors are interfering with the growth of the child. It needs careful examination. Women beneficiaries, according to these reports, figured between 60 and 70 per cent of the total registered women, which in itself appears little exaggerated considering their actual attendance at anganwadis, visited during the study.

The monthly progress report of the CDPO reveals that only 30 per cent of children in the 0–6 years age group had registered normal weight, thus on an average nearly 70 per cent of children suffer from various grades of under nutrition in both talukas (Table 14.6). It is noteworthy that the proportion of underweight children gradually increases with age, as shown by the decreasing proportion of normal weight children in the 1–3 and 3–6 year age group. This is despite the fact that around 70 per cent in Dharampur and nearly 60 per cent in Kaprada have been shown to avail food regularly. The data also reveals that even among the 3rd and 4th grade nutrient deficient children, some are left out of their entitlement. Thus three children each in the month of January and February did not receive double ration at Dharampur, whereas five and six children from Kaprada were left out of their entitlements respectively during the same period. Not to mention the poor record in the health checkup, the efficacy of the programme in improving the nutritional status of children holds little support.

Table 14.7 presents the overall performance of anganwadis and the perception of people about their services. It reveals that anganwadis functioned better in plains than in the hills. Proximity to taluka and easy reach probably renders better monitoring of the AWCs in the plains, while distant location and arduous reach to the hilly areas deride adequate attention of the functionaries, resulting in poorer provisioning

Table 14.6 *Status of Children and Women in Dharampur and Kaprada Talukas, 2005*

Variables	Dharampur				Kaprada			
	January 2005		February 2005		January 2005		February 2005	
	No.	%	No.	%	No.	%	No.	%
1. Total population	140,392	–	140,644	–	151,996	–	152,152	–
2. Population below 6 months	1,289	–	1,293	–	1,526	–	1,497	–
3. Population 6 months 1–year	1,398	–	1,344	–	2,014	–	2,028	–
4. Population 1–3 years	4,972	–	5,005	–	6,373	–	6,177	–
5. Population 3–6 years	6,034	–	6,156	–	8,001	–	8,120	–
6. Total 0–6 years	13,693	9.75	13,698	9.73	17,914	11.78	17,826	11.7
7. Total live births	160	–	147	–	165	–	156	–
8. Total deaths (0–6 years)	1	–	5	–	4	–	6	–
9. Supplementary nutrition								
Total no. of women enrolled	2,284	–	2,323	–	2,868	–	2,925	–
Total eligible children	12,404	–	12,505	–	16,388	–	16,329	–
Nutr. availed by 6 mon–6 year childr.	8,572	69.10	8,527	68.18	9,275	56.59	9,192	56.3
No. of childr. with double ration	109	–	117	–	150	–	144	–
No. of women beneficiary	1,576	69.00	1,567	67.45	1,644	57.32	1,701	58.2

(Continued)

(Continued)

Variables	Dharampur				Kaprada			
	January 2005		February 2005		January 2005		February 2005	
	No.	%	No.	%	No.	%	No.	%
10. Number of children weighed								
Below 1 year	2,414	89.8	2,325	88.16	3,101	87.6	3,014	85.5
1–3 years	4,766	95.8	4,653	92.9	5,640	88.4	5,455	88.3
3–6 years	5,137	85.13	5,037	81.82	6,236	77.9	6,308	77.7
Total weighed	12,317	89.95	12,015	87.7	14,977	83.6	14,778	82.9
11. Normal weighing								
Below 1 year	835	34.58	793	34.10	1,073	34.60	966	32.10
1–3 years	1,394	28.00	1,263	25.23	1,732	28.03	1,576	25.51
3–6 years	1,526	25.29	1,394	22.64	2,010	25.12	1,997	24.59
Total	3,755	30.48	3,450	28.70	4,815	32.14	4,539	30.70
3rd and 4th grade children	112	0.90	120	0.99	155	1.03	154	1.04
11. Pre-school education								
Enrolled	6,034	–	6,156	–	8,001	–	8,066	–
Attended for more than 15 days	4,229	70.1	4,223	68.6	4,410	55.11	4,497	55.7

12. Health check-up

Children	1,034	17.13	910	14.78	1,725	21.55	1,467	18.2
Pregnant women	149	–	105	–	218	–	188	–
Referred children	105	–	93	–	94	–	120	–
Referred women	37	–	18	–	29	–	19	–

Source: Monthly Progress Report 2005, CDPO Office, Dharampur.
Note: Only relevant percentages have been calculated and reported.

Table 14.7 *Perception and Overall Functioning of Anganwadis*

Parameters Infrastructure at Anganwadis	Dharampur (Figures in %)		Kaprada (Figures in %)	
	Plain Area	Hilly Area	Plain Area	Hilly Area
Own building	80	80	50	71
Separate kitchen	0	0	0	0
Learning & playing material	0	10	0	7
Storage facility for grains and other material	0	0	0	0
Adequate cooking ware	0	0	16	0
Profile of AWW				
Working experience for > 10 years	90	60	83.3	71.4
Not trained	10	20	0	21.4
Education below Std X	20	60	16.6	71.4
Avg. days for weighing newborn	4.8 (between 3 & 10 days)	4.2 (between 3 & 15 days)	23.6 (between 7 & 30 days)	33.57 (between 3 & 180 days)
Women's perception from FGD (proportion with clear 'yes' response)				
Regularity of AWW	100	80	100	70
Regular availability of Supp. Nutri.	100	80	100	85
Pre-school education	50	10	66	35
Monthly meeting	30	15	50	21
Advice to preg. and nursing mother	45	40	50	28.7
Home visits	30	30	50	30
Satisfaction	80	50	50	28.5

Source: Field Survey.

of services. The overall satisfaction of women from AWCs also reflects the same. The average was higher in Dharampur (65%) than in Kararada (35%), while within the taluka, it was poorer for the hilly areas.

From the perception of women, it is also clear that, despite various complaints, about functioning and quality of food, these centres are regular in most of the places, though other activities are poorly performed. While regularity in food supply is a positive sign, low attendance and negligence in other activities dilutes the comprehensive goal of the ICDS programme.

SUMMARY AND CONCLUSION

From the above observations, it is apparent that despite regularity in food supply, anganwadis have achieved limited success in attaining their objectives. The supplementary food for the targeted population remains underutilized as just a quarter of eligible population actually avail the food. Even according to official records, only 30 per cent of children registered with anganwadis are normally nourished, which means that 70 per cent of children are malnourished and hence are likely to suffer from some kind of functional physical impairments. The underperformance, however, points towards the following facts.

The dispersed habitation of the tribal villages does not provide easy access to the anganwadi by the targeted population. Aanganwadis too do not include all the population that are dispersed over a wide area into their coverage fold. They also differ within the same village in terms of coverage of the population, which often leads to a disproportionate burden on some anganwadis. To enhance the accessibility, anganwadis should be located within the easy reach of the population, and instead of following the population norm, two or three nearby located hamlets can be taken as a unit for the establishment of one anganwadi. Specific attention is required in the hilly and distant locations of anganwadis as people from these areas are more impoverished, and the demand for food is high. The infrastructural discrepancies such as inadequate space, poor ventilation, absence of toilet, playing materials and proper availability of potable water are some of the barriers that hinder the smooth functioning of anganwadis. AWWs, on the other hand, are also less inclined to pay adequate attention to ensure children's interest in anganwadis. This could be an important reason for poor attendance of the beneficiaries. Despite long working experiences of AWWs, they have not been able to motivate women and children to ensure their attendance for availing food from the AWCs. Besides, they are less likely to take up activities like preschool education, health advice, monthly meetings, home visits and other engagements with the population. Such negligence might have widened the gap between the community and the AWWs, affecting the services and their reach to the targeted population. Differential treatment by AWWs and lack of awareness among the population further restrict the flow of services. Their role as change agent in bringing about qualitative differences in the nutritional and health behaviour of women and children has yet to be realized. A regular training and proper orientation of AWWs will probably result in attitudinal change, which could be expected to improve their performance. The organizational structure too needs to be toned up to check the wastage of precious resources as indicated by the study. Effective utilization of food grains under the scheme should be ensured by mandatory social auditing and proper monitoring of the performance of the AWWs and supervisors.

For the success of any community-oriented programme, the participation of people is vital. The panchayats should be engaged to procure the produce from the local farmers to provide cereals for the supplementary food. This will not only reduce the transportation cost but will also improve the economic condition of the local farmers, enhancing their participation in the programme. The involvement of women will give a boost to the community-oriented activities of anganwadis. They can be invited for their suggestions in deciding on the menu for the food, improving the taste of the food, participation in health programmes where their own experience of specific health issues can be shared, and remedies could be discussed collectively. Their involvement can also be sought in organizing game competitions, cultural programmes, interactive sessions with children and their support in taking children out on a pleasure trip. By encouraging such participation, probably many of the discrepancies could be eliminated, and the positive impact of the programme would be realized.

REFERENCES

Adhar (2008). Report on Gram Sabha for social audit of ICDS programme in Ratakhandi Gram Panchayat of Loisingha block, dist–Bolangir, Orissa on 18 June, 2007. https://www.yumpu.com/en/document/read/48808443/report-on-gram-sabha-for-social-audit-of-the-icds-programme-in-.

Chaturvedi, S., Srivastava, B. C., & Singh J.V. (1986). Impact of six year exposure to ICDS scheme on growth and health status of target children in Uttar Pradesh. *Indian Journal of Medical Research, 12,* 766–774.

Fifth Report of the Commissioners. (2004). Retrieved from www.sccommissioner.org/pdfs/comreports/5threport.pdf

FOCUS (Focus on Children Under Six). (2006). Abridged report. New Delhi: Citizens' Initiative for the Rights of Children Under Six.

FORCES (Neenv). (2007). ICDS in Delhi: A reality check. www.righttofood.org/data/neenv2007icds-delhi-reality-check.doc

GOG (Government of Gujarat). (2006). Census of India 2001: District Census Hand Book, Part XII A & B, Series 25. Gujarat: Directorate of Census Operation.

———. (2004). Census of India 2001. Series 25, Gujarat. Directorate of Census Operation.

GOI (Government of India). (2006). Census of India 2001. population projection for India and states 2001–2026. Report of the technical group on population projections constituted by National Commission on Population. New Delhi: Office of the Registrar General and Census Commissioner.

Gragnolati, M., Shekar, M., Dasgupta, M., Bredenkamp, C., & Yi-Kyoung, L. (2005). India's undernourished children: A call for reform and action. *Health, Nutrition and Population (HNP),* Discussion Paper. Washington D.C.: World Bank.

Kumar, A., & Joshi, K. M. (2008). Family planning method among the tribal population in South Gujarat: A case study of access and usage. *Development and Practice, 8,* 258–66.

Mander, H., & Kumaran, K. (2006). Social exclusion in ICDS: A sociological who done it? www.righttofoodindia.org/data/manderkumarano6icds

IIPS. (International Institute for Population Sciences. (2001). *National family health survey (NFHS-2) 1998–1999.* Mumbai: IIPS.

———. (2007). *National family health survey (NFHS-3) 2005–2006.* Mumbai: IIPS.

National Nutrition Monitoring Bureau. (2002). *Diet and nutritional status of rural population.* NNMB Technical Report No 21. Hyderabad: National Institute of Nutrition.

Ramchandran, V. (2005). Reflections on the ICDS programme. *Seminar, 546,* 26–30.

Ratnawali, & Iyengar, S. (2005). *Working of anganwadi in the selected tribal taluka of Valsad district.* Mimeograph, Surat: Centre for Social Studies.

Saxena, N. C. (2004). Review of ICDS programme in Bihar. www. righttofoodindia.org/data/saxena-icds-biharreview.doc

Tandon, B. N. (1989). Nutritional interventions through primary health care: Impact of ICDS projects in India. *Bulletin of World Health Organisation, 67,* 77–80.

Chapter 15

Socio-economic Impact of Implementation of Mahatma Gandhi National Rural Employment Guarantee Act in India*

T. Haque

INTRODUCTION

The Mahatma Gandhi National Rural Employment Guarantee Act (MGNREGA), 2005, which is a rights-based flagship scheme of the Government of India, with effect from 2 February 2006, guarantees at least 100 days of wage employment in a given financial year to every rural household whose adult members volunteer to do unskilled manual work. The MGNREGA is also intended to create durable community assets which would enhance productivity along with an increase in demand for labour. The Act mandates 33 per cent participation of women. It provides a disincentive for underperforming states, as an unemployment allowance has to be paid by the state government if work is not provided within 15 days of demand. Also, accountability

* *Social Change* Vol 41, no. 3 (September 2011): 445–471.

This article is based on a recent research study supported by the Ministry of Rural Development, Government, of India and United Nations Development Programme.

of the delivery system has been built in through social audit. However, the key question is whether various provisions of the Act are being implemented properly for the desired impact. The present study attempts to analyse the impact of the implementation of MGNREGA in the past four to five years and also to identify the critical gaps and challenges.

Objectives

The specific objectives of the study are to:

1. Examine the impact of MGNREGA on employment, wage rates of rural labourers, out-migration, community assets, overall processes of rural transformation, including empowerment of marginalized social groups such as Scheduled Castes (SCs), Scheduled Tribes (STs) and women.
2. Find out the nature and extent of positive and negative effects (if any) of MGNREGA on agriculture, especially crop productivity and costs of production due to the rise in agricultural wages, if any.
3. Identify the key challenges in the implementation of MGNREGA and suggest appropriate measures for improvement.

Methodology

The study is based on collection and analysis of both secondary and primary data. While the analysis of secondary data covered the entire country, the primary data were collected from 23 selected districts in the states of Andhra Pradesh (AP), Bihar, Chhattisgarh, Rajasthan, Jharkhand, Karnataka, Madhya Pradesh, Maharashtra, Orissa, Gujarat, Tamil Nadu, Uttar Pradesh (UP) and West Bengal in the year 2010–2011. The districts were chosen from among the 200 backward districts which were selected for implementation of MGNREGA in 2006–2007 so that the impact of implementation could be observed over at least three to four years. The districts were selected purposively, keeping in view their representativeness mainly in terms of Naxalism, agricultural development and SC/ST population. Most of the districts selected for this study were in the Maoist-affected areas. These include Adilabad, Khammam, Gaya, East Singhbhum, Bastar, Dhamtari, Malkangiri, Sonbhadra, Gondia and Balaghat. Of the remaining districts, Dang, Chitradurga, Kalahandi and Banswara were tribal-dominated and Cuddapah, Lalitpur and Bankura were SC-dominated. All these areas were poverty stricken, under-developed and prone to extremism.

In each of the selected areas, the following exercises were carried out:

1. A survey of a minimum of 60 households in each block, covering a village or cluster of villages. Only those villages were selected where a minimum of 20 beneficiaries were available and most of them had worked for at least three to four years. The overall sample household was 2,200.
2. A survey of officials and panchayat functionaries to find out the constraints faced by them in implementing the MGNREGA. These involved structured interviews with officials of the district administration, block administration as well as elected panchayat-level administration. Both qualitative and quantitative data were collected and analysed.

ACCESS TO EMPLOYMENT

According to official statistics, the number of rural households which were provided employment under MGNREGA progressively increased over time from 21.02 million in 2006–2007 to 33.91 million in 2007–2008, 45.12 million in 2008–2009 and 52.59 million in 2009. In 2010–2011 (up to 2 December), the number of households covered by MGNREGA stood at 37.06 million. In 2009–2010, when agricultural output and employment suffered heavily due to severe drought in various parts of the country, it was MGNREGA which provided relief to a vast number of rural labour households in the country. In terms of geographical distribution, the states of Rajasthan (6.52 million), AP (6.16 million), UP (5.48 million), Madhya Pradesh (4.71 million), Tamil Nadu (4.37 million), Bihar (4.13 million), Karnataka (3.53 million) and West Bengal (3.48 million) together shared nearly 73 per cent of the total number of beneficiary households (Table 15.1).

Table 15.1 *Number and Per Cent of Rural Households Provided Employment under MGNREGA*

States	No. of Households Provided Employment (in Millions)	Percentage of Households Provided Employment	Average Person Days per Household	Per Cent of Total Districts Reporting That	
				Less Than 10 Per Cent Households Availed 100 Days of Employment	Above 30 Per Cent Households Availed 100 Days of Employment
	2009–2010	2009–2010	2009–2010	2009–2010	2009–2010
AP	6.16	48.58	65.67	13.64	22.73
Arunachal Pradesh	0.07	41.43	24.91	93.75	6.25
Assam	2.14	50.64	34.29	88.89	7.41
Bihar	4.13	32.60	27.55	84.21	0.00
Gujarat	1.60	27.12	36.65	76.92	0.00
Haryana	0.16	6.37	37.74	90.48	0.00
Himachal Pradesh	0.50	45.31	57.29	75.00	0.00
Jammu and Kashmir	0.34	28.93	38.30	86.36	0.00
Karnataka	3.54	52.96	56.67	73.33	0.00
Kerala	0.96	19.34	35.54	85.71	3.33
Madhya Pradesh	4.72	58.03	55.66	70.00	6.00
Maharashtra	0.59	5.38	46.38	81.82	0.00
Punjab	0.27	9.80	28.37	95.00	0.00
Rajasthan	6.52	91.11	68.97	27.27	24.24
Sikkim	0.05	59.04	79.92	0.00	25.00

Tamil Nadu	4.37	52.85	54.67	16.13	6.45
Tripura	0.58	106.82	79.83	0.00	50.00
UP	5.48	26.63	64.91	45.07	9.86
West Bengal	3.48	31.18	44.59	100.00	0.00
Chhattisgarh	2.03	60.31	51.41	83.33	0.00
Jharkhand	1.70	44.78	49.48	83.33	0.00
Uttarakhand	0.52	43.67	34.92	92.31	0.00
Manipur	0.42	141.24	73.15	100.00	0.00
Meghalaya	0.30	91.14	49.41	85.71	0.00
Mizoram	0.18	226.99	94.57	87.50	12.50
Nagaland	0.33	122.58	87.40	63.64	36.36
Orissa	1.40	20.62	39.63	93.33	0.00
Puducherry	0.04	55.92	–	–	0.00
Andaman and Nicobar Island	0.02	40.96	–	–	0.00
Lakshadweep	0.01	97.03	–	–	0.00
Chandigarh	NA	NA	–	–	0.00
Dadra and Nagar Haveli	0.00	11.41	–	–	0.00
Daman and Diu	NA	NA	–	–	0.00
Goa	0.00	4.69	–	–	0.00
All India	**52.61**	**38.03**	**52.51**	**69.33**	**6.04**

Source: Ministry of Rural Development, Govt. of India (website).

It may be seen from Table 15.1 that the percentage of rural households benefitting from MGNREGA was very low in the states of Haryana (6.4%), Maharashtra (5.4%), Punjab (9.8%), Goa (4.7%) and Dadra and Nagar Haveli (11.4%). The states of Rajasthan (91.1%), Chhattisgarh (60.3%), AP (48.6%) and the north-eastern states of Tripura, Manipur, Mizoram and Nagaland (100%) had relatively better coverage than all other regions. According to the official record, nearly 99 per cent of all rural households who demanded employment were provided employment during 2008–2009 to 2010–2011. It was only in a few states, such as Arunachal Pradesh, Assam, Karnataka, Manipur, Meghalaya, Orissa, Sikkim and UP that there were gaps between demand for and supply of work. However, one does not know how accurate these estimates are, as the demand for work is likely to be underestimated for various reasons in most places. It was also observed in the field that the delivery system did not often give information to the workers, as it had the commitment to provide unemployment allowance in case it failed to provide work on demand. It would be further seen from Table 15.1 that the average person's days of employment per household in a year ranged between 24.91 in Arunachal Pradesh and 94.57 in Mizoram in the year 2009–2010. It was above 50 days in Mizoram (94.57), Nagaland (87.40), Sikkim (79.92), Tripura (79.83), Manipur (73.15), Rajasthan (68.97), AP (65.67), UP (64.91), Himachal Pradesh (57.29), Karnataka (56.67), Madhya Pradesh (55.66), Tamil Nadu (54.67) and Chhattisgarh (51.41).

Table 15.1 further shows that as many as 69 per cent districts in the country reported that less than 10 per cent households could avail 100 days of employment under MGNREGA. In several states, including West Bengal, Manipur, Arunachal Pradesh, Assam, Bihar, Chhattisgarh, Gujarat, Haryana, Himachal Pradesh, Jammu and Kashmir, Jharkhand, Kerala, Maharashtra, Karnataka, Madhya Pradesh, Meghalaya, Mizoram, Orissa, Punjab and Uttarakhand, 70–100 per cent of districts belonged to the category where less than 10 per cent households had availed 100 days of employment under MGNREGA. It was only in 6 per cent of districts in the country where a little above 30 per cent of households had availed of 100 days of employment under MGNREGA. It would not be out of place to mention here that many of the districts having a low proportion of households availing 100 days of employment were economically backward and had a high incidence of poverty.

Also, most of the districts which were selected for the purpose of this study showed a much more depressing picture. Table 15.2 shows that the average person days of employment per household as per official data was highest in Cuddapah (82.35), followed by Sonbhadra (79.55), Adilabad (78.12), Lalitpur (75.03), Khammam (65.24), Dindigul (61.16), Balaghat (59.41), Chitradurga (57.61), Dhamtari (53.21), Dhenkanal (50.62), Raigarh (45.74), Gumla (45.47), Dang (44.99), Bankura (44.02), East Singhbhum (43.26), West Medinipur (39.33), Gondia (39.11), Malkangiri (37.28), Kalahandi (27.95), Bastar (27.24), and Gaya (14.03). However, based on the data from the villages, it was observed that the average person days employed per beneficiary household was higher in some cases and lower in some other cases. On the whole, even the village-level study shows that access to employment was much lower than the guaranteed level of 100 days in a year. The percentage of rural households availing 100 days of employment in the selected districts in the year 2009–2010 was highest in Cuddapah (31.43), followed by Lalitpur (30.36), Adilabad (28.68), Dindigul (28.17), Banswara (26.58), Balaghat (25.29) and Khammam (22.57). In all the remaining selected districts—such as Sonbhadra (15.39), Dang (12.77), Dhamtari (8.47), Gumla (3.95), East Singhbhum (3.82), Chitradurga (3.40), Raigarh (2.88), Khunti (2.69), Bastar (1.58), Gondia (0.91), Dhenkanal (5.68), Kalahandi (1.97), Malkangiri (3.26), Bankura (2.60), Gaya (0.58) and West Medinipur—this was very low (Ministry of Rural Development, Government of India, MGNREGA website). It would be seen from Table 15.2 that there is not much difference between what the official data and our survey data indicate about access to MGNREGA employment in most cases, although in several places the official figures were either overstated or marginally understated.

It may also be noted in this context that almost all these low-ranking districts are under the influence of Maoists/extremists. What does it really indicate? Do Maoist activities constrain effective implementation of MGNREGA? Or does the ineffective implementation of MGNREGA and other development schemes in these places result in the growth of Maoism and other forms of extremism? Both could be true in some cases. In several of our study areas, where Maoists were active, MGNREGA has proved to be a popular scheme if and when explained to the poor people properly. Unfortunately, there is a gap in communication between the officials and the people, and consequently,

Table 15.2 Access to Job Card, Employment and Unemployment Allowance in the Selected Districts

District	% of Households Having Job Card	Average Person Days of Employment		% Households Receiving 100 Days of Employment		% Households Applied for Unemployment Allowance	% Households Received Unemployment Allowance
		Official Data 2009–2010	Our Survey Data 2010–2011	Official Data 2009–2010	Our Survey Data 2010–2011		
Cuddapah	92.50	82.3	100.0	31.43	30.58	0.00	0.00
Khammam	84.17	65.2	100.0	22.57	20.30	1.67	0.00
Adilabad	93.00	78.1	50.0	28.68	25.15	2.30	0.00
Gaya	83.33	14.0	45.0	0.58	0.35	0.83	0.00
Raigarh	86.67	45.7	51.5	2.88	2.00	0.83	0.00
Dhamtari	88.50	53.2	41.7	8.47	6.25	0.83	0.00
Bastar	87.00	27.2	43.0	1.58	0.90	1.00	0.00
Dang	86.67	45.0	71.7	12.77	11.00	0.83	0.00
East Singhbhum	99.17	43.3	41.7	3.82	2.85	0.00	0.00
Khunti	85.00	22.4	33.0	2.69	2.00	0.83	2.25
Gumla	85.00	45.5	42.3	3.95	2.10	0.83	3.00
Chitradurga	83.33	57.6	85.5	3.40	2.65	0.83	5.83
Balaghat	94.17	59.4	33.1	25.29	28.50	3.33	0.00
Gondia	91.67	39.1	50.4	0.91	1.20	4.17	4.17

Kalahandi	88.33	27.9	1.97	2.18	0.83	0.00
Dhenkanal	88.33	49.9	5.68	4.55	0.83	0.00
Malkangiri	86.67	37.3	3.26	4.00	0.00	0.00
Banswara	95.00	76.7	26.58	28.26	3.33	0.00
Dindigul	88.33	61.2	28.17	26.12	18.33	10.00
Lalitpur	85.00	75.0	29.97	12.00	3.33	0.83
Sonbhadra	82.50	79.6	15.39	10.50	0.00	0.00
Bankura	88.33	44.0	2.60	3.10	0.00	0.00
West Medinipur	86.67	52.0	1.08	1.50	0.83	0.00

Source: 1. Official data obtained from the Ministry of Rural Development, Government of India (website).
2. CSD Survey data for the year 2010–11.

the MGNREGA remains poorly canvassed and implemented in many such areas. At the same time, it needs to be stressed that lack of development itself promotes Maoism/extremism in many places.

Table 15.2 further shows that about 82.5–99.2 per cent of households in the selected districts had a job card, but no adequate employment. For example, in the Singhbhum district of Jharkhand, 99 per cent of households had job cards, but only 3–4 per cent of households had access to 100 days of MGNREGA employment. Also, a significant proportion of the total households in Cuddapah, (55.8%), East Singhbhum (98.3%), Khunti (97%), Gumla (96%), Bankura (45%) and West Medinipur (63.3%), had reported that they did not receive a job within 15 days of application. Besides, in most cases, they neither applied for legally entitled unemployment allowance nor did they receive it in case applied.

Contribution of Income under MGNREGA to Total Household Income

Figure 15.1 shows various sources of income of MGNREGA-beneficiary households. As can be seen from the figure, wage incomes through MGNREGA work constituted as much as 44.25 per cent of total household income in Adilabad (AP), 43.18 per cent in Khammam (AP), 36.52 per cent in Sonbhadra (UP), 28.28 per cent in Dang (Gujarat), 24.85 per cent in Cuddapah (AP), 23.7 per cent in Lalitpur (UP), 21.23 per cent in Gaya (Bihar), 18.5 per cent in East Singhbhum (Jharkhand), 15.13 per cent in Chitradurga (Karnataka), 14.61 per cent in West Medinipur (West Bengal) and 10.89 per cent in Banswara (Rajasthan). In the remaining districts, it was in the range from 1 to 7 per cent. In several places, the share of MGNREGA income was higher than that of traditional agricultural and non-agricultural wage incomes considered individually. These districts include Khammam (AP), Lalitpur (UP) and Sonbhadra (UP).

Investment Priorities and Asset Creation

According to the official guidelines, water conservation, water harvesting, drought proofing, irrigation, renovation of traditional water

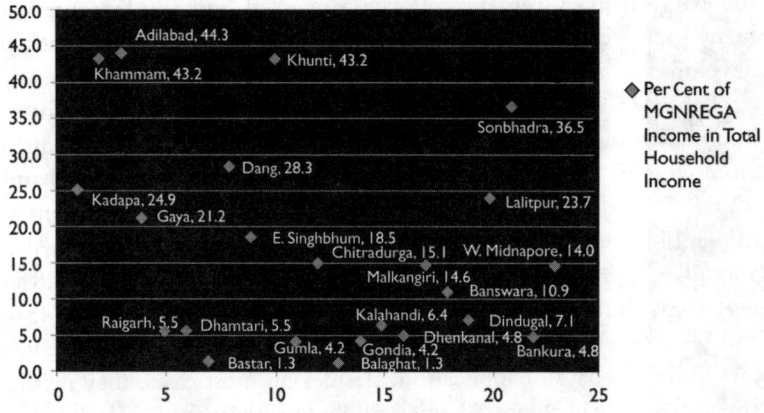

Figure 15.1 *Per Cent of MGNREGA Income to Total*
Source: CSD Survey data for the year 2010–2011.

bodies, land development, flood control and drainage improvement and rural connectivity would be the focus in order of priority. The data for the years from 2008–2009 to 2010–2011 reveal that about 35.8 per cent of the total MGNREGA expenditure was on rural connectivity, followed by water conservation and water harvesting (23.7%), renovation of traditional water bodies (12.6%) and land development (7.05%), respectively (Table 15.3). Irrigation canals accounted for only about 5 per cent of the total expenditure. However, it varied from state to state. The states where water conservation and water harvesting had the highest share in total expenditure include Jharkhand (40.1%), Madhya Pradesh (39.0%), Maharashtra (37.9%) and Gujarat (36.1%). The states of Orissa, AP, Tamil Nadu, Chhattisgarh, West Bengal, Maharashtra, Punjab and Puducherry rightly spent a sizable proportion of total expenditure on renovation of traditional water bodies as these states were once rich in water bodies which showed signs of decline over time. In fact, Tamil Nadu, Puducherry and Punjab put the highest priority on renovation of traditional water bodies. The states of Bihar, Orissa and West Bengal, which witness floods frequently, hardly spent much on flood control and drainage improvement, while this was one of the priority areas for MGNREGA work in Kerala, Uttarakhand and Goa.

Table 15.3 Pattern of MGNREGA Expenditure (Cumulative 2008–2009 to 2010–2011 up to 2 December 2010)

State	Flood Control	Rural Connectivity	Water ConServation and Water Harvesting	Renovation of Traditional Water Bodies	Drought Proofing	Irrigation Canals	Irrigation Facilities (SC/ST/ IAY/LR)	Land Development	Other Works	Rajiv Gandhi Seva Kendra
Orissa	0.60	52.22	10.75	19.11	2.36	1.95	3.42	1.03	2.60	5.97
Rajasthan	1.63	42.17	23.62	12.01	3.54	4.32	4.42	4.77	2.98	0.54
Chhattisgarh	2.99	40.19	19.01	16.37	4.51	7.26	4.65	4.57	0.46	0.00
Jharkhand	0.79	39.27	40.14	5.92	2.59	1.05	2.03	4.14	3.50	0.58
Madhya Pradesh	0.87	33.95	38.98	3.75	5.33	1.03	11.06	3.26	1.77	0.00
Tripura	1.51	37.68	14.37	2.73	5.49	7.77	0.94	15.11	14.27	0.13
Maharashtra	0.83	24.47	37.89	21.51	5.19	0.55	1.39	7.24	0.92	0.00
Gujarat	10.91	25.42	36.14	6.06	5.09	0.92	9.92	2.92	2.52	0.10
West Bengal	7.16	41.33	21.94	13.03	3.29	4.97	1.42	5.79	1.06	0.01
Kerala	27.08	4.50	11.84	15.24	3.35	8.77	4.08	24.48	0.65	0.00
Karnataka	13.62	15.65	19.33	7.70	8.99	11.21	5.59	12.45	5.40	0.05
Bihar	4.35	52.69	10.26	6.82	9.37	10.18	0.29	4.37	1.66	0.00
Mizoram	2.94	79.09	1.64	0.05	5.18	0.11	0.06	10.50	0.43	0.00
Haryana	3.43	33.60	23.22	7.00	5.19	7.22	0.10	11.72	2.66	5.85
Himachal Pradesh	15.29	44.26	13.18	3.09	0.73	11.26	1.16	8.37	2.64	0.00
UP	5.17	41.72	27.89	5.63	3.56	3.29	1.50	5.11	6.12	0.00
Nagaland	1.48	74.40	5.15	0.18	2.90	6.45	0.15	4.54	4.75	0.00

Assam	13.29	59.94	5.13	1.85	3.92	3.51	0.17	8.78	3.13	0.28
Uttarakhand	32.34	2.70	28.58	5.07	8.95	13.48	0.49	7.45	0.93	0.00
Meghalaya	5.74	61.12	17.29	1.48	6.21	2.56	0.03	4.55	0.90	0.12
Punjab	3.45	33.32	2.11	40.61	3.65	3.54	0.02	9.03	3.23	1.03
Tamil Nadu	0.67	18.91	20.52	47.48	0.02	12.20	0.11	0.08	0.00	0.00
Sikkim	14.55	25.08	0.83	0.40	29.34	13.59	0.03	14.99	1.08	0.11
Manipur	14.34	34.06	9.52	9.38	7.09	13.09	0.00	12.18	0.34	0.00
Jammu and Kashmir	23.31	39.63	9.02	1.84	0.43	6.87	0.27	17.63	1.00	0.00
Goa	32.27	32.08	2.26	7.34	0.00	0.39	0.32	25.35	0.00	0.00
Arunachal Pradesh	23.52	44.24	1.48	0.00	0.27	14.43	0.37	13.84	1.86	0.00
Lakshadweep	0.17	0.00	19.42	16.03	16.39	0.00	0.00	39.96	8.03	0.00
Andaman and Nicobar	8.27	23.29	35.65	1.36	0.31	6.64	0.00	24.49	0.00	0.00
Puducherry	0.00	0.00	0.00	99.04	0.46	0.50	0.00	0.00	0.00	0.00
Daman and Diu	0.00	0.00	0.00	0.00	0.00	0.00	0.00	0.00	0.00	0.00
Dadra and Nagar Haveli	0.00	0.00	0.00	0.00	0.00	0.00	0.00	0.00	0.00	0.00
AP	3.64	20.81	13.24	24.91	3.28	4.97	4.47	24.39	0.28	0.00
Chandigarh	0.00	0.00	0.00	0.00	0.00	0.00	0.00	0.00	0.00	0.00
All India	**4.57**	**35.82**	**23.70**	**12.56**	**4.03**	**5.00**	**3.87**	**7.05**	**2.97**	**0.43**

Source: Ministry of Rural Development, Government of India (website).

The states of Karnataka, Mizoram and Sikkim spent about 9–29 per cent of the total fund on drought proofing. Irrigation facilities for SC/ST/Indira Awas Yojana (IAY)/land reform (LR) beneficiaries accounted for a significant amount of total expenditure only in Madhya Pradesh (11.1%), Gujarat (9.9%) and Karnataka (5.6%). In the remaining states, it was more or less negligible. The result of our field survey also indicated that renovation of tanks, irrigation and land development formed priorities in most places.

Impact on Agriculture

The activities being undertaken under MGNREGA such as (a) water conservation and water harvesting, (b) drought proofing (including afforestation and tree plantation), (c) irrigation, (d) provision of horticulture plantation and land development facilities on the land owned by households belonging to SC and ST or below poverty line (BPL) families of beneficiaries of LRs, IAY or that of the small and marginal farmers, as define in the Agriculture Debt Waiver and Debt Relief Scheme, 2008, (e) renovation of traditional water bodies, including desilting of tanks and ponds, (f) flood control and drainage improvement in water logged areas, and (g) rural connectivity, are aimed at improving the resource base of the rural poor for sustainable agriculture and food security. Also, the recent expansion of the scope of MGNREGA to include works on the lands of small and marginal farmers is a strategic step towards increasing irrigation potential and drought proofing in rain-fed areas which will reduce soil erosion and loss of organic matter and improve crop yields (Sharma 2010).

It was borne out from the discussion with gram panchayat heads in most of the surveyed villages that renovation of ponds/canals using MGNREGA resources helped improve irrigated areas which impacted crop yields and income positively. The districts where such an impact could be observed prominently include Cuddapah, Khammam, Raigarh, Dang, Chitradurga, Balaghat, Gondia, Banswara, Sonbhadra, West Medinipur and Bankura. Also implementation of MGNREGA helped improve forests and other natural resources which would indirectly improve the environment and livelihood opportunities for the poor. An increase in the forest area was reported in Chitradurga,

Kalahandi, Lalitpur, West Medinipur and Bankura, while an increase in common property resources accessible to all was reported in almost all the places, excepting East Singhbhum, Gondia, Kalahandi and Sonbhadra. Besides, in the districts of Khammam, Raigarh, Chitradurga, Balaghat, Kalahandi, Banswara, Dindigul, Lalitpur and Sonbhadra, gram panchayat functionaries reported that there was a change in the cropping pattern in favour of crops such as fruits and vegetables, cotton and paddy, which yielded more returns. Also, with the implementation of MGNREGA, there has been a substantial increase in the market wage rates of agricultural and non-agricultural labourers. This has been true for both male and female labourers. The increase in the agricultural wage rates could be observed more prominently in Cuddapah, Khammam, Dindigul, Raigarh, Gaya, Chitradurga, Kalahandi, Lalitpur, Sonbhadra, West Medinipur and Bankura in both peak and lean seasons (Table 15.4).

In most southern districts, the non-agricultural wages of both male and female workers also increased substantially.

In this context, it should be noted that farmers organizations in AP and Tamil Nadu had made a representation to the Union Government saying that implementation of MGNREGA had affected the agricultural sector adversely for two reasons. First, it increased the market wage rates of agricultural labourers which resulted in an increase in the cost of production of various crops, and second, labour availability in the peak agricultural season became scarce, affecting agricultural operations adversely. While this may be true, it should be noted in this regard that in the rain-fed areas, improvement and water availability through MGNREGA work by way of renovation of ponds/canals and watershed development, land development, etc., has also helped improve agricultural productivity in some places. Also, the landless and semi-landless poor who benefitted from employment under MGNREGA would create additional demand for various agricultural products, resulting in rise in the farm prices of agricultural commodities. On balance, therefore, in the medium-to long-run, the agricultural sector would immensely benefit from MGNREGA. The additional cost of production due to the rise in agricultural wage rates should be compensated by the farmers by way of a proportionate increase in the minimum support prices, which would also impact the market

Table 15.4 *Per Cent Change in Wage Rates due to MGNREGA*

State	District	Increments in Agricultural Wage Rate due to MGNREGA (% Change During 2006–2010)				Increments in Non-agricultural Wage Rate due to MGNREGA (% Change during 2006–2010)	
		Peak Season (Male)	Peak Season (Female)	Lean Season (Male)	Lean Season (Female)	Male	Female
AP	Cuddapah	100	75	85	62.5	135	52.5
	Khammam	80	42.5	80	65	55	70
	Adilabad	88	45	82	70	72	80
Bihar	Gaya	46	46	46	46	50	50
Chhattisgarh	Raigarh	55	55	50	50	55	40
	Dhamtari	60	58	45	52	50	48
	Bastar	65	60	42	55	48	45
Gujarat	Dang	40	40	30	30	22.5	10
Jharkhand	Purvi Shinghbhum	9.5	9.5	9.5	9.5	9.5	9.5
	Khunti	10	16	7	19	9	15
	Gumla	7	15	7	18	10	5
Karnataka	Chitradurga	50	30	40	20	65	55
Madhya Pradesh	Balaghat	27.5	20	25	25	55	55

Maharashtra	Gondia	35	20	20	15	40	15
Orissa	Kalahandi	80	80	60	60	40	40
	Dhenkanal	80	83	57	49	57	35
	Malkangiri	80	85	50	43	57	29.5
Rajasthan	Banswar	26	26	12.5	12.5	26	26
Tamil Nadu	Dindigul	97.5	62.5	192.5	207.5	125	75
UP	Lalitpur	41	41	41	41	41	41
	Sonbhadra	31.5	31.5	31.5	31.5	31.5	31.5
West Bengal	Paschim Medinipur	36	36	36	36	55	40
	Bankura	40	40	40	40	35	40

Source: Based on Field Survey in 2010–2011.

prices of commodities, thereby benefitting the farming community in general. Regarding the scarcity of agricultural labour during the peak agricultural seasons in some places—particularly Punjab, Haryana, coastal AP and Tamil Nadu—due to competition from MGNREGA work, there would be a readjustment process in which farmers would now either do the farm work themselves or adopt more mechanization.

Impact on Social Inclusion

It may be seen from Table 15.5 that the shares of SCs and STs in total employment created under MGNREGA were disproportionately higher than their share in the total population in the country. The share of SC beneficiaries in MGNREGA employment in 2009–2010 was about 22.9 per cent as against their share of 16.2 per cent in the total population. Similarly, the share of ST beneficiaries in total MGNREGA employment was nearly 33.2 per cent against their share of 8.1 per cent in the total population. However, this kind of relationship should be read with a word of caution. In fact, the incidence of poverty among SCs and STs was much higher than others in almost all the states, and therefore, they needed greater employment opportunities than others from the point of view of equity and social inclusion. Considering the country as a whole, the poverty ratio among SCs and STs was 53.8 per cent and 61.3 per cent, respectively, against 41.8 per cent of the average poverty ratio. In several states, it was higher in the range of 60–84 per cent for STs and 57–78 per cent in the case of SCs.

Participation of Women

According to the provisions of MGNREGA, priority must be given to women in such a way that at least one-third of the beneficiaries shall be women who have registered and requested for work under this Act. The official data (Ministry of Rural Development, Government of India website) suggest that the share of women in the total MGNREGA employment in the country progressively increased from 40.65 per cent in 2006–2007 to 42.52 per cent in 2007–2008 and 47.87 per cent in 2008–2009 and 48.80 per cent in 2009–2010. In the current year, up to 2 December 2010, the share of women workers stood at 51.75 per cent.

Table 15.5 *State-wise Participation of SCs and STs in MGNREGA*

States	Percentage Share in Total Population		Percentage Share in Person Days Generated under MGNREGA		Poverty Ratio		
	SCs	STs	SCs	STs	SCs	STs	General
AP	16.2	6.6	25.0	14.4	41.8	60.3	32.3
Arunachal Pradesh	NA	NA	1.1	86.5	NA	NA	NA
Assam	6.9	12.4	10.8	31.7	45.3	28.8	36.4
Bihar	15.7	0.1	45.6	2.3	77.6	59.3	55.7
Chhattisgarh	11.6	31.8	14.7	37.9	48.6	65.5	55.1
Gujarat	7.1	14.8	13.1	39.1	49.3	57.1	39.1
Haryana	19.3	0.0	52.9	0.0	47.5	0.0	24.8
Himachal Pradesh	24.7	4.0	32.9	8.2	39.5	35.4	25.0
Jammu and Kashmir	7.6	10.9	8.5	26.3	14.7	26.5	14.1
Jharkhand	11.8	26.3	16.1	42.0	61.0	60.6	51.6
Karnataka	16.2	6.6	18.0	9.3	57.4	50.5	37.5
Kerala	9.8	1.1	17.5	5.7	30.8	56.9	20.2
Madhya Pradesh	15.2	20.3	18.5	43.9	62.6	80.0	53.6
Maharashtra	10.2	34.4	18.3	35.9	66.1	73.2	47.4
Manipur	NA	NA	15.0	57.1	NA	NA	NA

(Continued)

(Continued)

States	Percentage Share in Total Population		Percentage Share in Person Days Generated under MGNREGA		Poverty Ratio		
	SCs	STs	SCs	STs	SCs	STs	General
Meghalaya	NA	NA	0.5	94.3	NA	NA	NA
Mizoram	NA	NA	NA	99.6	NA	NA	NA
Nagaland	NA	NA	0.0	98.3	NA	NA	NA
Orissa	16.5	22.1	19.4	34.8	67.9	84.4	60.8
Punjab	28.9	0.0	77.4	NA	38.4	30.7	22.1
Rajasthan	17.2	12.6	26.1	22.7	48.5	59.3	35.8
Sikkim	NA	NA	7.7	42.0	NA	NA	NA
Tamil Nadu	19.0	1.0	49.0	1.9	51.2	47.3	37.5
Tripura	NA	NA	19.8	43.1	NA	NA	NA
UP	21.1	0.1	50.6	1.6	56.6	42.0	42.7
Uttarakhand	17.9	3.0	23.6	3.9	46.2	32.4	35.1
West Bengal	23.0	5.5	36.9	13.6	37.1	54.3	38.2
All India	**16.2**	**8.1**	**22.9**	**33.2**	**53.8**	**61.3**	**41.8**

Source: Census of India, Ministry of Rural Development website and Tendulkar Committee Report.

It would be seen from Figure 15.2 that the states where the share of women in total employment was disproportionately higher in recent years include Kerala (90.1%), Tamil Nadu (76.7%), Rajasthan (68.5%), AP (57%) and Himachal Pradesh (55.2%). It was very low in Jammu and Kashmir, UP and low in all other states. The states which failed to provide a one-third share of employment to women (as mandated by the Act) were Jharkhand (32.4%), West Bengal (31.2%), Bihar (29.8%), Lakshadweep (27.6%), Assam (23.2%), Mizoram (23.2%), UP (15.6%), and Jammu and Kashmir (10.8%). In fact, nearly 42 per cent of districts in the country failed to provide above one-third employment to women workers as mandated by law. Several of the districts selected for this study, namely Gumla (25.7%) and Khunti (30.8%) had less than 33 per cent share of women in MGNREGA employment while in Dang (48.7%), Chitradruga (45.4%), Bastar (42.7%), Malkangiri (42.6%), West Medinipur (41.9%), East Singhbhum (41%), Kalahandi (39.2%), Sonbhadra (38.6%) and Gaya (35%), it was in the range of 33–49 per cent. In other selected districts, the share of women was above 50 per cent (Ministry of Rural Development, website).

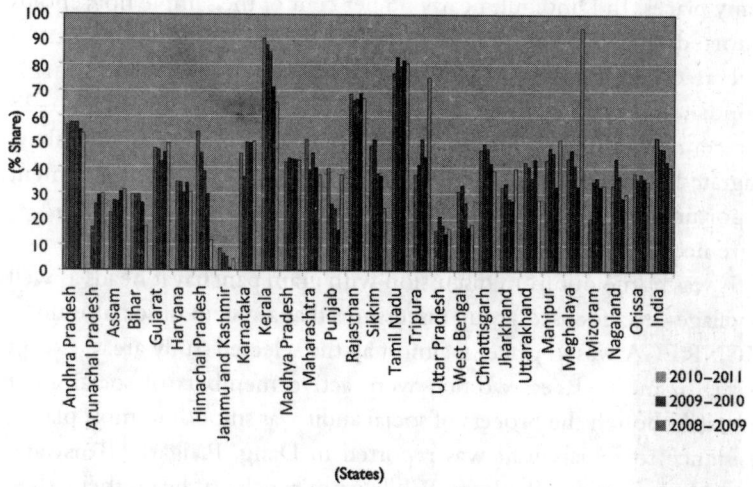

Figure 15.2 *Per Cent Share of Women in MGNREGA*

Source: Official data obtained from the Ministry of Rural Development, Government of India (website).

Impact on Out-migration

While migration of skilled workers from rural to urban areas or from underdeveloped to developed regions, for upward mobility is generally considered to be a sign of progressive economic development, any distressed migration of unskilled workers from rural to urban areas is a sign of underdevelopment. Hence, MGNREGA was intended to create adequate employment opportunities in the rural areas so that distressed migration of rural workers could be either prevented or reduced. The results of our field study also reveal—through analysis of both household and gram panchayat-level data—that there has been a decline in the incidence of migration of workers in several places in the post-MGNREGA scenario. Based on the interview of gram panchayat heads, a maximum decline in the incidence of migration was observed in Lalitpur (150%), followed by Banswara (88.4%), Chitradurga (86.5%), Dang (78.2%), West Medinipur (59.5%), Gaya (50.4%), Raigarh (50%), Dindigul (33.3%), Balaghat (30%), Bankura (29.5%), Cuddapah (25%) and Kalahandi (18.2%). In other cases, there was either no change or a marginal increase in migration, as in Sonbhadra (Table 15.6).

Still, the incidence of migration in search of jobs remained quite high in many places. In Dindigul, nearly 36 per cent of the sample households reported that they migrated in search of wage employment. In several other districts, including Khammam, Gaya, Chitradurga, Gondia, Sonbhadra, West Medinipur and Bankura, nearly 10–27 per cent of sample households reported that their adult members migrated for employment. This was mainly because the employment opportunities—including both MGNREGA and non-MGNREGA—were not adequate and also the local wage rates were lower.

It was borne out from discussion with gram panchayat heads as well as village-level focused group discussions that a system of social audit of MGNREGA was in place in almost all the selected study areas, except Gaya. In most places, women were active members of social audit teams. Although the process of social audit was smooth in most places, resistance to social audit was reported in Dang, Raigarh, Banswara, west Medinipur and Bankura. While gram panchayat heads themselves offered resistance to social audit in West Medinipur and Bankura, in

Table 15.6 *Impact of MGNREGA on Out-migration in Selected Survey Districts*

State	District	% Decline in Out-migration Rate from 2006 to 2010	% of Respondents Still Migrating in Search of Seasonal Wage Employment	The Main Reasons for Out-Migration
AP	Cuddapah	25.0	4.2	Inadequate employment
	Khammam	0.0	15.0	
	Adilabad	0.0	15.0	
Bihar	Gaya	50.4	18.3	
Chattisgarh	Raigarh	50.0	1.7	
	Dhamtari	54.6	2.0	
	Bastar	22.2	2.0	Low wage rate
Gujarat	Dang	78.2	1.7	NR
Jharkhand	East Shinghbhum	0.0	0.8	Low wage rate
	Khunti	33.3	4.0	Low wage rate
	Gumla	20.0	5.0	Low wage rate and inadequate employment
Karnataka	Chitradurga	86.5	10.8	Low wage rate and inadequate employment
Madhya Pradesh	Balaghat	30.0	6.7	Inadequate employment and low wage rate
Maharashtra	Gondia	0.0	26.7	Low Wage rate and inadequate employment

(Continued)

(Continued)

State	District	% Decline in Out-migration Rate from 2006 to 2010	% of Respondents Still Migrating in Search of Seasonal Wage Employment	The Main Reasons for Out-Migration
Orissa	Kalahandi	18.2	4.2	Inadequate employment and low wage rate
	Dhenkanal	40.0	14.2	Inadequate employment and low wage rate
	Malkangiri	66.7	26.7	Inadequate employment and delay in payment
Rajasthan	Banswara	88.4	6.7	Inadequate employment
Tamil Nadu	Dindigul	33.3	35.8	Inadequate employment and low wage rate
UP	Lalitpur	0.0	0.0	–
	Sonbhadra	–9.6	12.5	Interior nature of EGS work, inadequate employment and Low wages
West Bengal	Bankura	29.5	14.2	Inadequate employment, low Wage rate and job insecurity
	West Medinipur	59.5	26.7	Inadequate employment, delay in payment, job in security and low wage rate

Source: Our Field Survey in 2010–2011.

most cases it was both gram panchayat head and the material suppliers who put up resistance to social audit. Besides, the process of social audit did not seem to be truly participatory, as gram panchayat heads and official agencies dominated.

KEY CHALLENGES AND SUGGESTIONS

A critical analysis of the processes and impact of implementation of the MGNREGA in various parts of the country shows that it has performed quite well in several places in providing a safety net to the rural poor, although the average person days of employment provided per beneficiary household was much lower than the entitled 100 days in most cases. The very fact that nearly 5.26 million rural households (38%) availed of MGNREGA employment earning an additional income of ₹4,883 per household per year in 2009–2010 is, in itself, no small achievement. The overwhelming participation of socially disadvantaged groups such as SCs, STs and women in the MGNREGA activities further indicates that it has a tremendous potential to transform social and economic relations in rural India which, if properly utilized, may result in a much-desired social transformation. However, currently there are several gaps and challenges to the effective implementation of MGNREGA in most places, which could be briefly discussed as follows.

Bridging the Entitlement Gaps

The main objective of MGNREGA is to provide a right-based 100 days of unskilled employment for enhancing the rural poor's purchasing power and capacity to overcome hunger and poverty. However, this objective has not been achieved in any state so far at the aggregate level.

Most of the districts selected for this study exhibited a depressing picture. The average person days of employment provided per beneficiary household was as low as 14.03 in Gaya, 27.2 in Bastar, 22.4 in Khunti, 27.9 in Kalahandi, 45.0 in Dang, 45.7 in Raigarh, 43.3 in East Singhbhum, 45.5 in Gumla, 39.1 in Gondia, 37.3 in Malkangiri and 44.0 in Bankura. Also, several of these districts, including Dang and Sonbhadra had only 13–15 per cent households that had accessed

100 days of employment, while in Gaya (0.58%), Bastar (1.58%), Raigarh (2.88%), Gumla (3.95%), East Singhbhum (3.82%), Khunti (2.69%), Chitradurga (3.40%), Gondia (0.91%), Dhenkanal (5.68%), Kalahandi (1.97%), Malkangiri (3.26%), Bankura (2.60%) and West Medinipur (1.08%), less than 9 per cent households had accessed MGNREGA employment. All these low-ranking districts are also reported to be under the influence of Maoists/extremists mainly due to inadequate employment and scarce livelihood opportunities. Therefore, bridging the entitlement gaps in all such areas should be accorded priority by the government, as effective implementation of MGNREGA and other development schemes would help reduce the incidence of extremism. It is also not true that Maoists always interfere with the implementation of MGNREGA, as is generally believed in official circles. Hence, the communication gap that currently exists between government officials, PR institutions and local people needs to be bridged, so that the extremists-affected backward regions of the country can be brought within the loop of development.

Another related issue is the correct and timely payment of wages to MGNREGA workers. It was observed that a significant proportion of MGNREGA beneficiaries in East Singhbhum (19.2%), Sonbhadra (17.5%), Banswara (8.3%), Gaya (5%) and Dindigul (5.0%) did not have an account with either a bank or a post office and, therefore, received cash payment, leaving scope for corruption. Also, as many as 61.7 per cent of beneficiaries in Gaya and 43.3 per cent in Kalahandi reported that they had bank accounts at a distance of 10–15 km where the road connectivity also was not very good. In all such cases, the cost of travel, loss of working hours and non-cooperation of the bank officials discouraged them from opting for MGNREGA employment. Besides, there were reports of underpayments and fake payments.

The key requirement in this regard would be to create awareness among people about various entitlements of MGNREGA and mobilize support from all sources for their effective delivery. The result of our field survey (which could not be presented in detail here due to lack of space) reveals that the level of awareness about various entitlements of MGNREGA was very low in several places. Regarding the minimum 100 days of employment guarantee, about 42 per cent of families in Kalahandi, 35 per cent in Dhenkanal, 40 per cent in

Malkangiri, 28 per cent in Raigarh, Dhamtari and Dang, 22 per cent in Bastar and Khunti, 30 per cent in Chitradurga and Gondia and 24 per cent in East Singhbhum reported that they were not aware of this provision. Regarding other entitlements of MGNREGA—such as minimum wages, work to be given within 15 days of application, unemployment allowance, one-third of workers to be women, work to be provided within 5 km, if not additional payment, work site facilities, etc.—the level of awareness was extremely low. As a result, there are huge gaps between various entitlements and their actual realizations by rural workers. It is therefore, recommended that the Panchayati Raj institutions, civil societies and the concerned government departments should work hand in hand to create the necessary awareness among rural people about various entitlements of MGNREGA and mobilize support for their effective implementation.

Ensuring Productive Utilization of the Assets Created

The second most important objective of MGNREGA is to create productive and durable assets of irrigation, drought proofing, water conservation and water harvesting, increasing horticulture plantations and connectivity for generating a sustainable livelihood system. In practice, this objective has been pursued in most places as revealed from the priorities of MGNREGA expenditure (Table 15.4). But there has been hardly any planned effort to ensure productive utilization of whatever assets have been created. This is mainly because of lack of coordination and convergence, between various departments and programmes at different levels. Even though the Ministry of Rural Development has designed guidelines for convergence between MGNREGA and other departmental development programmes to facilitate better planning and investments in rural areas, there is a lack of seriousness about it in most places. Moreover, due to the absence of adequate socio-economic infrastructure such as roads, electricity, education, training, etc., the potential of assets created under MGNREGA remains either unused or underutilized. Therefore, there should be greater efforts to ensure not only increased convergence between MGNREGA, on the one hand, and agriculture, water conservation, irrigation and horticulture plantations, on the other, but also to promote education, training and skills of the rural people along with development of all-weather roads, markets, power connectivity etc. so that the assets created under MGNREGA could be more productively utilized for sustainable rural development.

No doubt, the present investment priorities of MGNREGA are in the right direction, given its emphasis on water conservation, renovation of traditional water bodies, land development and irrigation facilities in the lands of SCs/STs, IAY and LR beneficiaries and other small and marginal farmers and rural connectivity. All these have tremendous potential of raising farm productivity and incomes, apart from generating employment related incomes. In several places covered by our field study, it was observed that farmers have improved their irrigated areas and changed the cropping patterns to realize higher productivity and incomes in areas treated through MGNREGA works. But in most cases, productivity-enhancing efforts are missing. Therefore, proper utilization of assets created under MGNREGA should receive urgent attention by all those concerned at the state and local levels, through proper inter-departmental coordination and inter-programme/inter-activity convergence.

Addressing the Issue of Rising Wages and Cost of Agricultural Production

This study clearly reveals that the wage rates of agricultural labourers have substantially increased in recent years, under the impact of MGNREGA. At the same time, it has led to a scarcity of labour in the peak seasons. These two factors are reportedly affecting agricultural productivity adversely in some developed pockets of the country. While the additional cost of production due to a MGNREGA-led rise in agricultural wage rates should be compensated by way of a proportionate increase in the minimum support prices which also impact the market prices of agricultural commodities positively— thereby benefiting the farmers in general—the issue of seasonal labour shortage in agriculturally-developed pockets would be taken care of through a process of readjustment in which farmers would now either do the farm work themselves or adopt more mechanization.

Addressing the Issue of Social Inclusion

Although the shares of SCs, STs and women in the total employment generated under MGNREGA so far (as per official records) was found to be dispro-portionately higher than their share in the total population in most places, it should be noted that the proportion of households below the poverty line was much higher in the case of both SCs and STs. Considering the country as a whole, 53.8 per cent of SC households and 61.3 per cent of ST households were below the poverty line (based on the report of the Tendulkar Committee), as against 42 per cent in general. The incidence of poverty among ST households was invariably higher than the average poverty ratio in most states. It was as high as 80 per cent in Orissa, 73 per cent in Maharashtra, 66 per cent in Chhattisgarh, 61 per cent in Jharkhand, 60 per cent in AP, 59 per cent in Bihar and Rajasthan and 57 per cent in Gujarat. All these states also had a high incidence of Naxalism/extremism. Therefore, there is no reason why there should be any comfort saying that the shares of SCs and STs in total employment generated under MGNREGA is higher. In fact, there is a greater need for social mobilization, awareness-building campaigns and effective implementation of MGNREGA in all the extremist-affected regions. Similarly, in the case of women, their relative share in total employment is comparatively higher than their share in the total work force in most places. But here again, women, especially among SCs and STs, are more vulnerable than others and, therefore, need a better deal. Moreover, the inadequate facilities of drinking water, crèches, toilets, etc., at the worksite affect women workers most. Hence, providing decent conditions of work for women workers, even within the SC/ST working members, should be a priority.

Ensuring Good Governance

The MGNREGA guidelines provide for social audit and vigilance and monitoring mechanism for its effective, transparent and corruption-free implementation. However, the present system suffers from various inadequacies and weaknesses. In several villages where the field level survey was conducted, the vigilance and monitoring committees were dominated by the supporters of sarpanch/*pradhan* and ward members. This affected the proper functioning of vigilance committees. Similarly, in the case of social audit, the process of audit did not seem to be truly participatory, as gram panchayat heads and official agencies dominated and people's voices were often suppressed. Also, the reported social audits did not result in any mid-course correction. Besides, there were no technically educated persons in the teams of social audit who could understand the technicalities of works, and as a result, physical inspection of works and assets was generally conducted in a very non-professional manner. Moreover, at the public hearings held at the *mandal* or block level, not only the poor peoples' participation remained low, but also the uneducated people who still suffer from dependency syndrome in the villages did not open their mouths. Consequently, the entire show remained top-down and officially managed. It is therefore, suggested that the process of social audit should be people-centric and not sarpanch-/*pradhan*-centric and the civil society organizations should be actively involved to train the workers in articulating their grievances.

Building Capacities of Panchayat Functionaries and Officials

Appropriate training of panchayat functionaries and government officials is the key to participatory and effective implementation of MGNREGA. There are several well-established civil society organizations/non-governmental organizations as well as academic institutions in various parts of the country which can help build the capacities of panchayats and officials and support them in planning, implementation and evaluation of MGNREGA works. Also, such training will help the panchayats and officials to formulate appropriate strategies to achieve sustainable rural livelihoods through convergence of MGNREGA with other schemes.

CONCLUSION

The MGNREGA has provided a unique legal space for the rural poor, especially the landless labourers, SC, ST and small and marginal farmers, with a consequent legal obligation on the part of the government at various levels to deliver and improve the socio-economic condition of the rural people. However, there are several gaps and weak links in the implementation of MGNREGA in most places, which need to be bridged through sustained awareness-building campaigns about various entitlements, social mobilization, planning and convergence for proper utilization of the assets created for productivity enhancement, social inclusion and good governance through effective, albeit truly participatory social audit, vigilance and monitoring and capacity building of panchayati raj functionaries and government officials.

ACKNOWLEDGEMENTS

The author is grateful to Dr Amita Sharma, Joint Secretary (Ministry of Rural Development); Nilay Ranjan, Sr. Consultant, UNDP, and Professor Muchkund Dubey, President, CSD, for their moral support and guidance. Also the technical, editorial and secretarial help received from Sri Gitesh Sinha, Ms Rakhshanda Jalil and Ms Rita Khurana, respectively, is gratefully acknowledged.

REFERENCE

Sharma, Rita. 2010. Echoing the Green Revolution. *The Indian Express,* New Delhi, January 9, 2010.

About the Editors and the Contributors

SERIES EDITOR

Manoranjan Mohanty retired as Director, Developing Countries Research Centre and Professor of Political Science, University of Delhi, in 2004. A political scientist, China scholar and a peace and human rights activist with special interest in China, India and global transformation, he is editor of *Social Change* and distinguished professor, Council for Social Development, New Delhi. He is chairperson, Development Research Institute, Bhubaneswar and honorary fellow and former chairperson of the Institute of Chinese Studies, Delhi. He has taught or researched in many universities including California, Oxford, Copenhagen, Moscow, Lagos and Beijing. He is the author of many publications including *China's Transformation: The Success Story and the Success Trap, Ideology Matters: China from Mao Zedong to Xi Jinping* and edited or co-edited many publications, including *People's Rights, Class, Caste, Gender, India-Social Development Report, 2010, Exploring Emergent Global Thresholds* and *China at a Turning Point.*

EDITOR

K. B. Saxena currently a Distinguished Professor at the Council for Social Development, taught Political Science in Ramjas College, Delhi University from 1962 to 1964. He joined the Indian Administrative Service in 1964 having being allotted the Bihar cadre. As a civil servant some important positions he held included, Additional Chief Secretary, Government of Bihar and Head, Land Reforms Division in the Department of Rural Development, Additional Secretary in the Ministry of Agriculture, Principal Adviser, Planning Commission and Secretary in the Ministries of Welfare, Rural Development and Health in the Government of India. After retirement, he has been engaged in research, advocacy and writing on planning and development issues. His areas of interest include land reforms, rural development, agriculture, poverty (rural and urban), rural and unorganized labour, problems of marginalized sections, especially Scheduled Castes, Scheduled Tribes, minorities, women and children, and governance with a special reference to the implementation of government programmes and social movements. His publications include *Contemporary Pratices of Mahatma Gandhi National Rural Employment Guarantee Scheme: Insights from Districts and Health Policy and Reforms*.

CONTRIBUTORS

Satya Prakash Dash is an Associate Professor, Department of Political Science & Public Administration, Sambalpur University. He was formerly a Fellow at the CSD.

Arun Kumar Ghosh is a retired faculty member of the CSD.

T. Haque was a well-known agricultural economist, specializing in agricultural development and policy. He served as a Distinguished Professor and Director of CSD prior to which he was the chairperson of the Commission for Agricultural Costs and Prices, Government of India, and was appointed National Fellow of the Indian Council of Agricultural Research at the National Centre for Agricultural Economics and Policy Research. In 2016, he formulated the 'Model Agricultural Land Leasing Act 2016' in his capacity as Chairman of Land Policy Cell, NITI Aayog. His writings, as an author of a dozen books and reports, largely focused on rural development and monitoring agricultural policies to facilitate inclusive policy frameworks for developing countries.

S. R. Hashim is currently the Chairperson of both the Institute for Human Development and the Indian Association of Social Science Institutions. He has also served as the former Member Secretary, Planning Commission, and as the former Chairperson, Union Public Service Commission. He has worked extensively on issues relating to poverty and inequality. The Planning Commission appointed him the chairperson of the Expert Group to recommend a detailed methodology for identification of families living below the poverty line in urban areas.

Manju Khurana Project Officer, Department of Social Work, Jamia Millia Islamia, New Delhi.

Arjun Kumar is Director of the Impact and Policy Research Institute, New Delhi, and is currently a China–India Visiting Scholars Fellow at Ashoka University. He specializes in quantitative and qualitative research methods, econometrics and the use of statistical software to crunch big data. He is President of a Jharkhand-based non-governmental organization, Manavdhara, a youth social organization working for humanitarian causes in backward regions for marginalized communities.

E. Narayanan Nair No material or email id found. The article appeared in 1978.

Kamta Prasad As a former member of the Indian Administrative Service, he joined the faculty of the Indian Institute of Public Administration after retirement and conducted many studies on rural development and governance issues.

Ambati Nageswara Rao is Dean, Research and Publication Division, and Assistant Professor of Social Work, Gujarat National Law University, Gandhinagar. With a PhD from Tata Institute of Social Sciences, Mumbai, his teaching and research experience include social entrepreneurship, research methodology, human resource management and disability studies.

Ratnawali has been associated with the Centre for Social Studies, Surat, as an Assistant Professor. Having completed her doctorate from Ranchi University, Jharkhand, in 2000, her research work looks at socio-economic issues, especially the participation of marginalized groups in governance and the areas of health and nutrition.

Ramashray Roy was Director of the Indian Council of Social Science Research, New Delhi, and Senior Fellow at the Centre for the Study of Developing Societies. He is known for his studies of many elections, including those of 1998 and 2009. He had many publications on Indian democracy. He was also the founder of the academic centre in Ranti village in Madhubani district of Bihar.

Preet Rustagi served as joint director of the Institute of Human Development, and at the Indian Society of Labour Economics, she discharged many duties until her untimely death in 2019. She was an associate editor of the *Indian Journal of Human Development* and *Indian Journal of Labour Economics*, a quarterly publication of the Indian Society of Labour Economics. Her contributions, largely in gender studies, as well as child welfare and education have been widely used and cited.

Bijay Sarkar National Creative Research Initiative Center for Smart Supramolecules (CSS), Department of Chemistry and Division of Advanced Materials Science, Pohang University of Science and Technology (POSTECH), Pohang, Republic of Korea.

Helen R. Sekar is a Senior Fellow at the V. V. Giri National Labour Institute where she is the Coordinator of the National Resource Centre on Child Labour. She is the author of *Hard Labour at a Tender Age*; *Girl Child Labour in the Match Industry of Sivakasi: No Light in Their Lives*; *Child Labour Legislation in India: A Study in Retrospect and Prospect*; *Vulnerabilities and Insecurities of Informal Sector Workers: A Study of Street Vendors*, and *Forced Child Labour: A Study of Children at the Traffic Lights* and has co-authored *Rehabilitation of Child Labour in India: Lessons Learnt from the Evaluation of National Child Labour Project*.

V. B. Singh is a former Director of the Centre for the Study of Developing Societies (CSDS) where he was also a senior fellow. His interest in electoral politics led to many important publications, including a five-volume series on *Elections in India* that gave detailed results of Parliamentary elections held from 1952 to 1985. V. B. Singh also directed CSDS's programme on survey research and training.

Durganand Sinha was a leading Indian psychologist who set up the Psychology Department at Allahabad University. He was the Director of the A. N. Sinha Institute of Social Studies. As a central figure in the profession of psychology, he was the president of the Indian Psychological Association, the Indian Academy of Applied Psychology and also headed the psychology section of the Indian Science Congress.

Prashant K. Trivedi is an Associate Professor at the Giri Institute of Development Studies, Lucknow. He is the editor of *The Globalization Turbulence: Emerging Tensions in Indian Society* and co-author of *Backward and Dalit Muslims: Education, Employment and Poverty* and *Weapon of the Oppressed: An Inventory of People's Rights in India*. He is the volume editor of *Social Change in Contemporary India: Land and Labour in Indian Agriculture*.

Index

absolute poverty, 63, 115
  MGNREGS, xiv, xv
alleviation of poverty, 257
  cafeteria approach, 269–70
  delivery system, 265–6
  fund availability, 264–5
  growth, 266–7
  integration with area development
    programmes, 268
  land reform, 259–60
  main components of strategy, 257
  MNP, 263–4
  planning machinery, 270
  programme content, 268–9
  rehabilitation policy, 267
  SFDA, IRDP, NREP AND
    RLEGP, 260–3
  trickle-down strategy, 258
  welfare of Scheduled Castes and
    Tribes, 259
anganwadi centres (AWC), 272
  functional aspects, 282
  physical state, 282–3
  population distribution and
    coverage, 277–82
  provision and availability of
    supplementary food,
    286–92
  timings and attendance of
    children, 284–6
anganwadi worker (AWW), 273
  profile, 283–4

barrier free social environment
  deprivation, xxix–xxx
basic amenities, 76–8, 169
below the poverty line (BPL), 231
  percentage of people, 232

bridging entitlement gaps, 329–31
building capacities of panchayat
  functionaries, 334
burden of domestic responsibilities,
  107–9

capitalism, 229
child labour, 61
  causes and impact, 132–3
  consequences for the child, 133–4
  future prospects, 137
  health hazards, 134–6
  psychological consequences,
    136–7
city development plans (CDPs), 52
Constitution of India in Article 21,
  240

detailed project reports (DPRs), 52
development, 227
  Development as Freedom by
    Amartya Sen, 228
  Partha Chatterjee's argument, 228
dimensions of poverty, 59–62
  capability approach, 60
  child labour, 61
  disability, 61
  multiple deprivations, 59
  unidisciplinary approach, 62–3
  vicious circle, 62
dimensions of rural poverty, 5
  agricultural development
    programme, 7
  impact of British industrial
    revolution, 6
  local hierarchies, 8
  methodology, 8–9
  physio-climatic conditions, 7

pre-colonial traditional Indian
village, 6
Rural British India, 6
disability, 119
concept, 117–18
estimates, 123
medical model, 120–1
poverty, 61
prevalence in India's, 122–4
social model, 121
drinking water and sanitation,
179, xlix

economic reforms, aims, 230
education, xlviii–xlix
employment
self-employment, xlii–xliii
wage, xliii–xliv
Employment Guarantee Scheme
(EGS), 258
environmental degradation, lii
expenditure
composition, liii
social sector, lii–liii
Expert Committee on Consumption
Credit, 262

First Five-year Plan (FFYP), 50
Chandigarh, 51
Gandhinagar, 51
JnNURM, 51–2
Kalyani in West Bengal, 51
tenth, 50–1

Gandiali village
caste *versus* landholding, 13
correlation of ownership of land
with ownership, 12
employment pattern, 16
income distribution, 14
income distribution per capita, 15
occupational pattern of the
workforce, 10
gender discrimination, l–li

handicap, 119–20
head count ratio (HCR), 63–4
health policy, defined, 241
health services, xlviii
human development, xlvii–xlviii
Human Development Index, 60
human poverty, 64–5
human rights
defined by United Nations Centre
for Human Rights, 240

impairment, 118
India
policy establishment, 253
process of urbanization, 41
rural households access to basic
amenities in, 169–99
Indian Persons with Disability Act,
127
problems included, 127–8
provisions, 127
Indian state
development and poverty, 227–47
inequality, 165
growth, xl–xli
research papers, 166–7
rising, 166
infant mortality rate (IMR), 222–3
Integrated Child and Development
Services (ICDS) programme,
272
assessment of nutritional status,
295–301
methodology, 276–7
nutritional status of tribes in
Gujarat, 274–5
study area, 275–6
Integrated Rural Development
Programme (IRDP), 258

Jawaharlal Nehru National Urban
Renewal Mission (JnNURM),
51–2
sub-missions, 52

Jharkhand
  air pollution, 147–9
  annual release, 149
  common toxins and their sources,
    147
  concentration of pollutants from
    fertilizer plant, 149
  ground water pollution, 143
  growth of urban population, 145
  industrial pollution and health
    hazards, 141–2
  industries, 142
  industries maraud environment,
    142–3
  materials by deposit gauge, 148
  poisonous gas, 151
  preventive measures, 151–2
  profile of sanitation facilities, 144
  range of chemical characteristics,
    146
  Report on Labour Conditions,
    150
  river water pollution, 145–7
  safety of children, 149–50
  water pollutants, 150–1

Koraput, Balangir and Kalahandi
    (KBK) districts, 242
  census of families BPL, 236
  demand and sanction of additional,
    239
  demographic and literacy indicators,
    235
  functioning of MHUs, 240
  health status, 240–6
  left extremism, 246–7
  projected outlay for RLTAP,
    238
  socio-economic indicators, 234
  Special Area Development
    Programme, 234
  total population, 234
  utilization of RIDF programmes,
    239

macroeconomic policies for poverty
    reduction, liv–lv
Mahatma Gandhi National Rural
    Employment Guarantee Act
    (MGNREGA), 305
  access to employment, 307–14
  bridging entitlement gaps, 329–31
  building capacities of panchayat
    functionaries, 334
  challenges and suggestions, 329
  contribution of income under,
    314
  ensuring good governance, 333–4
  ensuring productive utilization,
    331–2
  impact on agriculture, 318–22
  investment priorities and asset
    creation, 314–18
  issue of social inclusion, 333
  methodology, 306–7
  objectives, 306
  out-migration impact, 326–9
  participation of women, 322–5
  per cent, 315
  rising wages and cost of agricultural
    production, 332
  social inclusion impact, 322
Mahnar and Hariharganj blocks, 26–7
  caste and land ownership, 28
  caste hierarchy, 29
  dependency ratio, 32
  education of children, 34
  foreclosure of future opportunities,
    35
  households, landholding and caste,
    30
  land utilization, 27
  landowning status of households
    and monthly income, 37
  marginal and small farmers lease, 36
  other expenditures, 34
  pattern of landownership, 29–30
  persistence of homogeneity, 33–4
  proportions of illiterates, 35

reflections of paucity of resources,
32–3
situation of poor, 35–6
two-thirds of the households, 32
type of farmer household, 38
Mica Manufacturing Industry
Report on Labour Conditions,
150
Millennium Development Goals
(MDGs)
basic amenities, 169
Minimum Needs Programme (MNP),
263–4
mixed economy of India
Jayati Ghosh's views, 230
mobile health units (MHUs), 242
monthly per capita consumption
expenditure (MPCE)
marital status of women heads, 81
sex ratios, 76
variations, 75–6
women-headed households, 80
Multidimensional Poverty Index
(MPI), 60

National Bank for Agriculture
and Rural Development
(NABARD), 237
National Nutrition Monitoring
Bureau (2002), 274
National Rural Employment
Programme (NREP), 258
National Sample Survey (NSS), 171
National Sample Survey Office
(NSSO)
61st data, 80
nutrition, xlv–xlvi

Orissa, 231–3
incidence of poverty, 233
infrastructural development, 233
KBK districts, 233–40
Planning Commission, estimation
of poverty, 231

Orissa State Integrated Health Policy
objectives, 241
other religious minorities (ORMs),
179

participation and social mobilization,
li–lii
People's Union for Civil Liberties
(PUCL), 231
persons reporting ailments (PAP), 223
pervasive poverty, 31
Planning Commission, 55, 63
estimation of poverty in Orissa, 231
incidence of poverty in India, 116
poverty, xix
agrarian distress retards,
xxxvii–xxxviii
alleviation programmes, xli–xlii
alternative estimates, xxi–xxii
approaches to define, xix–xx
barrier free social environment
deprivation, xxix–xxx
capability deprivation, xxviii–xxix
changing contours, xxxvi
child labour, 61
cognitive and motivational
concomitants, 155–63
cognitive dimension, xxxv–xxxvi
conflict dimension, xxxiii–xxxiv
defined, 1
deprivation of resources,
xxvii–xxviii
dimensions, xxv–xxvi
direct attack, xlii
eliminate child poverty, xxxvii
environmental dimension,
xxxii–xxxiii
feminization, xxxvii
gender-based deprivations,
xxx–xxxi
gradations, xxiii
growth, xxxix–xl
growth-induced impoverishment,
xxxviii

material deprivation, xxvi
measurement, xx–xxi
nutrition and incidence of child
    labour, xxxi–xxxii
phenomenon of multiple
    determination, 156
politics, xxv
powerlessness, xxxiv–xxxv
priority to human capital
    development over growth,
    xxxvi
profile of poor, xxiii–xxv
reduction, 63
regressive labour reforms, xxxix
rural and urban, 1–4
town size, basic amenities, 48–9
unprecedented unemployment,
    xxxviii–xxxix
urban, xxv
urbanization, 52–6
vulnerability and powerlessness,
    xxxiv
poverty alleviation programmes,
    253–6, xli–xlii
categories, 253–4
poverty and disability in India, 113,
    124–6
cycle, 124
definitions, 115–16
incidence, 116–17
limits access to education and
    employment, 114
methodology, 114–15
objectives, 114
policy interventions, 127–8
World Development Report, 113
Poverty of Philosophy, 155
public distribution system, xliv–xlv

regular employment in urban areas
differential access, 103–7
relative poverty, 115–16
Revised Long-term Action Plan
    (RLTAP), 234

rural households access to basic
    amenities in India, 169–99
caste and ethnic groups, 178–9
census of India, 171
database and methodology,
    170–3
decomposition by social groups,
    194, 197
determinants, 189, 194
economic groups, 178
economic groups and caste and
    ethnic groups, 179, 189
NSS housing conditions round
    data, 171
religious groups, 179
religious groups and livelihood
    categories, 189
summary of findings, 173–8
rural Indians, 11
Rural Infrastructure Development
    Fund (RIDF), 237
Rural Landless Employment
    Guarantee Programme
    (RLEGP), 258
rural poverty, 1
dimensions, 5–17
voicelessness and powerlessness, 2

self-employment, 261, xlii–xliii
social exclusion, xlix–l
social sector expenditure, lii–liii
social security system, xlvi–xlvii
Socio-Economic and Caste Census
    (SECC), 55
sociology of poverty, 63
core subject, 67–8
HCR, 63–4
human poverty, 64–5
problem of definition, 65–7
Special Area Development
    Programme, 234
objective, 234
strategic shifts in policy orientation,
    lv–lvi

structure of poverty
  Coates and Silburn define poverty,
    23–4
  cultural values, 24
  culture of poverty, 23
  Dantwala's view, 21–2
  education of children, 34
  homogeneity of lifestyle, 33
  intellectual exercises, 21
  Kuznets hypothesis, 20
  land utilization, 27
  Mahnar and Hariharganj blocks,
    26–7
  Meade's description, 25
  other expenditures, 34
  pattern of inequality, 25
  persistence of homogeneity, 33–4
  tendency of poor to get poorer,
    19–20
  Townsend, P. observation, 22
  unequal distribution of resources,
    25
  Valentine argument, 25
  views of Lewis, 23
  what constitutes poverty, 20
supplementary nutrition
  women and children, 272–301

Training of Rural Youth for Self-
    employment (TRYSEM)
    programme, 261
trickle-down strategy, 258

United Nations Development
    Programme (UNDP), 60
  Human Development Index, 60
  Human Development Report, 209
  rank of UP, 209
urban development and poor, 41
urban poor, xliv
urban poverty, 1–2, xxv
  voicelessness and powerlessness, 2
urbanization
  cities, 56

distribution of cities, 46–7
high level, 44
industrialization demands, 44
lack of industrial/manufacturing job
    creation, 44
pattern of urban growth, 45, 56
percentage of poor, 49
planning, 49–52
poverty, 52–6
selected small and medium towns,
    48
size and poverty, 57
slow pace, 42–4
urban growth in India, 42
Uttar Pradesh (UP)
  age at first marriage, 220–1
  caste differentiation, 212
  caste variations, 217–18
  disparity and development,
    209–24
  drinking water, electricity and
    sanitation, 224
  education, 216–17
  education and poverty, 218–20
  employment scenario, 214–15
  health, 220
  IMR and child mortality, 222–3
  land possession, 215–16
  morbidity and health facilities,
    223–4
  nutritional status of women, 223
  percentage distribution of
    households, 213
  place of birth, 221–2
  poverty, 210
  regional variations in poverty,
    211
  rural urban, 214
  structure of dwellings, 224
  total fertility rate, 221
  trend in poverty, 211

Village Gandiali case, 8–17
Vision 2010 document, 241

wage employment, xliii–xliv
women and poverty
  basic amenities, 76–8
  burden of domestic responsibilities,
    107–9
  concentration of self-employment,
    102
  demographic composition, 75–6
  distribution of all women persons
    across educational categories,
    84–5
  gender dimensions, 70
  income-based concept, 71
  industrial and occupational
    distribution, 96–103
  occupational distribution of poorest
    women, 102
  poorest women, 101
  poverty estimates, 72–5
  rural poverty, 70

  self-employed, 97–8
  UPSS, 99–100
  urban and rural contexts, 78–9
  women-headed households, 78–83
  WPR, 86–96
women-headed households, 78–83
  marital status of women heads, 81
  MPCE, 80
  status across MPCE quintiles:
    2004-2005, 83
  status of employment, 82
  work participation, 82
work participation rate (WPR),
    86–96
  poorest women, 91
  self-employed, 95
  share of regular employment in
    rural areas, 94
  UPSS for women and men, 90
  urban women, 91